As I Cast Out

As I Cast Out

AN ENGLISHMAN FISHING IN SPAIN

John Langridge

THE
MEDLAR PRESS
ELLESMERE

Published by The Medlar Press Limited,
The Grange, Ellesmere, Shropshire.
www.medlarpress.com

ISBN 978-1-907110-42-9

Produced in England by The Medlar Press Limited, Ellesmere.
Designed and typeset in 11 on 12 point Baskerville Roman.

Contents

INTRODUCTION
9

Part One - The North

CHAPTER ONE - NAVARRA
13

In which the author examines driving and walking into Spain, remembers Ernest Hemingway and the 1920s, fishes for trout in the hills, is visited by a ghost, wanders through ancient beech woods, encounters a Napoleonic arms factory and samples fine wines as the first snows fall.

CHAPTER TWO - THE BASQUE COUNTRY
33

Where the author reflects on Basque culture, its mysterious language and extraordinary blood, as well as its role in epic European human history. Then there are local fishermen's tales in a magnificent land of lakes, with their trout, pike and barbel, not to mention some remarkable aspects of gastronomy, a host of mushrooms and one or two more barbel.

CHAPTER THREE - ASTURIAS AND CANTABRIA
51

The author follows the coast, fishes with his father, chases sand eels, sea-bream, and sea bass, as well as fishing in harbours and quays for grey mullet, and meeting a local conger eel man before landing a record mullet, or is it a bass?

CHAPTER FOUR - GALICIA
79

An ovation to cuisine, octopus and white wine country, where abound the nase and black bass, not to mention witches and local prejudices. Messrs Chapman and Buck put in an appearance, and the question of angling luck arises as does a keenly interested crow. The author recalls Laurie Lee in the village of Mondoñedo, visits nearby trout streams, practises bubble and fly fishing, examines fire salamanders while the Spanish Civil War beguiles a blank day.

Part Two - Inland

CHAPTER FIVE - CASTILE
115

Castilian geography comes to the fore in the capital city of Valladolid, to which some history is added, featuring Cervantes and the Last King of Ireland. Something of local character is considered, especially that of the Ribera wines. Curiosities of climate and rivers arise, carp and barbel are fished for, in winter and summer. The humble gudgeon plays his part, as does yet another barbel and a serious storm. The author then follows a canal, encounters a blind pike, celebrates Carnival and other festivals, camps out and remembers other pike, both English and Iberian, all leading on to snake bite and cider.

CHAPTER SIX - THE EBRO (ARAGÓN)
171

Where the author discovers an angling Mecca, over Halloween and the Day of the Dead. Monster carp and catfish are conjured up, following a long bus journey, and more language curiosities arise before a Spanish breakfast. The Ebro ecosystem is examined, where carp and a catfish thrive, and the author makes a catfish film, as well as considering many catfish legends.

CHAPTER SEVEN - EXTREMADURA
205

Where the author looks into a region's history and biodiversity plus the country's sport of bullfighting and animal welfare in general. A cycling and fishing film is made, with bleak, carp and black bass and many famous British travellers in Spain are recalled as well as their writings before going afloat on Alcántara Reservoir and zandering from a boat.

Part Three - The South & South-east

CHAPTER EIGHT - THE EBRO DELTA, TARRAGONA, CATALUNYA
253

In which the author encounters the extraordinary leerfish in a Natural Park with horizon to horizon rice paddies. Further language curiosities come to light, along with giltheads, various sea bream and sea bass, which are caught on rubber lures. A mystery fish appears, and the author stops at an old town.

CHAPTER NINE - THE GILTHEAD SEA-BREAM, ALICANTE
267

Where the author fishes for gilthead sea bream, during his father's holiday in Dénia. They consider some local history and have a night fishing adventure. The British and Spanish *How To Catch Them* books are remembered, wrasse and painted combers, giltheads are caught in the dark.

CHAPTER TEN - ANDALUSIA AND THE GYPSIES
285

The author travels south to celebrate Mr Smith's birthday. Gypsy culture, language and Flamenco music loom large, as do bizarre holiday characters that have also flown south. The two friends fish on gypsy rivers and catch their barbel on the fly. Bloomsbury then turns up in Spain, before the author leaves Seville, and cycles to a secret lake after black bass, crayfish and an encounter with the largest carp he has ever seen.

FISHING AND TRAVELLING IN SPAIN
340

Fishing licences 340 - Arriving in Spain 346 - Where to go and where to stay 347

USEFUL SPANISH PHRASES
349

BIBLIOGRAPHY
350

INDEX
351

To Yolanda

Galicia

Castilla y León

Asturias

Cantabria

Pais Vasco
(Euskadi)

La Rioja

Aragón

Navarra

Cataluña

Islas Baleares

Valenciana

Extremadura

Andalucía

Madrid

Castilla la Mancha

Murcia

This book uses both English and Spanish spellings for place names (eg, Catalonia and Cataluña).

Introduction

The very lengthy process of writing this book began almost twenty-five years ago, long before I had ever published anything, indeed even before having seriously contemplated writing anything at all; one of the few, perhaps the only negative consequence of innumerable years studying English Literature. While wastepaper baskets were often enough filled to overflowing with screwed up scribblings, self-condemned as 'pretentious' or 'derivative', my angling notes always survived and were tucked away, in case I'd ever want to look back over them. From my earliest notebooks to those of today, the contents are surprisingly consistent, with Crabtree style sketches of swims I've been to, crudely drawn yet painstakingly detailed with diverse aquatic features and possible or imagined fish species; venues are named naïvely enough as 'perch corner', 'the big eddy', 'bass rock' or 'shark point'. Occasional captures, notable or otherwise, are lovingly described and scientifically recorded, at least as regards weight, and often with a photograph added as real proof.

One day, along the waterside of the river Duero in Spain, at a point where the waters widen above the dam of San José at Castronuño, I had been recounting some fishy memory or other to a good friend and fellow angler, the excellent Dr Stuart Park. I was enthusing about a particular water, its exotic wildlife, the fishing etc., when he suddenly said, "You should write all that up!" He was confident there were anglers as well as general readers who would enjoy reading about such piscatorial adventures around Spain. And so, in due course, I wrote down the episode I had been remembering on that occasion, expanding it and wandering off at tangents, then doing the same with other places, with constant reference to my old and tattered notebooks, until I had several hundred pages of longhand, altogether unmanageable and completely without direction. One of the later chapters became the novella *Lizarralde*, originally published in Spanish in 2003 (and then in English by Medlar Press) while others appeared in reduced form in *Waterlog* magazine but in the meantime, the great bulk of that original writing sat about largely neglected until Medlar Press expressed a guarded interest in it. That lead to an immense task of revision and editing which has brought us finally to *As I Cast Out*, which it is hoped will entertain readers at least half as much as Dr Park so optimistically anticipated and, moreover, encourage them to get to know Spain from quite another perspective.

My fishing has been done all around the Iberian coastline as well as offshore, I have angled up and down the rivers too and beside coastal briney lagoons and many inland lakes and reservoirs, sometimes in the company of my father or friends, who consequently feature in some chapters (apologies to all in advance).

On other occasions I have fished with Spanish TV film crews and local guides, days which almost inevitably provide much food for anecdote, not to say hilarity. Perhaps most of all, I have passed my fishing days entirely and blissfully alone, occasions when, surely, the angler finds himself most at peace with the world and when nature is at her most beneficent.

A final word might be said regarding layout and content of this book. In twenty-five years I have had, as suggested above, the opportunity to fish practically every waterway in the Iberian peninsula, where there are many freshwater fish species to be found, including an extraordinary eight varieties of barbel, though, surprisingly, not our beloved *Barbus barbus*, as well as almost every important European sporting species, all of which are introduced: the carp, rainbow trout, black bass, zander, pike, etc., among which the giant wels catfish stands out as the most formidable. The brown trout is native, as is the salmon, also the tench and the crucian carp, along with a number of small fishes such as inevitably turn up in any day's angling. Among sea fish, from the Atlantic coasts we have many species familiar to the British coastal angler: bass, mullet, etc; and from the Mediterranean coast and islands, several rather more exotic species, such as the many and varied sea breams or even tuna.

In this book I have confined myself to the Spanish mainland, forgetting for the present purpose the islands of the Canaries or Balearics, and have divided the territory into three geographical areas: the north, the interior and the south and south-east, divisions whose geographical and climatic conditions are so varied and extreme as to suggest three entirely different countries. I have attempted to cover all the major species and angling techniques as well as to communicate the wonder of what is, despite decades of tourism, a land full of never ending revelations and surprises. The cities, towns and villages encountered along the way are all easily identified and found, as indeed are the waters themselves, especially with the aid of the Internet. Inevitably, I have changed, my fishing has changed and the country has changed over the decades. Some of the chapters were written long before the advent of that particular revolution in cyber-technology and no responsibility can be accepted by the author or the publisher for things which may well have altered on the ground. At the end of the book there is an Appendix which gives some notes on licences and where to go fishing. Occasionally I have followed in the footsteps of famous visiting anglers, such as Ernest Hemingway, and on other occasions in those of literary travellers such as Laurie Lee or George Borrow, but the journeys and discoveries remain primarily a personal experience which, nevertheless, I hope may be enjoyed by all. Moreover, should the reader travel to Spain primarily for the fishing, there should be plenty here that will prove useful.

JDL

Part One

THE NORTH

Chapter One

Navarra

In which the author examines driving and walking into Spain, remembers Ernest Hemingway and the 1920s, fishes for trout in the hills, is visited by a ghost, wanders through ancient beech woods, encounters a Napoleonic arms factory and samples fine wines as the first snows fall.

Nowadays, most British tourists fly into Spain, to the innumerable coastal holiday resorts, yet there is also an important percentage of visitors that comes overland, following the most time honoured routes from France, across the Pyrenees. Ernest Hemingway was one of these and it is with him that we are going to start this Iberian adventure. The B road from Mont and through Salies on the French side will take you on to Roncevaux or Roncesvalles, scene of a historic battle in the year 778 when Charlemagne's army was attacked, or rather massacred, by the Basques. The famous Catholic Pilgrim's way of St James, leading to Santiago de Compostela in Galica, also enters the country here and, whatever it is that brings you, you will immediately find yourself in the wonderful countryside of Navarra.

Looking over the wooded hills from the high point known as el Collado de Nabala, it was easy to feel that it was just the same as when Hemingway first gazed across its rolling contours back in the 1920s. He had been only 25 years old then, and my first trip there had been in 1999, the centenary of his birth. So much had happened in the interim - the Spanish Civil War, the Second World War, a Nobel Prize and, somewhat before time, Hemingway's own troubled end; but here on the fringes of the Irati, the biggest and most ancient beech wood in Europe, an ancient ecosystem pursued its eviternal cycles, apparently unaffected.

Hemingway had come that first time in June 1924, it had still been spring and his character Bill Gorton in *The Sun Also Rises* complained of the cold. It was cold today, but at the other end of the year. The province of Navarra really has to be visited in the autumn, when the full rainbow glory of beech, oak, ash and a myriad other trees is at its height. Beech it was that stretched over the horizon to the south, but my attention was drawn to the towering darkness of black pine and larch, which backed away east. A thin path led into its shadows. I wondered how old this foreboding forest could be. Hemingway hadn't mentioned it in his description of this very spot; it simply can't have been there back then.

I was sitting on a soft mound of grass, leaning back against the only signpost there was anywhere along the 10 mile walk that Hemingway had taken from Burguete to fish the Irati river. The indicator boards were battered away to almost nothing, broken fingers pointing to un-named destinations. One, I guessed, was the Orbaitzeta direction, the middle one Burguete and the other presumably to the village of Aria I'd seen on my map, but there was no indication that this dark forest route had ever been marked.

The thin sun shone and the morning chill was beginning to lift. Like Hemingway, I had my rucksack, some wine and food, a couple of rods and a net. In an old photograph I had seen, taken in 1939 in Idaho, he was holding a fine old cane rod with an equally splendid Nottingham style reel. The brace of trout was impressive too, but for the moment I was satisfied with having brought along some old tackle, which, though not the same, was as near to that he would have used as possible. I had been walking leisurely for an hour or so and having reached this inviting spot, decided to pause for a biscuit and a drop of coffee.

"Come on! Let's get going. We'll never make it at this rate. You and your 'comfortably'."

I nearly slopped the coffee all over myself.

"*¡Buenos días! Perdone, ¿está usté perdido?*" A man, dressed in working clothes, had come up while I had been wrapped in reverie.

"No, no," I said, I wasn't lost. I was walking from Burguete . . .

The old man nodded, "Auritz," he said, that was the more lyrical Basque name.

" . . . on my way to the old arms factory at Orbaitzeta," I went on, adding that I would be heading down the north path, round to the left of the pinewood.

"*Así es, sí, sí, no tiene pérdida.*" He indicated over his shoulder, the way he had come, then waved cheerily and went on his way, south on the other of the three main paths, the one for Aria. He had looked a little quizzically at my initial incomprehension. How on earth I could have taken his accents and imagined an Idaho drawl I really couldn't say.

I had been reading the Hemingway novel on the train journey to Pamplona, or rather re-reading it, especially Chapter XII and felt really close to the days he describes there. 'Comfortably' had been Jake's word to Bill. "That's a nice word," Bill had said, adding "We'll have to go like hell to get there and back and have any fishing at all."

Jake was Hemingway himself in fact. Hemingway the doer, the man's man type, much fallen into disfavour since; the brutal fighter in adversity, blood-thirsty and heroic, who sought solace for his lost generation in Spanish wines and the bullfighting at Pamplona. But it wasn't that man that interested me. I sought another, the one who went fishing. There was redemption for the hunter-killer spirit in a river, as there had been for his old man, in the sea; but he himself never got there, it was as though he took the wrong path, and life became too much for him. Not until he watches his fish go, released after the struggle does the compassionate man in the angler find his true place in nature, and peace within himself. For me, it was a way to salve my own conscience.

Since arriving in Burguete the evening before, my mind had been full with Hemingway and this dilemma, and now I felt it even more strongly. I packed away the flask and shouldering my rucksack, stood looking into the dark limbo between the main paths. The narrow track led enticingly into the damp shade, trailing up and winding quickly out of sight. The way I had come and the two main choices before me were *pistas forestales*, wide and unmade, almost roads, which admitted the passage of 4-wheel drive vehicles for forestry as well as tourism. They were new, nothing like the paths Hemingway had taken 74 years before, even though my route followed his footsteps almost exactly. Here was a chance to try a walk more similar to that he had known. I decided I would investigate, I could always double back or cut through the wood north and pick up my way again.

The chill was striking as I entered the wood. Huge stark tapering trunks rose 60 feet at least, creating a seemingly impenetrable barrier of black verticals. Closer to, their barks were mottled reddish and brown. There was none of the twinkling yellow and green light, which had accompanied me through the beech woods; it was practically dark. The air was moist, wetting my nose as I breathed. Underfoot, the soft grass felt spongy and was finely cropped. It quickly thinned out though, giving way to clumps of ferns and low tangled briars. The larches were turning, their pendulous branches showing pale yellows and the needles were falling. A weeping deciduous conifer, it brought a sense of sadness among the silvery green pines.

"They're tamaracks." I imagined that voice again. "A magnificent tree, they get to 100 feet back home, up around the Idaho river, good fishing country too."

All was quiet, there wasn't anyone to be seen. The treetops rustled lightly in the breeze. Tamaracks - I was sure I had seen them, on the same page as larches in the field guide, but I had never seen a real one as far as I knew. And I was hearing voices! Perhaps the trees themselves would talk to you, if you listened.

The path wound gently upward and became thinner, finally disappearing altogether. I had reached the edge of the wood and came into the light once more. Before me opened out another area of beech wood, *hayedo* in Spanish, an airy sounding word, *haya* being the name of the tree. Here they were immense, the biggest I had seen so far. Huge twisted roots showed around the base of silvery clad trunks, prettily mottled with mosses. The girth of the nearest was at least 20 feet and had to be 200 years old. Casting around, I could see no path beyond this point. I had come about half a mile in and it seemed that the path led nowhere. I knew where I was though. The ground steepened ahead and tracing the contours on my map I decided to follow the depression, which descended through the trees to the left. It was named on the map as the Barranco Dindurrieta and a thin broken blue line indicated that it was home to a tiny spate stream. I had seen many already, but this one looked as though it hadn't run in a very long time. Hemingway too had seen dozens of streams that spring and those I had passed or crossed on my way, I tried to identify. He spotted tadpoles in one and finding what I fancied to be the same shallow pool, I half expected to see them too, five months behind schedule. Instead, at its edge wandered a truly bizarre creature. Fluffy yellow and hairy, it sported four white tufts in the middle of its back and a thin bright red one as a kind of tail. It was a 'Pale Tussock', the caterpillar an infinitely more dramatic sight than the adult moth.

The stream was the Sorulucea. All the spates here had extraordinary, evocative names, all in Basque, itself a rare, antediluvian tongue: Ollarburu, Patxaranberro and back at the village, the Xorinaga. That one ran behind the Hostal Burguete, where Hemingway had stayed. You can still get the room and the very bed, if you book early enough. Though it's no longer 12 pesetas with wine included!

It was there behind the Hostal, at the muddy edges of the Xorinaga that, in the early morning while Bill was still sleeping, Jake had gone in search of worms for bait. While he filled two tobacco tins, nearby goats had looked on. In my case it had been cows and their somewhat bemused herder.

I got going again, it was only another half mile to the main *pista* that was the way for the old arms factory. It was easy going but still cold under the pines and I began to feel the need of some sunshine. Fragments broke through occasionally, lighting up fronds of fern, *iratxe* in Basque; I loved these words, so non Indo-European. *Helecho* was the Spanish word and sounded similar, despite the very different spelling.

"You'll be out on the ridge again any minute . . ." The voice made me start. "The hills beyond aren't wooded, there's only gorse. Then you'll see the steep bluffs, dark with trees and jutting with grey stone, that mark the course of the Irati river."

Hemingway continued in my head, half from what I had read and half as though he were there with me. "I sure couldn't have better company," I said out loud. It was because of him I was here, a pilgrimage on the one hand, but above all, I was looking for a river, a 'Big Two-Hearted River', one I would never have known about otherwise.

"A trout river at that!" The accent came again; it was soft, I would have expected a rougher voice somehow.

I came to the edge of the dark wood at last and slid down a new scar of a ditch, cut to facilitate rain run off, beside the *pista forestal*, but the surroundings were still unspoilt and spectacular. With time this road too would blend in. It already looked better along the opposite side, where fallen leaves spread like a carpet of russets and yellows.

I started down hill; it was all down now, all the way to the ruined factory. Hemingway makes brief reference to the river, *el Río de la Fábrica*, the real name of which is the Itolaz, but says nothing about the factory itself. As my way wound down, I hadn't any idea what to expect. It was known on the tourist routes, for trekkers and mountainbikers mainly, but I had not been able to find any information about it. I hadn't been walking for long when the right-hand side of the *pista* steepened dramatically and, below, the tiny river Itolaz came into view. From here on it accompanied me, gradually filling out into a good stream. As the road descended I had a better view of its tumbling clear water and my eye lighted at last on a curiosity noticed in Hemingway's novel, and that I had seen no sign of thus far. Foot-logs, hefty trunks, sawn off flat and laid across the river as fords more than bridges. I was intrigued, and got down the bank, slipping and sliding through the fallen leaves to the water to take a closer look.

The logs were very deliberately positioned, like railway sleepers, as if to allow the passage of carts. The precipitous valley sides meant there was very little room for the woodsmen and so the old paths must have followed the river closely, these fords crisscrossing at intervals by necessity. A few rounded mossy rocks interrupted the river's babbling flow, creating little eddies and whirlpools. It was like a great river in miniature. Occasional clumps of grasses and ferns overhung the ripples upstream and fallen leaves busied along like rafts. Both steep banks were crowded with young beeches; there were no old trees down here. With plenty of forestry in the area, this valley must have been cut down a while since. These trees were perhaps 20 years old. Golden sunlight sprinkled the slopes and the river, the air full of the water's noise. I decided to walk along its edge. It was only a few inches deep, ten feet wide at most, but growing appreciably as I followed its course. As the ground rose and fell I strayed no more than a few yards from the water until I came upon the remains of an old path. The trees had become old ones once more, well spaced apart, massive and ancient.

"As though in a park, just like I said."

It was true. Where the biggest trees stood, they respected each other's space. The upper foliage touched gently here and there but admitted plenty of light. There was a tremendous sense of space in a beech wood. The mother of the forest. I peered into my *Observer's Book of Trees*: 'its drip destroys most of the soil exhausting weeds, its shade protects the soil from over-evaporation, and the heavy crop of leaves enriches it by their decomposition.' I stood for a moment on the old path, it was only barely visible; a slightly banked depression, leading up gently to the now nearer forest road. Glancing behind, I could see that it had come down alongside the river a little way back, just where the young trees gave way to old. Hemingway had trodden this very ground, I was certain. In all probability the newer route above had been made when those trees had been cut, only recently widened and rough-core surfaced, while this old one had been forgotten. I walked slowly along the 50-odd yards towards the *pista*.

I began to feel thirsty.

"That wine's probably filthy," came the voice, "not like the stuff in Pamplona . . ."

"No, no," I said, talking to myself, "this one's good, Gran Irache, a really fine wine."

I wondered momentarily about wines. What constituted a good one generations ago and what now, and then whether it was too early for a spot of lunch. There wasn't much further to go. I was on the road once more and had risen a good way above the river. I pressed on, eventually coming over the ridge and starting down again. The path became steeper and way below I could see the river exiting the wooded hillside. It looked a good pace to stop and I strode on, legs aching from the thudding down hill.

Eventually I came out on the flat and crossed the river via an ugly reinforced concrete slab which appeared to mark the end of the new roadwork. Only a few yards off was the old bridge - six huge beech trunks, planed flat on the topside, crossed straight as dies between big stone walls, almost invisible beneath the moss and ivy of ages. It looked sound enough too. It was picturesque in the gladed light, the timbers rotting but still solid. Thick with moss, it had lain untrodden through these last decades. An equally ancient ash tree stood against one wall disrupting the ivied stone. I had to get a photo, then tiptoed across and, somewhat relieved, rejoined the road.

Underfoot it was getting wet, with puddles and mud everywhere. Here the road was old but still much used. It was rutted by tyre tracks and pockmarked by a myriad sheep hoofs. Trees grew over, forming an arch and the air became musty in the gloom. My way meandered gently, past the odd dilapidated byre and small herds of grazing cattle, their dull bells clanking in the quiet air. I had lost sight of the river, but could hear it rushing somewhere to the left side of the road. There were low ruined walls there, wet and green with tangled plants, bright blooms of sunshine lighting pools of yellow. Lizards scuttled off the more exposed areas of stone into chill cracks and crevices.

The first hint I had of the factory was a looming, high crumbling wall to the right, hard up against the road, deep in its own shadow. A tree, a young beech had established itself precariously about eight feet up, its bulking trunk shattering the ancient lines of masonry. There were occasional doorways too but they led to nothing. Peering into them I found only weeded earth where the erstwhile chambers, storerooms maybe, had collapsed. The wall ran on and on, finally curving round and disappearing into banked ground. Behind it was nothing more than a field. A few startled sheep peered back at me, then carried on cropping the lavish grass. I was in the open now and the sun was hot. It had to be midday by this time and after four hours' walking I was experiencing definite gnawings of hunger. I came out on to a tarmac road and immediately saw a sign: *Orbaitzetako ola / fábrica de Orbaitzeta*. I had arrived.

To the left there were more ruins but nothing could have prepared me for what was to come. I followed the road round and the immensity of the site became suddenly apparent. Black faced sheep grazed among vast walls and portals, the spiral horned ram eyeing me with deep suspicion.

Spotting a convenient log, I sat down in the sun and set out sandwiches and wine. I poured a glass and drank in the view as well as the rich oaken flavour of the Navarrese grape. Ham and cheese, excellent staples, and the bread was good too. I thought about the *panadería* back in Burguete. It was nothing more than an outhouse, its bright blue shutters almost permanently closed. But those in the know would congregate at around 7am when the shutters were thrown back and a wizened old stick would dispatch *barras*, with the help of her pretty granddaughter, for the 15 minutes or so that they lasted. Fifteen for the bar / restaurant Maritxu, 30 for another, the Txikipolit, three for breakfast at my own *hostal* and so on . . . maybe a hundred loaves in all, crisp and vaguely scented with wood smoke.

I soon felt restored, packed everything away, and began to stroll through the ruins. The sheep bounced away to other corners, their dull bells clattering, as I made my way from one imposing structure to another. There were the remains of enormous kilns with reddish black interiors, stone arches as much as 20 feet high, vacant doorways and blank staring windows. The spirit of Ozymandias was certainly present: 'Look on my works ye mighty and despair!' they seemed to say. The stonework was decorated with cornices and scroll-lined plinths, making these very utilitarian, military buildings unexpectedly elegant. Cannons had been made here, all kinds of ordnance in fact, its heyday the Napoleonic wars; a vast stronghold for the French, only just over the border, but on the Peninsula side of the formidable Pyrenees.

Suddenly, the rush of the river became audible once more. Having walked right through the old arms factory ruins as far as re-established nature would allow, I found myself in a courtyard. The various exits were defended by briars and nettles, but one narrow gap lead to the river. I ducked through between walls and brambles and down a steep dirt slope. Reaching the bottom, I was astonished to find that the river ran right through these constructions, 10 or 12 feet below ground level. I stepped out on to rocks and stood amazed at my surroundings. Huge vaulted arches spanned the water, as many as 15 of them, at 10-yard intervals, linking the high walls that contained the river. The great stone blocks were coloured and stained with lichens, mosses and rust from iron rings and spikes. Plants sprang up here and there and light poured in from above making much of this interior bright with mottled tones. The river itself was strewn with bricks and stones, fallen or abandoned during the building. I set up the camera tripod and snapped several views of this extraordinary tunnel before clambering back up, elated by my find.

I really had to get on, if there was going to be any fishing. It wasn't far now to the Irati. The factory river ran into it about a mile downstream; all I had to do was follow the road. I felt a new spring in my stride and all the colours round about seemed intensified. Brilliant sloe berries, from which the Navarrese spirit called *patxaran* was made, hung in long ropes in the hedgerow, bright red with dizzy ripeness. The prospect of fishing the Irati was really exciting; I just knew there would be fish. Bill hadn't been anything like as optimistic.

"What would he know? Old Loeb was just the same."

"You came down with him and Lady Duff that first time in '25, didn't you?"

"Yeah, that's right, we had a wild time of it in Pamplona and came up here for a bit of a break."

Just then, I saw the river, steep hills to the far side. There was no buckwheat though, it looked like just grazing land. There was a white house - was it the same one I wondered - under some trees on the hillside. And there was the dam too, a weir, the water boiling furiously on the down side, after a drop of just a couple of feet. I could hardly believe it, little had changed here in the 70-odd years.

"There are the trees where we jointed up the rods, they're bigger, but that's the place all right."

I moved into their shade; it was getting quite warm. I put all my stuff on the ground and looked out over the water. What an extraordinary colour! A pale, soft turquoise, undulating mass, marbled with foaming white, after the weir. It looked rocky too, alive with hides and lies for trout. Downstream, at the far side, was a huge pentagonal boulder with deep black crevices seeming to form the shape of a gigantic lizard. The opposite bank rose quite abruptly, thickly treed with every variety - mainly oak and beech, already rust browned by the autumn, but there were yellowing fronds of ash, willow and alder, the occasional, brilliant green conifers and the glowing reds and oranges of sycamores and maples.

Wading was the only way. As far as the eye could see the river's edges were dense with vegetation, interrupted sometimes by abrupt rock ledges.

"You got any McGintys?"

I paused and listened, expecting the dialogue to continue, but it had been his voice again, not Bill's, as though he were asking me.

"Yes, yes I have. I've got one anyway." I hadn't originally known what one was in fact, but looking through my pocket guide I surprised myself by finding that I had one of these American bumblebee type flies in my wallet.

"Bill was determined to fish fly, a bit of a purist . . . You got worms too?"

"Yes, I got them where you got yours."

A light gust of wind came up the river stirring me into action. I went back to the gear and set up the rods I'd brought along. One with the McGinty and the other ready for a worm. I wondered whether to fish as he had. 'A good sized sinker' he said in the novel . . .

I decided on a half-ounce drilled ball, stopped by the knot, 18 inches of trace and a size 10 hook for the worm. I glanced over at the weir. It looked a little precarious to say the least of it. Taking the rods and the net, I walked over to see if it would, in fact, be possible to get out there. I had the worms in a tin too, an old tobacco tin with the green and gold legend 'Old Holborn, since 1798'. It felt authentic enough.

"What about the wine?"

The Gran Irache wouldn't need chilling that was for sure and I said so.

"Come on then, let's see if you're half as good a fisherman as that Harris guy."

"What about you?" I said, "Your luck wasn't in that first time, back in '24!"

"Yeah, well, poetic licence. Anyway, stop avoiding the issue and get on with it!"

I stepped gingerly out on to the slippery stonework, the torrent blasting away all other sounds. It was exhilarating. The gate was up, and I sat on one of the squared timbers and watched the smooth apron of water before the river tumbled into the falls.

"Plagiarist!" came the voice again, laughing.

"Poetic licence," I said. "Come on, give me a break, I can't concentrate on the fishing."

As I baited up I had half an eye on the little waterfall at the gate. Would a trout leap for me too? There was no sign - it would have been far too perfect. I dropped the baited line down into the deep water at the foot of the weir and waited to feel a trout strike. After a few moments I lifted the line a fraction, felt the lead buffeted by the swirling undercurrents and lowered it again, *donk*, on to the bottom. 'The trick with this worming for trout,' I thought, thinking now of Bernard Cribbins's voice . . .

"Whoah!" I jumped up, the rod tugging over with what felt like a good fish belting away through the white water.

"Hey, what about that!"

My fish went well, eventually veering hard round to the nearside. I got the net down to the water and over its rim came a battling brownie. A wild looking fish it was too. Beautifully coloured, purple sheened with exceptionally large, cream bordered blotches of red and black. I got the hook out quickly and lowered it back to the water. His gills puffed and blew where he lay in the net, nosing forward once or twice before settling. I looped the hand strap on to a jutting bit of timber and waited to see if the arrangement would hold. It seemed OK. I ran for the camera, in my haste nearly toppling in. There were ferns behind the trees and I wrenched free a few of their big feathery fronds and doused them in the chill water, ready to complete the photo.

I couldn't believe my luck, a really good fish of a pound and a half, practically first chuck. I soon got the picture and lowering the net again watched the trout a while, paused at the rim. Then with one good thrash he shot out into the stream, away from the weir.

"What are you, nuts! You let him go!"

"I'm only in it for the sport," I said, "I feel bad enough about that. I don't want to kill my fish, I get a portrait, that's all."

There was a silence in the din from the weir. I thought about the contradiction, the hypocrisy and all the conversations I'd had trying to justify myself to friends that accused me of 'torturing wild life'. For me, I had to connect. I had to fish, but at the same time I had to return them to the water, that was my deal with Nature.

I went back on to the wet wall and tried the same hole again but time passed and there were no takes. I began to cast around, fishing the white water, the weight tumbling around between rocks and boulders. The fish started to come, not as big as the first, but fast, exciting half-pounders. I fished on until I'd had six and stopped. It had been a while and I was getting hungry again, and tired too. It had been a long day. And I wanted to give the fly a go. It could wait though, until after a break and some food. I fancied another glass of the superb wine too.

I sat back against the trunk of two of the trees . . .

"You're doing it again."

"Hello there, I thought you'd gone. Did you really have that A.E.W. Mason book along with you? I remember the lovers and the glacier thing."

"Sure did, I liked that story and reading it gave Bill plenty of time to catch his fish!"

I laughed and opened up my picnic - roast chicken and hard-boiled eggs. I poured the wine and ate hungrily while the lowering sun shone up the river. There was a sign a way down the bank and I pulled out the binoculars to be able to read it: *Arrantza Barrutia (Hil Gabe) Coto de pesca sin muerte*. Well, what about that - 'without death', it was a catch and release water. Above these words was the crest and shield of the *Nafarroako Gobernua*. I understood that all right, Navarra Government, but without the Spanish for the rest I'd've been in the dark. I pulled out my licence, yes, the same name and crest. There was a rather nice silhouette of an angler too. It had been a somewhat complicated business to procure, I remembered, unlike today, when you only need go to the website at: *www.navarra.es*

Back by the water, the autumn warmth was going from the air and I had to get some fly casting in before the long walk back. It wasn't dark until eight, but I guessed it was a couple of hours' hike back to Burguete.

I left everything under the trees and headed for the water with just the fly rod and net. My waders were good but the cold of the water very soon made itself felt. I was a fair way down from the weir and only thigh deep but the current was tremendous. I persevered for a while but gusts coming upstream and the pervading cold soon brought a halt to my endeavours.

"Brrrr! Makes your eyes ache," I said aloud.

"That was the wine," came the voice, "tasted rusty too, but it was good against the cold."

"I'm packing up," I said, "I'll walk down the road to Orbara, then take the path that cuts through the woods. I'll give this another go tomorrow."

I had seen that there was another of the *pistas forestales* running back up to the Collado de Nabala, the one for Aria. It joined up with the ancient country roads, which connected the villages in the old days. It should be pleasant walking and once I got to Nabala it was only a couple of miles to Burguete.

I collected together my gear and by the time I got going it was after four. The road wound along close to the river eventually rising sharply into the village of Orbara. I took a tarmac side road, which was the start of the forest path and soon came to the point where the Canal de Betolegui passed beneath. The woods began to thicken as I left the Irati valley behind. Looking back I had a last spectacular view of the river, a broad meander some way below. There were the white dots of grazing sheep in the pastures either side and a ford, the path from which disappeared into thick woods on the far side. The warm autumn tones extended from there over the horizon east, rising dramatically into the Sierra de Berrendi. My way took me into the valley of the river Aztapar, which for the moment was below me in the dense forest. Above were towering dark cliffs, heavily stratified, home to the vultures whose straight winged silhouettes I could just make out high up.

I knew from the map that I had to leave this road a couple of kilometres out, on a simple footpath, which might not be marked. I passed a few that disappeared abruptly downwards but I pressed on - my path ought to go straight on at a point where the road hairpinned into a steep climb.

Suddenly, there it was, and signposted too, with a path number and colour code, though no named destination. I plunged into its wonderfully thick overarching vegetation and within yards came to another path. It turned back, heading down I guessed, to the river, in the direction of Orbara. The other path looked infinitely more inviting; overgrown damp green and steep sided to the left, where there were traces of ancient stonework. It had the added advantage of seeming to go my way. I hadn't time enough for a dead-ended diversion.

I knew immediately that I was into something special; untrodden, forgotten maybe. The light was low, the thickness of foliage saw to that. Glossy sharp holly, occasionally heavy with blood red fruit, and bushes of thick green leaved box crowded into the spaces between oaks. The branches of these were doubled in thickness by the most outrageous growth of lichens I had ever seen. The ground was littered with fallen branches, unable to support the weight of their fleshy grey green fronds. Fallen leaves extended in every direction filling the air with the pungent scent of damp and decay.

I could hear water. The path was dropping along a gentle ridge towards the river. As its dark course came into view, still a way below, I heard a nearer smaller trickle. The path was suddenly black and muddy under the brown carpet of oak leaves where a spring emerged in the rock to the right. Under an amazing variety of mosses and lichens the wet rock ran with crystalline sparkling water. Reddish browns, yellows and infinite greens crowded together in wisps and clusters, broken here and there by black tree roots from higher up. Ahead was a great dome of almost luminous green in the middle of the path. Soft deep piled moss completely obscured the rock beneath which itself very nearly obscured the path. There were signs that the obstacle had once been skirted on the downside, but a bundle of fallen branches, thick with ferns that had pushed their way through, blocked the way. I decided to leave the path a moment and drop down to the water.

This was the Aztapar, another of the shallow black streams that traced their way through these uplands, searching for an escape. It was extraordinarily pretty, mostly overgrown and seemingly devoid of residents. There were certainly no fish. No light penetrated, even with the branches bare around about - the *barranco* was steep sided and the sun too low in the winter months; once it was high enough, the foliage was dense once more and shaded the rippling waters.

What light there had been was now fading fast and the temperature was falling appreciably. I followed the river and soon found the path again. The two ran parallel for a while and suddenly came out into the open. The water widened and ran over flat stone, though it could still have been leapt over, with a good run up. Bare spindly bushes appeared along its grassy banks, with the woods distant, away up the hillsides. It was beech once again which I would soon be entering on my way up to Nabala. The path turned and the remains of old paving appeared leading to a bridge. There was an old barn with horse-shoes wedged into many of the crevices in its stone walls, doubtless to bring luck. The door was arched and above was a large stone carved with the '*lauburu*', like a four-leafed clover, representing the Basque speaking provinces on the Spanish side. It was an ancient sign symbolising the elements and the four winds. The building was clearly still used, for wintering cattle probably, and as I passed it I came upon the road, with some sense of relief. It was the Aria road, once tarmac paved but now fallen into considerable disrepair. It cut a picturesque line south, rising in the distance into the woods. My direction was north to the Collado and then west to Burguete.

The dusk came on and the world became a solitary place of moving shadows and mysterious nocturnal noises. I whistled to myself for comfort, as I had done as a boy, but the truth is, I was enjoying myself immensely. After passing through the cold but richly scented beechwoods I eventually came out into the open, high up. It was an arduous climb and I felt exhausted. The signpost at Nabala stood out black against the night. Stars spangled the heavens and I paused to name constellations to myself in the darkness.

"You going to give the fly a try tomorrow then?"

This time the voice fairly startled me and I didn't reply at first.

"Yes," I said, "yes, we'll give the McGinty a go tomorrow."

I turned away from the black pines and the tamaracks. So much about that wood was chilling, as though it were haunted, haunted by the spirits of other trees and of men, unable to rest after being uprooted from this landscape in the face of progress. Here among these alien verticals, they were waiting, in this no-man's land between signs. Waiting for some kind of way out.

I remembered reading that Hemingway had been terribly disappointed on his second trip up here, only a year later, in 1925. Logging had not only ruined the country but the Irati too. The pools had been destroyed, the dams broken down and the river full of trash. But it had all been part of the cycle. Today, much was back as it had been, as though nothing had ever happened. My mind turned on the fact all the way back to Burguete.

It was dark by the time a pale glow from the village told me I hadn't far to go. But well before its lights came fully into view, the first thing that greeted me was the warm scent of beech wood fires. I came out at last on to the road and was soon approaching the bar Maritxu, at the top of the village. Wood smoke hung heavily over the roof. The night air was still and a golden glow shone from the windows. I eased open the old wooden door and after pushing my things into the corner by the window asked for a tot of *patxaran* and some *txistorra*, the famous Navarrese sausage, spicy and warming. My hands were cold and it took a little while before I could raise the glass to my lips. The people were friendly and asked where I had been walking. As I told them and asked the names of various peaks round about, an old woman, well wrapped up against the cold, came into the bar.

"It doesn't look like snow, does it?" she said doubtfully, to no one in particular.

"A thousand metres and above, they said on the weather," said the barman.

All ears turned to the conversation.

"It's a clear night so far," said a big, bearded man at the far end of the bar, "but it's definitely cold enough."

The old woman came past me and peered out at the sky.

"There's thick cloud coming in over Ortzanzurieta," she said.

A general murmur ensued around the bar with everyone talking about the prospects for snowfall. I sipped at my *patxaran* and listened. The talk was of the animals and the late crops. Winter had to be pretty hard up here; once the snow set it in it might stay for months. Burguete stood at 900 metres and the great peak the old woman referred to, only 6km away was nearly 1600 metres, that was 5200 feet! It was only 30th October though, and the river ran a couple of hundred metres lower than Burguete; surely the next day's fishing wasn't really at risk.

Warmed and fortified against the cold, I wished everyone '*buenas noches*' and ventured outside. It was around 0° C and a biting wind was coming down from the mountains. I pulled up my collar and trudged down the street into the village. The strong smell of wood burning was everywhere and my breath billowed out like the smoke from the chimneys. I passed the tall white façade of the Hostal Burguete, booked up for the weekend by a group of hunters from Madrid, its green shutters closed against the chill. The houses along the village's single street were exquisite, little changed over centuries, each with a name and as often as not a date - 1780, 1810. Each house, or *etxea*, had a sprig of hawthorn over the door, traditionally a charm to ensure plentiful harvests, now for good luck in general. I rather thought I should cut myself a twig against the snow.

Opposite my *hostal* was the Etxea Arretxe, 1885, with red painted shutters that seemed to glow against the whitewash behind. Almost all the buildings were white, with the woodwork in red or blue, green or yellow. It was warming, even though the windchill factor was dropping well below freezing. I bundled in through the wide front doors of the Hostal Juandeaburre and was greeted warmly by Doña Rosa, who assured me that the heating was on full blast. The hall smelt of family cooking and I thought the sooner I got washed and changed the sooner I would dine.

It wasn't long before I was braving the elements once more, up the road to the Jatetxea Txikipolit, a really splendid restaurant. I found a small table beneath a painting of country people from the last century and passed my eyes eagerly over the menu: *amurraina*, that was trout, locally caught too, but I rather thought I would go for the duck, with a dish of red bean broth called *babarrunak* to start. Feeling infinitely warmer, I ordered a bottle of *txakoli*, a white wine from San Sebastián, known as *Donostia* in Basque. The words on the menu, the names of cities and villages, all made me think again how I would love to learn something of their extraordinary language. Akin to a handful of others in odd pockets around Europe, invariably isolated by their geography such as in the Caucuses, these languages survived. No one knew if they were original to their lands, survivors from pre-history or whether they were derived from the common tongue of a travelling people, settled and somehow never ousted by the marauding Indo-Europeans.

All such speculation vanished with the arrival of the food. I took my time, enjoying my meal and the baronial hall style of the Txikipolit. I somehow managed all the wine too, and as a consequence slept soundly after a hurried, vaguely blurred walk back to the *hostal*.

The church bell in Burguete woke me at eight and the smell of coffee too. Opening the window was like opening the door of an upright freezer cabinet, a heavy pool of icy air gathered around my legs. I shivered and rushed to get dressed without daring to swing back the shutters and see outside. I imagined I could smell snow. Washed and clothed, I went again to the window. The street was clear. I leaned on the ironwork of the balcony and watched the narrow torrent of icy water below in the roadside channel carrying leaves.

Down in the breakfast room was a young French couple who were doing a bit of the pilgrims' route, El Camino de Santiago. They were planning to spend the day visiting the monastery at Roncevaux, just up the road. It was just a long weekend for them, France was only fifteen miles away. They were from the little town of Sommiers in Provence and we talked of the films *Jean de Florette* and *Manon des Sources* that had made it famous, not to mention Lawrence Durrell's living most of his life there. '*Du Relle*' they called him, and told me all the scandals known of him in the town. For my part, his *Alexandria Quartet* had been a major landmark in my adolescence but I suspect my part in the conversation was a ploy to delay having to venture out. We enjoyed our breakfast, that was for sure - warm croissants, toast and plenty of hot coffee.

I got all my gear together, food too, not forgetting the flask, of hot soup this time, and left the hospitality of Juandeaburre around nine. The church was chiming again, nearly deafening me as I passed its stone walls, half obscured by the young plane trees in front. There were a few light white clouds about but the day was bright and by the time I was out of Burguete and taking the *pista forestal* once more, I began to feel the warmth of the sun. The walking helped and once I was off the road I cracked on much more quickly than the previous day, soon coming out on to the ridge, which gave such a splendid view. I could see snow behind me, high on the peaks of Ortzanzurieta. The water would be colder than ever, the wading might have to be a matter of brief sorties followed by prolonged periods on the bank.

There was the conifer wood, straight ahead, an imposing sight. Its darkness made me shudder. All the same, I decided I would at least go a little way in and follow its perimeter south. I would be able to pick up the Aria road and short-cut my way to the Irati towards Orbara. That way, I would get at least a couple of hours more fishing and anyway I wanted another look.

The long sad and yellowing lower branches of the larches drooped almost to the ground. Most of the ferns near the edges of the wood were brown and dead-looking and as I picked my way through them and between the tall trees, the cold air penetrated to the bone. Enough was enough. I bounded down the grassy bank and back out into the sunshine.

"This your last day?" came the voice at last.

"I thought you'd forsaken me," I said.

"No, I'm intrigued, I'm wondering how many fish you're gonna let go today!"

"It's got to be the last day," I said, "I have to get down to Pamplona tomorrow for the train. I should get an hour or so in the Café Iruña too."

"Still there is it? I loved that place."

"Yes, it's still there and unchanged by and large, big ornate mirrors, chandeliers and the same chequered floor."

"Good coffee too, and a great view of the square."

"Anyway," I said, "in answer to your question, I'm hoping for a good half a dozen, at least as big as Bill Gorton's, if they're fool enough to fall for one of your crazy McGintys!"

"The McGinty's a good fly, I've used it down in Colorado, but keep in mind it was Bill's choice, not mine."

Up the road ahead came the man I had seen the day before.

"*¡Muy buenos día*s!" he saluted me cordially, but again there was that doubtful expression in his eyes. I couldn't help thinking that my striding along in the hills talking to myself might well form part of the evening's talk in a bar somewhere.

"*¡Buenos días!*" I waved back and asked how long it was to the Irati valley by the Aria road.

"An hour or more," he said, "but you've got to leave the road at la Borda de Irarte and follow the stream, there's a big barn to the left."

"*Muchas gracias,*" I said, "*¡Adiós!*" and headed down the hill, leaving the conifers behind and entering anew into the *hayedo*. Silvery grey trunks, softly thick-matted with moss on their north sides stood mute to either side of the road. The upper branches, as thick as the trunks, twisted like huge serpents and reflected near white in the brilliant sun. Coming into a grassy hollow, I surprised a few breakfasting rabbits that soon scuttled to their holes.

"Good hunting up here," said the voice. "There are wild boar, deer and partridges too."

"I can't be doing with hunting," I said, "not that I haven't been, but one day I just decided I didn't want to kill anything ever again." Like Ted Hughes I thought. He never stopped fishing though, it was different somehow. I felt I agreed with that and I had become committed to always returning the fish.

I wandered on in my thoughts and out loud, in the eternal debate about harm done to fish, efforts to minimise the impact on them and nature. Lead-free shot, barbless hooks, de-hooking mats, antiseptics, biodegradable materials etc. etc. . . . justifying myself to myself. It was either that or give it up altogether.

I came upon a patch of grass where autumn crocuses showed in pale purple and white round the base of an old walnut tree. The remains of a rustic ladder seemed to grow out of the very bark of the trunk. A substantial beech branch formed the single upright to which four crosspieces had been nailed, to act as rungs. Littered about were black rotted leaves and empty walnut shells, shaded by the ever present ferns. The tree had gone wild and was overrun with ivy. No pruning or harvesting had gone on here for a while. I paused to photograph its strange, decadent beauty and hurried on.

Time skipped by and I was soon into the glorious walk I had found on my return the evening before. Jewels of golden sunlight flickered here and there, but it was remarkably dark and damp. I set up the tripod and snapped the curious forms of branches laden with lichens and the narrow undulating path that despite being known, seemed untrodden in ages. Again I went down to the river and followed its course a short way, its ripples running like thoughts through my mind.

Once out of the Aladdin's cave and on to the Orbara road it was no time before the magnificent Irati valley came into view. I passed through the village and leaving the road, took the path down to the ford I had seen from above. It was marked on the map as Puente Zubialdea and was the focal point of a number of paths that traced across the country between villages. Among them, Aria, and Aezkoa Iriberri, beneath the great peak of Olloki Ate, places unreachable by modern roads. Reaching the old ford, I came upon another sign, '*Arrantza Barrutia*'. I didn't need the Spanish translation this time. Here the fish could be taken away, killed. The river ran over rocks above and below, the banks thick with trees warmly painted with autumn. This point looked accessible enough. I set up my gear, tied the McGinty and struggled into my waders. There was no sense stopping to think about it.

"That's the way, it's all part of the thing, being there, being in touch, connected to the natural cycle," came the voice again.

Those could have been Hughes's words I thought, as I pushed out into the stream. An involuntary shiver coursed up my legs to the back of my neck. It was bitter, the trout would be sluggish. I fished the fly down the stream, between bulges in the flow, looking for lies. It was rocky and I had to wade with much caution. A soft breeze from behind helped me place the McGinty long; sometimes just clipping overhanging branches before dropping into the water. There were no takers. My gear was safely stashed under bushes, so I moved away down water, searching methodically for fish.

I was out of sight of the ford and the river deepened. I fished on, and after a while found myself coming into shallows over great flats of stone, cut and divided as though worked by man. Ahead was a huge square block like an altar, breaking the surface, the water boiling on the down side. I let the fly back into the lee and stopped it there. I waited and was rewarded with an arm-wrenching jerk on the rod, the reel spun, the bone handles belting my fingers as I shifted grip to thumb the spool.

There was no drag on this old reel and I wished momentarily for a modern one. I was suddenly down to the backing, the fish now careering left and right across the width of the river. I moved down, recovering line. A big fish, I hadn't expected that.

"Good old McGinty doesn't let you down."

I laughed. It was true. Who would have thought a bee imitation would take a fish in November! Wading was easier over the flats and little by little, I was closing in on my fish. There it was, only a few yards off. What a trout! I had never had a brownie that size; the rod was arched over, yanking down again and again. Then a leap, I caught my breath. If I lose it now . . . The fish plunged back into the water and swung away, making for the overhangs. Reaching round behind me I got the net, looped the strap over my arm and pushed against the current across the stream. I had the rod down nearly flat over the water, still hooped right round. Out it came, up jumped the rod and the trout wavered in the current, letting me bring it in. I scooped the net under it and brought the rim to me. I was waist deep, the fish panting in the gentle water before me, a big olive brown wildie. Very dark above, turning golden yellow down the sides, his fins were rather battered, jaws hooked. He looked a serious customer.

Easily double figures, and as many seasons probably - it was the biggest brown trout I had ever seen. I slipped out the fly from his upper jaw and keeping the fish in the water fumbled for my pocket scales. I weighed it, net and all - 12lb! Even taking a pound off, it was a tremendous catch. I lowered the rim of the landing-net and the trout inched forward to liberty.

"Just look at that," I said out loud, "watch him go."

No reply came this time. The trout dropped through the water slowly and rested on the bottom under our gaze. I shuddered from the cold and my movement startled the fish away. A powerful lunge forward and it disappeared.

I had to get back to the bank. I felt sluggish and heavy, my gear cluttered about me. Trudging against the flow, my progress towards the shallows was painfully slow, the water icily weighted. I longed for that soup and wondered if I actually would venture out again after it.

My fingers were numb as I twisted the cup off the flask and poured out the life giving warmth. I sat down on a rock, the chill taken off it by some hours in the direct sun. It was covered in lichens, like gold and silver coins, even some green tinged, like oxidised coppers. The soup was piping hot, I sipped it carefully, my hands closed around the cup, absorbing the heat. Winds had sprung up and the sky was clouding over from the direction of Ortzanzurieta. I looked across the waters, leaden grey, reflecting the now near white sky as it shifted irrevocably south. It looked misty over the nearer hills.

Much restored, I felt ready to brave the stream once more. I waded out and started to cast. Snowflakes in ones and twos began to waft by me on the air. I fished the water, concentrated, searching for one more fish. The wind turned and buffeted me. More snow came with it, silver and dark, in the failing light. I began to think I had better call it a day. I looked around - snow was falling. It was falling here, it was falling to the west in Burguete, and in all probability it was falling too in Idaho, where Ernest Hemingway was finally laid to rest.

Chapter Two

The Basque Country

Where the author reflects on Basque culture, its mysterious language and extraordinary blood, as well as its role in epic European human history. Then there are local fishermen's tales in a magnificent land of lakes, with their trout, pike and barbel, not to mention some remarkable aspects of gastronomy, a host of mushrooms and one or two more barbel.

Very few visitors to Spain get to know anything at all about the Basques or their country, Euskal Herria, in Spanish *el País Vasco*. From international news, all most people have ever heard about is the bombings and other outrages committed by the separatist terrorist group ETA against the Spanish state, although there are those who may point to the stunning modern art museum, the Guggenhiem, in Bilbao as a monument to Basque culture. Modern art lovers may also be aware that Picasso's 'Guérnica', which represents the horrors of civil war, makes specific reference to an attack carried out by German warplanes at Franco's behest on a Basque town of that same name.

Innumerable visitors to Spain have certainly heard of and passed through Bilbao, the well known port town on the northern Spanish coast, and capital of the province of Vizcaya or Bizkaia (from whence the name Biscay), which is one of the three Spanish Basque Country regions, the others being Álava and Guipúzcoa, in Basque *Araba* and *Gipuzkoa*. This latter region is home to an international road transport company, which many holiday-makers, driving in Spain will certainly have seen, and, as the huge, green TIR truck rumbled by, doubtless wondered as to its possible pronunciation: *Guipuzcoana*.

There are two other Basque territories: Navarra, the autonomous region to the east; and over the border, the French Pays Basque, itself made up of Lower

Navarre, Labourd and Soule. The three Spanish Basque provinces and Navarra are symbolised, as we have seen, in the lauburu or Basque cross, which is a leaf-like design similar to the Japanese *tomoe*, and is often seen on houses and in bars across the region. The word *lauburu* means 'four heads' and the intellectual Imanol Mujica suggested that the heads represented spirit, life, consciousness, and form.

Many Basque homes and shops display the symbol over the doorway for good luck and the symbol is generally held to signify prosperity. In Basque mythology the right-facing lauburu is in its positive form and symbolises vigour, where in its left-facing negative form it represents death. For this reason, in many Basque cemeteries the tombstones feature left-facing lauburus. The use of the lauburu as a cultural icon fell into disuse under Franco's nationalist dictatorship, between 1939 and 1975, when almost all elements of Basque culture were forcibly repressed. It was a dark period for the Basques, a period which gave rise, among other things, to the foundation of ETA, which was originally a resistance organisation operating against Franco's Fascist state.

There is something deeply mysterious about the whole Basque phenomenon. The most obvious difference between the Vascongados, as they are sometimes known, and their neighbours in France and Spain has to be their extraordinary language, which the Basques themselves call *Euskera* or *Eusleera*, depending on which dialect they speak. Although, over the years, this language has absorbed individual words from both French and Spanish, its basic vocabulary and structure bear absolutely no resemblance to either.

A phrase taken at random from a phrasebook may serve as an example: 'The table is laid, you can bring in the food.' The French '*La table est mise, vous pouvez apporter le déjeuner*' would be comprehensible to many, with memories of their school days, and perhaps the Spanish too: '*La mesa está puesta, puede traer la comida.*' The Basque, however, is another matter: '*Mahaia gertu dago. Liar dezakezue bazlearia.*' The look and imagined sound of these words is utterly alien, with not a single recognisable syllable, and the grammar and syntax are no less exotic.

If the reader will forgive for a moment the language teacher in me replacing the travelling angler, I will explain a little. The definite article 'the' is not a separate word in the Basque language but a suffix, coming at the end of the word like 'ly' in an English adverb: quick, quickly. Nouns used with numerals, moreover, remain in the singular, as one egg, three egg. Auxiliary verbs vary according to the number of objects as well as the number of subjects, and prepositions are also suffixes in Basque, or prefixes, which alter according to whether the word to which they are attached represents something animate or inanimate. Such are the complexities of the grammar that the author of the first modern Basque grammar book, an eighteenth century priest and scholar by the name of Manuel de Larramendi, entitled his work *El imposible vencido* (1729) or The Impossible Overcome.

Coming once again from a slightly more fishy angle, one sixteenth century Sicilian author was convinced that the Basques' strange tongue enabled them to communicate with the monsters of the deep. Perhaps knowing a few words would help us charm the finny denizens of Basque rivers and lakes into our landing-nets. 'Fish', for example, is *arraina*, 'angling' is *arrantza* and 'Caught anything, mate?' would be *Zerbait ortu duzu, lagun?* Moreover, learning to count from one to ten might be a useful pastime while waiting for a bite: *bat, bi, hiru, lau, bost, sei, zazpi, zortzi, bederatzi, hamar*.

It has always been understood, or at the least suspected, that Basque was a language of great antiquity. In the Middle Ages, it was believed that the various languages of the world were the product of divine intervention at the Tower of Babel. A number of scholars have argued that Euskera was the language which Noah's grandson, Tubal, was said to have taken to Iberia and that in ancient times, it must have been spoken throughout the Peninsula.

Long after the Biblical explanation of the origin of languages had been called into question elsewhere in Europe, it continued to be strongly supported within the Basque country itself, largely because of the immense authority there of the Church, particularly the Jesuits, whose founder Ignatius of Loyola was a Basque. Some Basque authors went as far as to claim that theirs had been the original language of the whole of Europe or even the world. There is no doubt that Basque was once spoken over a much larger area than it is today, an area which almost certainly included the entire Pyrenees, since it is known to have been current in parts of Aragón and Catalonia during the Middle Ages.

Modern scholarship has demonstrated that Basque is indeed an extremely old language. The mainspring of modern philology was the discovery towards the end of the eighteenth century that almost all European and near Asian languages subsequently grouped together under the name of IndoEuropean came from a common source. Throughout the nineteenth century, Basque resisted all attempts to find it a place in the IndoEuropean family and philologists have eventually had to reconcile themselves to the conclusion that Basque predates the migrations from the East which brought the IndoEuropean languages into Europe around 3,000 to 5,000 years ago. But there is also evidence that the language may be much older even than that. It has been suggested, for example, that words like *aitzkor* (axe) and *aitzur* (hoe) which derive from *aitz*, meaning stone, date from the time when tools were made primarily from that material. The Stone Age is generally thought to have covered the period from around two million years ago to approximately 3000 BC.

Recent research has concentrated on trying to find a link between Basque and other pre-IndoEuropean languages (such as those which still survive in parts of the Caucasus in Eastern Europe, and among the Berbers of North Africa) using a method invented by the American linguist Morris Swadesh, whereby a hundred-word passage in one language is compared with the same in another language to discover the percentage of similar words. Up to five per cent is regarded as no more than coincidence. But it has been found that there is more than a seven per cent overlap between Basque and two of the three Caucasian languages, Georgian and Circassian, and a ten per cent overlap between Basque and certain Berber languages, which would seem to suggest that there was indeed an ancient link.

While linguists have been puzzling over the singularity of the Basques' language, doctors and scientists have been discovering that they have other, less evident, peculiarities. To understand these, we need to make a brief detour into the world of serology, or the study of blood.

On occasions, when the blood of two individuals is brought into contact, it coagulates. This is because the blood of at least one of them contains what is called an antigen. There are two types of antigen, A and B. Some people have both and they are classified as type A/B. Other people's blood contains only one antigen and they are classified as either A or B. But there is also a third category (0) whose blood contains no antigens at all. There are two reasons why all this is of importance to anthropologists. Firstly, antigens are hereditary - no one can have either A or B in their bloodstream unless at least one of their parents had it in theirs. Secondly, the proportion of each blood type in the population varies significantly from place to place. As we move across Europe from East to West, for example, the percentage of As increases while the percentage of Bs decreases. The Basques conform to this pattern, but to an exaggerated degree. The percentage of As is higher and the proportion of Bs lower than we would expect for a people living on the Atlantic coast.

In 1939 an American researcher opened up new fields for exploration when he discovered a substance in the blood of the Macacus Rhesus monkey which was also found to be present in the blood of some humans. According to whether or not their blood contained the new substance, people could thereafter be divided into Rhesus positive (Rh+) and Rhesus negative (Rh). It was found that in Europe the percentage of Rhesus negatives was higher than in other parts of the world and that throughout the continent it was a more or less uniform 12 to 16 per cent. The relevance of this to the Basques was discovered, not by researchers in the Basque country, but by an ordinary general practitioner working thousands of miles away in Argentina, who was concerned with an entirely different problem - eritroblastosis. This is an often fatal illness which affects newly born children whose blood is incompatible with that of their mothers. In most cases, the problem arises because the mother is Rh while her child is Rh+, having inherited the substance from its father. The GP, Dr Miguel Angel Etcheverry, noticed that an unusually high proportion of these unfortunate mothers were, like him, of Basque descent. To confirm his thesis, he took samples from over one hundred Argentinians who had four Basque grandparents and discovered that fully one third of them were Rh, which was an abnormally high proportion even for a group of European descent. After his findings were published in 1945, a series of studies in the Spanish Basque country all produced figures in excess of 30 per cent and one, carried out in the French Basque country, put the proportion of the population who did not have the Rhesus substance in their blood at 42 per cent, the highest figure recorded anywhere in the world. As far as blood grouping was concerned, the Basques were emerging as exceptionally 'European' (by virtue of their Rhesus count) and very 'Westerly' (by virtue of their antigen pattern), therefore pre-dating all other peoples of western Europe.

Throughout history, the Basques have been thought of by their neighbours as being bigger and stronger. A great deal of measuring and weighing by anthropologists, especially during the early part of this century, proved this to be the case. The Basques were found to be, on average, two to three centimetres taller than the average in France and Spain and, although they tended to be more muscular, their limbs and in particular their hands and feet were inclined to be quite delicate.

The anthropologists also established that the typical Basque had a distinctive 'hare's head', broad at the top and narrow at the bottom, and that he or she was likely to have a high forehead, a straight nose and a distinctive bulge over the temples.

These findings, when put alongside the archaeological discoveries of that period, are very interesting indeed. Shortly after the First World War, two Basque researchers, Telesforo de Aranzadi and José Miguel de Barandiarán, had begun excavating a number of dolmens dating from around 3000 BC, the time of the IndoEuropean migrations. The bones they found in them suggested that the people who had lived in the Basque country at that time had the same physical characteristics as the Basques of today. But even more interestingly, a skull found in the mid-Thirties by Aranzadi and Barandiarán in a cave near Itziar in Guipuzcoa dating from the late Stone Age, about 10,000 BC, also displayed several typically Basque traits, further suggesting that the Basques of today could be the direct descendants of earliest European man.

The Basques, therefore, along with other peoples in the Caucasus and among the Berbers, are certainly the most ancient communities of Europe and North Africa, considerably predating the westerly spread of Indo-European peoples and their language.

Needless to say, even fewer anglers than tourists have heard of the Basque Country or have ever considered fishing there. As is frequently the case when we first visit any such lesser known regions, we are apt to feel we have discovered them just for ourselves. I certainly felt this, since there are some wonderful, seemingly secret locations here, with, moreover, the most extraordinarily evocative names. My first fishing excursion into the País Vasco took me to some spectacular lowland lakes, the *embalses* or reservoirs of Zadorra, just to the north-east of Vitoria or *Gasteiz*, the capital of Álava or *Araba* and indeed of the whole Spanish Basque Country. The most notable of these waters are the Ullíbarri-Gamboa and Urrúnaga reservoirs.

Getting a licence for fishing in the Basque Country can be a complicated affair, as each of the provinces has its own rules and regulations, and its own licences both for sea and freshwater fishing. Searching the Internet throws up horrible quantities of nearly indecipherable information in Basque and Spanish but relief came when I finally made the discovery that the Caja Vital, a bank of Vitoria and Álava, handles freshwater licence applications for the whole region. Finding the address of the nearest Caja Vital to where you are in the Basque Country, as well as elsewhere around Spain, is easy enough, via the Internet or the *Yellow Pages* and much to my surprise and pleasure there was one in my home town of Valladolid. I spent no more than ten minutes in the bank, where a passport or other identifcation was required, and had to pay very little (€15 - in 2013) for my licence.

Travelling by road from Castile into the Basque Country, you get a strong sense that you are leaving one country and entering another. My girlfriend Yolanda was driving. Not an angling enthusiast herself, she was joining a group of ramblers early next morning, leaving me to 'bother the fishes'. We both thought the change in the landscape was spectacular, from the immense wide open plains, in tones of brown and yellow ochre for the most part of the year, where there is hardly a tree to be seen under a burning sun, you suddenly find yourself among the forest-clad foothills of mountains, lush green with purplish shadows hiding waterfalls and rivers, where cloud and rain are never very far away. Then the language of the road signs is distinctly foreign, and the people, when you first stop at a roadside café or restaurant, actually look different too.

Most of us like to acquire a little of the local language when travelling: 'Yes' and 'no' are respectively *bai* and *ez*. *Kaixo* is 'hello', *egún on* is 'good day', 'thank you' is e*skerrik asko* and *agur*, 'goodbye', and so, we might begin to feel that we are at least making a start at immersion in a foreign culture. Although the traveller will certainly hear many of these words, particularly *kaixo* and *agur*, in this area, in neither the province of Álava or the capital, Vitoria-Gasteiz, is Euskera very commonly spoken. To hear much more of the language you would need to take the road north-west to Arrasate/Mondragón into Guipuzcoa.

There's no better place than the bars anywhere in the Iberian Peninsula for cultural immersion and, more importantly still, for finding out something about the local angling. I have found over the years that wearing a fly fisherman's vest or waistcoat, one of those things with dozens of little pockets, a few 'D' rings and several zingers, complete with dangling snips and forceps, will attract the attention of the best informed local enthusiasts. Perhaps it would be as well to insert a warning at this point. I once read a piece called 'Bad Advice', a hilarious account of encounters with local angling opinion, by the American writer and *New Yorker* contributor Ian Frazier. 'People will tell you any damn thing,' he says as he recalls those all too familiar moments when you 'ask a touristy, greenhorn question'. You will be told for starters that your car will never make it up 'that Forest Service road' and that anyway, you're 'headed in the wrong direction'. Who among us hasn't been helpfully advised that it's the wrong time of year for the fish you're after, that you need a completely different rod and reel set up, different tackle and a special kind of bait you've never heard of. There are folk out there who just don't want you anywhere near their angling backyard. 'It's much better further up,' they'll tell you, 'the other side of the motorway bridge . . .' or 'You'll never catch anything round here on bread, mate . . .' or on surface baits, or even worms. I remember one sour-faced individual who bellowed: 'There ain't no fish in 'ere, pal!' Extraordinarily, I didn't get another bite after that. Nevertheless, there is nothing, we assure ourselves, as invaluable as local knowledge. It just depends on who you talk to.

Around the great lakes of Ullibarri-Gamboa and Urrunaga there are many small villages with delightful *casas rurales*, where bed and breakfast accommodation is first class and where, perhaps, the proprietor is an angler. One word to watch out for is *jatetxea* or 'tavern'; these are often converted farmhouses, which are superb places for good food and wines, typically by an open fireside, and of course, small cafés and bars are everywhere. With any luck mine host at the *jatetxea* will offer some local knowledge. As often as not, however, their experience will be limited to the highland rivers, where there are plenty of trout, but I was irresistibly drawn to a number of the coarse species to be found in the reservoirs.

I found a cosy little bar in the village of Marieta, where I deliberately didn't order *gaztanbera* or *mamia*, the legendary breakfast dish of the Basque country vaunted by many travel guides, since I suspected that 'sheep's milk junket' wasn't going to agree with me half so well as coffee and a toasted croissant. Junket was popular once in Britain, as a pudding, and whenever I have looked it up in a dictionary, failing always to remember just what it is, I find the description concurs with that of curds and whey, another delicacy lost in British tradition, except in the tale of Little Jack Horner. They are both as near as anything to yoghurt, that ubiquitous breakfast, tea and supper pudding substance which I, personally, have never warmed to. Since I have begun this gastronom-ical digression, I shall continue, with . . . quince, or quince jelly. This rather solid, grainy, jam-like conserve, made from large, heavy and rock hard yellow pears called quinces, has also vanished in Britain, except in another rhyme, in which the Owl and the Pussy Cat went to sea. In Spanish it is *membrillo*, and it is very popular everywhere, particularly in the north. Here in the Pais Vasco it is called *irasagar* and is absolutely delicious, as are the quinces themselves when cooked with sugar or baked in the oven stuffed with currants, an invention entirely my own I might add, since no Basque or any other Spaniard I have met has ever considered doing such a thing.

Inventiveness, nevertheless, has become a distinguishing characteristic of modern Spanish and very particularly Basque cuisine. The most famous chefs in the Iberian Peninsula are Basques, from the affable and entertaining Karlos Arguiñano, who has popularised Basque food, along with his incredibly corny jokes, all over Spain through his TV shows and books, to Juan Mari Arzak, a restaurateur in Vitoria/Donostia, who became the most famous exponent of New Basque Cuisine and who ran one of the first three-star Michelin Guide restaurants in the country.

In the 1970s and 80s, Basque chefs were considerably influenced by French nouvelle cuisine but very soon began to produce something entirely their own. This Nouvelle Cuisine Basque was certainly original in form, often highly com-plex in terms of flavour and textural combinations, even exploiting chemical and strict temperature-controlled interactions, and extraordinarily artistically creative in appearance, but continuing to be decidedly Basque in substance, featuring less weighty and less rustic versions of traditional dishes and flavours. The influence of this new gastronomy spread quickly across Spain, rapidly becoming, in effect, the nation's national style of *haute cuisine*. Many tapas bars, especially in San Sebastián, serve modern-style *pintxos* employing thoroughly modern techniques and ingredients, but the little dishes on offer are not cheap. They are a radical departure from the very economical, traditional pinchos and tapas that were once a national institution.

In recent years, new young chefs, such as Martin Berasategui, are giving fur-ther impetus to Basque cookery, pushing back frontiers in order to internationalise it, particularly in France, where Basque Cuisine is even more highly regarded. Most famous of all, however, is the Catalonian chef, Ferrán Adrià, who took the techniques pioneered by Arzak and other Basque chefs to even greater heights of sophistication. The Bulli or Bulldog Restaurant in the picturesque Cala Montjoi on Barcelona's Gerona coast, was originally estab-lished in 1962 but when Ferran Adrià joined the kitchen team in 1984, the restaurant quickly became something special, and was awarded a number of Michelin Stars before soaring to international recognition in 2002, when the prestigious Pelligrino World Top 50 List and *Restaurant* magazine declared it the entire world's Number One restaurant, an exceptional honour, which it then repeated in 2006, 2007, 2008 and 2009. Ferrán Adrià brought ever more innovative and adventurous techniques to cooking and when the restaurant eventually closed in 2011, a new business sprang up, the Bulli Foundation, dedicated to creative and scientific gastronomic research, including the so-called culinary 'deconstruction' method, which centres on the isolation, via physics and chemistry, of individual flavours, and the invention of Molecular Cuisine.

Meanwhile, in the United States, Basque chef Teresa Barrenechea pioneered her native cuisine in a restaurant called Marichu and has published two influential books on the subject. Elsewhere around the world, in cities with large numbers of Basque émigrés, such as Buenos Aires or São Paulo, there are several Basque restaurants and visitors there will also notice the Basque influence in local dishes. Back in Spain, new Basque-style tapas bars are now a common sight in Barcelona and Madrid, as well as other large cities around the country but my own taste continues to be decidedly simpler and more rustic.

In the bar in Marieta I enjoyed my breakfast, and chatting with the bartender, soon found out who to speak to about fishing. Old Patxi, the Basque equivalent of Paddy in Ireland, looked every inch the expert, advanced in years, with weathered features, a cropped and grizzled beard and a sparkle in his eye that might belie brotherly enthusiasm, or innate wickedness, bent on deception and a stroll up the garden path. Nonetheless, he had a good countryside air about him, clothed in something approximating to an Arran sweater and wellington boots. I felt, overall, he might know what he was talking about, even if he did look a little too much like Frazier's experts 'Pappy' and 'Cappy'. The first thing I learnt from him was that pike had been introduced some years before by 'some biologists'. This was said with considerable disdain, biologists were clearly the epitome of despicable city types poking their noses in where they weren't wanted. I hastened to assure him I knew nothing of the damnable subject. A couple of others joined us and it soon became apparent that there was general consensus and the demon *Esox lucius* had effectively annihilated the local fish population. The other interesting piece of news, however, was that there were also monster trout in the lakes, six- to eight-pounders, which could be taken on small spinners, and one man claimed to have caught a giant ferox over sixteen pounds! It seemed that many of these monsters were thoroughbred proper brown trout, but there were also plenty of huge rainbow ribbed pirates. Then there were barbel too, one man affirmed, probably Graells barbel, *Barbus graellsii*, which I knew could be a big fish, certainly of ten pounds or more. I also remembered having once read of one specimen measuring nearly three feet in length and weighing over twenty-five pounds. One or two older folk in the bar mentioned the much smaller red-tailed barbel *Barbus haasi*, a fast-water fish, usually found in the upper reaches of mountain rivers in the region and across into Catalonia. It seemed that where some rivers entered the lakes here, usually when in flood, the red-tail was occasionally caught on a worm. That sounded like very pleasant fishing indeed.

Autumn was the season I had chosen, the trees were decked out in a splendid array of golden tones and the weather was still mild, if a little change-able - my old pocket barometer was falling. There had been a good deal of rain and more was forecast. There was no doubt I had to make the best of the blustery day's current sunny intervals.

On my map from the tourist office, I found the main expanse of blue very clearly marked as *Uribarri-Ganboako urteguia*, which is the Basque name for the Ullibarri-Gamboa reservoir. However, on other maps it appeared, a little con-fusingly, as the Otxandio or the Legutiano (from the name of a large town on the northern shore of the Urrúnaga reservoir a short drive to the north-west). Names varied according to which maps I consulted; I found a very Spanish name on one, the Santa Engracia reservoir, which was, moreover, described as the water most favoured by local anglers. Ullibarri-Gamboa is the larger of the two most important waters here, and is bordered by the spectacular scenery of the Landa, Garaio, Lubiano and Mendixur natural parks. The other, Lake Urrúnaga, is bordered by the Sorgimendi and Zabalain natural parks and the countryside around both reservoirs, lying between the provinces of Araba and Bizkaia, is a haven for all kinds of wildlife, as well as being glorious territory for hiking and mountain biking. The reservoirs lie in the shadow of Mount Gorbeia, which, at 1481m or 4813ft, is a very impressive peak, forming a spec-tacular backdrop, as well as being the high point of the Gorbeia Park. The open mountain pastures that surround the cross on the summit are dotted with old stone-built shepherds' refuges, while lower down the mountain sides and in the valleys there are extensive beech forests, where you may come across aban-doned charcoal burners' huts. There are also innumerable and timeless oak and yew trees, together with much younger conifer plantations. There is a remarkable variety of wildlife in these places, including most exotically, the European wild cat, the wild boar and the beech marten, although you would be lucky indeed to actually spot any of them. September is rutting season and it is well worth taking a day off from the waters and spending time in the park to listen to the deer bellowing in the distance. I've never got close enough to actually see one.

Taking a stroll that afternoon along the eastern shore of Ullibarri-Gamboa, I found a remarkable variety of conditions in a short distance, from a long rocky outcrop of near vertical sedimentary layers extending into the apparently quite deep water, to a very shallow broad bay surrounded by black muddy margins into which my wellies sank almost to the knee. There is a footpath all the way around this reservoir, a total of 30-odd miles in the form of a figure of eight, obliging you to cross the water at Azúa, where there is a sturdy footbridge, known as the '*aqueducto*'. At Azúa there is also an impressive ruined church and tower at the water's edge, contained within a sheep farm, but perfectly easy to photograph. A little further on after crossing the lake east to west, there is another wooden slatted footbridge passing just inches above the water across a series of small pontoons. This very attractive causeway is *La pasarela del Zadorra*, which apparently was once crowded with local anglers, but from which fishing is now prohibited.

I was desperately keen to fish yet could not stop walking on and on, investigating every inch of the shoreline. As I enjoyed my walk, I was struck by the huge number of crayfish remains scattered everywhere along the shore. I had noticed signs marking areas where fishing for them was permitted but I was also aware that all permits had been suspended a year or two before, to allow the population of crayfish to recover after over-fishing. It certainly seemed as though that recovery had taken place and local birds, including herons and cormorants, were making the most of it. I imagined being plagued by crayfish if I chose to fish a bottom bait anywhere and resolved to try my hand with spinners to start with. One of those really big trout, if they actually existed, would be a tremendous start.

I had already set up a five-piece travelling spinning rod and, reaching another rocky outcrop which commanded a broad bay of deepish water, I started casting, covering the water in that classic fan shape recommended in so many 'How to catch them' books. I worked the water hard but there was no sign of a fish. I began to notice sunken tree stumps and clumps of weed here and there and cast as near as I dare, hoping to locate some predator jaws lurking by them. The water meanwhile was becoming distinctly choppy, with the sky darkening from the west. I was well prepared in wellies, leggings and a waterproof jacket but, noticing that kind of thundery dark curtain, to which no manner of clothing was impervious, descending over the hillsides, I really didn't fancy trudging the banks in such torrential rain.

I recovered my spinner quickly, the little silver Super Vibrax No. 2 skipping across the surface, just as a huge thunderbolt shattered the relative silence buffeting me about the ears. The lightning crack was wonderful, its resounding aftershock rumbling in all directions. I jerked the little rod up, about to swing the spinner into my hand, when there was a violent squall in the water right at my feet and a huge pike lunged head and shoulders out of the water, a deep-green camouflage blur, its toothy maw agape and its bright golden eye drinking me in. Every detail in a split second of slow motion, then a red flash of gills and a further eruption of water splashed on to my boots, before it turned away and vanished into the depths. The rain was suddenly hammering down; I pulled my hood up and made a dash towards a line of spindly trees, where I hoped to at least get out of the worst of it. I ducked down on the leeward side, where most of the rain seemed to be driving horizontally over my head. The sky was now dark as dark, from horizon to horizon, the wind mercilessly thrashing the branches.

The situation was far from comfortable and I looked about for some hope of relief. I recalled that back at the aqueduct footbridge there had been another path, an avenue of trees either side, which ran up the hillside towards Larritzar where Yolanda had dropped me off. There was a ruined tower which I had seen when coming down to the water along the earlier path. I might find some shelter there and then make a dash for the car. I ran back along the path feeling pretty wretched. There were cold trickles running down my neck and chest and my wellies were squelching. Nevertheless, I got to the path and in the avenue, found I was relatively sheltered keeping under the right-hand-side overhang. I made my way up the slope and came within sight of the tower much sooner than I had expected. The path I had taken when coming down was clearly more circuitous. I ran for the tower and had to negotiate some old barbed wire but was quite soon standing in a dry patch beneath the entrance arch of the building, breathing hard.

What a pike . . . it must have been a 20-pounder. I really hoped I would get another chance at that fellow. The rain didn't seem to bother him. It was coming down harder than ever now. The hollow tower was open to the sky but was so densely packed with brambles that there was virtually no updraught to pull the rain into the entrance. I was safe for the time being. The tangled briars looked hundreds of years old, with huge thorny limbs spiralling up towards the sky. It was just like the abandoned entrance to the castle of the Sleeping Beauty; nothing short of a sword would have any effect either.

I was reminded that the Basque country was also a land of witches and sorcerers, where long ago a huge black goat had been an idol of worship, and where mysterious rites and festivals were celebrated in lonely places. A marvellous painting came to mind, Goya's *The Witches' Sabbath* of 1798 which depicted a small crowd of hags, some individuals clutching voodoo-like fetiches - one holding forth a skeleton babe and another her own infant in arms - gathered at the feet of a huge black goat, with a garland of oak leaves around its spiralling horns. The scene represents a climactic moment in necromancy, in which Satan presides over a grisly rite of child sacrifice, one forehoof extended to touch the offered child, beneath a gibbous moon, as huge black bats flitter over their heads. The work is a precursor to the artist's later 'black paintings' of the 1820s; images never commissioned or even intended to be seen in public, they give imaginative rein to the artist's awareness of the darkest forces at work in humanity: terror, fear and hysteria, perhaps best symbolised in his 'Saturn Devouring His Son'.

The wind howled eerily overhead and a crow cronked complainingly some-where beyond. The rain continued to hammer out its fury on the surrounding bushes and trees, while the sky appeared to offer no hope of respite. Suddenly, a terrific crash of lightning broke overhead and resounded down the tower, rattling the nerves of another pair of crows that flew off complaining even more loudly than their predecessor. Just then I heard a car. It was Yolanda with the lights on full beam, crawling along the track. I dashed out from my cover - scaring the daylights out of her, she said afterwards - yanked the door open and jumped in.

"I thought I'd come and look for you," she laughed. "You look like the proverbial drowned rat!"

"Boy, am I glad to see you!" I said.

"How about an open fire and some tavern fare?"

I agreed heartily to that and we drove back the way we had come that morn-ing and then through the villages, heading for Eribe, where we had been directed by our landlady. The tavern there did not disappoint and I soon dried out by the fire while we were waiting for our dinner. We couldn't resist the homemade *txistorra*, made from pigs kept at the end of a long straggling garden, and mountains of *patatas bravas*, sautéd potatoes drizzled with the common combination nationally of spicy chilli-tomato sauce and cheap salad cream style mayonnaise . . . superb!

The following day at first light the rain was still heavy and it began to look as though our last day would be a washout. The breakfast at our B&B in Murguia was superb: coffee, fruit juice and an enormous basket of all kinds of continen-tal pastries, from croissants and *petit pain chocolat* to apple filled turnovers and deliciously crunchy plain bread rolls. There was plenty of butter and various jams along with them too, such that I began to count up to myself the many advantages of not being able to go fishing at first light. I laughed as I did so, remembering our friend Stuart's having a similar list: The Advantages of Forgetting to take your Rod along when going Fishing. These included, if I remembered correctly, not having to tackle up and cast out, when there were other, more enjoyable things to do, such as dipping into the lunch box. And above all, not having to sit about waiting for a bite when you could take the binoculars and go for a bird watching stroll instead.

Miraculously, as we came to the end of the breakfast bounty, the rain stopped and the overcast sky began to break up into recognisably cloudy shapes with wondrous fragments of blue coming through between them. Yolanda said she would join me and go off on a hike around the lake shores, if the weather allowed. It sounded ideal.

My choice of a water to tackle for my last day in Araba was easy. The third of the Zadorra reservoirs was also the smallest, lake Albina, and it was a very short drive north-west from the Urrunaga, following a minor road, the A2132, which went to Mondragón. After just a couple of kilometres this road comes to the lake and follows its shoreline. Before reaching this point, however, we spotted a turning and found ourselves on a somewhat rutted forestry road, which, since we weren't driving a 4x4 all-terrain vehicle, immediately brought back to mind Frazier's helpful locals and their advice. The track followed the considerable ups and downs of the hillside, occasionally dipping us into gulleys running with muddy water. Finding a wide spot on higher ground, we decided to stop. Yolanda, after some skilful manoeuvres to turn the car about, parked as tight to the woodland as possible, in case any vehicle came by. No sooner had we set off than I immediately descried the lake some way below.

As we scrambled down the bank, we found ourselves skidding through a dense carpet of fallen beech leaves, almost psychedelic in colour, and ducking under branches, amid the voluptuously twisted trunks of ancient trees. The air was rank with the bittersweet aroma of decomposing vegetation and mossy moisture. There were toadstools everywhere, large red ones, their flat tops flecked with creamy yellow, just like the one the blue caterpillar had sat on in *Alice Through the Looking Glass*.

I certainly had no intention of nibbling at the edges of any of these. In fact, I had always been deeply suspicious of all things mycological. The mushroom seasons of the year, principally the spring and autumn, are periods of intense activity in Spain, with many rural communities, and even cities, organising events around the picking of field mushrooms, exhibitions of the many species, edible and otherwise, and gastronomical extravagances based entirely on them. There are many experts, who praise the culinary delights of mushrooms, and on my many fishing trips I am invariably encouraged to pick and take home the numerous mushrooms I come across. I never do so. Every year several of these experts find themselves in the intensive care units of hospitals or even in the cemetery. I definitely prefer my mushrooms shrink-wrap packed and labelled from a reputable supermarket.

I remember once standing before a large poster at one mushroom event, a full colour informative sheet which featured pairs of photographs showing virtually identical species, labelled either as edible or non-edible. There were occasionally minor, very easily missed details which helped to distinguish one from the other but the key factor as often as not was location, i.e. where exactly the mushroom had been found. A certain species occurring in a beechwood for example *might* be quite safe, I emphasize the word 'might', and was therefore classified as edible; another, in all visual respects identical but occurring in a pinewood for example, would be dangerous at the very least, and perhaps lethal.

Names, I have found, do not help a great deal. The Trumpet of the Dead, not a bad title for a novel perhaps, is the literal translation of *Trompeta de los muertos*, the Spanish name for *Craterellus cornucopioides*, the black chanterelle, which, as can be imagined, has a distinctly funereal black appearance and yet is edible. Apparently, they have to be dried and ground to a powder, when they will then serve as a condiment for meat. I am confident I would prefer black pepper any day.

Good old *Agaricus campestris* or *bisporus* is an entirely reliable little fellow, the small white and nicely rounded mushroom we are most familiar with, the *champiñón* in Spanish, and *barrengorri* in Basque. I'm particularly fond of the 'button' variety and yet, when I come across small crowds of them in the countryside, I avoid picking them just as surely as death's trumpets.

Quite the most popular on Spanish menus are the larger, darker and very fleshy mushrooms known universally as *setas* (*Pleurotus ostreatus*), *perretxikos* in Basque, which in English are usually called oyster mushrooms. These are good eating and certainly the meatiest mushrooms I have ever eaten. When served in a stew or some kind of sauce, they could almost be confused with slices of pork or chicken. The next favourites in the Iberian Peninsula are probably the *níscalos*, which are usually smaller than *setas* and distinctly redder in colour. These are the saffron milk caps or red pine mushrooms, *Lactarius deliciosus*, called *esnegorria* in Basque and which are delicious indeed.

Finally, the porcini or cep mushroom, *Boletus eduli* is highly prized, particularly in those culinary circles where design and decoration, a balance of colour and minutely exquisite flavours are paramount, the kind of meals which invariably leave you hungry and craving for something to get your teeth into. The *boleto* in Spanish, is *ondo beltza* or *ondo undua* in Basque but I'm afraid I have learned to avoid any restaurant where the menu includes references to '*esencia de boletus*' (essence of the boletus mushroom) or '*espuma de esparragos*' (esparragus foam), on the grounds that I would prefer something to eat.

Having managed at last to get down the hillside, we gazed out over the thick pea-green water. We found the bank to be very muddy, only slightly inclined but terribly slippery. Yolanda picked a decent walking staff from the washed up jetsam of branches and leaves, to help her along the margins. The water showed not the least ripple since it was protected from the elements by the steep and thickly wooded hillsides all around. There were no signs of fish either, yet I was full of that special optimism inspired by a completely new swim, on a completely new water. I quickly set up my rod and chose a cork bodied float with its small antenna topped of with a bright yellow bauble. This was going to be a worming day, and as soon as I had tackled up, I cast out and gazed with that special angler's satisfaction at seeing the float suitably positioned, cocked and ready for action.

Yolanda went off exploring and I watched my float, waiting expectantly for something to happen. *Bat, bi, hiru, lau, bost . . .* one to five I had mastered, then it was *sei, zazpi . . . zortzi, bederatzi . . .* and *hamar.* I started counting again. Suddenly, I pulled up my line and wound in. I couldn't help hearing my father's voice, 'You're not patient enough for fishing! You are supposed to wait!'

I sauntered off along the bank in search of some feature of interest or anything at all that might lead to fish. I soon came to a small peninsula, slightly elevated by a mass of tangled tree roots, from which I could see the tail of the reservoir. At the far end, a small but turbulent, chocolate coloured river was rushing in. To the near side, a broad eddy opened with a gathering of floating leaves gently turning and drifting at its centre. It was just the sort of spot I was hoping for. There had to fish there.

Getting into position, I cast to the far side of the eddy and watched the float lean and wander with the current from the inflow. The yellow bobble suddenly vanished and I struck but there was nothing. I wound in and checked the bait. It had been snaffled. The thrill of knowing it had been a real bite, that something fishy was at work down there where the bait had been, was more than sufficient recompense for the lack of a fish. I re-baited and cast anew. Again the float vanished and this time I wound in to find just half a worm on the hook.

I snipped off the size 8 and quickly tied on a 10, rebaited and cast again. The float wandered and stopped. Then it slowly sank, almost certainly snagged. I lifted the rod gently and the float reappeared, wavered a moment and then renewed its drift, only to vanish again almost immediately. This time my strike was met with a bouncing rod tip and the zigzagging dashes for freedom of some little fellow, whom I would be delighted to see, no matter how small he was. After a few moments, up to my hand came a pretty little barbel of around six ounces. It was a red-tail, the first I had ever caught, indeed it was the first red-tail I had ever seen in the flesh. The truth is they hadn't been around for very long, in scientific terms that is, not having been described and classified as *Barbus haasi* until 1925, by the biologist Mertens. Its autumn colours would have pleased old Bernard Venables, I fancied. Perhaps not as gaudily swaggering as his perch but this fish's golden flanks, speckled with dark brown or black flecks, were very autumnal indeed. Then there was the species' most characteristic feature, the lower part of the pelvics, pectorals and tailfin were as though they had been dipped into an orangey red dye.

I took the mandatory photo and released the little red-tail as quickly as I could. It zipped away, doubtless to tell its companions in a breathless burbling voice what had happened to it. They would never believe his tale from the other element, of a huge horribly dry monster with no barbels or even fins, so I was sure I would be in with a chance of hooking one or two more. My hope now was for a bigger one, of course. The angler's hope is always for a bigger one, as Bernard Cribbins once observed. Although on that occasion, at Redmire if my memory serves me correctly, a certain Mr Yates was excepted on the grounds that he was the British carp record holder. This was certainly not my case, even given the fact that there was no record for the redtail, as far as I was aware. The field guide book said they reached a respectable 30cm, perhaps weighing a pound or so.

My next cast led to a re-run of the action and another redtail came to the bank, a smaller one. I fished on, undaunted, until I had bagged, metaphorically, about a dozen, the best of them at least three-quarters of a pound until I began to wonder seriously if there were any bigger ones. It was delightful angling, yet I could not stop thinking about bigger fish, different species perhaps. I would probably not have an opportunity to fish this lake again for a long time. I had to make the most of it now. Perhaps a change of tactics would get results.

I tried fishing shorter, longer, deeper, shallower . . . all to no avail. I stood perplexed and yet gazed admiringly across the water. The lake was long and narrow; for all the world it seemed a river from where I was standing. Yet the upper part of the gently shelved banks, exposed by the water was that uniform brown coloured rock and earthy mud typical of reservoirs. After all the rain it was surprising that it was not yet full, wanting another three feet or so of water. All the forest around me was beechwood, beautifully painted in its autumn colours, but down the lake on its northern side, this changed to conifer of some kind, tall freshly green pines.

A swirl at the surface caught my eye and I immediately remembered that pike I hadn't been able to go back for. I pulled off my rucksack and quickly set up the spinning rod with a barbelly looking Rapala. It flew out beyond where I had seen the movement and I started to bring it in. Almost immediately it snagged. I thought it had been hit by a pike but soon found it was held solid in seemingly shallow water, probably by a tree trunk. I tried all angles but there was no shifting it. I waded out a little way but it was soon too deep for my boots. Then, as I pulled harder, with half a mind to snap the line, it came free and I wound in a good sized chunk of waterlogged tree bark. After that I was able to cast several times, avoiding the snag but there was no response. I abandoned the cause and returning to my other rod, flung the yellow bobble out to the same area, freshly baited with a pungent brandling.

I settled back on my haunches and setting the rucksack down on a reasonably dry rock, took out my flask and made a cup of tea. The sun peeped through the skidding clouds and I enjoyed the feeling of its heat on my shoulders as I ate one of the B&B's bread rolls, a few biscuits and an apple. A couple of jays were making a sudden racket behind me and both flew out over the water briefly before thinking better of it and fluttering white rumped back among the trees.

I glanced back at the water. I couldn't see my float. Jumping up I scanned the water, picking up the rod as I did so. There it was, it had drifted rather too near the stump I had snagged before. I wound in and immediately found I was into a fish, a bigger fish too. Then, just as suddenly, it was off.

Recovering my line, I found the worm intact. It must have just mouthed the bait as I started to bring it in. I set the float a little deeper, put a second brandling on to the hook, re-cast and waited for it to settle, giving the line a few tugs to sink it as much as I could, aided by the ripple. It seemed to stay put this time and I again set the rod down, clicking on the baitrunner, so as to be able to return to my tea. Time passed, the float and the angler remaining alert. 'Be a Lert!' I thought, 'The Nation needs Lerts!'

Patience is a peculiar thing. I was now disposed to sit and wait until doomsday if needs be. There was a fish out there, a bigger fish of some kind, and it was at least interested enough in a brandling to mouth it. Two brandlings might be irresistible. I kept my eye on the yellow bauble but my other senses were engaged elsewhere. The jays were squabbling again. The sun was warming. The scent off the water was richly verdant. Something heavier was moving in the wood, another crack of a branch . . . I looked round. Yolanda was coming out of the trees. It would be nearly time to pack up. In a few moments she was next to me and I offered her the flask and a tea bag.

"Anything doing?"

"Yes, I've had a few red-tails . . ."

"Any size?"

"Well, hard to say. The best was nearly a pound. I'm not sure they get any bigger."

We both jumped as the baitrunner jerked and the spool spun. I grabbed the rod which arched over nicely. It wasn't a red-tail this time. Whatever it was hugged the bottom and veered right, luckily away from the snag. The rod bounced as it lunged away looking for deeper water. I dare not let it run, there were certainly more submerged trees around. The rod did the work and suddenly the surface broke open and a tail splashed in the sunlight. It was a barbel - not a red-tail but surely a Graells. It would be another first. I hardly dared to think about it.

The fish battled valiantly but the rod and line were too powerful and it soon tired and slid towards the net, which Yolanda had ready. After the netting, photographing and weighing we watched the fish go. At 4lb 9oz it was a fine note to end on. We finished our tea, I packed up and soon Yolanda and I were walking back to the trees. All that remained of our weekend in Euskadi was an easy drive home, back to the high plains of Castile.

Chapter Three

Asturias and Cantabria

The author follows the coast, fishes with his father, chases sand eels, sea-bream, and sea bass,
as well as fishing in harbours and quays for grey mullet, and meeting a local
conger eel man before landing a record mullet, or is it a bass?

Language is a tricky business in Spain. There is Euskera in the Basque
Country, Catalán in Catalonia, Gallego in Galicia, and, in Asturias, there is
. . . Bable. Not the biblical Tower, nor yet an official language, Bable is a
ragged blend of dialects that has been regaining force ever since the death of
Franco in a wave of reassertion of Asturian regional tradition. You may not
hear it in the streets of Asturias but it is taught in schools.

Asturias and Cantabria are both northern mountainous and coastal regions
of innumerable fishing ports, small villages, Alpine style pastures, mining towns
and summer beach resorts, the latter favoured by the Spanish social elite for
generations. Once-flourishing heavy industry, mining, steel and shipbuilding
have dropped away and out of the inevitable social and economic ruins has
risen the phoenix of rural tourism. There are charming and exquisite small
B&B houses everywhere, some not so small, being the converted mansions of
the *Indianos*, those who long ago made their fortunes in the Americas. These
can be rented as self-catering retreats and often sleep up to as many as fifteen
people. Another immediate feature of the landscape are the *hórreos*, large,
square, wooden slatted corn stores on tall legs, found everywhere. They allow
the free passage of air, essential in drying the corn, and are on stilts to avoid the
attentions of rats or other rodents. Over the border into Galicia, the *hórreos* are
suddenly a very different shape, oblong, often of stone, and usually rather taller.

One mainstay industry all along the north coast is, of course commercial fishing, although the ludicrous dictates of the European Community, invariably completely out of touch with any reality, have meant there has been serious disruption to the business over the years. It is difficult to know which of the regulations handed down are worse: those banning the capture of particular species, which often leads to the out of control proliferation of others; those dictating quotas, which never take into account proper scientific evidence; or those reinstating one or the other, when the given species is showing only the merest signs of recovery. Fortunately, anyway, angling from the shore is rarely much affected.

It was a Sunday morning and my father and I had the whole day ahead of us. We were actually in Mondoñedo, Galicia, but our intention was to fish in Asturias, a short drive eastwards along the coast. We had risen early and breakfasted in a café in the village. Walking up the narrow streets from the Hospedaxe Santa Catalina, we had seen in a shop window the famous tarts made in the village by *O Rei das las Tartas*, the King of Tarts. They were extravagant looking things, covered with dried fruit and were thoroughly unappetising as a prospect for breakfast. The place, though, was small and cosy and also offered excellent coffee and croissants. While Dad was enjoying his second espresso ("If I'd known it was going to be so small, I'd've ordered a *café con leche!*") I made a quick phone call from the still mist-shrouded village to enquire into the weather along the coast. After years of summers visiting the area, I had got to know many people and one such acquaintance had a souvenir and fishing tackle shop in Luarca, about 50 miles away. It was a bright and sunny morning, so Paco had said, adding that it looked a good day for a bit of fishing. What better news could there be?

The kindly old lady café owner knew all about our fishing trips and was deeply sceptical, since we never brought anything home. Maruja, her name was, and she wasn't a bit impressed by our extravagant tales of success or of putting our fish back into the sea. This last was palpably absurd, as far as she was concerned. Until something fishily tangible was produced for her table, she considered us no better than indolent time wasters or at worst charlatans.

"What's the point of spending all day with a baited line in the sea," she laughed, "if you don't ever bring anything home to eat?"

Fishing for the sheer pleasure of it was an impossibly difficult concept to get across, not only to her but to almost anyone anywhere around the country. Catch and Release had never really become established in my 25 years in Spain, except for some trout waters, and where it had caught on, it was known as *Pesca sin muerte*: Fishing without death, or without killing, which somehow summed up the whole problem, as though it were hunting without killing, a notion quite demonstrably ridiculous.

"Why not leave the poor things in peace then?" was her parting shot.

Unperturbed, we headed down the road to the supermarket, which was just opening as we got there. Shortly afterwards, we loaded up the car and took the coast road out of the village. A few miles north was the village of Villamar where a picturesque country road led to the seaport of Castropol. As we drove down the valley of the river Eo, the sun began to make itself felt. The morning mists, which could stay put the entire day up in the hill valleys, gradually began to thin and disappear. Castropol's situation on a protruding section of the coast in the ría de Ribadeo, made it look like an island, when seen from the huge bridge that took the main road over the sea border between Galicia and Asturias

Then, suddenly, there was the sea, a deep blue expanse, extending into the seeming infinity of the horizon. We breathed in the salty air and sighed with the pure pleasure of it. Leaving the ría behind us, the road followed the irregular and much broken coastline. These were the Rías Altas, given their name by the numerous river estuaries or *rías* along this stretch of coast. Following round in the opposite direction and going south towards Portugal you would come to the Rías Baixas, both had popular tourist resorts. Their real charm though, especially for anglers, was the remarkable number of lesser known beaches and rocky inlets, including the mouths of smaller *rías*, where both tranquillity and fish abounded.

It was a spectacular coast, all the better seen from the minor, squiggling roads that kept within sight of the sea. The main road thundered on in the near distance, safely out of harm's way. There were always plenty of fish to be seen, especially surface feeding mullet or mackerel, but we were reconnoitring the stretches of sandy beach and sudden coves in search of likely habitats for sea bream and bass.

Conjured up in my mind's eye, I was envisioning a sweep of Cornish beach on the north coast at Tregardock, and suddenly I called out as just such a scene came into view.

"That'll do us. It looks plenty fishy enough to me!" I said, pointing eagerly through my window.

"We'll have to watch out not to get fried," Dad said.

It was true, too. The sun was already quite high and burned down seriously on our exposed necks and legs as we sorted out our tackle from the back of the car. Sun hats and factor 20 were the first things out in fact, constituting tactic number one in the pursuit of Spanish summer fishing. Dad had been busy long before though, in his favourite stamping grounds around the boot fairs of Kent and Sussex. I had virtually no sea fishing tackle in the country at the time and he had acquired a couple of light, first-rate beachcasters. I had my old faithful Mitchell multiplier, still as good as when it had first been used back in my childhood, and

Dad had an even older reel, one of those huge purply brown centre-pin things made of 'ebonite', which swivelled round to a fixed-spool position for casting. It was a splendid invention. I ribbed Dad about its antiquated appearance and he retorted that it was miles better than my newfangled multiplication effort!

We got the rods tackled up, 2oz ledgers on sliding booms with 3-foot traces after the beads and no. 5 bronze hooks, with good long shanks. I had artificial sandeels too but we decided to have a rummage around for natural baits first. We had bought a couple of small boxes of ragworm at a tackle shop back along the coast a few days before, just in case we found nothing.

It was already very hot, and making our way down the dunes between rocky outcrops towards the sea, the heat reflected off the sand and shallow pools left by the recently receded tide. The hint of a breeze off the sea was welcome, but the very air seemed to be burning. To our left was a useful outcrop of rock, which ran from near where we were parked, right across the beach and some yards into the sea, forming a natural pier. A freshwater stream trickled alongside from a depression in the grassy banks above and cut a little channel across the sand flats to the sea. This was one side of our cove, which was five or six hundred yards wide, extending to where some great rock arches strode over the sands and into the sea.

Tuned to every feature, the angler sees in a way nearly unique to himself, only the hunter really sees the world in the same way. Gulls and a little group of stilts busied themselves along the submerged banks of the stream, some yards out. Beyond, another 30 yards or so, there were small white capped breakers with rocks occasionally showing or creating turbulences. Otherwise, it was sand; broad trouble-free stretches where I was sure there were sandeels, shifted by the turbulent breakers, dashing hither and thither for cover. It was almost low water.

We strode down over the near rocks and laying our rods down, began searching for bait. I washed my hands thoroughly in the brine, keen to be rid of any traces of factor 20. There were innumerable shallow pools and we soon found a few sandeels. Not that we could catch them. One of us would throw one up in great handfuls of dripping sand and then we would both scrabble about madly trying to catch it. The sandeel is certainly one of Nature's masters at the art of not being seen, vanishing from view as soon as they come into contact with the tiny grains of their native element. Once we had that first one safely in one of the bait boxes, with some moist bits of straggly seaweed, we set to again. Dad, after a few not entirely positive philosophical observations on sandeel fishing, headed for the rocks, and there, turning them over, went in search of peeler crabs.

The sound of the sea was magnificent. A constant dull boom in the background, with higher pitched hushing and shushing that came and went in intensity. It put me in mind of some music by the Finnish Misha Alperin; haunting piano, jazzy, slow and very moody with shimmering cymbals like breakers. There were horns and things too, but it was the piano and cymbals I remembered. I was originally attracted to the CD *North Story* by the cover, which has a beautifully active, black and white photo of anglers. They are fishing off rocks, maybe six of them, into a foaming ocean, under a lowering sky. The nearest figure is almost dancing, his back to the sea, like a Morris man in wellies. His light spinning rod is arched over, an unidentified fish swinging in the air, about to be lowered into a niche in the rocks for unhooking. The others are casting or retrieving, one with a handline, held high as though he were flying a kite. But it was the music that was most strongly with me, there among the rocks. Gulls and other sea birds cried and sometimes came near enough for the flutter of their wings to be heard.

After a while, we had done as well as we were able and decided to try a cast. With our bait boxes tied round our waists, we waded out into the shallows, having left our gear as high out of harm's way as we could. The tide had moved only fractionally since our arrival and would turn at any moment. High water was due at 19.56 in the tide tables for the port of El Musel, Gijón; that meant somewhere around half past along here. We had a good long afternoon's fishing ahead. Not only was the timing propitious, but we were in for a spring tide, 4.06 metres in the book, with a full moon. The rocks down at the water's edge were heavily grown over with deeply browned kelp that only rarely received the direct light of the sun.

Our first casts weren't of the best. It had been some time since either of us had handled great big rods like these. We were about ten or fifteen yards apart (beyond that we couldn't hear our voices) and casting a bit away from each other, we aimed to hit the water around where the surf was breaking, keeping as near to the visible rocks as possible without snagging. As it was, we cast over each other and I had a nice bird's nest to keep me quiet for a bit. Dad was faring better altogether, with that strange old reel, and had time to practice several casts and slow retrievals while I picked away at what must be one of the biggest banes of a fisherman's life.

With the angler's almost infinite patience and the near clairvoyance needed when it comes to tugging at certain loops and not others, the tangled chaos was cleared. I then launched into another. Though very much a committed traditionalist in those days, one among my many and increasing concessions over the years, had been to tie on a length of shock leader - a good thing too! Fortunately, it wasn't half as bad this time. The lead fell short, but the whirling muddle of monofilament pulled through and fell out, as I let the line drift a bit. Dad was saying that perhaps we should try the live bait. We had artificials on, since we hadn't collected that many crabs or eels for the long session in prospect.

I wound up my line and I couldn't help thinking how convincing my little silvery white sandeel looked, as it approached through the sandy shallows. I waded over to Dad and he decided to try a peeler, while I opted to stick to the artificial a bit longer; at least until I could manage a decent cast. Anyway, it was always good policy to have different baits or presentations out there.

I tightened my spool ever so slightly, feeling that it was running a fraction loose and made a tentative third cast. Luck was with me at last and the line fairly flew away beyond the breakers. I felt the lead thud gently on to the sand and as I gently recovered line, I could feel it tumble from time to time, then drag a little, as it travelled over the sandy contours. I pictured the imitation sand eel weaving about, wriggling and flipping over provocatively amid the little clouds of sand thrown up by the tumbling lead. A memory from childhood flashed through my mind. I remembered being fascinated by the action of a flounder spoon, baited with ragworm, I had watched skating over the bottom. I had been fishing from a boat swinging gently at anchor on the low tide, in a quiet cove somewhere along the Kent coast. My old school chum Gary Denham's line had passed under the boat. I had wound in and was looking down into the clear water when I saw the spoon approaching. The lead skipped along, sending up little silty puffs, and then the spoon, looking for all the world like a fish. I had jumped, about to say it was a fish, when I realised. Not a very healthy fish perhaps, but that undoubtedly made it all the more attractive. It was a moment of vision. I saw for the first time what these little contraptions of metal and swivels had to do with catching fish. I saw too, that the speed of their movement, the pauses and the angles, were all important.

My sandeel lure was now approaching the point where the undertow, back from the gently inclined beach, had carried the food churned up in the raking surf, to where the fish should be feeding. I brought it along a foot, a couple of feet and waited, then wound again. Suddenly, there came a distinct knock. I struck, a bit late, taken incomprehensibly by surprise.

"A bite!" I called out.

"Weed!" Dad called back, exactly as I expected.

"Might've been a bass," I said.

"You're just imagining things," he said and I chuckled to myself; I always enjoyed going fishing with my dad.

I continued winding and waiting until I had passed through the fishiest area. Glancing again over to Dad, I could see his rod bent over under the weight of something.

"Fish?"

"No, I've picked up some weed or something."

The rod certainly wasn't giving any sign of life. Dad had begun to pump against the dead weight, which had swung round to his far side. I re-cast and began once again to comb the likely spots, jerking from time to time and varying the rate at which I reeled in, all in the hope of arousing some interested response out there in the surf.

Dad called out for me to look and he held up a string of weedy material, apparently all welded together by mussels, several of them really big ones. He pushed his way through the knee-deep water to show me. The line, the hook and bait were all apparently bitten by the tightly closed shells.

"They'll make good bait, I should think," he said.

I felt another hard tug and responded quickly, a couple more small knocks, and nothing.

"Another bite," I called to Dad, as he waded back to the rocks to sort out his line.

"Pure imagination," he said, "I've never known anyone like you for thinking everything's a bite!"

I yelled back that I was quite sure it was a fish, and Dad did his disbelieving old man Steptoe face. I wound in and inspected my rubbery fake sandeel optimistically for bite marks. Nothing. I re-cast, rather more confidently, getting a good 20 yards beyond the breakers. It felt much deeper there, the lead taking appreciably longer to hit bottom. Another peck at the eel came as soon as it did so. I left it and waited. A moment passed and I twitched the lead forward, waited, and then repeated the pulls, convinced that there were fishy eyes there, watching. I wound on slowly but nothing happened. It was time for a bit of real bait.

Dad was once more in position and I watched as he cast into the furthest of the breakers. It would be good to have a photograph of his casting technique. Styles in casting were as different as fingerprints. I had pictures of a few rather nice fly line casts; I made a mental note to take more. I envisaged a whole album of action casting shots with floats, leads or even a measly single maggot. I watched Dad's rod tip on and off, as I slid away, pocketed the sandeel and poked around in my baitbox for a crab. It soon seemed secure enough on the hook, so I risked another hard cast, and again the lead took its time to bump on to the seabed. I let it stop there a moment. There was no sign of anything now, on Dad's rod or mine, whether of weed or mussel gangs. I went through the motions of retrieval and as the weight and dangling trace approached, I saw that the bait was gone.

"Let's try the worms," I called out to Dad, moving over to where he was about to launch into a fresh cast.

"You're not going to catch much with that," I said, laughing and pointing to his bare hook.

"Oh, I had some mussels on, they must have fallen off."

"Silly ol' fool," I laughed again, "mind you, the same thing's happened to me."

We walked back together to the rocks, where I had left the worm boxes tucked into a crevice. We baited up again and had the little cardboard boxes tied round our waists in plastic bags. We certainly looked absurd, like one-man bands in shorts, as we headed back out. We had put our Spanish holiday straw hats on too. We were really quite comical; it was just as well there was no one to see us. The sun was fierce and the salty air had us both rather red faced, not to say thirsty but we were set on a few casts more, before taking a break.

Back in position, I put everything into my next cast and got well out beyond the breakers. Maybe food was being pulled out that far, I didn't know, but from there I could at least cover more ground. After the same longish drop through the water, I felt the lead bump on to the sand and a small knock came almost at the same instant. I struck, and again nothing, and I decided to wait, tensed, poised, ready for another touch.

"You didn't have a bite!" Dad called over, "it's weed, that's all," and he too suddenly struck, but nothing.

"Nor did you, then," I shouted back.

We both chuckled. What a lark we had, fishing together, and the fish too, come to that. We were both exaggeratedly opposite in temperament, optimist v. pessimist. My glass was half full and Dad's half empty. Not that he ever drank, we were opposites in that too.

I felt another touch. Something was going on out there, albeit not very bass like. I hadn't bothered to wind in at all as yet, on this cast. I had just taken up the slack when the weight shifted. Another nibble; there was definitely something out there.

The next bite was sure and I struck once more. Yes! Something tugged away in a bid for freedom, it seemed miles away, down the 50-odd yards of nylon.

"I've got one," I called to Dad, winding in carefully.

"Fat chance! A crab more like."

The resistance certainly wasn't much, but it was definitely a fish, jagging about in the surf. It coasted repeatedly on the incoming waves and the little chap was soon with me in the shallows.

"It's a bream," I shouted and looking up saw Dad approaching, his rod high, the line straight out into the breakers.

"You've got a bite there, Dad!"

He pulled tentatively and sure enough something suddenly hit hard. Dad left me to my bream and moved away a pace at a time, his rod tip bouncing.

"It's only another tiddler," he said, "poor little mites."

I slipped the hook out of what proved to be a nice little white bream, *sargo* in Spanish, of no more than half a pound, and away he flipped, to warn his chums. Dad was still bringing his in. I smiled to myself. Ever since he'd caught a 24lb cod on a boat trip with his Work's Angling Club, all other fish were deemed to be tiddlers. It had been a good cod though.

Dad had his fish in at last, a bright orange and brown mottled wrasse, a painted comber in fact. A really pretty fish, with a big pale blue patch half way down its flank, where doubtless some legend told of its being handled by a Martian. Dad slipped it back and we both rebaited.

"Well, it's a start," I commented, and Dad agreed, though he added it was probably the finish too.

As if by way of justification for this view, we were plagued throughout the succeeding half an hour by weed bites and crabs. Dad moaned in complaint and was for packing up. I replied with the angler's perennial plea, that we would just have one more cast. Luckily the annoyances vanished as suddenly as they had come, and we were both instantly happier. We took up new positions, some yards down and Dad's tackle flew once more into the breakers.

"There's something nibbling," he called over, and I agreed though we were certain they were still small fish. Then, suddenly, I felt a harder thud and struck into something rather more interesting. A good fight ensued, but somehow I was sure it still wasn't a bass. It was too erratic, short lunges and flips among the muddled currents. Bit by bit I brought it closer, the light gear responsive to every turn. Soon enough, a bigger white bream splashed and flapped about in the shallows.

"Shall we keep it?" I shouted. "They're good eating."

The fish's eyes seemed to implore an immediate switch to vegetarianism and as Dad called back that he didn't really like fish anyway, I let it go. I fancied I saw a look of relief in that pale yellow eye. He was a good fish - $1\frac{1}{2}$ perhaps 2lb. We felt somewhat encouraged at last and fished on expectantly for nearly an hour, but with nothing more to show for it.

The tide was coming on and we had backed up the beach several yards. Fortunately there was enough of an incline to slow its progress and allow our fishing to continue. Not like that beach I had remembered back in Cornwall. I had fished that superb spot any number of times. It was a completely flat beach and the tide raced in dangerously, as soon as it turned, cutting off the unsuspecting angler completely. I had been forced to clamber up rocks and earthy banks on numerous occasions in face of its treachery. It had always been worth it though, half a dozen school bass up to three or four pounds, more than good value for the risk to life and limb.

Dad was making his way back towards the rocks and I pulled in and followed. We slaked our thirst with thankfully still-cold orange squash from Dad's thermos and tucked into some bread, cheese and *jamón serrano*. The latter really set us up. If ever I move away from Spain, I think I would have to have that excellent ham imported.

"I'm going back in," I said, smothering myself with yet more suncream.

"I'll be there in a bit, you might have scoffed yours but I've still half a *bocadillo* to go!"

I waded back through the warm ripples, my mind set on trying one of our precious sandeels. I extracted the wiggly little devil with care and with my guilty conscience turning its habitual blind eye to live-baiting, was soon ready for another cast. The higher water meant that the deep spot was now out of reach and so I cast into the white-flecked surf alongside where we had noted rocks earlier. The lead bumped and bounced around in the turbulence there as I slowly recovered the line.

Dad had said he would carry on with the ragworm and some minutes later he was wading through the shallows, soon to have his line back out. He had a good bite immediately and his rod arched over quite dramatically. He pulled and recovered but immediately had to allow the fish line. He pumped again and the old reel spun backwards, the loud clicking ratchet ringing out over the waves.

"That's a bass!" I shouted.

Dad certainly didn't dispute the fact, not that he was being allowed time to even think about it. The fish careered back and forth in great long runs, just to our side of the first breakers. Dad kept up the pressure and began winning the battle. A beautiful silvery flank flashed through the sun-bright shallows and was soon near enough to land. Dad got a hold and held it up to show me.

"What a beauty!" I hollered.

It was too - a good four-pounder, shimmering in the brilliant afternoon sun-shine. To my surprise, it had an equally silvery lure dangling from its gaping mouth by a small treble hook.

"I decided to give the old spinner a try," he said.

"Deadly secret tactics eh!" and we both laughed.

I nearly lost my rod then, as a sudden terrific lurch on the line had me stum-bling in the sand.

"Blimey!" I yelled, "there are more of them, Dad."

I was nearly over, one leg bent and water splashing up to my chest, but the rod was up and the fish very much still there.

"Grab the net, Dad," I spluttered.

Unbeknown to me, Dad had bopped his fish on the head, with yet another boot-fair treasure, a brass, mahogany handled priest, probably a hundred years old, and had already made his way back to the rocks. We had brought a flick-open trout net with us and while I was looking round in a bit of a panic, Dad approached with it.

"Stop messing about!" he said, "it's only a tiddler."

The bass, there was no mistaking its wild power, still hadn't given an inch. It was coursing left and right, some 30 yards off, in dangerously rough water.

There was method in it, too. I was minute by minute nearer the rocks. I applied more pressure, bringing down the rod and hoping the sidestrain would ease the fish over the sand. The rod was hooped over marvellously and slowly began to make the required impression. Now, only about 20 yards out, it suddenly broke the surface in a tremendous leap. The line slackened and my heart dropped, but no, it was still on, making yet another run. That had been close. I kept the rod down, trying not to bring the fish near the surface, the light, hollow glass forming a surprising arc. Dad was casting occasional aspersions on my angling skills, and with good reason. I just couldn't get this fellow any nearer to us. As soon as that thought passed through my mind I felt the pull beginning to abate. It came up, showing near the surface, and I was able to bring it in on the waves towards Dad, who had meanwhile waded out a bit, net at the ready.

"That's a good fish," he said.

"A personal best, I think, I've never had a bass the size of that one."

"Do you remember that fish in the Medway estuary, that nearly had me out of the boat?"

I did indeed. Apart from occasional trips to Cornwall, my only other bass fishing had been with Dad in a rowing boat, off Kingsnorth power station.

"That was a five-pounder, I think," Dad added, "but I'd say this one goes a bit more than that."

We made our way back to our perch on the rocks and soon had the fish in a bag. Down went the marker, past the lines and the dots on the Little Samson. 'To weigh 7lb x 2oz, Made in England', it said, and true to its word, the indicator nudged at the limit.

"7 lb!" I said, delighted.

"6 lb 14$\frac{1}{2}$oz," Dad said, "you're forgetting about the bag."

"Ow . . . all right then," I said, laughing, "come on, there must be more where this fellow came from. It'll be high tide in under an hour, I should say."

I was thrilled to pieces, it was definitely my best ever bass.

"I reckon the café lady will be impressed, don't you?"

Dad did the honours, employing the priest's good offices. With a brace of *lubinas*, there was no doubt that our credibility as fishermen would be enhanced at the Rei das Tartas café.

"I'll take them up to the cold box," Dad said.

"I thought you didn't like fish," momentarily rather puzzled.

"I don't, I'm not going to eat it. Horrible things! But aren't you a bit fed up with her taking the mickey every time she sees us and saying we never catch anything?"

I had to agree and smiled at the thought of what would happen. As soon as we presented her with the fish, there would be an invitation to come and dine. Such would be the invitation that there would be no way at all of getting out of it. Bass for supper and the motherly attentions of Maruja - I had my doubts about how Dad would feel about that.

'She's a nice enough woman," he said, as he picked his way across the rocks towards the car, with our fish in an incongruous Sainsbury plastic bag (I hadn't seen one of those for years).

I rubbed in some more suncream and pushed out into the gentle sea and baited again with an eel, leaving only one in the box. The water was now rippling up to where our rocky refuge emerged from the dunes, leaving interlacing arcs of tiny fizzing bubbles. There was an occasional wash too, against the freshwater stream's trickling progress. It was nearer high water than I had thought. I got in quite deep, hoping my last few casts of the evening would be able to reach the fish.

I felt the ledger sway through the water and touch bottom, it then lolled and turned as it slowly approached the breakers, 40 yards off at most. There was nothing doing though, and as Dad took up his position, I was inspecting my eel for a second cast. He was soon back out there and using more of a spinning method, was almost instantly into another fish. I watched a moment but Dad had everything under control. The fish ran well though, and Dad moved off a way to bring his fish away from the rocks. He soon brought another nice looking bass alongside, of a couple of pounds.

"They're definitely still out there," he beamed, "what are you messing about at?"

"Oh, I'm just here, waiting for a whopper!"

I had my line back in and the eel was in good order, so I prepared to cast again. This time, I tried to the left of where I hoped the rocks were. The rising tide was a little disorientating, as the rocks disappeared under ever-deeper water and the surface signs showed less and less. I was fairly sure I was safe, when the lead banged against something hard, snagged and moved, then caught up again. I doubted a minute, then risked a pull. Luckily the weight bounced free and tumbled across sandier contours. A small touch immediately followed and I experienced that surging thrill of expectation, the angler knows so well. My concentration redoubled; I could feel the lead quite distinctly tumbling right, perhaps towards the rocks. Another nibble came like a tingle of electricity, then a banging take. Up jumped the rod, a struggle ensued, the drag hummed and then stopped. I had lost it. I looked over to Dad; he had his fish in another Sainsbury's bag, the handles looped through his belt, and was about to cast again.

I wound in and inspected what little remained of the sandeel. It had been fairly munched, the head only remaining. I always suffered those inevitable qualms so many anglers feel when using live bait but it was a fish eat fish world. All those lengths gone to: barbless hooks, thought essential to avoid the ghastly mutilation of fishes' mouths, lead free shot, fine mesh knotless nets and so on; yet here I was live-baiting. My mind ran on with the problem while I rebaited. I thought about how angry I would get, over discarded line, shot and leads. All my efforts to protect our beloved fish and all the waterside species from harm jarred against the worst dilemma, baiting up with live creatures, even worms. It's pretty grim really, impaling the poor things on hooks, slinging them out into the watery mire to drown or be eaten alive by ferocious fish. The fact that animals live, 'instinctively and unreflectively, untouched by higher awareness', to quote Laurence Catlow, the fact that they may not be imbued with our sense of pain, didn't really help me and my conscience at all.

I threaded the last eel on to the hook with an involuntary shudder. As an angler, my own stance was a preference to see myself as taking part in the cycle of predators and prey. Able to avoid those above me in the food chain, I chose to pursue fish. I killed and ate them rarely in truth, but partook actively in the chase. At the moment of capture I was able to show compassion, unlike other predators, and release my prey. I felt confident that I played the part of no more than a scare in the lives of my fish, that at least was my mitigation. Maybe I would have to one day abandon live-baiting, for all that.

I had cast again in the meantime, again as far as I could, hoping inexplicably for deeper water. It was odd how deeper water always seemed so attractive, even when logically enough, I knew there would be fish in the shallows, immediately behind the breakers, at no distance at all. Some primeval notion, to do with the mystery of the depths drove me to fish there if I could. There were odd fragmented recollections too, of fish taken deep down, from over the years. Even though they were surely fewer, they held a curious magic.

I noticed suddenly that Dad had moved way off and was struggling with something. I had backed up and was close to the rocks, so I sloshed through the ripples and lay down my rod, leaving the drag optimistically slack. I grabbed the net and splashed heavily over towards him. A broad oval shape broke the surface as I approached.

"Another sea bream," Dad said, as soon as I was alongside, "though it looks a better one."

Although they grew to maybe 5lb and a length of 18 inches, we had never had them over two pounds. This one was looking to be the exception. A few moments more and I was able to slip the net under it. It was indeed a splendid fish. There was no trace of the vertical bands that marked the juveniles, which could still be seen on the smaller fish we had caught already. It was thick set too, heavy in the body, most definitely worth weighing, though we decided we would release it afterwards. The Little Samson registered a fraction over four pounds.

"3 lb 14½oz," I announced.

"Hmmm," Dad made his Mr Grumpy face.

We had certainly never seen such a fine white bream and we watched with great pleasure as he puffed his gill a moment back in the net and then thrashed away through the foam towards deeper water.

It was getting on and we had to be back at the *hospedaxe* (guest house) for dinner between nine and nine-thirty.

"One last cast?"

How I enjoyed those words. There was something magical about them, such as might be felt for 'shall we have just one more tipple?' Especially for me, since I didn't drive.

"Not me," Dad said, "I think I'll start packing up. It's nearly 8 o'clock, you carry on a bit though, if you want."

"OK. It's nearly high tide," I said, "so I won't be long."

I clambered across the rocks to where I had left my rod and immediately saw that the line was pulling off steadily and silently. I had left the spool lock off! I pounced and struck, clicking the gear release on, and the ratchet howled. There was an enormous amount of line out, a hundred yards at least, but I had contact. An erratic jagging fight suggested another bream. The line seemed to go straight for where the submerged rocks were but I could feel nothing dangerous. I let the rod's full length do its job and increased the effect by backing up the ledges behind me. I wound and wound, taking what seemed an age to bring my fish within reasonable distance and away from the snags. He swung in a powerful surge towards the top of the beach, just where Dad was starting in with the net. I continued winding interminably and getting back down to the water, headed up the beach.

"Was it already on?" Dad asked.

"Yes, it's amazing it didn't all tangle up out there. There was a whole load of line off."

"Here it comes," Dad pushed forward and netted our fish, "another tiddler!"

"I'd left the spool undone, instead of clicking the ratchet on."

"Go on, get back there for your last cast," he said slipping out the hook and letting the bream go in the shallows.

"Right," I said, "I'll just try one last chuck for a bass."

'The one,' I thought, with the angler's eternal optimism, 'that catches the big fish.'

"I reckon they've moved off. Tide's too high now."

Dad was probably right, but I had to have one more go. All I had left was rag, so I baited up with a couple of big ones. Back in the water, I let the bait and ledger rest up on the rocks and launched into a good cast, my sights set on the deeper area. I was sure there would be bass there still. A sickening snap echoed out over the air and the lead flew menacingly, rising to the horizon, the baited hook flailing wildly. I saw the small white point of its splash easily 150 yards away. I sighed and began winding up the slack, guiding the line on to the spool as tightly as I could. What an idiot. I then realised I had tightened the spool instead of the drag and moreover, as the end came in, drifting on the salt air, I found it to be badly damaged by abrasion. The last ten yards was cut to shreds, doubtless dragged across the rocks by that last fish. How it hadn't occurred to me to check it, I couldn't say.

I made my way over to where Dad was almost finished packing up and he ribbed me about the inadequacies of modern tackle, as I disjointed my rod.

"Never mind though, we've got some good fish to impress Maruja with."

"She'll be over the moon," I said, "there's around twenty pounds of *lubinas* there, enough to feed quite a few people."

We dried ourselves off, changed our clothes and got our sandals on, before strolling back across the sand to the dunes. We stood at the top finally, and looked out across the sea. There was no one to be seen, there had been no one all day in fact. It was incredible really, such a stretch of seashore. Gulls wheeled overhead and one or two had already landed down where we had been and were poking around for any bits we may have dropped. Bits of bait maybe, the scent of fresh caught fish, but there was no visible sign that we had ever been there.

* * *

Fishing with my father has always been entertaining and on his numerous visits to Spain, we have fished all manner of waters together. On one occasion, when he had taken the 24-hour ferry crossing from Portsmouth to Santander, the ship arrived at a very early hour and I suggested we went along the Cantabrian coast in search of somewhere to harry the finny denizen. We were considerably attracted by the small port town of Llanes and Dad parked the car in the shade, alongside a rusting, abandoned loading bay, at the harbour end of the quay. I visited the place again, more than twenty years later, to find it utterly revolutionised, with fresh planes of smooth concrete everywhere, and everything thoroughly modern. It was a million miles from the way it had been when my father and I first saw it. On that occasion, there had been cranky pallets stacked up along the wharf, and great muddled piles of orangey brown nets with big plastic floats running along their tangled edges. They were baking in the sun and gave off a salty sweet odour reminiscent of tar and dates. There was no one about as we stalked, as only anglers can, along the edges of the harbour walls watching the water. So fixed was our attention that I at least only narrowly avoided plummeting into the water as a result of tripping over guy ropes or mooring capstans.

"You should look where you're going," Dad said, "anyone would think you'd been drinking!"

Dad didn't drink at all himself, and during his summer visits out here to Spain he was astonished how much alcohol people managed to get through. Not least his own son and heir. As it was Saturday, and I had no afternoon classes at the summer school where I was working, I had enjoyed a glass or two of wine with our lunch. Dad had drunk *gaseosa*, a sort of lemonade, and the truth is I did feel a bit light headed. I clearly wasn't immune to the perils of lunchtime drinking even after nearly ten years in Spain. I decided to watch my step.

Along the quay, summer bright fishing boats rested on the rising tide, emerald green and yellow, Mediterranean blue and white, with shining orange buoys dangling, at intervals, over the sides. High up, brilliant white reflecting masts, their cables clattering in the offshore breeze. Under prows and sterns lurked some startling shadows, backing out of sight at our approach. In the open water between vessels teemed countless alevins, the fry perhaps of these cautious giants. I had a *barra* of crisp white bread with me which I broke open and threw in a few chunks of, just to see what might happen. There were half a dozen more sticks of this excellent bread in the car, which we had bought at a little *panadería* we had stopped at on the road. If the fish weren't interested, we wouldn't let it go to waste.

There was no sign of anyone fishing; one or two old salts milled about, retired trawler hands, or captains perhaps. Their faces were browned and wrinkled from a lifetime at sea. Puffing quietly on black tobacco, they seemed in contemplative mood, their eyes shaded by the peaks of seafarers' caps, always looking out to sea, as though remembering a bygone age, like characters from old sea stories by Conrad or Melville. As they passed, voices hailed them from the shadows. In the shade of a dilapidated crane, three old men in suits and black berets were talking. These, I felt, were landlubbers. They sat facing the town, watching the old clock tower as they spoke; they seemed quite a different species, noisy and gesticulating.

"What are they arguing about?" Dad enquired.

"They're just talking" I said. "From what I can make out, family, neighbours, football, that kind of thing."

"What do you think about the fishing?"

"It looks promising to me, the tide's not long started to make and it's a pleasant enough spot."

"OK, let's get the gear, shall we."

Following a none too musical warning, the town clock boomed out the hour. 10 o'clock in the morning - 9 in the Canaries, I thought. The islands are Spanish territory of course and so on national broadcasting they always give the time there too. On the drive down, a radio announcer, famous for his clowning around had said:

"*Son las nueve de la mañana, ¡ las ocho, cuarenta y cinco en Canarias!*"

It's 9 in the morning, 8.45 in the Canaries.

Due to an ongoing and apparently permanent hitch in local and national radio broadcasts, at the moment when they unite for news bulletins, I have frequently heard the very funny but entirely useless and meaningless announcement: '*Son . . . las canarias.*' 'It is . . . the Canaries.' A truncated consequence of the ineffective use of a digital editing suite to produce, for example: 'It is 10 o'clock, 9 o'clock in the Canaries.' Sometimes, we are informed that 'It is 10 Canaries' or 'It is 10 in the Canaries' (When in fact it is 11.) I often catch myself listening hard, not for the time but for the latest variant in the gaff.

We walked back towards the car along on the seaward side, looking deep into the iridescent turquoise water. Deep down there were huge shadowy shapes moving, apart from larger groups of shoaling fish. I dropped more bread into the water, compressing some lumps of the doughy centre and watching them sink. Some violent thrashing suddenly caught my ear and I trotted over to the harbour side to see some very nice looking fish ripping the now sodden bread to shreds. Grey mullet, and some of them looked really big. I nipped back to tell Dad.

"They're on the bread down there too," he pointed along the wall where more mullet were boiling round the crusts that had washed along on the incoming tide.

"This is going to be great fun!"

"Hmm," Dad murmured, "their taking the bait is one thing, keeping them on the hook is quite another."

This was certainly true, of course. Those soft mouths and funny lips didn't make effective hooking easy. They also tended to be very wary and would vanish at the sight of an angler.

As we went to get our rods and tackle out of the car, I remembered my first ever fishing book, even before I discovered Mr Crabtree. It was an album for Brooke Bond tea picture cards of Freshwater Fish, with descriptions by A. F. Magri MacMahon. It included one or two estuary species like the mullets and for me, as a small boy, the alarming observation that they were 'notoriously difficult to catch by fair angling'. Thoughts as to what unfair angling might be plagued the rest of my childhood, but the information was a terrible blow. Having, at that time, just graduated from eels to flatties, I was keen to catch a proper fish. I remember gazing with wonder at these metallic blue and silvery marvels cropping green algae off the piles round Strood pier in Kent.

My memory of that place had been partly evoked by the scent of diesel here; it permeated the air and rainbow coloured patches of the water. Strood had

had no fishing boats though, instead there were tugs which worked down at the oil refinery moving the huge tankers around. At the pier, there was a rickety old wooden walkway which led down, the angle depending on the state of the tide, and terminated in a floating pontoon, which boomed with the echo of my footsteps. No sooner would I appear than my quarry vanished. My offerings of garden worms or shrimps, that plummeted to the bottom with the help of a nut and bolt, were totally ignored.

A lot of mullet had swum under the bridge since then. Mr Crabtree's *In All Waters* soon came to my aid and with due care and attention, worthy opponents though they were, good catches began to be made. I had high hopes now of a closer look at some of the beauties Dad and I had spotted.

"Come on," Dad called out.

I had wandered off beyond the car to a small fish processing building. On the ground was a pile of ice below an outlet chute.

"Just coming," I said. "There's something interesting here."

On the seaward side, well below the water line was another outlet. An enormous sand bank had formed, making this point rather shallower, and on the sea bed I could make out odd fishy remains, heads and bones, all picked clean. I imagined the feeding frenzy that took place when the plant was operating. There were hundreds of small mullet packed tightly together in the fast rising tide, hanging optimistically in mid water, down current of the outlet, but I could see no big fellows.

"Where do you fancy trying, Dad?"

"I'm not sure. When the tide is running we'd be better off in the harbour."

"It's running hard now," I said, "let's try between the boats, up there, where there's a reasonable gap."

"Right, give us a hand then, I'm not carting all this lot on my own."

The boot of the car was crammed with our gear, the bulk of which had rather less to do with fishing than with creature comfort. Having decided on where to set up base camp, we struggled along loaded down with folding chairs, a table with a parasol and a cold-box full of goodies. It was a real treat to go fishing when Dad was visiting; usually I could take only what fitted on to my bicycle rack.

We soon tackled up, baiting our no. 8 hooks with big doughy lumps of bread picked out from inside the crust. We squeezed the bread hard round the eye end of the hooks to stop it falling off, but left it soft and flaky at the points, with plenty of surplus. Mullet are notoriously tackle shy. If they detect the presence of hook or line, they turn briskly away, as often as not scattering the shoal. As a boy, lying flat on that old pontoon, I had watched them often nudging the baited hook repeatedly as if looking for the trick. All too frequently they would find me out and disappear, and I would be back to dabs.

We were between two capstans, the guy ropes well out of our way, with a bit of open water in front as well as the interesting shady corners between the boats and the wall. Keeping well back from the edge, Dad and I were ready for our first casts. These were no more really than lowerings into the water between the boats, then letting the slow sinking baits drift, some six feet below the floats, under the nearest prow or stern. I had picked up the big cork bodied floats in a '*Todo Cien*', the Spanish equivalent of a Pound Shop. (Although, at the then rate of exchange, *cien* (100) *pesetas* was only 42 pence, or 0.60 Euros . . . about midday in the Canaries.) The floats stood out wonderfully in the blue grey rippling shadows, bright red with long yellow, red and black antennae, bobbing gently on the light harbour swell.

It wasn't long before slight nibbles began knocking our floats sideways, rapid little tugs making them bob and jerk as the fish pulled at the soft part of the bread. Odd crumbs and flakes disintegrating and falling through the water would hopefully attract the attention of the bigger fish skulking under the keels. We wound in occasionally to replace the bait, as often as not reduced to a hard white nibbled hook shape by tiddlers. I threw in a couple more crusts and we sat back under the little sunshade, our floats just visible over the edge.

"This is nice," Dad said. "I could just about cope with this kind of fishing - a warm sunny day, nothing much going on, lovely!"

I had to laugh.

"Do you remember that day last summer on the Admiralty, at Dover?"

"Argh! Don't remind me! You and that Chris are raving mad, tipping down with rain, four hours in a force 10 and nothing to show for it!"

That Chris was Chris Ryan, probably my oldest angling friend and companion, of at least 30 years' standing.

"How do you know? You spent the whole afternoon in the car!"

"Well, I wasn't staying out there with you nutcases. Chris would have done the same if you'd've let him."

"We had a few nice pollack . . . "

"They looked more like bibs to me, poor things. You should've put them back."

"But we made a jolly good fish pie with them that night, remember?"

"Not me, I didn't eat it, I don't like fish!"

I was laughing again. How could I have fallen for that again. Dad never missed a chance to point out the pointlessness of angling especially to one who didn't even like fish.

"OK," I said, "But you've got to admit this place is nice."

"Perfect," Dad admitted. "Just as long as no fish turn up to spoil it, horrible, slimy, smelly things!"

Suddenly, the stillness was broken by an eruption in the water round some of the bread that had drifted out a way into the harbour.

"That looks like a good fish, Dad."

"Tch, typical!" he groaned "with any luck he'll stay out there."

"I think there's more than one," I said, "They're demolishing that bit of bread."

"Well, if you want to catch anything, you'd better sling out some more and move your float, it's no good down there."

My float was rubbing against the hull of the fishing boat along to our right. Dad's was in open water, halfway to where those fish were feeding.

These new arrivals might well have been the rather wilder fish that came in with the tide, usually smaller than those that took up permanent residence in the harbours. These open sea fish were excellent eating too, unlike the port fish that ate all manner of filth and as often as not reeked of diesel. The attraction of the latter though was definitely size; at least one of those we'd seen earlier was three feet long, and might weigh as much as 12 pounds.

Just then, my float pulled away under the boat as though snagged. Taking up the rod, I pulled the line round to the right so as to clear the keel. Like a rocket, the float shot out from the dark side of the boat, skipping across the wavelets into open water. The drag emitted a shrill wail of distress, and Dad jumped up as though yanked from a half doze by a grappling hook from a passing plane.

"Hello! That looks interesting," he said, blinking into the sparkling reflections off the water. "Just as I was nodding off, trust a fish to put in an appearance when you're least expecting it!"

A good size, hard fighting grey mullet on a light 12-foot freshwater rod and 6 lb line, this was going to be something. It was a pure stroke of luck he hadn't run under the boat, the line would have been keelhauled and, '*Adios*'. The old hollow glass was hooped over, the line singing at maximum pitch as our fish careered back and forth, the float surfing sideways over the ripples. The drag was still giving line but only a little; at each turn I was able to recover a few feet. As the skirmish went on, we began to wonder how on earth we were going to land it. The water was at least 15 feet below us. Spot the deliberate mistake, I thought to myself.

"We need a drop net," Dad said. "I've got one in the garage."

There wasn't anything that Dad didn't have in the garage, or in the shed. In fact it had been more than twenty years since it had been possible to get the car in there.

"Grab the landing-net, Dad," I called out, "I've had a brainwave."

"Oh no, not like one of your short cuts I hope!"

Dad was screwing the handle on to the net as I battled to get the mullet in to the wall, between the boats and away from trouble. I couldn't help chuckling to myself. After years of experience, if ever I proposed a short cut, like the day we cycled to Reculver Towers, the ruined abbey along the coast from Herne

Bay, instead of following the road, Dad would say 'no thanks, I'd prefer to go the long way round.'

With the rod in one hand I struggled down the remains of a rusting wharf ladder. Some of the rungs were non-existent but this aided rather than hindered matters since I was able to hook my arm through and deal with the fish. It appeared to have got wind of my predicament and made a number of spirited bids for freedom before I got near enough to the water. Dad was muttering the while about wills and life insurance.

I now had my first Spanish mullet within reach and I called up to Dad to pass down the net. With the rod in my left hand, the same arm round a good rung, I took hold of the lowered handle and let its length slip through my hand. If my fish made a run for it now I'd be in trouble. For a second I held on to the net handle with my teeth. Dad was saying I was mad, and I think he was right. The green slimy rung I was standing on was being gently lapped by the water, my toes squelched. I could feel my foothold slipping.

If the worst came to the worst, I thought, there was a dinghy a few feet away, tied to the ladder, I'd be able to make a grab for it. I switched hands and began to play the fish towards me which involved some of the most cack-handed winding in the entire history of angling. It was a beauty of a fish, now rolling on the surface as I brought the rod right up to my face, the butt pushed into the waistband of my trousers. My left hand, the one connected to my tiring, life-saving arm, held the end of the landing-net pole, the net itself in the water. With the rod held vertical, my fish slowly approached and then, finally, it was in.

Cheers and applause suddenly sounded above me. I remained stuck some moments in that last position, not able to move my left arm, the mullet looking up at me calmly, but with some measure of expectation. Getting back up was horrible. My arm was all pins and needles and I managed to get the line wrapped round everything. Dad took the rod once I had managed to get within reach and we could at last have a look at our fish. A family group had gathered, fascinated by our antics. We were heartily congratulated on our success before they went off back to their pre-lunch strolling.

Suddenly, Dad's rod dragged across the concrete and thudded into the nearest capstan, the line pulling the tip down dangerously. He bounded over to it and was immediately into a fish. While his reel was singing out on the harbour air, I unhooked my mullet and got it weighed, 4lb 4oz, a fine first fish. Seconds later, I was back down the ladder with both fish and net. Dad was having a tremendous battle trying to keep his fish from getting under the boats, let alone bring it along to me. I slipped my fish into the water and watched it flash away into the depths. I hung on once again to the ladder, this time with both hands, both arms round the net, waiting. Then suddenly, Dad had his fish under control, splashing a little on the surface, approaching me. I got the net to it and in no time was back up the top admiring an identical capture.

"They are terrific fighters," Dad said, "I'm not sure if I've ever caught one before. They go more like bass than anything else."

"Especially on this light tackle," I said. "But just imagine a really big one, there are fish at least twice this size right there under our noses!"

"I could do with a rest, I don't know about anything else. What does that one weigh?"

I held up the spring balance, the tail of Dad's fish sticking out the top of the bag.

"4lb 4oz," I said.

"Isn't that what you said yours was?"

"Yes, maybe the hungry ones are all the same size!"

"I could do with a bite to eat," Dad said as he baited up with a fresh bit of bread. "What's in the cool-box?"

"Hmm, good idea." I took Dad's fish back down the ladder in the net and released it. His silvery blue flanks caught the light as he headed for the underside protection of the nearest boat. That tiny flash of light, before it disappeared caused another, bigger fish to start from the shadows, deeper down. A mullet I supposed, it looked huge for a split second, then sunk from sight.

Dad was back under the parasol.

"I'm on my holiday!" he said as I reappeared.

"Quite right too, let's have English lunchtime now, since it's gone 1 o'clock, and then Spanish *comida* a bit later on!"

We sat back and relaxed. In order to help us do so we had cast out a way and were able to watch our floats bob about while we sipped our beers. We broke open another of the lovely fresh-smelling *barras* and tucked in to some fine local cheese and *jamón*. I threw a bit more bread over the side, in case anyone else was hungry.

"I've just seen a monster down there, Dad, under the boat."

"This bread's far too good for the fish," Dad said.

"The woman in the *panaderia* was somewhat taken aback when I told her I wanted it for bait. I'd said that we were going fishing, but then, since I'd asked for six *barras* she wanted to know how many of us there were."

"I'm not surprised, imagine what she'd think if you told her you put the fish back!"

"That's true," I said. "Mind you, with the enormous offshore fishing industry, they don't take these mullet very seriously, and local anglers tend to go after bass mainly. But that fish I've just seen, I wonder how big they get."

"They get pretty big off the coast of Africa. Do you remember that documentary about, where was it, Mauritania? Where they fish for mullet with dolphins.

They were big fish."

"Yes, they beat the water with sticks to attract the dolphins which then drive the fish into nets," I recalled. "But I honestly think that fish I've just seen was much bigger, maybe a 20-pounder."

"I think you'd better lay off the drink!"

We both laughed. The air was warm and salty, overhead wheeled remarkably quiet gulls. The entire port seemed half asleep as the tide reached high water. Our floats sat out in the still, reflected blue, the lines wiggly across the surface. A few hazy clouds drifted by, occasionally forming fishy shapes, a john dory, a marlin, even a white whale.

Along the quay came an old, but powerful looking man in a beret and a past-its-best brown suit. He was carrying a hefty bamboo boat rod to which was fixed a huge and seemingly brand new fixed-spool reel, by means of jubilee clips. As he came closer, I saw a ledger of at least a pound dangling from a steel hawser and a 12/0 shark hook.

"Any luck?" he half shouted.

Dad visibly jumped in his seat. I answered that it was quiet for the moment, but that we'd had a couple of mullet. I used both the words *muxe* and *mugil* which were frequent synonyms for the standard Spanish *mujol* anywhere along the coast from Cantabria to Galicia. His expression immediately changed to one of scepticism, and even disgust.

"I'm after *congrios*," he boomed. "I've fished here all my life and I've never seen anyone catch a *mugil*."

A bit surprised, I replied that there were lots of them but he said they were impossible to catch.

"Soft mouths you see," he said, knowingly.

"How about the congers?" I enquired.

He told us how a young boy had been dragged across the rocks over yonder, pointing to a slipway a hundred yards off, by a conger which had emerged from a hole and taken the lad's crab fishing bait, a bit of mackerel strip.

"I'd never have believed it if I hadn't seen it with my own eyes. I'm after him," he said, showing us his bucket full of bait; he had half a wet-fish counter in there.

Just then, Dad had a bite and struck, only to reel in a bare hook. As he baited up, the old man nearly fell over laughing.

"Bread!! You won't catch anything on bread," he spluttered, tears in his eyes.

Mr Crabtree's words suddenly came to mind, 'bread is by no means the only bait that mullet will accept - in fact it is difficult to find a bait they won't sample!'

Dad lowered his line into the water instead of casting and something about the way he did so had us all watching to see what he was up to. The float drifted gently under the high looming prow to his right. My Dad's eyes and mine were expectant, the old man's were still watering with barely suppressed derision.

Dad put his rod down and reached over to the table for his beer. I glanced at my float and thought I would re-cast. As I wound in, we watched as a seagull swooped momentarily after my float. The old man was about to move on when all three of us jumped to see Dad's rod leap off the ground into the harbour! There were exclamations of various kinds of astonishment all round.

"It's snagged the bottom of the boat," the old man shouted.

"Now that's a good fish, Dad," I said.

Dad was only concerned about his rod. But I said he shouldn't worry, I was sure we'd get it back.

"It's like the days when the fishing rod was first invented," I said. "If the fish was too big to deal with then you threw in your cane and went off along the bank after it. It wouldn't be long before the fish would tire and you would get him."

"There it is!"

The cork handle had just popped up a few yards beyond the boats, in open water. Then it started away from us, jaws style, in fits and stops, helplessly dragging behind the unhappy mullet. I yelled out to a local man who was skulling towards a little pleasure boat, moored a short distance off.

"*Oye señor,* Grab that rod, if you can!"

The man was as amazed as the rest of us (another small crowd was gathering) but seeing the cork handle approaching, he crouched down in his skiff and positioning himself, soon had hold of the rod and was struggling with what was clearly a very fine fish.

"He's going to lose it," I said.

The rod was hooped right over and the man was winching away with all his might.

"Careful!" I hollered. "The line'll snap."

But it was no use. He had the mullet alongside his rowing boat by this time and Dad and I watched in horror as he attempted to lift the fish bodily out of the water. The rod bent double, the line tensed and I was just imagining the singing agony of the monofilament, when the inevitable 'snap' suddenly echoed like a whiplash round the harbour walls, along with multitudinous groans of disappointment.

"Line was no good," bellowed our conger angler, "too thin for bass."

Treating with contempt my observation that it had in fact been a mullet, he showed us his line. That was what we needed for bass, he told the assembled onlookers.

"The strongest in the shop, 44kg breaking strain."

He hung around a few minutes longer until the boatman kindly handed over

Dad's rod. I shinned down the ladder to get it, thanking him profusely for saving it.

"Never seen anything like it," said the conger man, when I was back at the top. "A bass pulling along a rowing boat!"

"It was a *muxe*," shouted the boatman, "biggest I've ever seen!"

The murmur '*muxe*' buzzed through the assembled onlookers as they began to disperse.

With that, the 44kg man set off towards the end of the wharf in search of his *congrio*. The last of the small crowd, two families on holiday, chatted with us for a while, then set off in search of ice-creams, and we were finally alone once again.

"What was all that about the Congo anyway?"

"He's after a legendary conger eel," I said. "But I think Congo is more like it, this harbour is that fellow's very own Heart of Darkness!"

"It was an incredible fish, wasn't it? I wonder if it was that one you saw."

"I don't know," I said. "What a shame, eh?"

"Well, at least I got my rod back!"

Dad and I got back to our fishing. A few more tourists sauntered by on their after lunch walks. They were mostly from other parts of Spain, and I tried to place their accents; one or two Germans and a Dutch family were rather easier to identify. As the afternoon ticked gently by, clangingly measured by the town clock, we continued to fish between the boats. We had several more, smaller mullet, but those really huge fellows or their shadowy shapes failed to put in any further appearances.

A few more local anglers turned up and were fishing in a huddle off the far end of the harbour wall. Apart from one or two tiny flatties, nothing much seemed to be going on except crossed lines and a great deal of shouting. Our earlier, ancient brother of the angle was slightly apart from them. I thought I would go and see how he was getting on.

As I approached I realised that he too was yelling at the top of his voice, though at no one in particular. His conger fishing technique was remarkable. He baited up with a whole sardine or mackerel; he had, as we had already seen, a good stock of both. Then, with sinewy lust and determination, he cast savagely at the water. The ledger thundered directly into the innocent sea at a distance of 20 yards or so. The lead kaploomed, creating a tidal wave in every direction. Nearby gulls, cautiously out of range, waited a second, then swooped in to snatch up the shattered sardine corpses off the surface. The fish heads, as far as I could see, stayed on the hook. Then, all the crabs for miles around, having been alerted by the commotion, moved in on the bait. The old man's rod tip danced in response to their pickings and he struck aggressively into the phantom conger, that would certainly have lost his teeth if not his head, had it been anywhere near. Frantic reeling, accompanied by considerable vocal disappointment then brought to his eyes the appalling proof that his arch rival had again outwitted him, having gorged himself on the best part of 25 wholesome fish so far that day.

The real heat of the day had passed, and the breeze off the sea was cooling and pleasant. It was late afternoon by this time and, as I walked back to see how Dad was getting on, there were a few more people about, taking their postprandial exercise on the wharf.

"Anything doing, Dad?"

"They are on the bread I threw in a minute ago," he said, "we might get something."

We sat once more and concentrated on our lines. A couple of local wise men sauntered by and chuckled at our innocence as we pressed fresh bread on to our hooks. For the moment there seemed to be no fish in close, as there had been at the top of the tide, but further out there were several powerful looking rises to the crusts Dad had thrown in. I said I would have a go at a long cast, hoping the bread would stay on. The tackle looked very ungainly as it flew out to within a few feet of the floating soggy remains of the bread. In my mind's eye I saw my bait sinking slowly, as though broken from one of those pieces, down to a feeding fish. The float bobbed gently on the imperceptibly falling tide. Our onlookers, having overheard us speaking English, began a few not entirely good natured observations on the remarkable ignorance of foreign fishermen.

"*Vorsprung durch technik!*" said one, just as my float, unseen by them, began a slow but steady pull across the surface. I grabbed the rod and struck, and the fish took off on a tremendous run towards the big fishing vessels moored further out. I couldn't afford to give any line or else the fish would put them between itself and us. The rod curved over like a weeping willow, the line whining in the wind.

"Much too light a rod," came a squeaking voice behind us.

"Not a hope of catching a fish with that," said another.

"He's snagged up on something."

"Using bread for bait! Ho ho ho!"

I tried some sidestrain, the rod lunged repeatedly. I could feel a powerful tail beating the water, but it was swinging out, away from danger

"Blimey, it looks like a good ''un," Dad said.

"It sure does," I muttered, hardly daring to speak, I was gaining a little line.

One of the local experts decided I had hooked a guy rope.

Suddenly, my fish broke the surface and ran away across the harbour ripping line off my reel. The accompanying music of the drag, so loved by all anglers, drew noises of appreciation from our onlookers. Again the fish slackened its pace and all of a sudden I was frantically recovering line. Word had spread along the wharf, and the sceptics were now joined by a cheering band of local people and sightseers as the glistening silver, grey striped flanks of the mullet flashed through the spray, only a few yards off.

"He's caught my conger!" sounded a voice we knew. "On bread! I'd never have believed it."

"No, no, no, it's a bass," it was the squeaky chap speaking. "Anyone can see that."

"A shark!" came another voice.

"Very like a shark," I felt inclined to agree with this latter. It was beyond doubt the biggest mullet I had ever had on, but for how long, that was the question. I manoeuvred the giant as best I could; the truth was, the rod really wasn't up to it. Every movement from the fish put rod and line in jeopardy. It was in our patch of open water and I began to debate with Dad concerning the business of getting down the ladder. A good way off to the left were some steps down to a landing point which was visible under a few inches of gentle ripples. Before, it had been under five or six feet of water, and the top step was a good drop down from the wharf. The real problem though, was that there were a couple of dinghies between it and us, their ropes slopping on the water.

Keeping a tight line on my fish and the drag set soft to cope with the sudden lunges he was still very capable of, I moved off along the wall. Dad went ahead amidst myriad suggestions from the crowd, one or two in French, to which he responded, delighted at the chance to practise. With the help of a newly made friend from the Gallic province of Landes, he got down on to the steps. I called out for him to go carefully. He made his way down, testing each slippery green step as he went, passing the net over and under the tangle of guy ropes. Now, I had to get down the ladder and on to those dinghies. I was practised enough at this stage and at least I didn't have the net in my teeth. I stepped on the nearest rope, my weight pulling the first dinghy near enough to step on to. I crossed and clambered over to deal with the renewed struggles of the mullet. It had sensed something and was thundering off towards the propellers and rudder of the nearest trawler. I really thought I was going to lose it then, but he went deep and though the rod bent double and the drag grudgingly gave, he stayed on. I battled on and clambered over the rocking dinghies until I finally got to the last. Dad was only six feet away. I played the fish round between me and the looming trawler, keeping tighter control than ever. By pure chance the mullet made a tremendous run in just the right direction and was in the square of open water off the landing stage. Dad had the net in the water, which had dropped now to a foot below the landing. All I had to do was bring the fish round towards Dad for netting. As it came nearer, it palpably increased in size; this was the fish I'd seen surely, under the boat. Above us there must have been 20 people, gathered to see the spectacle. Plenty of advice was forthcoming, but for at least half an hour we'd been oblivious.

"Pull it into the boat!" one voice called out.

"Light tackle," I said. "The line would break."

"Ah," and the conversation returned to the surprising ignorance of foreign anglers. Wrong rod, wrong line, wrong bait, wrong everything, they explained to each other at the tops of their voices. I couldn't help smiling as I sweated and strained with this splendid creature, the odds rather in its favour as a result of my foreign inadequacies. To the amazement of all, us included, the huge fish slipped over the rim of the net and Dad visibly struggled to pull it up on to the landing-stage. An incredible arm-ache suddenly manifested itself as I left the rod and pulled on the ropes to get myself over to the landing point. In a flash I had gone for the bag, the scales and the camera. The picture and the weighing done, to the bewilderment of our onlookers, we slipped our fish back into the water - 12lb 14oz! A specimen thick lipped grey mullet, a record even. We sat back on the drier upper step, completely exhausted.

"They let it go!"

"No idea, these Germans."

We couldn't really move or say anything. Above us the crowd was breaking up, several voices calling out congratulations on our success. Eventually, all was quiet once more, and I thought I had better go and get my rod. One of the old men we'd seen earlier, in shirtsleeves and wearing a sailor's cap, dropped down on to the step behind us. We were enveloped suddenly in the rich tangy scent of his pipe smoke.

"A beautiful fish that," he said. "Good to see it go, been around a few years I'd say."

His voice was soft, and his manner thoughtful and deliberate.

"They hang around the harbour when they get to that age and size," he went on. "But I've never seen one caught, they're too wily. I was happy to see that one go, back under my old ship."

I followed his glance over to the old trawler, the name *Narcissus* brightly painted over the bridge. He wished us all the best, and I did the same. We were delighted to have met him. Despite his years, he hopped back on to the wharf and was gone.

I told Dad what he had said and we set about collecting our gear.

"The old fellow was right. Well done," Dad said. "What a fish!"

"Call it a day, shall we?"

"I think so, don't you?"

Chapter Four

Galicia

An ovation to cuisine, octopus and white wine country, where abound the nase and black bass, not to mention witches and local prejudices. Messrs Chapman and Buck put in an appearance, and the question of angling luck arises as does a keenly interested crow. The author recalls Laurie Lee in the village of Mondoñedo, visits nearby trout streams, practises bubble and fly fishing, examines fire salamanders while the Spanish Civil War beguiles a blank day.

Galicia is perhaps Spain's most famous region for fish. All over the country, wet fish and seafood from Galicia is held in high esteem, particularly such delicacies as *percebes*, or goose barnacles, and *pulpo*, octopus, neither very well known to the English. The men who harvest the *percebe* tell an amazingly dangerous harvesting story, to rival those of the Himalayan honey gatherers of Nepal or the Tiger Cave nest gatherers of Thailand. The fishermen abseil down the cliffs into a foaming sea, with a netted bag tied around their waists, and selectively cut the *percebes* off the rocks at the water line. Above, their companions hold the ropes and will help to bring them back up. There were incidents enough of fishermen having lost their lives at this practice and, needless to say, *percebes* are usually a very expensive appetiser.

Octopus was known almost everywhere as '*pulpo gallego*', as a *tapa* or a main dish, comprising tender chunks of reddish-purple-skinned white meat and tentacles, spiced with paprika and invariably served on a bed of Galician *cachelos* or sliced, boiled potatoes. It certainly deserved all the fame and praise lavished upon it. Fishermen might be found almost anywhere along the coast working with a long handled hook, like a gaff, with which they would wrench the unfortunate cephalopod out of the rocks, or using a fiendish looking multi-pointed and lead-weighted hook, lowered into the water in harbour corners. If working at the waterline, these men would frequently be seen wearing white wellington boots, a curious characteristic that I soon discovered was attractive to the octopus, which would often launch itself from its hiding place and actually attack the feet of the fishermen, at which juncture it would be rapidly impaled with the gaff. Being thus impaled, however, was only the beginning of the creature's sufferings. Next came the tenderising process. The fisherman would smash the octopus repeatedly against the rocks or any solid ground for a considerable period, finally ripping the bulbous head and body section from the rest and dropping the desired parts into a bucket before moving off in search of another. A good deal more tenderising would be required before cooking, a labour which would usually fall to the lady wife at home. Once, during a food fair in a Galician village, I was drawn to the extraordinary sight and sound of three somewhat battered looking front-loader washing machines, their drums tumbling around in full wash process. The din was tremendous and on closer inspection I found that each had a house-brick inside, and a few octopuses. Upon enquiry, I was laconically informed that they were 'tenderising'.

There are so many small and picturesque sea ports in Galicia, as well as the huge, more industrial centres such as Vigo or La Coruña, and all the wild year round, many fleets of trawlers head out to fish, mainly in the North Atlantic but also very much further afield. Sportfishing along the Galician coasts is rather less known about, particularly from the perspective of anyone from outside the country. Although there certainly are local anglers to be seen, fishing from high vantage points on the rocks, for the Spanish angler a great deal of Galicia's most famous fishing is inland, for salmon and trout. There are some quite surprisingly remote and wonderfully pretty rivers, often shrouded in the dank green cover of overhanging lichened branches, with streams and rills tumbling over wildly rocky stream beds, rarely far from the coast. Moving further inland there is quite another sort of river, the Síl, which I originally visited more years ago than I can now recall.

Breezing down into the valley of that river for the first time, the immediacy of my thoughts then makes it seem as though it were actually happening today. As I write, everything is as fresh to me as if I were actually there. I recall my thoughts drifting away from wondering whether I have forgotten anything, if the tackle is in good order, if the bait is OK or even from considering the prospects for catching a good fish. Instead, my mind is drawn into the world of wine. The sides of the valley are decked with brilliant greens, hectare upon hectare of vines that climb the seemingly unending heights of terraces, hanging as precipitously as those ancient Gardens of Babylon. Just like that wondrous extravagance of the great Queen Shammuramat, these terraces are also reflected in a river; not the Euphrates of course, but the exquisite río Síl, which winds its way like a great serpent at the valley floor, glistening in a deeper, darker, olive green than that of the vines.

I am in the heart of La Ribeira Sacra, among the vineyards of the Síl canyon in the mysterious hinterland of Galicia, land of monasteries, mystery and magic. Dare I ask myself if I believe in '*as meigas*', the famous witches that haunt this country? Put that question to a native of these lands and they would cautiously reply: '*Eu non creo nas meigas . . . mais habelas hainas . . .*' 'I do not believe in witches . . . but such things as may seem, may be.' Upon first hearing this well-known refrain, I was reminded of an equally extraordinary remark somewhere in Hardy, perhaps *Tess of the D'Urbervilles* . . . 'Life is but a series of seemings, and what things seem, they are.' Seeming to be quite alone at the waterside, the angler may be blissfully oblivious to the presence of others, a hiker perhaps, or bird spotter, and they equally of him. Therefore, they are in fact quite alone in their communion with themselves and with nature. This might be especially so in such a place as the Síl valley.

There is, above all, something uncommonly exotic in the atmosphere of this place, a kind of enchantment, which resounds in the names of the vines cultivated here: Albariño, Treixadura, Godello, Loureira and Torrontés, white grape varieties, from which the region's most famous white wines are made; and then there are Mencía, Brancellao, Merenzao, Garnacha, Mouraton and Negreda, all black varieties, which produce red wines, some of which have recently been cited by international wine guru Robert Parker as among the best in the world.

The valley is calm and quietly apart from worldly affairs, a place of tranquility and peace, yet the very air seems to whisper inscrutability. The dramatic orography, contour lines piled one upon another, where lands surge up and valleys plunge as though commanded by wizards, make viticulture here a challenging prospect. Just walking the narrow paths between the steep terraces is a vertiginous experience. At any moment you imagine yourself falling hundreds of metres, down to the snake-like river below.

It was spring and mid-day was approaching as we entered the scene. I was seated on the passenger side of an old Volkswagen beetle, driven by Aurora, an old friend from Lourenzá, near Mondoñedo. She had business that day in the far off city of Orense and had offered to drop me off on the way, at a bridge that arched high over the San Esteban reservoir, on the Síl. After cheerful thanks and a promise to be back at the same spot late that evening, I stood by the roadside and watched the old car where it confronted the phenomenal climb up the other side of the valley. It was soon lost to sight and so, walking on to the irresistible bridge, I looked down at the water. Tiny fry were very active at the surface, apparently chasing something even tinier, flies probably, that scattered in all directions, sudden flashes of silvery sides, then just as suddenly disappearing, leaving the surface quite still again. Elsewhere on the river, there were other patches of similar activity, certainly alevins of the *Perca americana* or black bass, which I had been told were abundant in this stretch of the river. Moreover, they had been here a good number of years and according to local stories, had grown to considerable size. The largest of them were said to haunt the concrete piles below the very bridge I was standing on.

Nevertheless, on this sunny April day, it wasn't the bass I was after. The attraction of the Síl lay in another, genuinely autocthonous species, known locally as '*os peixes*', simply 'the fish', which were in fact *Chondrostoma duriense*, the nase of the Duero, one of a number of species of '*bogas*', or nase, found in the Iberian Peninsula.

The subject of the Iberian nase is possibly even more problematic than that of the Iberian barbel. In my fishing diary, I have a section dedicated to the nase which notes, first of all, the extraordinary and quite amusing list of names for these fish around Europe as a whole.

The Spanish *boga* is 'nase' or 'nose' in English, although no representative of the species occurs in the British Isles, which is perhaps just as well: 'I'm a nose man', has a more ambiguous ring to it than, 'I'm a carp man'. The fish is *nase* in German and *soiffe* in French, *naso* in Italian, *nesling* or *næresi* in Scandinavian countries, *hotu* in Hungary, *sneep* in Holland and *syrtári* in Greek, to name but a few. Almost all of these words mean 'nose', stemming quite naturally from the notable protuberance of the snout in most of the Chondrostoma family. Europe is home to various different species: the most widely distributed common nase, *Chondrostoma nasus*, the French, *C. taxostoma*, the Italian, *C. soetta*, the Bosnian, *C. phoxinus*, the nase of the Caucasus, *C. colchicum*, the Terek nase, *C. oxyrhynchum*, the Southern European nase, *C. genei*, and the Dalmatian nase, *C. knerii*. Once we move into Spain and Portugal, most guide books agree in adding the Iberian nase, *Chondrostoma polylepis*. However, the list does not end there. The rarest of all the nase species, currently and perhaps irredeemably on the verge of extinction, is the 'loina', *Chondrostoma arrigonis*, which is found only in the immediate basin area of the river Júcar in Valencia. The populations of this species are, moreover, considerably fragmented and reducing rapidly. Meanwhile, Iberian species which are rather less at risk are the Guadiana nase, *C. willkommii*, the pardilla nase, *C. lemmingii*, and finally our Duero boga, *Chondrostoma duriense*. The Chondrostomae also include a number of fish unafflicted with prominent noses: the little Iberian bermejuela, *Chondrostoma arcasii*, well known to all fresh-water anglers in the northern half of Spain, the madrilla, *C. miegii*, common in Catalonia, Navarra and the Basque Country, and finally the madrija, *C. turiense*, found only in the Turia and Mijares river basins, north of Valencia.

Both Spanish and international scientific communities have considered the re-classification of the Iberian Chondrostoma family but, combined with the fact that sufficiently detailed information is scarce, and research funding limited, there is the problem of hybridisation among certain members of the group, specifically *Chondrostoma polylepis* and *C. lemmingii*. One of the reasons for possible re-classification is the occurrence among certain populations, particularly of *C. lemmingii*, of important variations in genetic and morphological characteristics, considered sufficient to justify their description as new species.

The question which had brought me to the Síl on such a fine spring day was the need to establish whether the *'peixe'* was indeed the nase of the Duero. *Chondrostoma duriense* is common throughout the Duero region, occurring in all the tributaries of that river. To the north and west, its distribution extends to the border between the Castilian province of Zamora and the Galician Orense. At this point, a further population extends throughout Galicia. The Síl and the Miño are the main rivers of the south-east of Galicia and form a quite separate ecosystem, making it perfectly possible for the *peixe* to be quite another species.

I am very familiar with the Duero nase, since it is not only common around Valladolid but also great fun to fish for. The best bait is silkweed, or a worm, and despite having proportionally small mouths, they are not difficult to hook on a size 10 or 12. My tackle on this day included a light but long match-style rod, 14 foot being ideal for fishing deep at only a short distance from the bank.

Having studied the river to my satisfaction, from my vantage point on the bridge, I began looking for a way down and soon found a narrow, steep and stony goat track, which seemed to lead to the water. Progress was far from easy, amid brambles, hawthorn and dog rose, which was becoming thicker at every step, when suddenly I came face to face with an old woman, who was ascending the path in front of me.

"*¡Boas tardes, Xoan peixeiro!*"

This sudden salutation in broad Gallego, employing moreover, the Galician form of my own name, *Xoan* for John, 'John the angler' in fact . . . stopped me dead in my tracks.

"*Ehh . . . ¡Boas tardes!*" I replied, a little disconcerted.

"*A pesca de hoxe hache ser boa . . .*" the old woman asserted - the fishing would be good. "*A xornada de hoxe apresentase xeitosa . . . E a lúa está minguando,*" she added, - it was such a propitious day, and under a waning moon.

She must have mistaken me for someone else, I thought, for some other 'Xoan', who fished there. She looked very old, perhaps her son or even grandson was a *peixeiro*.

She was dressed as a simple country woman, quite timeless, and she had a stout walking stick, more like a mountaineer's staff. As she passed close by, I heard her mutter under her breath, "*Mouchos, coubras, escaravellos, cun chisco de peixe . . .*" - Owls, vipers and beetles, with a scrap of fish . . .

Then I noticed the head of the staff was carved with figures or symbols, cut deeply into the wood.

"*Ha ter boa pesca, xa verá,*" she said aloud, - The fishing will be good, you'll see. Then she looked me fixedly in the eye. "*Os peixes andan a tres metros namáis,*" - The fish are three metres down, no more.

She turned and reached the road and there, she seemed to vanish, behind the bushes.

I stood there watching a moment, then continued down the track. She had to be a *meiga*, if anyone was . . . Such as things may seem, they may be . . .

'*A lúa está minguando*' - 'A waning moon' - she had said. I loved the soft sound of this language, so much gentler and more musical than Castilian Spanish, sounds that had much in common with the neighbouring Portuguese. I had learnt a good deal over the years but, as with Italian, I tended to respond in Spanish, merely mixing in any verb endings or vocabulary I knew.

The *lúa* . . . I hadn't checked on the phase of the moon before coming on this trip. Occasionally I do. Some anglers considered a full or a new moon, even a crescent or a gibbous, most propitious, or indeed the very opposite. I would be glad of any phase when it happened to coincide with good fishing, and would be thoroughly put out when it didn't. The old woman's auguries were favourable, there was no doubt about that, but nothing substituted for local knowledge, or better still, close observation of the water in question. With that thought I found I had arrived at an opening and had the river before me at last.

Settling my gear among the rocks, I set up the rod, threaded a light line through the rings and tackled up with a float, a few shot and a small hook. Then, as though performing some mysterious rite, I prepared to plumb the depth. Setting the float at about six feet, I cast gently to six or seven yards and observed the float vanish, just at the last minute, below the surface. I gauged the depth there to be only another foot at most. Making the adjustment, I cast again and, sure enough, the float stayed upright at the surface. I wound in once more and, removing the plummet, baited with a few twists of rich green silk-weed I had collected that morning from the old water mill near the village of Mondoñedo, where I was staying. I snapped the lid closed, to keep the weed moist, and cast again to the same distance from the bank but some 20 yards upstream. The float ran gently with the current and, keeping a gentle check on the line, I attempted to maintain the distance from the bank, as I walked slowly towards the towering pillars of the bridge. Reaching the end of the swim, I wound in and returning to the starting point, trotted the same stretch again. Halfway along the run, the float wavered, as though the bait had brushed some obstacle at the riverbed, but then continued on its way. But it was only momentary, for, with a sudden lurch the float pulled under. As fishing writers have often observed, there were few things more delightful to behold in the angler's field of vision than the appearance of his float, nicely positioned against a lily pad for example, yet, certainly still more delightful, was its sudden disappearance.

I upped the rod and immediately felt the tugging turns and dives of the first fish of the day. Not a big one but the sense of contact and success was gratifying. Moreover, the swift finned nase put up a most valiant and exciting defence of its liberty. Soon, though, the fish slid over the rim of the net and I let it rest there a moment until it became calm. I then crouched down for a closer inspection. It assuredly looked very like *Chondrostoma duriense*: the characteristic snout, head shape, long in the body, perhaps ten inches in this case, and silvery pale grey in colour. The flanks were speckled with irregular dark flecks, a characteristic said to be peculiar to Galician and Portuguese populations of the species. The lateral line was clearly visible and I carefully counted 71 scales along its length, which accorded with the references in guide books of between 63 and 74. Furthermore, the tail and dorsal fins each had nine branched rays.

There was little in these first impressions to suggest that the pretty little fish might be anything other than the nase of the Duero. A more scientific study would be required to establish the exact species, something which even my considerable angling curiosity hardly warranted. Even so, since a few of the fish's tiny scales were left in the landing-net, as I flipped the fish back into the water, I decided to keep them and dispatch them in due course to the Natural History Museum in Madrid.

"Why d'ya throw it back for?"

The strident, aggressive voice came from up on the bridge.

"You should kill 'em."

This pleasant fellow I soon heard crashing down the little goat track towards me and as soon as he emerged from the thicket, he immediately demanded to know what I was doing there.

"There's good trout fishing further up," he bellowed, without waiting for a reply, and waving a stick up the valley. "I killed thirty only yesterday."

I decided he had to be the blood brother of the Conger Man I'd met on the coast some years before. He went on to explain that down here near the bridge there was nothing but rubbish, just worthless fish you couldn't eat.

"You've got to kill 'em, kill all of 'em!" he added. "They do no end of damage. They're a plague, and they ruin my trout fishing."

Fortunately, after opining in this way for some minutes more and then commenting on the dismal quality of the tackle I was using, he marched off, back up path and moments later, silence reigned once more along the hushed valley of the Síl.

Such contempt, so typically expressed by trout fishermen, and not only in Spain, towards other species, which they swear at, throw into the bushes or even stamp on, reveals their true attitude to Nature: one of domination and exploitation, of disdain and destruction. They kill all their trout too, of course, all too frequently ignoring the regulations of size. 'They are the best eating!' I have heard them say. They kill all they catch, even if it is with a shade more respect than that shown to inferior species. As they wade through their slaughter, mercilessly thrashing the river, their trout slowly suffocate, crushed together in their creels. Then come the complaints: 'Useless, no fish here!' 'Only these worthless rainbows!' These latter, of course, have been introduced following their decimation of the native fish.

I stood pensively for some moments but then soon consoled myself, considering the fact that there were other kinds of fishermen, plenty of trout men among them, who understood the balance of the natural world, respected all wildlife and fished in accordance with the philosophy of catch and release, which, little by little, was making some headway in Spain as well as elsewhere.

Then, I suddenly remembered reading in Chapman and Buck (that intrepid pair of nineteenth century hunters and occasional fishers in Spain) that, 'A land without Trout labours, in our eyes, under grave physical disadvantages.' My immediate reaction to that was 'poor devils, if only they knew'. Although I have certainly enjoyed the jig jig jigging of a trout on my line, it has never done that much for me, although it has to be admitted that the intricacies of fly-tying and exquisite dry-fly casting have great charm. Hook into a barbel, let's say a gypsy of a couple of pounds, on light fly gear, and the angler, whether Victorian or present day, would quickly see what a real fish can do.

Even so, those two illustrious gentlemen, to their great delight, certainly did find trout in Spain but nevertheless went on to tell readers, in their excellent works *Wild Spain* of 1893 and *Unexplored Spain* of 1910 that, 'No one . . . who has other lands open to him, should ever go to Spain expressly for trout-fishing.' Wrong again, I muttered to myself. But, like everywhere and anywhere, a fellow really needs to know exactly when and precisely where to go a fishing. 'Who, but an angler,' they ask at a further juncture, 'can appreciate the heaven-sent joys of casting one's lines on "fresh streams and waters new"?' In this instance I cannot but concur, and absolutely so, but what a pity it is that their piscatorial catholicism did not extend beyond merely new waters, but rather to the new fish species to be found in them.

It is also amusing to read how the intrepid pair complain of Spaniards killing everything they catch or, come to that, anything they see in the landscape, a practice even more prevalent way back then than today. But what is funny is that Messrs Chapman and Buck were in Spain to do exactly the same. During their breaks from hunting down ibex, bear, wild boar or chamois, they were busy murdering every trout they came across. To be fair, though, they also initiated hunting restrictions and started the notion of the protection of endangered Iberian species, particularly the ibex, which led to a dramatic recovery in numbers and the eventual renewed success of the species. Chapman and Buck were also instrumental in the founding of Spain's first natural park, at Coto Doñana, originally a hunting reserve with extensive wetlands, which were and are home to innumerable species of birds, as well as being the major European breeding ground for flamingos. The park was later acquired by the Spanish state and is still managed as a nature reserve today.

In a much later book, D. A. Orton's *Where to Fish*, published by *The Field* and Harmsworth Press for the years 1978 and 1979, Spain is described as follows: '. . . a well-endowed country, offering the most southerly fishing for Atlantic salmon in Europe; brown and rainbow trout, coarse fish including large carp and barbel, both in rivers, and shore fishing for sea-bass, mackerel, mullet, conger and other species. Black bass, pike and Danube salmon are comparatively recent additions.'

At the close of the section, Orton reflects on the fact that Spain, 'has not yet become as notable for high-grade coarse fishing as it may at some future date.' Prophetic words indeed.

Feeling decidedly positive once more, after these reflections, I renewed the silkweed bait and returned to the start of the swim to fish gently and quietly, with no thought of ever bothering anyone anywhere. After having made a further half dozen passes down the river with no result, I re-set the float and shot some 18 inches deeper and cast a little further. The bottom dropped away abruptly but was marked by a progression of small terraces. Since the dam had been constructed downstream, the water here was very much deeper than in times gone by and the terraces below the water line were remnants of the same agricultural, or viticultural, practices seen higher up. These convenient ledges were ideal places for the fish to search for food and very easy for the angler to trot a line along.

The change of tactics worked well and over the ensuing couple of hours I managed to catch half a dozen more nase. They were graceful, elegant fighters with their sparkling twists and turns in the deep water, genuine *señoritas* of the stream, not unlike the beautiful grayling of more northern climes. Each fish seemed prettier than its predecessor, bright and silvery under the afternoon sun, with their decorative sprinkling of dark metallic specks. After a further adjustment of 18 inches in depth the fish had been bigger until suddenly I struck into a really fine specimen. Again, the fight was a series of fast weaving spirals and flourishes, and I had to respond with care and patience, in order to tire the fish just sufficiently to bring it to the bank. Once in the net, the nase measured 15 inches in length and weighed an impressive 2lb 4oz. Laying down the rod, I suddenly realised I was now fishing at a depth closer to ten feet. Three metres in fact, just as the old woman had said, '*Os peixes están a tres metros . . .*'

After removing the hook, I decided to keep the fish momentarily in the landing-net, which I laid across a convenient rock so the mesh was held in the water, and fetched the camera. I snapped a few pictures, including one with the tripod, in order to show the proud captor with his fish but all as quickly as possible. Moments later, I released the nase once more and glanced at my watch. Six o'clock. Due to the height of the valley walls, the opposite bank and water margins were already deep in the descending shadows. The warm evening light of the sun gilded the plants and bushes at the far side of the river, creating a scene worthy of further photographs and so I left the fishing for a bit and continued snapping away with the camera. Once the sun had dropped further, the magic was gone and so I settled back among the rocks and pulled my flask out of my rucksack.

It was definitely time for some tea. I filled my special fishing mug with piping hot water and dropped in a couple of 'rooibos' tea bags. This South African infusion, rich in flavour, was best made strong, which, since it was naturally caffeine free, wouldn't keep me awake all night, even if I drank a litre of it, which was likely enough. Accompanying victuals consisted of traditional María biscuits, a nut-packed munchy bar and an apple. Fishing being famously 'the contemplative man's recreation', as I sipped my tea, my thoughts turned to the mysterious old woman I had almost bumped into coming down the path. She had been quite right about fish at three metres, the best of the day's fish anyway. It would be good to have more of her auguries.

My mind then wandered to the many caprices of fortune associated with fishing, strokes of luck and coincidences, that marked so many waterside days. Like all anglers, I had my particularly 'lucky' rod or float, and in one of my timeworn fishing boxes, I had an old pike lure made by Heddon, called a 'Tadpolly'. It was a relic from many years past, before the omnipresent 'Rapala' had managed to catch practically all the world's predator anglers, such that the name was now universally applied to almost any fish shaped lure, just as with 'Hoover' for any vacuum cleaner. The Tadpolly was plain silver, with no other markings, and dived quickly, with a wobbling movement, such as that of an injured or moribund fish.

One winter day, perhaps fifteen years ago, that lure had brought more pike to the bank than I had ever caught in a day before. It seemed as though, as soon as it hit the water, any Esox within earshot would come rushing in and strike. Day after day, piking excursion after piking excursion, that lure was the lucky one, succeeding where all others failed, until its condition had seriously deteriorated. Now it was a scratched and scarred vestige of its former self, brutalised by the myriad teeth of so many pike, and it remained in the box, merely an amulet, a lucky charm, no more to be cast into the jaws of the dreaded *Esox lucius*.

It was certainly possible to make our own luck, of course. Careful and thorough preparation, attention to every aspect of weather and season, of the nature of the water to be fished and its finny residents, yet, there were certainly other less tangible factors. It seemed impossible not to recall those famous lines from Sheringham, so often quoted yet never superfluous. Every angler would do well to abide by them, even recite them, before any day's fishing, whether for carp or any other species.

So far as my experience goes, it is certain that good luck is the most vital part of the equipment of him who would seek to slay big carp. For some men I admit the usefulness of skill and pertinacity; for myself, I take my stand entirely on luck. To the novice I would say: 'Cultivate your luck. Prop it up with omens and signs of good purport. Watch for magpies on your path. Form the habit of avoiding old women who squint. Throw salt over your left shoulder. Touch wood with the forefinger of your right hand whenever you are not doing anything else. Be on friendly terms with a black cat. Turn your money under the new moon. Walk round ladders. Don't start on a Friday. Stir the materials for Christmas pudding and wish. Perform all other such rites as you know or hear of. These things are important in carp-fishing.

Had the old woman on the path a squint, I wondered. Probably not, but she was almost certainly on the best possible terms with a black cat.

Coincidence was another mystery, apparent flukes of fate, which were equally extraordinary. The first fish I ever caught in the Iberian Peninsula holds a special place in my memory and is honoured in my notebook with a special entry headed, 'The No. 2 Fish', and takes up a full page. It was a mirror carp of exactly two kilos, not a gramme more or less, caught on two grains of corn, not on the 2nd of February but of March, two months to the day, after my arrival at Barajas airport in Madrid. The bite had come at two o'clock in the afternoon and in the photo can be seen just two glistening mirror scales on its flanks.

Another well-known case of coincidence concerns the capture of a splendid common carp at Redmire Pool, which is not only well documented but actually recorded on film, since it occurs in the 'Redmire Legends' episode of Britain's most celebrated TV fishing series, *A Passion for Angling*. Bob James, in company with Chris Yates, is fishing Redmire for the first time, and he succeeds in landing a 20-pounder which, when it reaches the bank, is found to have no pelvic fins. Bob remarks that it is surely a known fish and Chris not only agrees but has, in fact, immediately recognised it as his own first big carp from Redmire, captured over 20 years before. It weighed 21lb then and now swings the balance around to 24lb, which is no surprise since every carp they catch during the filming of the episode also weighs 24lb.

Smiling to myself, remembering other delightful moments from the series, my attention was suddenly drawn to a dark shape, high in the sky, a crow, which suddenly emitted an incredibly loud and raucous croak and dropped sharply through the air before landing on the high railings of the bridge. There, the stately bird remained perched, its glossy plumage reflecting metallic blue-black in the low light. It turned its large ebony eye upon me with an expression of the most extraordinary, uncommon, intelligence. It seemed to absorb every detail, even to read my very thoughts. With a slight inclination of its head, the bird seemed to glance at the rucksack, then return its penetrating stare once more to me. I reached into my bag and taking a few biscuits, threw them towards the bridge, below the bird and waited. With feathery dark flit and flutter, the crow swooped down to the ground and began to break them up and gulp them down rapidly before flapping powerfully back to the railings. Then with more deafening caws, perhaps of thanks or farewell, the enormous bird flew up high, out of the valley and disappeared from view.

There was still an hour to go before I had to be back on the bridge, where Aurora would pick me up on her return from Ourense. An hour's fishing, to be made the most of before the light failed, and so I took up the rod once more and approached the water. Freshly baited, I again cast to the deeper run and followed the float's progress, slowing it periodically, to keep the movement of the bait as natural as possible, and attentive to its every movement. I repeated the process several times without result and found I was letting my attention wander; I was searching the sky for any sign of the crow. Such a bird was hardly a typical sign of good purport, but it had been so extraordinary. If it had been a magpie perhaps . . .

With each trot down the swim, I rather lazily allowed the bait to run closer to the piles of the bridge, before winding in and starting again. Just fifteen minutes remained now before I would have to be back on the bridge, and so I walked slowly back to the starting point intending just one last cast.

The float resumed its journey and just as it closed in on the pile of the bridge it slowly pulled under, as though caught on some snag at the bottom. I lifted the long rod, not wishing to pull hard, since I expected merely to lift the hook free and avoid jamming the point firmly into what was, in all probability, the dead wood of a sunken tree trunk. Unfortunately, the line did snag, but to my great surprise, the initially dead weight slowly moved against the current. As I increased the pressure, it suddenly became very much a fish and a series of deep thuds came resounding down the length of the rod. The strong carbon fibre doubled over dramatically, line pulling off the reel. This fish was no nase, it was staying down and pulling obstinately for yet deeper water. In no time at all the fish had gained a thirty yard advantage. If it was a nase it would make the headlines, but it was much more likely to be a bass.

Whatever it was, the fish continued to fight hard, staying between 10 and 15 feet down. The lightweight rod was managing well but I was more than a little concerned. Then, suddenly, the fish seemed to tire and stop pulling, only to rush to the surface in a dramatic change of tactics. It was definitely a bass. The fish erupted through the surface ripples, spraying water all around and leapt two feet into the air. It was a big one, and while in the air shook its head violently in an attempt to rid itself of the hook. But where was the hook? The bass jumped again and tail-walked backwards in a display of aquabatics so typical of the species. The position of the line suggested it was foul-hooked, certainly not anywhere in the gaping jaws. I had dropped the rod and was holding the tip under the water in an attempt to stop the frantic leaping. Then it seemed as though the battle was nearly over and suddenly the bass slid across the surface to the net. It proved to be a further switch of tactics, the fish suddenly diving anew, pulling strongly for deep water.

The rod survived the run in part because I had cautiously loosened the drag, thereby allowing line to pull off the reel. It was very light gear for tackling a bass of this size but patience was surely what would win the day, giving the fish line and time to tire itself out. Just as long as the hook didn't pull free. It was only a size 12 hook, moreover, which could just as easily open under such pressure.

It had been hard to see but it seemed that the hook was either somewhere in the gill cover or around the right side pectoral fins. Since the bass was foul-hooked, controlling it was doubly difficult. It was a fine specimen, perhaps five or six pounds. The rod had an action of only 50g and could not exert much influence at all. It was a matter of time. I kept up as much pressure as I dared, hoping to convince the bass by repeatedly changing the angle of sidestrain, rather than direct pressure. Gradually, the fish began to lose ground and again rushed for the surface. It seemed it hadn't strength enough this time, only managing a half leap from the water. I had to act quickly, bringing the rod to the vertical and steering the fish across the surface towards the net. Just as it was about to slide over the rim, the bass again recovered and thrashed its tail violently, which more by chance than anything else, drove itself into the mesh.

With the net still in the water, I knelt down and contemplated the bass with some pleasure, even though it had not been caught fairly, not a properly sporting capture. The bass had certainly not snapped at the silkweed bait but had been hooked in the gill cover, perhaps when making a lunge at a small nase that was intent on the bait. The hook had opened a little but all the while it retained some bend; it was so well embedded in the bone or cartilage, it would never have pulled free.

The thick set, dark-green bodied fish was well marked with its characteristic black patches, freckled with golden specks along the lateral line. The most significant feature of the species, though, was its large head, a third of the animal's length, and enormous mouth, capable of swallowing whole, a prey fish nearly as big as itself: the large-mouth bass, as it was known in its native North America, thereby distinguishing it from other, otherwise very similar, members of the bass species. Grabbing my pocket balance, I quickly weighed it, with the aid of a plastic bag, and jotted the result down in my notebook: 7lb 6oz. It was a personal best for the species but between brackets I added the all important detail: '(foul-hooked)'.

Black bass, like most members of the perch family were jolly good eating but, all I wanted was a few photos, preferring to see the fish returned afterwards to its own element. Something which often occurs at this moment in angling, whether it be from sheer joy or from an attempt at revenge, the fish, upon being returned to the water does not drift away quietly but rather just pretends to do so. Once it has a few inches of water over its head, it gives a tremendous kick with its tail, splashing water everywhere but mostly over the angler, drenching him from head to toe.

On this occasion, in order to go for the camera once again, I left the bass nosing into a bottom corner of the landing-net, which was held in place over the same rock as before. When I returned only a few seconds later, I was astonished to find the fish gone. Though it was not the first time I'd had a fish jump from a net left in this way, it was odd not to have heard a splash or some other sound. Moreover, the net was pretty deep, with the frame well out of the water. It was most certainly an escape worthy of the Great Houdini. I checked the net for holes and even returned to check again, as if I had imagined its disappearance, but the fish had definitely gone. So, I had no photo. Just then, I heard the discordant cry of the crow, very high overhead. I searched the sky but it was nowhere to be seen.

I shrugged my shoulders and quickly packed up before hurrying back up the track to the road and on to the bridge. I sat down on a low stone wall that lead on to the bridge and suddenly shivered. Deep shadows had now completed their invasion of the valley; only the vines on the very crests of the heights glimmered weakly in the last of the sunlight, against a backdrop of dazzling blue. Stillness reigned as time breathed, until I heard the solitary sound of the Volkswagen engine echo down the valley and, shortly afterwards, the old beetle swung into view.

Soon, I was once again in the passenger seat, with all my gear under the bonnet, except the rod which was too long, and had to travel in the back. We hurriedly and excitedly exchanged greetings and questions about how the day had gone for each of us. And as we climbed up the valley towards Lugo, I was suddenly stopped in my effusion of praise for the Síl and its fish by what I saw before me - a figure walking by the side of the road. It was the old woman, now dressed in glossy black and waving farewell, while in her other hand she held by the tail, a splendid black bass.

"Look!" Aurora exclaimed. "You weren't the only one fishing here today!"

"Indeed," I said, quite astonished. "So it would seem."

* * *

Galicia is very much in my blood. For seventeen consecutive years, I spent the calendar month of July, or *Xullo*, working in a village there, teaching English on a summer camp, to youngsters from Valladolid, where I lived during the rest of the academic year. I cannot bring this section on Galicia to a close and move inland without recalling an extraordinary day there from early in the 1990s.

Unlike those amazing days when a big fish is taken or when surprising numbers are caught, blank days tend not to linger long in the memory, nor obviously enough do they figure much in angling literature. However, as Arthur Ransome once observed, 'There is no such thing as a blank day for the fisherman . . . no one could call that day a blank on which he has seen a kingfisher'. The angler, as another literary fisherman, J.W. Hill's famous words highlighted, is particularly 'receptive' to those kinds of experiences where something far greater than the moment communicates itself, when 'veils' are withdrawn. I can certainly recall with ease such a day, without so much as a bite, when both time and history seemed to accumulate on the banks of a Galician river.

The truth is, it all started well before I got anywhere near the water. It was my first trip to Galicia, in the north-western corner of Spain from Valladolid, and the journey was, in a way, a sort of back-to-front pilgrimage in the footsteps of Laurie Lee. I had read his famous autobiographical novels of course; *Cider with Rosie* had been a set text at school. But like many who came out to Spain from England, other titles were essential reading. *As I Walked Out One Midsummer Morning*, which recounts his Spanish adventures in the early 1930s, had started in the Galician port of Vigo, from whence he walked the nearly 300 miles to Valladolid, then on to Madrid and beyond. Eventually, the outbreak of the Civil War had forced him to abandon the country from a village near the southern port of Málaga. On his return visit fifteen years later, *A Rose for Winter* took him around Andalusia, and then there was also his horrific experience with the conflict itself, *A Moment of War*, fighting with the International Brigades, which was published very much later.

In 1990, I had not been long in the country, and I had very little fishing gear with me. Since my boyhood, however, I had learnt never to go far without at least something to fish with. On this occasion, during the long bus journey, I had bought a sort of kiddies' starter kit, made by Grauvell, in a roadside service area supermarket. It consisted of rod and fully loaded reel, and the unlikely combination of a small diving plug and one of those very cheap, red and white plastic, bung style floats which registered the bite of Godzilla in the latest Hollywood remake.

For that month of July, the Galician village of Mondoñedo, specifically the historic seminary of Santa Catalina, would be home for me and my fellow teachers on an English language summer camp. As soon as I had a bit of free time I was away round the village in search of anything I could find out about the local fishing. I had already done the most important thing, which was to obtain a local authority licence from the Xunta de Galicia. This entailed my having a wine in The Green Bar, filling in a form they had there, handing it, along with the fee, to a bus driver whose route early the following morning took him into the provincial capital A Coruna. There, it would be left with another driver, whose wife worked next door to the offices of the Xunta, the regional council. Her cousin worked at those same offices and had coffee with her every morning. She would hand over the papers and the payment and would receive back, at the same time the following day, the fishing licence, duly stamped and certified. Then came the return bus journey and the original driver would drop it off at the bar the following evening. Marvellous though this arrangement undoubtedly was, nowadays the whole thing can be done in any branch of the Caixa de Galicia bank or at various offices of the Consellería de Economía e Facienda or Consellería de Medio Ambiente.

The Green Bar is so called because it was once painted green and sported no other name or sign outside. In recent times it has become 'El Fugitivo', has been woefully modernised and been painted white. Nevertheless, it is still called The Green Bar by locals and visitors in the know. Next door but one, there is a newsagents, which also doubles as a bookseller's and souvenir shop, and there is also a fishing tackle section.

On that day, when at last I had a few free hours from teaching, I repaired to the newsagents, bought myself a couple of bubble floats, a few small silvery spinners and a motley collection of local flies. Try as I might, looking through my pocket guide to trout and salmon flies, I was unable to identify any of them. One was perhaps a sort of camole, dressed on an eyeless size 10. In fact, they were all on eyeless hooks except the handful of *saltamontes* which had rather caught my eye, being nearly fluorescent green, rubbery vinyl grasshoppers, which the man in the shop assured me were 'deadly' for the trout which abounded in the local rivers. We would see soon enough.

Saturday was my first proper free day, although it was only a half day in reality, since we had classes in the morning. Nevertheless, I had a good number of free hours in prospect. On the previous evening, a couple of the other teachers and myself had been on our way back to the old seminary for dinner, after a couple of the local white 'Ribeiro' wines. We were coming down the narrow little main street towards the village's market square and the magnificent cathedral, a monument to considerable past wealth and glory, when one of my colleagues spotted a bundle of old fishing rods just behind the glass door of a gifts and jewellery shop. The proprietor was just closing up for the night but said he was in no hurry at all if I wanted to have a look at the rods.

Leaving my companions to go on down to dinner, I went into the shop. The shopkeeper had meanwhile pulled out the ramshackle old bundle which consisted mainly of bamboo poles as well as a couple of not so old telescopic hollow fibreglass river rods. Each of these lovely old bamboo poles was in three sections adding up to some nine or ten feet with a solitary eye at the tip and it was easy enough to separate them out as the whipping at the ferrules and the top eyes was a different colour for each rod, once bright greens, reds and yellows, now faded with the years. The ferrules and the very nice butt pieces were made of darkish tarnished brass which reminded me of something else, although for the moment I could not think what. As we sorted them out it soon became apparent that they were in disastrously poor condition; the butt and middle sections were splitting, most of the spindly top sections were either hilariously warped, broken or missing altogether. In the end there was only really one pole in reasonable condition and as I looked along its pale golden lengths I found that near the butt end were the tell-tale tiny holes of an earlier skirmish with woodworm. The man told me that he had treated the job lot with 'Rentokil' some years before when he had bought them and was confident the rod was sound.

They came from a house clearance sale when an old man had died who used to live at the top of the village. There had been all kinds of wood and bamboo things in a kind of dilapidated workshop next to the house, most of it abandoned and rotten. It seems that the old man used to make furniture and other items of carpentry, years ago when he was younger, and at some stage had made these fishing rods, seemingly from the bamboo poles generally used in gardens around the village for runner beans. No one really knew anything about it, since as far as anyone could remember the old fellow never fished and they had never been offered for sale. They had probably stood there forgotten in a corner of the workshop ever since the old man had taken it into his head to try his hand at rod making. There had never been much demand in the village for fishing tackle either, most things, until recent times, having been bought away in the city of Lugo or down at the coast.

The old house itself had stood empty too, since the old fellow's death, there being apparently no other family and the clearance sale had been organised simply to raise the money for the funeral expenses. In response to my query he told me that indeed the house itself was now pretty much in ruins and I could hardly have missed seeing it because of its striking position overlooking the village.

We stepped outside a moment and he pointed up the valley. I had indeed noticed the house before, with its lean-to style out-building and *hórreo*, an enormous structure on two-metre high pedestals. The house stood at the top of steep grassy slopes chequered with old *corredoiras* or paths, and ancient walls, above the part of the village known as *Os Muiños*, or The Mills, and there were still some old stone workings in the houses there, for milling flour. Behind the old house rose great threatening ranks of eucalyptus trees which marked the border between the village's outer limits and the higher mountainous territory beyond.

Evening mists were gathering, threatening to swallow up the old house there on the hillside. I really had to be on my way. Having selected the one decent pole, I said I would have it and the price was very reasonable indeed. I commented that it had hardly been worth his while staying behind for so little business, but he told me that although he had not fished for donkey's years, since he had been a boy, he still had a soft spot for it and anyway the story behind those old rods was a curious one. He was not bothered about having one for himself and now rather thought he would dump the rest, delighted to have sold the only one that had turned out to be any good, to someone genuinely interested in it. He even found me an old, but strong looking rod bag which fitted the three pole sections nicely and refused to take anything for it. I made a mental note to go back there before the month was out and buy something or other with a little more profit for him in it. After some warm farewells and a handshake I headed off through the narrow streets back to the seminary and the dining room, only just arriving in time.

All this had been the evening before. Now it was Saturday and having whisked through the working morning, I decided to skip lunch and ran down to the labyrinth style kitchen, reminiscent of a Peter Greenaway film, with its seemingly endless rows of shiny ovens, grills and huge cauldrons. My intention was to filch some fruit and chocolate but, being caught in the act by the kindly and jolly old head cook, Montse, I had slices of chorizo, York ham, a lump of cheese and some crisp fresh bread, still warm from the oven, thrust upon me as well. She wished me luck and unfortunately added that she looked forward to seeing some nice fresh trout in the kitchen for dinner.

After profuse thanks, I was soon back upstairs wondering if my chances were blighted by her well-intentioned wish as I made my way along the old arched cold stone corridor to the Teachers' Room, where I had my bike. My typical angler's mind dwelt momentarily on the vicissitudes of fate, Sheringham's marvellous omens and the like. Galicia is perhaps Spain's only truly superstitious region, with *meigas*, magicians and every imaginable imp and pixie.

I decided to tie the old bamboo rod on to my crossbar, using the strings of the rod bag, and take it along as a sort of good luck charm, feeling it would not be of much practical use. Apart from having no reel fittings or intermediate rings, it was far too long to fish the place I had in mind. I swung my rucksack on to my back, with its rather meagre weight of fishing gear compared with the bulk of my picnic lunch - though my old Russian binoculars and my camera weighed a ton - and wheeled along to the huge front doors and out into the warm early afternoon.

Galician weather, like the landscape, is radically different after the blinding merciless heat of Old Castile's wide open arid plains. Here, especially inland among the verdant hills and valleys, the humidity could be really high, like the rainfall. It is a land of mists, grey light and low cloud which only briefly give way to a drier summer in the month of August. As I cycled out of the village, down through the part known as 'San Lázaro', it was overcast and still but definitely warm. Then, as I rode up the first hill, which would take me out of the valley of the river Valiñadares and towards my destination, the río Masma, a light breeze sprang up, which was very welcome, since I was beginning to perspire somewhat under the weight of Montse's provisions.

I knew exactly where I was going, having already been out a couple of evenings during the week to reconnoitre the surroundings. This part of the country was fairly riddled with running water; the sound of babbling brooks or small idyllic waterfalls was never far away. So, armed with my 1:50,000 scale Spanish military map, I had gone to investigate some of these wonderfully exotic sounding waters; streams like the 'arroyo la Margarita' or 'arroyo Campicero', and rivers such as the 'río Coubeira,' 'río Eo' or 'río Miño'. The river I was heading for, the Masma, was well known for its various trout fisheries, and a way downstream there was even a salmon stretch, although it had apparently been some years since a salmon had been seen there.

The map had proven invaluable and although it was out of date as regards new main roads, it was ideal for me in these lesser known backwaters. I was reminded of many excursions back in Britain with an Ordnance Survey map, in search of likely new fishing spots. It was curious to think that both sets of maps had originally been produced with rather less peaceful objectives: 'Ordnance', military hardware, artillery targets, all of which seemed so far removed from the tranquil landscape around me, even less the old Kentish stamping grounds of my boyhood. Yet, the old map I had was dated 1973; Franco had still been alive then and perhaps memories of the Civil War would have been much more recent. As far as I knew, the war had in fact comparatively little impact on Galicia, in terms of direct action, although there would have been many young men from villages in these rolling green hills and valleys who went to fight in other parts of the country. Throughout the war, Galicia was firmly behind the anti-Republican military uprisings, and there were certainly attacks made from here by the '*sublevados*' into Asturias. Franco was in fact from Galicia, born in El Ferrol, only 60-odd miles away. I recalled having seen a picture of his statue there in a leaflet in Mondoñedo's little tourist information office.

Anyway, I had come out on this road late-ish one afternoon and had found a number of very attractive looking spots though none that really inspired me. I was returning as the evening came on through the tiny village of Marquide, which consists of maybe half a dozen dwellings, of which at least three were bars. As I was passing through I saw a small sign which read 'San Andrés 2km' and indicated a narrow road heading steeply down. I pulled out the map and saw that there was a good stretch of the river Masma in open country before the next village, so I decided I would just have time to go down there for a quick look. What I found was absolutely stunning.

Now, I was on my way back there, with plenty of time to investigate. I left Mondoñedo behind me and was out into open countryside, dominated in every direction by the devastating armies of eucalyptus. I had been told that this Burnham Wood of tall slender trees had been introduced under Franco in the post war years, to supply the timber industry. The huge local wood processing factory dominated the borough of San Lázaro, and the trail of white smoke drifting up the valley bore constant witness to its presence. The eucalyptus was now seen by many as, at best, a mixed blessing. There was no doubt that it provided employment, but it is a species with very low needs, is terrifically fast growing and along with a formidable rate of self dissemination wipes out all indigenous trees in its sway. It alters the pH of the soil, introducing an intolerably high level of acidity and its peculiar habit of shedding bark in great long strips suffocates the ground beneath. These undeniably magnificent trees are like a mercenary army scourging Galicia and posing a major threat to its ecosystem. The trees accompanied me on my run to Marquide as though it were Dunsinane and I thought once again of local witches and bad omens.

Marquide was only about forty minutes of fairly gently undulating road out of Mondoñedo and as the final climb came into view I was helped along by a little tail wind and whisked into the village. I pulled over at the first of the bars and bought a couple of bottles of water. Outside, I gulped down about a litre, to the apparent amusement of the two or three people in the bar, and putting one bottle on the front rack and the other in my bag pushed off towards the San Andrés turning. Passing the other bars, I was reminded of a little place called Wouldham I used to cycle through as a small boy on my way to some fabulous fishing at a nearby reservoir. It too was a tiny place in those days, consisting of barely more than a single street of terraced houses. As I recall, every terrace had a pub at one end, and at least one had a pub at both ends. They were very small places of course, nothing more than the living room really, with a door and little porch round the side instead of an entrance off the front garden. They had names like 'The Nag's Head', 'The Hart', 'The Cooper's Arms' or best of all 'The Angler's Rest'. This apparent excess of pubs probably wasn't really so remarkable but the house numbering system was surely bizarre. Each terrace on either side of the village high street began at No. 1, so there were any amount of No. 1's, 2's and 3's, High Street, Wouldham. The postman doubt-less managed by virtue of being on first name terms with everyone in the village. Moreover, I later realised that the letters would have been addressed to No. 1, So and So Terrace, etc. thereby solving the problem I had imagined for him. But, then there was Forge Terrace, the five houses of which were numbered 1,2,3,2,1, both the No. 1s being pubs. Many years later, when I happened to be passing through that old High Street, I saw that all the numbering had been standardised, running from one end to the other, odds and evens on their appropriate sides and that all the pubs had gone. One of the terraces had gone also, and on the site was a monster three storey thing called 'Gators Disco & Pub' with a huge green neon crocodile on the roof and a shiny No. 94a next to the letterbox.

Thankfully, Marquide had not fallen foul of these modern developments. In fact, there was not a door number anywhere to be seen. I reached the turning for San Andrés and flew away down the hill into the first of a series of hair rais-ing hair-pin bends, hurtling only moments later on to the little bridge at the bottom, where I skidded to a halt. I dismounted and gazed over the old rusty green railings at the dark tangled waters of the river as it tumbled over mossy rocks and clumps of weedy vegetation under the shadows of the trees. A sign by the bridge declared '*Vedado de Pesca*' and prohibited fishing from this point downstream for how far I didn't know, but as I was heading upstream where my licence was all I needed, I felt I had nothing to fear from the Guardia Civil.

I got back on the bike and tackled the final hill which would bring me out on the fabulous sight I had come across just a day or so before. The narrow lane at last brought me out of the trees and there, not far off, ran the river. It emerged from a thick wood of deciduous trees, deep in the valley bottom and widened to race over gravel shallows, punctuated by the long trailing tresses of water crowfoot which lent a deep green hue to the water. On either side lay freshly mown hay fields like the lawns of some Capability Brown arcadian garden, finally bordered by more indigenous woodland into which ran the river on its way round to the bridge where I had been standing a short time before.

I cycled on to where a narrow, high sided and grassy path left the road leading riverward. The air here was cool and refreshing. I freewheeled silently over the moist grass, then hopped off. The path was recently trodden down and before I had gone more than a few yards, an enormous hay stack came walking up towards me leaving odd strands of itself on the bushes to either side. Beneath the load emerged two stout brown woolly stockinged legs, wooden clogs and a heavy blue skirt, whose owner was clearly quite unaware of my presence. I leaned back with my bike into the brambles in order to let her pass, not even daring for a minute to think that such a load might be any lighter than it looked. Behind her trailed the thick golden scent of fresh cut hay, nearly dizzying in its intensity.

Righting myself once more I was confronted by a second figure, this time it was an old man, without doubt the husband, who, by the look on his face was as weighed down with the worries of the world as his wife was with the hay. All he was carrying though was the scythe, the use of which I had no doubt, from what I had seen on my cycle runs around, was all his wife's, the operation directed by himself. Once he saw me he greeted me cheerfully with '*Buenas*', the '*tardes*' being omitted, and I responded with the same short form, common enough more or less everywhere in rural Spain. He too was wearing enormous clogs, reminding me more of a painting by Bruegel than something of the present day. With the musical accent of his '*Hasta luego!*' in my ears I proceeded to where another, virtually untrodden, path cut directly down to the water. I pushed my bike into some bushes, more out of habit than from any sense of a need for security, and stealthily approached the river.

The air was thick, dank and mossy with a pervading sense of damp and cool trickle. Ivy grew on every trunk and underfoot the abundant stray leaves were never dry enough to crackle; the vegetation was wet and peaty. Under the last of the great overhanging trees before the river glided out into the open, I saw a number of small rises and my heart nearly skipped a beat when a loud crashing rise sounded from upstream.

Overhead vaulted a great canopy of trees, their sinewy branches forming the nave of a colossal sylvan cathedral, its immense woven columns of browns and greens extending away from me. It was a place of refuge from the world. I had entered as though seeking deciduous sanctuary from the marauding eucalyptus infantry. I crept by the ancient pillars, watching the water and half listening to the tinkling melodies of bird calls above me, until I suddenly became aware of dozens of little frogs, leaping in all directions, mainly waterward, in response to this Gulliver suddenly appearing in their low-lit world. After a brief damp scrabble in the undergrowth I soon captured one or two of them for a photograph. Once over the initial shock of my acquaintance, these little chaps became quite docile and I was able to sit one on my bag where I got a lovely picture of it in a shaft of light that broke momentarily through the dark.

I continued on my way scanning the water. From time to time further shafts of shimmering light shone down from great leafy, stained-glass windows. Often enough they lit up limpid, golden-tinted areas of water in which I caught occasional glimpses of small trout hanging expectantly in mid or high water, just hoping for some tasty looking morsel to come by. I spotted several likely looking swims along the way: outcrops of roots where parts of the bank had collapsed, the half submerged trunks of old fallen trees and pools of invitingly deeper looking water. After a while, I eventually arrived at the apse end of this extraordinary interior. Here, the branches of the trees hung right down and trailed in the water across the whole width of the river. Beyond this veil, fragmented sunlight showed through from the river where it cascaded over jagged black outcrops of slate and other rocks. The sound that filtered through to my ears was like the opening drone of some baroque organ toccata that seemed to swell round me drowning out the bird song.

Making my way back to what I thought might be a perfect spot to try my luck, I noticed through breaks in the trees across the far side, the recently cut green sward where the mowers had been at work during the morning. The curious, gently angled undulations of the fields had been revealed, like shallow green gables with thin dark irrigation channels running along their tops and spilling down over the slopes. The water was taken off the river higher up and channelled, via a network of ditches, into the various meadows. I felt sure it was a system as ancient as land terracing, both of which had doubtless remained unchanged here for centuries.

I got back to the place where I had decided to have a go, where an outcrop of heavy roots formed a comfortable looking perch with command over a nice stretch of river. I slid carefully down on to the tangled mass of thick coils which lay like anacondas grown unusually heavy through years of struggle with both bank and river to keep their towering master in position.

I tackled up the little five-foot telescopic rod with a bubble, then one of my locally bought flies, the semblance of a tiny Chief Needabah, and a Greenwell's Glory as a dropper. My swim had a couple of fallen saplings downstream off the opposite bank, a big tree down a way on my side, which created an eddy behind, and in the centre, about 20 yards down, what I thought to be a deep pool. I could see small rises in the tail of it and imagined that the big splash I had heard when I arrived had come from its centre. Fishing at last! I made my first cast, slightly upstream and only narrowly missing some spindly briary-looking vines which I had not really noticed, hanging down like bell ropes over the water. It was lucky the rod was only a five-footer.

I was into a nice looking patch of clear water ahead of the fallen trees. I let the flies drift round and sink; they were about a yard down from the float and I was pleased to see that it didn't drag or zip along too fast. I mended the line which for the moment was dry and floated, and watched the little bubble like a hawk. I inched the flies back, more or less with the current until I gauged I was near enough to the spindly trees in the water; I let them waver there provocatively as long as I dared, then I snatched them away from danger. I made a few more similar efforts in the same area but there did not seem to be anything doing, so I again cast over the far side, switching to a point just beyond the snags. This time I tried to steer my flies under the far bank. I managed to scare out a couple of little trout with the clumsiness of my efforts. Little by little my technique improved and I was able to work that stretch of water quite well, but it seemed they were not going to be deceived. I tried once more and to my surprise a slightly bigger fish appeared and briefly followed my flies on the retrieve but there was no take, and then he vanished away downstream.

In the mottled light the stream bed was a glistening patchwork of irregular coloured stones and pebbles, stretching away from me. There were some very small trout darting here and there in the gentle current, gradually coming nearer. I decided to cast beyond them and drift down to the deeper water. I had a couple of rises straight away but no contact, so I worked the pool as thoroughly as I could, turning an occasional fish and even provoking several more near misses. It was maddening. And, I began to suspect it was the same fish just backing down the stream, one step ahead of me. I decided to move.

Keeping well out of sight I walked all the way down to where this lofty midnight arch of trees ended, or as near as I could get. The light there was blinding after the dark, but I could clearly see smallish fish rising to flies that I couldn't quite make out, even with my binoculars. The flies seemed to be a pale yellowish colour and were certainly popular with the fish so I looked amongst my harlequin collection, which unluckily was all wet flies, and selected what my angling chum Chris would have called an 'LYJ' . . . a little yellow-rib job. I soon changed it for the rather gaudy Chief Needabah lookalike and stepped down to the water. At my feet, there were convenient outcropping heavy ledges of slate, one slippery plane of which went out a yard into the water. From there I could see the bottom dropping away dramatically into a dark series of hollows. Watching my step I made a cast, carefully avoiding the low trees. The cast didn't have to be far and as soon as it touched the water, I gave the rod tip a twitch letting the stream gently place the flies over the last rise, just as my line straightened out. The rise was so sudden and so massive I half jumped with surprise and half struck - not a happy combination. Especially when that rise was way off the flies. The little bubble float leapt into the air and into the open arms of the willow above and I watched as the flies wrapped themselves almost gleefully around the leaves and twigs. A few determined tugs later and they were still there, firmly entrenched. I had to pull hard finally and the leader inevitably snapped. Miraculously, so did the offending tackle laden twig; it splashed lightly on to the water and drifted only a few yards before reaching the deep pool where, doubtless, there were other eyes watching. The twig's leaves twirled around slowly and then slipped gently towards the bank. I quickly trotted along, negotiated a great grassy mound and more jutting slate before I could get down to the water, and, with the help of a stick, retrieved my flies. There was no sign of the bubble though and I was glad I had bought more than one. I sauntered back to where I had left my bag and cut the flies free, being careful not to lose too much line, and retied them.

One thing was clear, there was at least one big and decidedly sharp witted trout in this water.

I thought it best to leave it for a while to gorge itself on what I could now see were yellow mayflies, one having drifted into the shallows over the slate. I paused to get a picture of it, mottled pale yellow and brown, gripped in the surface tension of the water.

All in all, I spent a couple more hours working up and down the stream, finding new spots and frightening the fish out of every kind of cover. I had one dramatic take, struck and felt the briefest tussle before the line went slack. It just wasn't my day. But it really was the most extraordinarily beautiful and timeless place. In my wanderings I fished the open end several times more and on the last occasion saw great crowds of flies in the then paler, yellowish arch of light. An early evening hatch had begun and was being enjoyed by a pair of pied fly catchers and a wagtail. Odd darker flies had also begun to appear, coming from some point upstream and dotting the surface of the water under the shadows. A desire to sit down once more and have a bite to eat brought me back to my first choice pitch on the roots, and I could see quite a big fish was there, only a short cast down, rising repeatedly. I quickly got into position and cast once more, off to the far side, bringing the flies round towards the intended spot. Needless to say there was no joy, and so leaving my flies muddling around in the lee of the tree on my side, I got stuck in to my lunch, since I was starving. It had to be at least six o'clock and I had been fishing hard for a good few hours.

After eating, and finishing off the bottle of water, I leaned back to watch the watery world go by. It was then I noticed a figure approaching along the bank. He was still some way off, having just entered my arboreal cathedral at the west end and paused, fishing rod in hand, to observe the water. I remained quite still on my perch as the old man moved stealthily along the bank towards me, keeping low and stopping every now and again to look for fish or to ponder a rising trout's behaviour. He was dressed in country working clothes, dark brown trousers, heavy shoes, a green and brown checked shirt and a tatty old tweed jacket. On his head he wore a '*boina*', the black beret so typical of old Spain. As he drew nearer, I could see his face deeply creased from a lifetime outdoors, peering into mists or squinting into the sun but, there were also the lines of laughter, of an optimistic disposition, it seemed to me. He was close now, and looked about to cast when he spotted my indolent bubble; his eye followed the direction of the line and . . .

"*¡Coño!*"

This colourful exclamation, uttered at finding an intruder in his swim, might be loosely rendered as, 'Blimey!'

"*¡Buenas!,*" I responded.

After expressing his surprise further and saying he hadn't seen me and so on, he enquired as to my luck and I admitted that I had failed to get so much as even a bite in the entire afternoon.

Discovering quickly that I was '*¡Inglés!*' he was yet further surprised and apparently delighted. He then bade me a most convivial welcome to Galicia, and hoped I would enjoy my time there, especially the fishing. Coming to the edge of the bank he shook me heartily by the hand and examined my hastily retrieved flies. He told me, predictably enough that they would never do here under the trees and what I needed was a grasshopper. Live ones were best, though he said that those he tied at home worked well and showed me the ones he had on. I had a couple of passably similar hoppers in my box, and upon seeing them the old man said they would be fine.

I had been using the formal '*usted*', but he told me not to, that his name was Serafín and that as a boy he had met some Englishmen, back in the war years. They were good people he said and wished me luck with the *saltamontes*. I offered to abandon my efforts and let him try where I had failed so singularly but he wouldn't hear of it, saying he would head off upstream beyond the trees where he knew the fish would also be rising well.

"*¡Hasta logüiño!* . . . *¡y suerte!*" he called out as he headed off.

"*¡Adiós . . . y gracias!*"

He waved and I sat down to copy the set up he had shown me. I tied my two hoppers on droppers and fixed the bubble float, half filled with water, about three feet below. Looking back across my patch of water, I could see a good fish rising in the ripples that radiated out from the fallen trees opposite. I cast out, convinced I would never get him. I let my line out on the current and once again began to swing the flies into the window over the trout's dining room when a movement at the water's edge suddenly caused me to look away. Just a few feet from the roots where the water lapped gently against the muddy, mossy underbank, an eel, about ten inches long slithered very snake-like on to wet land and towards me between the stones and pebbles.

'They're giving themselves up!' I thought, laughing to myself. Now, only inches from my right foot the eel began to follow a groove where a pair of roots grew tight up against each other, ascending confidently to where the trunk proper began and disappeared in the wet grass. Where on earth he was going

I couldn't imagine, perhaps in search of food or to tell his extraordinary family history, of epic journeys and transmogrification, to a toad.

Suddenly, there was a jerk on the line, I struck and soon wound in a long wiggling green leaf from a bulrush. I sighed and decided to pack up; it was getting on, and although there was still plenty of light, I decided to call it a blank day. I couldn't help thinking that it was just as well I wasn't fishing for my supper. Montse would have to be appeased; perhaps I could get something on the way home. Maybe buy a couple of trout!

Clambering up the bank, I paused where the eel had disappeared in the lush wet grass. I lay the rod down and took a look to see if I could find it. I rummaged about in the soft turf over a big enough area and found a fire salamander, a common toad and several of those small frogs, not to mention the odd worm or slug. The fire salamander is a marvellous little creature which, over the centuries has been persecuted and victimised, suffering horribly at the hands of *Homo sapiens*. I was greatly interested to find one, since they do not occur in England or my part of Spain, and I had only just seen one for the first time a day or two before in the village. Being strictly nocturnal and mainly terrestrial, there's nothing they like more than a little light, night rain, especially the fine *barruza* or *orvallo* of Galicia. I had spotted one in the light of a street lamp on our second evening in Mondoñedo, and going for a torch soon found several more. Much to the amusement of my colleagues, I kept them overnight along with some wet grass and moss, in the en-suite bath tub. Then, after morning classes the following day, I got some good photos before taking them back to their underground nooks and crannies, and releasing them. Unfortunately, the local people kill them on sight because they are deemed to be poisonous. This is in part true, in as much as they protect themselves via an abundant, noxious secretion from the skin which irritates the mouth and eyes of potential predators, but short of sticking one in your mouth they are really harmless to us. On the subsequent countless occasions I have handled them, always admittedly with great care as with any creature, the skin secretion has never been provoked. I have found dead ones, trodden on at night, which were covered with this milky mucous like substance. I have also read the dubious assertion that they are able to squirt this venom a distance of 200cm into their attackers' eyes.

These creatures have the most endearing faces of any European amphibian and after a glance at their history, it rather surprises me that they don't wear a more bitter and twisted expression. Since Aristotle (who, incidentally, and little to his favour, believed that elvers spontaneously transmogrified from horses' hairs) salamanders have been thought to be able to extinguish fire, and ghastly experiments were undertaken in the mediaeval period to prove the fact. The very name 'salamander' means 'fire lizard' in Greek, the English name of this particular species being therefore somewhat tautological, but the 'fire' in this case refers to the brilliant warning yellow markings on their glossy black skins. In other parts of their distribution, these marks vary tremendously between orange or reddish spots or stripes. Here they were intense, nearly fluorescent yellow, in broken stripes, although in my nocturnal, torchlight excursions I had found the odd almost completely yellow or black individuals. I took a few pictures in the just adequate light and continued my foraging.

As I was crawling around on all fours, the old man in the *boina* came back along the bank. He didn't seem at all surprised by my antics and without the least hint of triumph, produced from his old wicker creel a real beauty of a brown trout, a good pound and a half, dark coloured and spotted with purple. He had a couple of others too, around the three-quarter pound mark, really lovely fish, all bedded together in fresh moist grass. He said his wife would make a splendid supper of them, and when I said I was about done for the day, asked if I would like to join them. Such kindness and hospitality to strangers reminded me of Patrick Leigh Fermor's travel masterpiece *A Time of Gifts*, tracing his travels across Europe in the 1930s. After a similar instance of kindness in Holland he remarked that 'it was to occur again and again' as he made his way to Constantinople.

The old man and I set off along the river together and I explained how I was expected back at the seminary for dinner at nine and so would have to decline his kind offer. As we walked along the damp path, the old man related in his sing-song accent, his battle with his splendid trout and how he had failed to catch it at least twice when it rose to his flies. Finally, by sheer chance, the take had come just as he had started a final retrieve, before going for a fresh cast. He recounted with enthusiasm several dangerous moments with roots and an overhanging briar, before getting his fish.

He then offered me a swig from his '*bota*', a small, dark, kidney-shaped leather drinking bottle, and we both drank to fish and fishing. In my case most of the wine went in my eye and down my shirt. I wasn't very practised in the technique of squirting the thin jet of red liquid from a foot away. Don Serafín laughed and cast doubt on the perspicacity of the English beer drinking tradition, as opposed to that of wine.

"You don't know how to drink," he said. "This is Ribeiro, good Galician wine!"

My not knowing how to drink it at least, was certainty.

Back in the Civil War, he said, in the Thirties he had met a number of *ingleses* in his various displacements around Spain, and had learnt then of this dismal state of affairs.

He then began to tell a tale of those old days, as I stopped to pull my bike out of the bushes, and seeing it he said that as I wasn't walking back I would have time at least for a drink. I agreed of course, and in fact it was only just seven, so I had plenty of time. He walked slowly ahead of me up the narrow grassy lane and turned right into the path which led to the hay fields.

"There's another fine stretch of river up here," he said, and continued his story. He had begun telling me that at the end of the war, in March 1939, when he had been just 17, he had found himself in Málaga. "My mother was a nurse," he said, "she was working in the hospital there. My father had gone to Madrid in July '36 immediately after the Melilla rising and we hadn't heard anything from him since. When my mother volunteered for the Red Cross I went with her and we ended up in the south. She cared for me and I met many young men, often no older than myself who were heading for the ports and escape."

I remembered reading in Ian Gibson's *Fire in the Blood* that there were all kinds of people, including foreigners, who were fleeing the country at that time. Franco's 'Law of Political Responsibility' made all those who had supported the Republic, criminals and this meant trial, imprisonment and what turned into massive scale executions. There was in fact a purge, carried out by Franco's Guardia Civil, which lasted from the end of the war until at least 1942 and in many parts, a good deal longer. Those men who had fought against Franco found that their lives were in great danger, and from all parts of Spain began to undertake the precarious return journey to their villages. Once there, they had to go into hiding, in many cases just long enough to pick up an escape route and get away to South America. Others though, had to, or wanted to, stay and decided to '*echarse al monte*', i.e. go into hiding in the mountains. There were those who dedicated themselves to trying to continue the war, forming small resistance groups, and others who simply couldn't leave their families or their places of origin.

The people in hiding, who were active against the Franco regime, became known as '*Los Maquis*' - *maquis* being a word which originally described the dense kind of bush or woodland they preferred; others, those who sought refuge from persecution, often hiding in tunnels, were called '*Los Topos*' (i.e. moles). I had read a short book about the life of one of the last and most famous of these men, Juanín, who held out in the high country around the town of Potes, Cantabria, about 160 miles west of Mondoñedo, until being finally ambushed and killed in 1957, nearly 20 years after the end of the war. Then there was '*El Piloto*', José Castro Veiga, *jefe de Estado Mayor de la guerrilla*, who was killed in a confrontation with the Guardia Civil, even later, in 1965, fully 26 years after the end of the war.

Serafín knew the story and said there were many tales of men who had spent weeks hidden in barrels or hollowed out walls. We had arrived at an opening where the river tumbled over rocks, out of the trees and into a dark, reflecting pool. We sat on the grass in the mild sun and, after another slug of wine, Serafín went on to say that one of those he got to know at the hospital was a young lad from Mondoñedo.

"His name was Anxo, he had run away to the war in '37, having no family hardly, except for an uncle who had taken him in and cared for him as best he could after the death of his father. He had no recent news of his mother either; after the loss of her husband she had found life too hard in Galicia. She had nursed his father to the end, and since the boy was grown up, she had gone back, before the war, to their family's village in Asturias. His uncle, a hard working, powerful kind of man, had expanded his small carpentry business and did just about well enough to keep the boy. He told him stories of the old family, their mining town traditions and songs, and taught him the words to 'The Pit of María Luisa', a rousing miners' ballad. He told the boy how he had brought his mother and father together, at a village on the coast in the summer of 1920. He and his father had in common a passion for woodworking and became good friends. The next step was a move to Galicia where they had set up the workshop together. He told him how happy they had all been in those years, but when the Asturian miners rose against the government in '34 and were brutally crushed by the military, things went awry. Many members of their family were killed in the incident and, as though in sympathy, his brother-in-law suddenly fell ill.

"News of the massacre of the miners was suppressed nationally but people knew, and despite having always got on well with his neighbours, they had been like family after all, the atmosphere changed and he began to take advantage of his house's being set a little apart from the village. He worked hard in his workshop and only went down to the square on market days. Although privately at odds politically with the villagers, he never had any personal difficulties although there were terrible stories from up the valley. Not long after the outbreak of war, the people of Meira had dragged the village butcher, a man much disliked for his meanness, out of his shop and shot him as a 'Communist'. This very incident had been the last straw for Anxo though, and one morning, some days later, his uncle found himself alone. A scrap of paper that had been slipped under his bedroom door sometime in the night said simply 'Gone to the war'."

Serafin paused and took a mouthful of wine, his profile in half silhouette in the dimming light, the air cooling and seemingly scented somehow with the past.

"Anxo," he continued, "had been all over the country since then and had won the respect of the tiny band of International Brigade comrades he had eventually found himself with, in some front line action, but now he had been wounded, he was hoping to get back to Galicia. He had half a dozen like-minded friends with him, and as I had entered into his confidence, he told me their plan. He wanted to get to Mondoñedo, to the cathedral's old abandoned vaults, or if that wasn't safe, then to get to his uncle's, but stay only long enough to organise passage out of Vigo. His best option for the first leg, since they were certainly wanted men, was to walk cross country, avoiding the roads. He told me this coolly enough. I said it had to be more than a thousand kilometres. '1166 to be exact,' he said, 'we should be there in a month!'

"I never saw him again," Serafín said, "but I know he got at least this far. It must have taken him nearer three months in the end and even though it was spring time, the northern cold would have been murderous. I can't really imagine what that journey must have been like. Ours was no more than a series of trains, from Málaga to El Ferrol . . . although we were vetted by the Guardia Civil at least a dozen times on the way.

"My mother was no longer needed at the hospital and we ourselves returned to San Andrés a few days later. Our old house needed work doing and it was because of this I found myself, some weeks later in Mondoñedo, in the market square in front of the cathedral. While I was enquiring about timber for windows I suddenly realised that the swarthy thick set man before me, with that trace of an Asturian accent to his Gallego, had to be Anxo's uncle. I ordered some timber, cut to size and arranged to go up to his workshop the following week to pick it up. As soon as I got to his place I was eager to tell him about Anxo, but in the end felt afraid to do so. The political climate was far from good and so I did no more than enthuse about wood and the work I had on at the house and we became friends. His name was Esteban and he came over to the house once or twice that summer with materials or with tools which he lent me.

"One afternoon in September - it having been some while since I had seen him - I had finally finished with a number of his planes and a drill, I decided I would walk over to Esteban's and return them and perhaps go down into Mondoñedo afterwards for a Ribeiro. It was evening time and beginning to get dark when I reached the top of the village and the path which led away up to his place. I could see the long slanted red tiled roof outlined against the sky, there being nothing much behind but low bushes and broken down walls. The lower edge of the roof projected beyond the walls, and was supported by old wooden pillars, some with carved capitals at their tops. Smoke, carried by the wind, drifted down the green, yellow autumn valley."

As Serafín spoke I easily imagined the whole scene. The house then, without the usurping eucalyptus behind, in the shadow of Peña da Roca, the great peak that rose beyond like a colossal guardian. I imagined mysterious impenetrable places of refuge up there. Serafín knew from his boyhood that there were certainly caves, in the rocky outcrops amongst the dense woodland. Many of them led to labyrinths of tunnels carved out by rippling underground streams which then emerged, gushing through deep crevices and on into steep sided pools, often full of trout.

I had closed my eyes. Serafín's disembodied voice made me feel as though it were me standing there, on the path looking up to Esteban's, back in 1939. The much lower, nearer slopes were deep brown and sienna in the late evening light, their shadows turning purple and grey. Dark lines of vague stone walls and bushes marked out time honoured *corredoiras*, pathways that criss-crossed all over the hillside. As he had been heading on up the path, two black silhouettes suddenly emerged at one of these junctions, caped and hatted figures that paused and seemed to look up towards Esteban's house.

"I was in the shadow and I too paused a moment," he went on. "The two Guardia Civiles were armed with rifles and were clearly patrolling the narrow pathways between the village and open country. I waited and watched them go. They eventually disappeared in the direction of 'Os Muiños' and doubtless into the *taberna*. I started on my way again only to pause almost immediately; a light appeared in one of the workshop windows, showing intermittently like a signal, then vanished again. I crept ahead carefully and quickly got close to the house. From the cover of a tumbledown bit of wall I saw Esteban emerge from the side door with what seemed to be a bundle of poles. He reached up and slid them silently on to the low roof of the workshop, then glancing around nervously ducked back inside. I heard him securing the doors and decided I would leave, returning his tools for another day. But my curiosity about the bundle of poles was too much and, after waiting a safe period, I sneaked up to the house to investigate. I hid myself momentarily against the supports of the house's huge *hórreo*. There was a hefty old chopping block next to the lean-to; I crept silently over and got up on to it. There on the roof I found at least half a dozen bamboo fishing rods, all tied together. Esteban had used old shell cases to make the ferrules and the same thick braid I had seen on soldiers' uniforms for the whipping. There was also a canvas bag with what seemed to be food in it. I suddenly felt scared and hopping quickly down, got away back to the wall and crouched there, my heart in my throat, and just waited.

"It was soon very dark, and there was no moon but maybe an hour later I thought I saw movement. I stayed stock still, my back aching against the cold stone. Someone, two people, were approaching the house. I felt sure one of them had to be Anxo, but I could only make out vague shapes. They collected the rods and the bag and in a few seconds disappeared into the night."

Serafín passed me the *bota* and rather more expertly now, I took a taste, more to alleviate the dry sensation in my mouth. It had been a marvellous story and I told him so.

"What would you think if I told you I had one of those old bamboo poles?" I said, and I got up and untied the rod from my bike. I undid the bag and held out the three pieces to Serafín.

"Just have a look at that," I said.

His eyes widened; I think he thought I had been joking. As I told him about how I had come across it, all he was able to say was, "*¡Coño!*"

I asked him if he would like to have it as a souvenir of those old days, but he said no, he thought I should keep it. He then asked me if I could guess why those old bamboo rods were so long. I had no idea and he explained that many of the mountain pools were steep sided and inaccessible. These three-metre poles were ideal for fishing them. Anxo and the others would have tackled them up with the same length of gut, a single hook, and with a live grasshopper as bait: deadly! I said I needed a bit more practice with Galician trout by any method.

It was time for me to get going and leaving the river we returned by the same paths back to the road. His house was just up past the church; he said I should drop in next time I was nearby, and I promised I would. He refused to let me go until he had gone to the house for something and he quickly returned with a bottle of Ribeiro. He would take no refusal and so I thanked him, promised again that I would call and jammed the bottle into my bag. We said goodbye and, wishing him all the best, I cycled off, my head full with the day, back to Mondoñedo.

"Catch anything?" Montse called out as I passed the kitchen.

"No, nothing," I said. Nothing tangible, I thought. "Nothing for the table anyway!" I added, as she beamed at me from the doorway. Then I thought of the Ribeiro. "Except this," I said. "I caught this!"

I handed the bottle over and Montse's face really lit up.

"Well, well, well, that's a good enough catch," she laughed and with profuse thanks interspersed with her characteristic chuckles, she ambled away towards a cooler cabinet.

Blank day it may have been but it had been a day that would certainly never be forgotten.

Part Two

INLAND

Chapter Five

Castile

*Castilian geography comes to the fore in the capital city of Valladolid, to which some history
is added, featuring Cervantes and the Last King of Ireland. Something of local character
is considered, especially that of the Ribera wines. Curiosities of climate and rivers arise,
carp and barbel are fished for, in winter and summer. The humble gudgeon plays his part, as
does yet another barbel and a serious storm. The author then follows a canal, encounters
a blind pike, celebrates Carnival and other festivals, camps out and remembers
other pike, both English and Iberian, all leading on to snake bite and cider.*

An old Galician shepherd, in a moist and deeply verdant valley in the province
of Lugo, once told me that as a young man he had, on a single occasion, been
to Castile. He said it as though he were claiming to have been to the very
centre of the Earth, or to some other planet, beyond Alpha Centauri. He added
that the bony, dull-woolled sheep there spent long periods of time staring at the
ground, staring at the parched arid earth in the faint hope that a blade of grass
might eventually appear.

Castile is vast. At 95,000 square kilometres, the politically autonomous region
of Castilla y León covers an area 30 times greater than, for example, the
English county of Kent. Indeed, the whole of England is only around 30%
bigger than Castile. It is a highland region with mountains over 2000m all
around an immense central plateau, known as the Meseta, which itself lies at
an average altitude of almost 700m. The climate is virtually continental, with
very low precipitation and very long periods of clear, blue skied days. Summer
temperatures reach the high 30s centigrade, even 40°C in August, and winter
lows more than 10°C below zero, with occasional dips to -20°C. The most

important river is the Duero but the rivers Duratón, Pisuerga, Esla, Ebro and Tajo also have all or part of their courses in this region, along with numerous much smaller tributaries. There are also many huge reservoirs, such as Ricobayo, Almendra and Linares. The fishing everywhere is excellent with almost every Spanish freshwater species represented, from huge numbers of trout in the mountain streams of León, pike and black bass in the canals, lakes and rivers, to barbel and carp practically everywhere, particularly in the great reservoirs.

During my many years in Spain I have lived and worked in this region's busy capital city, a place of high-rise blocks and crowded streets, abruptly separated from the surrounding country as though from an inhospitable desert. Roads leaving the city become suddenly unaccompanied black asphalt lines into a blank wilderness, although in the boom years before the crash, many housing estates sprang up at various points along these roads. Valladolid, the capital city of Castilla y León, with a population of close to 400,000, lies at the centre of the Meseta, a huge tableland of around 45,000 square miles. All kinds of rivers and streams descend from the distant mountains and snake their way, often invisible in their little ha-ha valleys or '*riberas*', across the inhospitable terrain. They are often pretty, green, oasis-like places where wildlife abounds, precariously safe at the margins of vast extensions of agricultural land, and where the fishing is not only wonderful but happily, very much under-exploited.

Getting a licence to fish anywhere in Castilla y León, or day-tickets to the '*cotos*' or restricted fishing areas, was always fairly straightforward, if you happened to be in Valladolid, since it had to be done there, in person, at the offices of the Delegación Territorial. (See Appendix for further details.)

To date, it is still perfectly possible to get the licence or permits in this way but doing battle with the bureaucracy and paperwork used to take hours. Once you had obtained a form from these offices, at the Caza y Pesca counter on the ground floor, you then had to go to a nearby bank and pay the fees, a trifling amount for the year, and return again to the office to have your tickets typed up with every imaginable detail, including your mother's maiden name. You were also required to queue at every stage.

Nowadays, the procedure is greatly simplified. Once you have provided your details, the form, including the actual licence, is printed off and you go across to the bank to pay roughly €6.00 or £7.00 and have it stamped. The actual cost for 2013 is €15 for Spanish nationals and resident foreigners but in the case of non-resident foreigners, the price is substantially higher, at €50. Be advised that you will need your passport at the initial stage of the process.

In very recent times the process of obtaining a licence has been dramatically improved and all that you need to do now is provide your personal information at any one of the offices of the *Servicio Territorial de Medio Ambiente* or Territorial Environment Service, anywhere within the nine provinces which comprise

Castilla y León. This can be done in person, by post or by phone. The details which must be provided are your full name, date of birth and address, ID document or passport number and phone number. The address you provide must be Spanish, since the form will be sent only to an address within Spain. The address of your hotel, or other accommodation will serve perfectly well. The service will then provide the form to be filled in and taken to any branch of the banking services indicated on the rear of the document, where, following payment, the licence will be stamped and returned to you. The application form can also be completed online.

Although it is no longer necessary to give yourself a leisurely morning to get your licence, it is still worth coming into town and heading for central cafés, around the Plaza Mayor main square for example, to enjoy the excellent coffee and soak up a little Castilian city atmosphere. Having lived in Valladolid for more than 25 years, I might pause a moment to give a little information about a city which is very little known in the UK or indeed almost anywhere outside of Spain. First of all, the pronunciation of the name Valladolid causes some consternation for English speakers, since the V is a B, the double L a Y and the D a soft TH. For UK visitors it might best be given as 'Buy a dollith', with the stress on the first and last syllables. The city is the capital of the region, the largest politically autonomous region in Europe, as well as being that of the province of Valladolid itself. The origin of its name is subject to some dispute. It may be from the Latin *vallis* for valley and the Celtic *tolitum* meaning 'of waters' or 'of clouds'. The Pisuerga and Esgueva rivers certainly meet in the city and the reference to cloud coincides with the fact that the city's airport is at Villanubla, which might be rendered as Cloud- or Fog-town. Prolonged periods of winter fog, especially the *cencellada* or freezing fog, do occur although they are less common nowadays than they once were. A second possible etymology for the city name is from the old Spanish *Valle do lid*, 'Valley of the battle', and, finally, a third dates from AD 705 to AD 715 when the city was ruled by a Moorish caliph and so the Arabic origin, *balad*, or town, of Al Walid is a reasonable derivation, but scholars have failed to agree on which might be the true origin. To make matters worse, the city also has another popular name, *Pucela*, the origin of which is equally problematic. One story is that this name is derived from the French *pucelle* or young girl, a reference to Joan of Arc who during a battle reputedly went to the aid of some knights from Valladolid. Another etymological yarn tells of a mediaeval hostelry in the town, called Pintia or Puntea, possibly meaning 'well house', which was Latinised as *puteum*, and the diminutive *pucelum* supposedly became a popular traveller's name for the locality. As the excellent Ask Oxford specialist Dr Samantha Schad once informed me, 'Etymology is not an exact science.'

In the year 1074 King Alfonso VI granted the town to Conde Pedro Ansúrez, nowadays considered the city's founding father. Ansúrez established the collegiate church of Santa María de la Antigua, one of the city's most attractive monuments, and built the Puente Mayor, which is the main bridge over the Pisuerga river. Valladolid quickly became a bustling bureaucratic centre and from the reign of Alfonso VII through to that of Felipe II, from 1130 to 1598 was frequently the seat of the Castilian court. The period of Valladolid's greatest glory began in 1469 when Queen Isabel of Castile and King Ferdinand of Aragón, the so called Catholic Monarchs, were married here and the city became the seat of the Spanish Court and de facto capital of the country for the next two centuries, a period when Spain was dominating a good part of the known world. Both Felipe II and Felipe III were born in Valladolid, and it was Felipe III who properly established Valladolid as the capital of Spain in 1601 but this was short lived, as he then moved the court definitively to Madrid in 1606. After this transfer of power, Valladolid went into prolonged decline. In a little over a century, the city which had once boasted a population of 100,000 had been reduced to some 20,000.

Among the city's most famous historical residents are Miguel de Cervantes, author of perhaps the world's most famous novel, *Don Quijote de la Mancha*. Cervantes lived here briefly towards the end of his life and his house, now a museum, is well worth a visit. The Italian explorer Christopher Columbus is said to have died in Valladolid, in 1506, in a house known as the Casa Colón, which is now also a museum. The truth of this is uncertain, however, since the death of Columbus is claimed by numerous other localities around the world, including the Dominican Republic. The character, nevertheless, who stands out to me as the most remarkable in the city's history is almost entirely unknown: Aodh Rua Ó Dónaill, or Red Hugh O'Donnell (1572 - 1602), who was the last of the Gaelic kings of Ireland. Red Hugh led the Irish forces against the English conquest of Ireland from 1593, particularly the Nine Years' War from 1595 to 1603. Following the battle of Kinsale in 1602, O'Donnell escaped to Spain, where many other Gaelic chieftains were already exiled, and travelled to Valladolid to seek the support of Felipe II against the marauding English. Aid was promised but it never materialised and O'Donnell, upon leaving Valladolid, died suddenly just a few miles out of the city, at Simancas, the result, or so it was rumoured, of having been poisoned by the British agent, James Blake. O'Donnell was buried in the chapter of the Franciscan monastery in Valladolid, the exact location of which is uncertain, since it was demolished early in the eighteenth century, although some old maps place the monastery close to the Plaza Mayor, behind or under the buildings which line its south side. Curiously, it is the same spot which is claimed by some to be the burial site of Columbus.

Coming more up to date, in 'Antimony,' one of Italian writer Leonardo Sciascia's *Sicilian Uncles* stories, the hero finds himself hospitalised in Valladolid, during the Spanish Civil War:

> Valladolid is a beautiful and ancient city, I could have stayed there for ever. I like small, ancient cities, and I hope to end my days in a city like Valladolid, such as Siena: a city in which man's past is in every stone.

In the story, he is a Sicilian fighting on the side of Franco against the Republic and perhaps this is why he is so enchanted with Valladolid, which in my time I have often heard being referred to as Fachadolid, *Facha* being Facist, due to a long history of right-wing political tendencies. Moreover, the city so embraced Franco's 1936 military uprising that the conflict, which lasted three years nationally, lasted barely four days in the provincial capital of Valladolid.

The view of Sciascia's character contrasts markedly with the comments made by most writers who at some time or another have visited the first city of Old Castile. In *As I Walked Out One Midsummer Morning*, it was 1934 when Laurie Lee arrived in Valladolid, where he found:

> A dark square city as hard as its syllables - a shut box, full of the pious dust and preserved breath of its dead whose expended passions once ruled a world which now seemed of no importance . . . My last night in Valladolid sustained the sick fever of the place . . . the whole city seemed suddenly corroded with misery.

In Ernest Hemingway's short story 'The Capital of the World' the author refers to a bullfighter:

> . . . a matador . . . short and brown and very dignified . . . who ate alone at a separate table and he smiled rarely and never laughed. He came from Valladolid, where the people are extremely serious . . .

The city always seems to have suffered from this somewhat bad press but things have most certainly changed. In the 1940s, following the hardships of the post civil war period, the city experienced spectacular growth, due to industrial development, especially in the car manufacturing industry, stimulated by the French. There is a huge Renault plant and numerous ancillary industries such as Michelin tyres. Then there are sugar-beet processing plants and a large wood or chipboard factory.

Unfortunately, most modern guide books still have little that is positive or indeed little at all to say about Valladolid. 'Dreary', 'industrial', 'unattractive city centre', 'nothing to write home about' are just a few comments I might pick out, but the truth is that Valladolid in the last few years has experienced a transformation that the guide book writers seem not to have experienced. There are new museums, art galleries, concert halls, theatres, hotels and restaurants all over the city, and historic buildings, streets and parks have been cleaned up, restored and laid out to produce the effect of a thoroughly modern and attractive city, with plenty of history to show off. There is the inevitable element of globalisation about much of the newer urban landscape, so many cities in Europe and the world looking practically the same, but nevertheless, there is no doubt that the city is now well worth visiting. Night life, with bars open till dawn, is today one of the most notable characteristics of the city, and the cuisine is excellent, although my preference will always be for the heavy traditional Castilian rather than the now ubiquitous, decidedly scanty and expensive 'nouvelle cuisine' style offerings.

Historic cities, with their several World Heritage sites, like León, Burgos, Salamanca and Segovia, as well as Madrid, are not too far away, especially now there is the AVE high speed train network connecting them. The people of Valladolid, moreover, have always been famous for speaking the purest Spanish, known as Castellano or Castilian, and so increasing numbers of students of all ages are coming to the city and the wider region to learn the language. The University of Valladolid is large, with over 30,000 students, plus a considerable number of exchange students from across Europe and the USA, all lending a spirit of youth and vitality to the city, with ever more opportunities of live music, night clubs, discos and theatre etc.

Despite all these developments, the national perspective of Valladolid has not changed much. The people are still considered to be reserved and serious, which is certainly true compared with other parts of the country, and there are still a good number of monasteries and convents, albeit with rather few inmates. An angler I got talking to on the Ebro one day, a Catalonian from Barcelona, asked me incredulously, "How can you possibly live in such a place? There are nuns walking about the streets!" There was certainly much truth in this. Where I lived at that moment, I was surrounded by them; I overlooked a convent, a school and two university residences, all run by nuns, the Royal Salesians, the Carmelites, the Teresians . . . there was no getting away from them. On the positive side, many of the nunneries offer delicious pastries and cakes for sale, as often as not through a complicated mechanism of sealed and revolving hatches to avoid any of the closed orders being subject to contamination from the outside world, or vice versa.

Perhaps the city's and indeed the region's most outstanding attraction though is its wine. The valley of the river, the Ribera del Duero, produces a complete range of superb wines, with three *denominaciones*, or officially denominated quality marks of guaranteed origin and vintage: Ribera del Duero, for red wines, Rueda, for White wines and Cigales, for rosé wines, known as 'claretes'. The most famous of all are the rich red wines known simply as Riberas, produced by many prestigious *bodegas*, or wineries, which compete to be No. 1. The undisputed champion for many years has been Vega Sicilia, whose wines have become far too expensive for almost anyone to even sample nowadays but there are numerous others: Abadia Retuerta, Emilio Moro, Peñafiel, Pesquera, Yllera, etc., all absolutely superb and markedly cheaper. The majority of these fine wines come from a part of the Duero valley known as 'The Golden Mile', and nowadays there are many wine tour holidays available, with accommodation in the city and visits to all the most important *bodegas* along the valley, with wine tastings included, of course.

Outside the city, and away from the valley vineyards, much of the stark, open countryside seems abandoned at first glance, although in fact it is cultivated from horizon to horizon with sunflowers, wheat or sugar beet. Local geology is mostly gravel, shingle and sand. For the angler, the various abandoned and flooded gravel pits are certainly attractive features, although many are private working quarries, without public access. The Castilian landscape is mostly composed of softly contoured, flat-topped hills of soft calcareous rock, sprinkled with mica and the small glittering shards of arrow-head quartz. You may even find an occasional desert rose, not the red coloured variety common in the Morroccan Atlas mountains, but paler, sometimes white rocks which are a pleasure to go hunting for. In this landscape, whole villages lie as ghost towns of crumbling adobe and shattered red clay roof tiles, and the abandonment of these old rural communities has been a political problem for many years. You hardly see a soul throughout most of the year, especially at any distance from the city. The climate is to blame, at least in part. 'Nine months of winter (*invierno*), three months of hell (*infierno*)' is how the local saying goes, and even when the weather is pleasant, the new, modern Spaniards prefer their city suburbs' swimming pools and leisure centres to the bathing holes of old, in those small river tributaries flowing to the Duero and on into Portugal. Before emptying finally into the Atlantic, these unassuming little streams will have flowed for around 300 miles and dropped from as much as 4500 feet above sea level. These rivers are the real jewels in the crown for the visiting angler, since hardly anyone from the city fishes them.

The river Adaja is one such, and one afternoon, as I cycled out of town, there was that typical combination of Castilian high summer weather, a complete stillness of the air and scorching sunshine. What was not normal was that this should be the case in only the second week of June. From around mid-morning the temperature had risen steadily to stand at 36°C by 2pm. The sky over to the east, however, was blue-black with the threat of thunder and lightning or torrential rain. These summer storms, more generally a feature of the month of August, rarely had both. The dry electric storms could be staggering in their power and intensity. Away to the north, a similarly malevolent prospect loomed. Elsewhere, it was dazzling blue sky, the sun high and burning down, ferociously stinging my neck and forearms. I was almost covered with total block and wearing an indescribable hat, yet, despite it all, the sun's rays came on like lasers. It was certainly *un sol de justicia*, a 'sun of judgement' as a local saying has it.

As I approached the river it was worse, the very air seemed to penetrate the body, burning into my eyes, and into the very pores of my skin. Fractious sylphs of smouldering breeze squabbled along the dusty paths, like Lilliputian dust devils, seeking shelter from the tormenting rays. Then, once down at the bank, my glances up and down stream, were met with a blinding, halogen-white, strobe effect off the rippling water.

This was the little río Adaja, probably my favourite among the local rivers. It rises in Ávila, 80 miles to the south and runs into the Duero a stone's throw further down from here, near the village of Villanueva del Duero. At its highest spate, it torrents along its tiny valley, up to 15 or 20 feet deep, leaving quantities of flotsam high in the deciduous trees along its course. The often steep sided edges of the *ribera* are dotted with heavy old pines, whilst down at the water there are aspens, poplars, willows and the occasional alder, often standing at odd angles on unstable, sandy islands. Many places are nearly impenetrable but are always worth investigating. Sudden idyllic clearings can be found, which command promising looking stretches of water with weedy, overhung pools or deep racing channels, lined with bulrushes or the giant 'carrizo' reeds. There are lush grassy banks, erratic clumps of wild plants and spindly willow saplings everywhere along the water's edge. The onset of water over the winter sometimes washes away whole islands, trees and all, or tears into soft cliffs making ever wider meanders. Then in high summer, in the near Saharan heat of August, it is often reduced to such a trickle as you could easily step across.

The sound of the river at least was refreshing, and though it was prematurely low for the time of year, barely a foot deep over the wide open sandy flats before me, there was definitely water enough for some fishing. Here and there it coursed deep and fast, especially in the shade opposite, where it ran under abundant bushes of crack- or brittle-willow. Curiously, the twigs of this very common, frequently bush-like, waterside tree, would snap off easily when brushed against, the twigs then rooting themselves at whatever point they washed up at downstream. This brittleness is an unexpected delight to the angler who, following an unlucky cast, sees his tackle dangling from the twigs of one of these trees on the other side of the river. A sharp tug is all that is usually needed to save the day.

For a few brief weeks in the spring every year, the city, which lies in a wide-open valley where the rivers Pisuerga and Esgueva converge, is inundated with fluffy seed bundles, partly from these brittle-willows, though mostly from the white poplars. Blizzards develop which carry them for miles on the air down the *riberas* and become something of a plague for the house-proud, whistling in on the breeze, through every opening and collecting, along with other darker conglomerations, under beds, wardrobes and even inside tackle boxes.

Back under the bushy banks of the river, the occasional slurp of a feeding carp was music to my ears, rather more melodious than the raucous froggy din of the dialoguing reed warblers. The place was alive with sounds, the erratic fluctuating racket of marsh frogs sometimes blotting out everything else. Some of their sounds were frankly hilarious and more than once their chuckles would be heard after a less than competent cast. This was also true of green wood-peckers and mallards, though their paroxysms were usually reserved for inelegant slips into the water or lost fish. Such laughter tends to reinforce that feeling that wildlife is full of critics. The Romantic poets knew all about this deep empathy with Nature, which John Ruskin styled somewhat pejoratively as the 'pathetic fallacy', rain with spells of sadness, sunshine for joy etc., but nevertheless, the angler could not help but suspect that frogs, ducks and green woodpeckers knew a great deal more about the antics of man than was generally believed.

It was time to get my rod and bag of gear, not forgetting the water bottle, and to leave the bike and lunch pack in the shade of a particular, huge old stone pine, I knew well. The trunk was massive, and the thick green canopy extended a shadow at least ten yards in diameter. A couple of huge headed soldiers of the harvester ant family were patrolling the cracks and crevices in the chunky red-dish bark and I paused a moment to watch them. Their seed cracking jaws looked formidable, yet although I have had the odd one wander across me, thankfully they seem not to be aggressive, for I have never been bitten. The very much smaller common black ants are a different matter. They tended to turn up along the riverbank carving their ingenious dual carriageways across the sand and, apart from taking considerable umbrage at the bare legs of an angler stretched across their highway, they really needed no excuse to bite away gleefully. They were also very good at locating packed lunches.

I left the harvesters to their business and moved from the shade back into the burning air and down to the river. Overhead some fluid chirruping caught my ear and a small flock of maybe a dozen bee-eaters dotted the blue sky, suddenly perching, in rainbow colours, all together on the uppermost dead twigs of a bleached white lombardy poplar which stood lifeless near the water. They would be able to hunt nicely from there; these slopes were alive with grasshoppers, butterflies, an occasional mantis perhaps, not to mention the damsel flies and other insects at the water's edge but, I am not sure they would want to tackle the huge purple carpenter bees that would drone by from time to time like B52s, cruising between their dead wood tunnelings and the abundant yellow broom blossoms higher up the slopes. It would be easy enough just to sit back and watch all this frenetic activity but my old split cane drew me to the water like a divining rod.

Some of my favourite haunts on this stream were little ox-bow style pools often overhung with trees where trapped fish tended to fall victim to hordes of herons, as well as occasional foxes or a wild boar. Like all the small rivers of Castile, the Adaja is home to plenty of fish: spiny loach, gudgeon, pumpkinseed sunfish and the little Iberian roach known as the *bermejuela* swarm in considerable numbers. Of greater interest to the angler though are the carp, barbel and to a lesser extent the small Iberian chub, or *cacho*, as well as the common Southern European nase, or *boga*.

In May and June there were quite a few carp, which in spring began their move upstream from the deep silty pools of the Duero, not seeming to mind the cool, clear and much faster water. I have had many an epic battle with mere three-pounders, the rod really being tested as they turn their deep sides into the racing current. There is always the guarantee of shrill reel music almost anywhere on the river and the carp here were always brilliantly golden coloured, but it was the barbel I was after today. They weren't big fish really, a few pounds at most, but disproportionately powerful; and it was thrilling fishing for them. Precious little information is available in guide books or anywhere else regarding many of the at least eight species of Iberian barbel. That some of them reach a formidable size is well known, 20-pounders being the norm in the huge reservoirs of Extremadura or Andalusia. The common species for me locally is *Barbus bocagei*, resident in all the local rivers and said to exceed ten pounds, though I have only very rarely seen one over six pounds. A characteristic of this fish, the Castilian *barbo común*, is an exceptionally developed anal fin, not only much larger than normal but with a thicker, very strong spine at the leading edge, which acts as a deep cutting rudder, making them very serious opponents in these hard running waters. My personal best, a lean, winter fish taken on a sub-zero winter afternoon, weighed 6lb 4oz. It had taken over half an hour to bank that fish.

The memory of that arduous battle brought me back here to the Adaja time and again. And what a gruelling experience it had been. On a freezing cold morning in February, I had cycled out of the city horribly early, some fit of madness upon me. The moisture of the *cencellada*, or freezing fog, had formed into ice on my eyelashes, and in the scarf across my mouth. There had been hoar whiteness everywhere, thicker still down the slopes towards the steaming river. Icicles and the elaborate filigrees of Jack Frost's work were on the bare twigs and branches, and in the still, muddy shallows, ice glinted on the water's surface. I really had wondered what on earth I was doing outdoors at all.

I had lit a small fire, I remember, warmed my hands and put my pot on to boil for coffee. All this before the first cast, which may give an idea of how cold it really was. Normally the fishing would come before everything else. The water temperature had been well above that of the air, a sign I took as positive, a chance that the fish might be moving; slowly, slowly, but moving, and seeking out some morsel to stave off their pangs of winter hunger. I had set up my line and swung out a big lobworm on a No. 8 hook against the stream, but into a bit of protected water, my side of a bare branched outcrop of dead-looking willow. There were roots and trailing weeds at the top end covering what I knew to be the haunt of good barbel. Unfortunately, it was also the occasional playground of half a million or so sunfish. But that was during the rest of the year; on that winter day there had been no sign of life at all. I put the rod on the rest, sat back and supped my coffee, nearly scalding the roof of my mouth. A robin appeared, watching me across the babbling downstream water. He began ticking at me, a sort of Morse message asking about the worms, or so I fancied. A rustling at my back caused me to look away, and slowly turning I found a water vole, sitting upright, puffed up furry against the chill, then cheekily tugging away at the flap of my rucksack. My camera was in there of course but his interest had more to do with my sandwiches. He returned my look, a calm unwavering stare, a few whiskery twitches and then he ran off into the roots of the poplar towering above and behind me.

My float had swung round a fraction, rubbing shoulders with the current slipping by at the edge of the swim, but there was no sign of fish. I made more coffee and nibbled at a biscuit. I threw a few crumbs over to where the vole had hidden himself and some more towards the robin, my side of the river but well within his view. I had some mash groundbait and I threw a ball or two into the waving weeds, in the hope of encouraging someone fishy to start their breakfast.

The morning slipped by and eventually a few small fish appeared, darting about at the edge of the weeds, doubtless attracted by my free offerings. They were small barbel by the look of it and I rather hoped they would look upon the lobworm as too big a dish. But it wasn't long before I started getting bites. My hook was too big though and as they nipped at the bait, I began to regret having stimulated this plague of hungry little mouths. I re-cast, a little dangerously, away from the frenzy and into a hollow, very nearly under the overhanging bare branches. The tactic worked, there seemed to be no sign of tiddlers there. The shoal gradually thinned out, just a few stragglers staying on to take what they could of the groundbait that trundled into the main stream.

Time wore on; lunchtime came and went. I replaced the bait a few times, but there had been no sign of any larger finny diners. I began to consider calling it a day. The frost had gone, though it was still very cold in the shadows, pools of chill air occasionally wafting out to make me shiver. The sky was blue and the sun had warmed my bank well enough, but now the deep shadows of the trees began to creep over me, bringing back the cold.

A big shadow, a dark torpedo shape showed itself a second or so. I had quite literally just put my hand out to take up the rod for the last retrieve. A tail wavered slowly and disappeared under the long braid of trailing weed. My breathing stopped, my heart too.

I took up the rod, moving very slowly and taking so very long that my arm and shoulder began to ache. I pulled the line, dragging the float away from the corner and letting the bait slide towards the weed. I put it down again. I knew exactly where the big lobworm was, I couldn't see it but I knew. It moved by tiny fractions into the backwater stillness, now engulfed in shadow. I saw the big fish again, moving tantalisingly baitwards but still keeping his distance. His dark shape skirted the weed edge, moving into the overhang, then disappeared again into the darkness. That thrilling tension was almost unbearable. There is nothing quite like knowing that there's a good fish there; you, the angler, being transfixed by your float, and just waiting. The bright yellow tip seemed to know how important it was and wavered very gently from side to side in the slight backwater motion.

A few more shivers ran through me. It was getting colder, the wind would be with me on the cycle back, only an hour or so, to home. I began to yearn for cups of piping hot coffee or freshly brewed tea, Highland Muscatel Darjeeling or Assam Latakari. I emptied the flask, sipped the horrid, half-cold dregs and shivered some more.

The float began to move away towards the far side vegetation, where it hesitated. I waited. Very slow motion. It moved again, moved, moved differently.

I struck and the fish thundered straight into the cover sending a bulging wave through the weed and out into the main stream. I pulled hard, sidestraining out toward running water. It was a risky manoeuvre but the snagging tangle of roots under the willow would be a greater problem than the main current. The barbel flashed gold and turned, ploughing through the trailing weed into the open river. Strands of straggling green dragged on the line, but the fish was free and powering hard into the current. This was a very lucky moment; the only proviso was just how long it would last. It pulled away steadily, looking big, very big. The rod was arched over and bouncing with the barbel's thrusts up-river, the line pulling into the overhanging branches. There was no room to keep the line free from them. I had to go in.

I pulled off my trousers and shoes and stepped into the icy water. The shock ran right through to the very core of my being. I waded out over painful pebbles and slippery weed to get clear of the obstacles. My feet quickly numbed, the sensation inching up to my thighs and I felt my teeth grind against the cold. I was in as deep as it went, ahead was a sand bank and the chance to get a sounder footing. No sooner had I reached it than my fish began to weaken against the stream. Suddenly it turned and flew down towards me. I recovered the line frantically, keeping taut contact, and loosening the ratchet with remarkable forethought, considering the cold. The fish swung past me, down-river, thrashing wildly and gaining dangerous speed. The reel screamed as 20 yards stripped off even as I stumbled to the bank after it. He got into the pool below me. It was good and deep and looked likely to be the final battleground. It was overhung with thin branches but there was room to move the rod.

The dark shape of the barbel slid around the bottom of the pool, seeming tired. I looked for the net. It lay alongside the flask, back where I had been shivering earlier from incomparably less cold than I was feeling now. Keeping the rod high, I got back on to the bank and stretched for the mesh. The fish was still pulling hard as I half crawled, finally sitting down and shunting myself across the ground, at last getting hold of the net and dragging it towards me. All of a sudden it was easy. I took up line and approached the pool. The fish thrashed as deep as it could go then rolled, coming up gasping before another diving bid. On the next rise I clumsily pushed the net under it. The fish was too big for it, its bulk tumbling over the rim but a great broad tail flapping free. I dragged it to the edge of the river, letting the mesh wrap over its broad glistening gold flank.

What a day that had been. It had been a real whopper, my best *bocagei* barbel by a long chalk. Seconds later I'd had it ready for a portrait. I had set up the tripod and got a picture of myself with my prize in the prematurely gloomy evening light. Then I had returned it to its element and stood there shaking. I remember how I had shuddered uncontrollably, my teeth chattering like castanets. It had been a spare bodied and hungry looking fish; I couldn't help thinking what kind of weight it might attain in the spring. I fished the place again and again through the ensuing year, but never saw that fish again.

Back on that chill day, I had dried myself at last and dressed. With the night gathering, I had packed up as quickly as I could, my fingers useless with the split-shot and line loops. I remembered pushing my heavily laden old bike up the steep slopes to the path and cycling, heaving my body weight one side then the other, climbing the winding track up, across the side of the cultivated valley to the pines and holm oaks above. I had never felt so cold, and the wind had bitten so deep. Reaching the top, the view across the dark grey valley had been tremendous under a leaden wintry sky. With the city in the distance, I had peddled off, staving off pneumonia by planning my supper of Irish style hot whisky, with cloves, honey and lemon, and Welsh rarebit of local cured ham, tomatoes and strong cheese, and deliriously dreaming still of steaming dishes of exotic tea.

There had to be a difference of almost 40°C between the bitter cold of that day and the ferocious heat of this June afternoon. No wonder the great open expanses, the gypsum and mica landscape of the province, were so barren and scarred. Such extremes of temperature, such terrain, made for a thoroughly inhospitable environment. It was no wonder that everyone nowadays lived in the cities.

With the memory of that fine winter fish fresh in my mind, I set up my rod, clipped the little flick-open landing-net on to the waistband of my shorts and with a few essentials in my pockets, including a baitbox, I was ready for some rather different tactics. It was a day for stalking. I crept off upstream along the baked hard and cracked waterside keeping down and watching from behind bushes or reed beds. Every now and again a barbel would emerge, drifting out on the current, having perhaps detected some intrusive vibration, even though I was trying to be as light-footed as a heron. The lovely, slightly coppery toned shape with those characteristic angular fins would pause, alert, the head a light grey against the sandy river bed, then reversing, relaxing and slipping once more out of sight. There, hidden in a pale gravelly hollow they would await some drifting food item, driven into these edges by the current.

I had on only a tiny drilled ball ledger, the line running directly through it to a No. 10 barbless hook, which would be baited with a plump, shop-bought brandling soon enough. At this time of year, digging worms was practically impossible. The ground was like concrete and the water's edge yielded only tiny things of little or no use at all. So, I had gone into the city's only tackle shop the previous afternoon and bought a good supply of these dark red worms with their distinctive yellow bands. These extremely active little fellows and their unmistakable aroma reminded me of my boyhood, scrabbling around with a trowel in neighbours' compost heaps or in further off gardens and allotments, without permission of course, which led invariably to being seen off in true Anglo-Saxon style.

I had gone no more than a hundred yards and seen a half a dozen good fish when I reached an open stretch of bank, the outside edge of a slight bend, where I thought I might make a start. I slipped my bag under the green filigree fronds and pinky catkin-like flowers of a gorgeous wild tamarisk bush at the near end of the clearing. At the far end there were grassy mounds, lush green in the shade of young willows. I could fish from here into the lower edges and work my way back downstream taking advantage of occasional breaks in the cover for casting. I should be able to get my bait to tumble along to the ever cautious barbel from a distance safe enough to avoid spooking them. The river flowed hard into this section of bank where it met with sudden resistance and was forced to turn slightly in its course creating a deep channel where the current was trying to undercut the rounded outcrops of rock that kept the edge intact. From this point the channel ran away under the lower branches of another tamarisk bush and on to the various fish lies I had spotted before. The force of water would easily whisk my ledger along so, keeping well back, I first tried the deep water, where it cut under the rocks, from my vantage point under the willows.

My rod was light and it was easy to feel the bounce and roll of the lead over the little undulations of sand and gravel. Gudgeon bites came fast and frequent and it wasn't long before I brought one glistening and panting to my hand. I quickly had several more, popping them back immediately and trying further and further down the swim. Nearing the end, just where the tamarisk overhung and threatened to snag, a different kind of bite came down the line, a more tentative nibbling. I held on, the rod tip curving round with the slight pull of the river, and the nibbles came harder. I struck and the bouncing felt like a big gudgeon, and I remained convinced that that was exactly what it was until I brought it to the bank, where it turned into a pretty, baby barbel.

A moment later, I moved a little downstream and without getting too close, could fish more comfortably into the overhang. The clip of the net was digging into me as I crouched down and so I laid it at my feet within easy reach and applied myself to this promising little spot. I soon had a couple more young barbel, as well as several more gudgeon, but patience and time would hopefully bring something bigger. The gudgeon, however, had other ideas and devoured every brandling I sent along, before it managed to reach any bigger barbules. Arriving at the corner near the overhang and peeking over a small bunch of spiky rushes, I could see about a dozen gudgeon darting here and there against the pale river bed, on the edge of the gulley. Peering through the thin branches I saw there was a particularly good looking swim just the other side of the tamarisk. A long waving mare's tail of water crowsfoot, dotted with its white, yellow centred flowers, stretched out two or three yards in the stream. To the left was open water and tall green reeds formed a protective barrier on the bank.

I cast out into the flow, giving plenty of line and followed the lead's trundle along and gradual descent, diagonally down the sand bank toward the swim bottom. Halting its progress gently, I imagined the tempting brandling drifting in a slow arc round and under the weed. As my eye arrived at the spot I suddenly focussed on a frog sitting nonchalantly among the flowers watching my every, evidently highly suspicious, move. Beneath him, under his green matted garden, was what I felt sure to be the shadowy lair of a large barbel. I waited, the line between my fingers, my eye now on the rod tip, and felt the lead nudged inquisitively by the current. It inched away little by little, finally reaching the tail end of the weed, where it stopped. Beyond, I could see nothing fishy in the open water. I repeated the operation several times, checking the ledger somewhere under the trailing ranunculus and waiting, but nothing happened. At least the gudgeon were leaving me alone. Finally, I let the bait stop there, lay the rod down and tightened the line at such an angle as would prevent the current pulling it away.

Keeping an eye and a half on the rod, I let what was left unoccupied wander back to the frog. There were quite a few now, enthusiastically getting to know each other and exchanging various discrete chortles and chuckles of general well-being. I uttered a sort of imitation of the louder resonant croak they commonly made. To my surprise they fell immediately silent; a few individuals, males probably, gave a little jump and all faced upstream. I repeated my call, sounding better, to my ears at least, than the first effort. A reply came from across the river, rapidly followed by more and then my companions broke out in unison. What a din! Almost certainly they were combining forces to teach the intruder a well-deserved lesson.

A breath of air ruffled the bushes behind me, coming from up-river bringing with it a watery, wading sound. Upstream, two branches of the river wove around a sandbank island and joined again at a point some 20 yards distant. The far side stream was visible but something was creating a disturbance in the other. I jumped up and light footing across the baked mud, hopped on to the grass mounds and peered over the willows. I was amazed to see a big male wild boar, chest deep, pushing his way against the stream, heading away from the island. My camera, like a landing-net, was never to hand when needed, so I just held my breath and watched.

It's not that the *jabalí* is a rare animal, they are quite common, particularly in the *encinares*, those dry smelling, dense woods of prickly leaved holm oak, the most ancient woodlands of Castile. However, they are elusive, mainly nocturnal animals, rarely seen and generally feared, even though their legendary ferocity manifests itself only when persecuted or injured. They are, under normal circumstances, retiring and inoffensive. During the night they root around after the *bellota* acorns which are their principal food, and lounge like hippos in the cooling mud of the *riberas*, when they can find it.

I had come across tracks and diggings often, but to see one, especially a full grown male, in broad daylight was something else. Their excellent sense of smell and hearing meant they would normally detect my presence long before I was near enough to see them. This big fellow was upwind and had the rush of the water in his ears. His overall length of at least six foot, and a weight of some 120kg (over 18 stone), made an impressive bow-wave in the stream. His head was up, tusks and truffling snout just above the surface, as he waded towards the reeds and thick willow bushes on my side.

I glanced around as he vanished into the cover in case there were any sign of his family. I had seen groups of females and their striped youngsters occasionally, only ever at dawn or dusk, usually at a distance, invariably at the muddy margins of the more remote pools and rivers around, but the older males tended to be solitary, though rarely very far away. He will have picked up my scent by now and doubtless have made for the safety of the dense *encinar* to await nightfall.

I looked at my rod, then scanned the water. I needed a drink, and another layer of suncream. From the shade of the tamarisk I saw a good-sized barbel slip out from the willow overhang opposite and start diagonally upstream. His big tail fin slowly inched him along, over the sand bank that dominated the centre of the stream, pectorals and pelvics hugging the riverbed. I stayed stock still as he then let the current draw him over the sand in barely four inches of water, his arrow-head dorsal cutting the surface. The stream buckled round him and he let himself be carried, passing only ten feet from me. His eye fixed on mine, or so it seemed, as he glided into the channel, reversing gradually as if about to park there, under the tamarisk. What had he seen with that beautiful bright yellow ringed eye? Not an expectant angler, hopefully, something more like a tree stump maybe, in a dark green T-shirt and khaki shorts, spying on him from half behind the reeds.

My bait was another 20 feet downstream, but he had gone that way. I crouched down and watched the rod. Was that a twitch on the line? The rod tip remained still but the line did seem to be tightening almost imperceptibly. It was just the current. I took the line between my fingers, waiting to feel the resistance of the small ledger and sensitive to every tiny undulation. I took hold of the rod carefully and risked a slight tweak of the line; the lead tumbled an inch or two and settled again. Then came a small knock. The tension was agony; another tap, cautious, tentative and . . . The bait was taken and the old ratchet sang out, deafening the frogs. The first run went with the flow, well out into the stream, sweeping over the shallows. The fish broke the surface thrashing dangerously, churning up sand and sharp gravel before ploughing right towards the nearside bank. My line was heading directly for the tamarisk. I kicked off my plimsolls and keeping the rod up, plunged into the river, wading with effort against the surprisingly powerful current. The cool water was soon up to my waist, the barbel, head down was battling away from me still taking line. Quickly up on to the midstream sand banks with the water tearing round my ankles, I felt much more in control. My fish had the rod arched over impressively as I eased in the drag and went with it, not daring to apply any more pressure. It swung back towards the centre splashing wildly. Up on the surface it seemed as though the barbel was following my every move over the riverbed's varying topography.

I was waist deep once more holding the rod high as the fish powered for the overhanging willows. Sidestraining and striding ahead I ascended another bank, the gravel swirling around my ankles and washing out from under my feet. The barbel traversed the stream seeking refuge first one side then the other. We had come maybe 50 yards already and I was trying to steer it towards some shallows, where the river panned out 30 yards further down. The fish was tiring as I pressured it away from the deep runs, the far side willows and reed beds. A magnificent dorsal cut the surface, shark like, with more and more frequency. I approached carefully, loosening the drag slightly.

With the net back on the bank, my only chance was here in the shallows where the huge lifeless poplar skeleton towered, its few remaining branches thrust skyward. Bee-eaters flapped into the air, alarmed by our approach and cruised down over the water to see what was going on before chirruping away over the bushes. All my senses were heightened. Over the rush of the water I detected the drum roll of distant thunder and fitful puffs of wind danced upstream into my face, carrying the unexpected yet unmistakable scent of rain.

I closed in on my prize. It was tired out at last and soon came alongside. I picked it up with both hands, the rod under my arm, and strode joyfully back to the bank. My second best barbel from this river and a really superb specimen. The fish was quiet and easy to handle. I kept it a moment in the landing-net among the reeds back at my pitch and set up the camera. I got a shot of myself, beaming with satisfaction and a couple of fish close-ups too. It was in terrific condition, creamy white bellied, rich golden flanks and once again those exquisite yellow irises. All that remained was to slip it back. I held it, gills pumping in the stream, before gradually letting go. The barbel rested there a moment, unsure of this new liberty, then slowly nosed forward watching me, as though remembering. At last it shot out into mid river and paused again, before vanishing into the willow shadows.

A far away boom sounded. Sprite like gusts twisted round the treetops and skipped over the water. The heavy aroma of a summer storm was getting stronger. I left my gear and clambered up the crumbling bank, holding on to the exposed gnarled roots of pines, and on up between the trees. Underfoot lay a patchy carpet of pine needles with squirrel-stripped cones scattered around. The air was warm and perfumed with pine. I came out into the open, higher up, where the banks of wild thyme commanded a wider prospect. There was a sweep of fallow farmland ahead of me, aglow in the sunlight. Tall spikes of canary yellow flowers rose above the scattered blue-tinted bushes of viper's bur-gloss. Like an army of Triffids these taller plants, known in Spanish as *gordolobo*, literally 'fat wolf', were splendid examples of that extraordinary wild plant known in English as the Great Mullein (*Verbascum thapsus*), and which here, appeared to have occupied the land like an invading army. Though not actually mobile, these ten foot giants did indeed have their sting, a toxin, most curiously a piscicide, the employment of which was banned throughout the country. Centuries past, country folk would wrench these vegetable monsters from the ground and, seeking out a suitable backwater would plunge the enormous flowery spike into the water and, holding the plant by its powerful woody stem, agitate it vigorously up and down as though it were an enormous plunger. All the fish in the immediate vicinity would suddenly go belly up, suffocated by the plant's extraordinarily effective chemicals, apparently absorbing oxygen at such a rate as to effectively suffocate any fish nearby.

The plant's fish killing powers were known as long ago as the times of Aristotle, whose *Historia Animalium* of the fourth century BC remarked that, 'If mullein be introduced into water it will kill fish in its vicinity. It is used extensively for catching fish in rivers and ponds; by the Phoenicians it is made use of also in the sea.'

The storm, meanwhile was coming on hard, its grey curtain blotting out the southern horizon. I realised I would have to pack up. I skidded back down the dusty slopes and collected my gear, then half ran back to my bike. I de-tackled under the huge lone pine, which over the years had sheltered me more often from the summer blaze than from rain. The wind was getting stronger, whipping up dust and twigs while in the distance the rain hammered down, vanishing deep into the parched Castilian plain. It became suddenly dark while I loaded up the bike and, as I left the tree's shelter, big drops of rain thudded into the fine sandy soil making little dark hollows and causing occasional pine needles to perform mini somersaults before blowing away on the breeze. I also noticed, luckily enough, a few spiky seed pods of the *abrojo* plant blown into my path, often known in the villages of Castile as '*abre ojos*' or eye openers, a notion which is indeed justified in the Latin etymology, *aperi oculum*, since their visciously sharp points would easily penetrate the soles of inadequate footwear and most definitely the tyres of a bicycle. I don't believe the plant actually occurs in Britain but *Tribulus terrestris* does have a handful of English common names from elsewhere in its area of distribution, in much of Africa for example, where it is known appropriately enough as devil's horn or goat's head.

Meanwhile, pandemonium was breaking out among the harvester ants as I started up the hill. While going peaceably about their business they were suddenly startled by great drops of rain, making them dash for cover. Then their tidy mounds of husks were being scattered, the entrances to their underground nests blocked. They were running about frantically as though engaged in organising relief workers and search parties.

It seemed it might be better to wait a while and so I freewheeled back to the old pine, where my decision was almost immediately justified. I sat with my back against the trunk and watched the river boil under the impact. Although a few trickles got through the dense canopy above me, I was certainly out of the worst of it and opening up my sandwiches, I sat back to enjoy the spectacle. It was fabulous. The river ran coffee-coloured in no time, the trees and bushes lost their summer hues and tones, taking on instead a uniform dull-grey. No bird song or insect buzz could be heard, only the incessant tattoo of the deluge.

It was short lived though, time enough only for two sandwiches. I still had half a Granny Smiths to go when the sun burnt through once more. The retreating dark veil now hung over the hills, behind the trees, far away. The ground dried instantly, hard underfoot but no longer dusty as, a little while later, I set off up the slope pushing my bike past the crumbled adobe ruins of La Casa de las Hornías, a house with a story, perhaps to be told another time. The pines dripped, the fields of sunflowers glistened and at the top of the valley, the great panorama of holm oak smelt rich and wonderful. White rose-like flowers of the 'jara' family fairly shone from their bushes of succulent fleshy leaves, and there were *scoliidae* bees back at work. These huge hairy fellows with bright yellow spots on their abdomens don't occur in Britain and nor does the flower (*Cistus salviifolius*). I had to stop and get a picture of the two together. Jara was symbolic to some extent, of the countryside of the region, associated always with field pursuits, first and foremost with hunting.

Despite the recent downpour it was still very warm as I followed the paths back through the pines but upon reaching the road, it was clear that another vast storm system was threatening to the south. An immense, glossy, purple-black shadow was progressing north directly for the city. I would have to make the most of the time I had. Unable to resist a view from the highest point of Monte Blanco, where a forest fire observation tower dominated the crest of the rise, I peddled wildly up the track away from the road. The view then was breathtaking, a vista, a hint merely of the immensity of Castile, but cowering beneath the forces of Thor's irresistible onslaught. My mind ran on fragments from *King Lear*. Sulphurous, oak-cleaving, cataracts and hurricanes seeming to strike flat the thick rotundity o' the world. Thunder exploded as tremendous blinding lightning flashes suddenly lit up the nearest village, the church tower, a patchwork of red roof-tiles and the higgledy-piggledy of surrounding allotments. The wind and rain were advancing with great strides, with the sweeping destruction of some immeasurable scythe blade in the hands of a gigantic reaper, threatening the catenaries of power pylons, beating down and blasting the crops. It was truly apocalyptic and I stood staring some minutes before turning and flying back down the track with a furious gust of wind behind me, pushing me to hazardous speed. I hit the road with a jolt and then my tyres hummed delightedly over the tarmac, down hill towards the village of Puente Duero. The bike was old, though far from ancient, unlike Chris Yates's 1911 model in his story of 'Hercules and the Storm'. The incident recounted there must have taken place at almost the same time, early in the 1990s but, unfortunately, my tale ends rather less luckily. Nevertheless, my Saracen Conquest was truly herculean, every joint, every cog, every spoke, pitted against the speed of the storm.

The wind continued buffeting me about the ears as the full fury of the tempest bore down like an insanely destructive dragon. The briefest possible glance behind showed just how close it was. I was on the cycle path now, that ran the ten kilometres or so between the village and the city. Not surprisingly, the way was clear, not an idle Sunday afternoon walker nor a family on roller skates to be seen. Putting my head down I pedalled like never before in my life in an attempt to outrun the weather. Kilometre markers blinked by in astonishing succession. If I could just make the city, there would be shelter enough. I could hear the rain hammering behind me . . . 500 yards, 400. My chest, my lungs, seemed about to burst as I hopped the verges and kerbs and sped madly on to the large roundabout that marked the city's outer ring road. It was decision time. I had friends near here; I could spin left and rush for their house but the rain would reach me first. Or else I could thrash on and perhaps be lucky.

The startled and surprised faces of an entire family were a sight to see, when only minutes later they beheld a wild-looking, thoroughly drenched and mud-splattered angler, propping up his bicycle in the entrance hall of their tranquil Sunday afternoon home, looking much more like a drowned giant stick insect than anything remotely human.

* * *

As well as the ubiquitous barbel, there are pike everywhere in Spain. They are not always easy to locate in the rivers and reservoirs around the country and there are, of course, wonderful legends. Close to home I have fished for them every winter for over 20 years in the Canal de Castilla, but I have never actually caught a big one. My best was just 12lb but I knew of larger fish having been caught up to 25lb and perhaps more. The problem is that anglers' imaginations often run away with them. Nevertheless, I had an experience once, which still echoes round my mind as wholly real, yet it surely was part dream and part imagination. I jotted down a few words at the time and when I got home, this is what I wrote:

> 'As flies to wanton boys are we to the gods . . .' [Shakespeare *King Lear* Act IV scene i] I saw a pike today . . . I touched it . . . Over three feet long, lean, pale, dappled drawn camouflage . . . kingly and huge!

I was fishing a light float with old style Jardine double-hooked worm tackle, which lay quiescent under the nearside bank, awaiting perhaps a good sized barbel; and at the same time, spinning a silver, Blue Fox Super Vibrax No. 3, methodically fanning the water, risking loss under every overhang, those stealth places for pike, when the great beautiful thing appeared, touched in light water-colours, easing slowly against the flow. Five yards away he came, near the midway channel, through darker, deeper water. I paused stock still, and watched as he shifted course slightly towards the far side, slowing to a stop where I could but barely see him.

It was a mist shrouded day. I had cycled from the city along the broad gravel path with the twinned worlds of night and day still veiled. A confusion of the senses reigned in monochrome tones, in a limbo of time and of place where shapes and sizes were uncertain, suggesting doubt, or madness. It was frosty; trappings of spun ghost hung among the threads of webs, their braids made silver and tensed among the bushes. I had come an hour before and with eyelashes wetted and cold I had blinked, watching the smooth flow of the water.

It was not so cold now, 4°C, pleasant, foggy over the hills around but lifting, and above me a small opening oval of blue calm, sunny sky.

I had taken many pike here, but none ever so big as this one, it had to be 35 pounds or more . . . The noble creature was moving again and I stalked him, ready to cast. I dared not put the spinner too near. Another cast, landing nearer, and nearer but ne'er a twitch from that great predator snout. I dropped the Model Perfect and ran for the other rod. I checked the hooks were good and the big lobs glistened appetisingly, then I shunted the float up a foot.

Worms! How did I dare present such an offering, such ignominy to this monarch of the stream? It was absurd; I felt like a court jester trying to divert my sovereign with the baubles of a fool. True, I had once in a while, managed to trick a pike with so humble a bait, jacks usually, or one distracted a moment from bigger prey, but surely now it would be no less than insulting.

There was movement. I could just make out his regal majesty as he made his way through the penumbra under the far bank. I headed upstream waiting my chance for a cast between the stunted elms, and recalled suddenly another encounter I'd had with mere worms and a pike.

Then too, I had been fishing this same canal, further north near the village of Dueñas. A day's stalking, after fine looking barbel, the golden chain-mailed knights of these waters. From my hide amidst the undergrowth of a gloomy damp place under ancient trees, I had descried a pike in the crystalline water of that early spring day, some years before. It hung there motionless, perfectly blended in the stippled verdant light, its snout just below a straggling mane of water crowsfoot. I watched with an angler's patience, then noticed that the weed trailing along its near side seemed to start at the scissored commissure of the pike's jaws. I straightened up a fraction and, startled, the fish lunged forward a yard, taking a great stream of weed with it. Either this was the only vegetarian pike I had ever heard of, or something was up. I stayed quite still, watching. The pike began to gnash awkwardly, to open and close both jaws and gills in a series of brusque movements, clearly trying to rid itself of a throatful of something, whether the weed or some other nuisance. Compared to the pallid giant this fellow seemed a mere squire-at-arms, four pounds perhaps, no more. It seemed that the fish had not been long in this condition either, judging by it wholesome colouring and the freshness of the uprooted viridian streamers.

The raucous din of a reed warbler jolted me suddenly back to the present. There was no sign anywhere of the great pale pike. Upstream the early light revealed a bare patch of the canal bed, free of weeds and shadows. At the moment of his crossing there I would see him readily. I scanned the waters but he was nowhere to be seen. He was deep meanwhile, in the dark underbank opposite, I had no doubt of that. I would wait.

My thoughts returned to the youngster. Similarly, the only bait I'd had with me that day had been worms, big ones searched out by torchlight over a rainy night. I remembered slipping up the bank a way, to get above the little pike and cautiously throwing a lively worm into the water ahead of it. The young fish meanwhile remained on guard at his station in the slowish run. The worm landed in the weed and moving slightly, drifted down twisting itself through the green filaments, carrying slightly on the current and dropping slowly towards the bottom, less than a yard ahead of the rapacious jaws. The effect was instantaneous. The pectorals quivered and the pike shifted forward to within inches of the bait, fixing his cold stare on the unfortunate worm. Upon contact with the bottom, the worm had stopped still, for which he could hardly be blamed. I too held my breath.

Then its tail wound round and down, slipping off the last strand of weed and resting finally on the soft silt bed. The pike dipped its head down, the tail coming up towards the surface. All the fins were busy now, its nose nearly touching the invertebrate, which just then decided it was safe to move. A lunge and a snap of jaws was then succeeded by more troubled gulpings, before the fish dropped back into its haunt, waiting. I tried two or three more worms over the next half an hour, and then crept away for my rod.

I was set up for barbel, with float tackle, a very light trace and a 10 barbless hook, not really adequate but the 6lb reel line would easily cope. What I didn't have was a wire trace against the young fellow's very sharp teeth. I would just have to take a chance.

Since swallowing the last free offering the pike had not moved. I baited with a lobworm and returned to my post. With consummate care, I swung out the worm and dropped it on to the trailing ends of the weed. My young jack performed the same ceremony as before and to my great joy snapped up the worm. I struck immediately and he powered out into the fast water, upped to the surface and began to leap into a series of somersaults like a black bass, ghastly memories perhaps firing his fight. This fish was powerful for its size, doing more than enough to impress the royalty at a jousting match. A more than worthy opponent, the jack knew every skirmishing manoeuvre . . . and how to escape. But this time the match was uneven and only a little later his green bony brow and angry eyes came over the rim of the net.

Now for the moment of truth, I thought. With the loss of tension the hook fell free as I got the fish up to the grassy top of the bank. Armed with forceps for a little investigation, I turned him over and opened up the fearsome mandibles, though this time they were only those of an Esox squire-at-arms. More than a foot of bent and twisted trace wire led to a pair of barbed size 8 trebles. I couldn't say how long they'd been there, but they were rusty. Down in the gills was a small, still shiny spinner too. It was an arduous business to get the lot out, but out it all came. I held the valiant little pike back in the water, while it panted through to recovery, still a little panicky. The fish soon settled though, and seemed fit. I let go, and it glided away out into the full current and held his own there a while. I watched with satisfaction how it sought out the current and chose immediately a suitable hide for ambush. There the young pike awaited his prey, invisible nearly and ready to pounce anew. I hoped some distracted fish would come by soon and start again the predatory cycle. That way he would become one of the big fellows soon enough.

I recalled sitting there a while and watching, wondering if the pike had any feeling or notion at all of the whole experience. It seemed not, none whatsoever. Reputedly, with a fish's memory span of only a few seconds, the most likely thing was the pike would lunge again at the very next spinner that was well enough presented. Something we could always say of a pike was that they were single minded. As I had stood up finally, the fish had pushed away and made against the stream, disappearing into the far side shallows, where the rippled reflections and dancing shades had soon hidden its Esox camouflage from me.

There he was! Suddenly flashing back to the present moment, at last the colossus was coming slowly but surely from his refuge. Keeping low I tracked him as he made again for the central channel, where I would have a chance of reaching him. I got ready to cast. Soon the worms wobbled by him, failed . . . and were cast and wobbled nearer . . . too near, bump . . . and stopped him in his tracks. Then, of a sudden, moving again, he changed course, a gentle angle towards my bank. I crept behind the towering reeds but my shadow crossed him. There was no reaction and then I saw . . . I saw why . . . this great fish was totally blind.

Worse, his eyes had been poked out . . . or in. There was ugly torn flesh in the sockets, I remembered suddenly the local method for landing a pike, by the head, with the fingers embedded in the eyes . . .

This king of pike, then, came closer and closer. I scrambled along the bank through reeds and brambles, stumbling in my haste. He stopped, as though to rest, behind a clump of brown, half dying weeds. Right under the bank he drifted, huge fins steering, feeling . . . I reached down, wetting my jacket to the elbow and stroked. I ran my hand along his back, unhealthy, colourless green. He moved not. How he was alive really I couldn't say. Had he escaped in this condition I wondered, wrenched free, mortally blinded, or had his captors and tormenters freed him thus, to die . . . of hunger, slowly?

My hand now without feeling in the icy water, touched the top of his bony skull and he suddenly spooked. He powered out into midwater again and settled a moment, in safety, before resuming his progress. Unhurriedly, he took to the underbank opposite, there to vanish in its shade . . . and I came away. I no longer felt like fishing that day. I slowly collected up my gear.

A day's fishing, I reflected, a day of complete immersion in nature and of contemplation, was a day that led to a clearer vision of the world and to understanding. A pale sun unveiled the valley of Cabezón, its pastel scents and colours wakening. The timid calls of winter birds provided gradually a backdrop to a cold world where a great blind pike drifted, just as Gloucester had done across the heathlands of Kent. In *King Lear* the honest Duke of Gloucester's eyes were ripped out by his pitiless torturers; falsely he was accused of treachery to the absent king. It was a barbarous act, from a period of ignorance that forms part of a human tragedy in which a kingdom is governed badly. Gloucester is turned out, banished into the unknown, condemned to wander in agony and perdition through the realm. Later, he is reunited briefly with his demented sovereign but finds no solace. The king raves so that he fails to recognise his one faithful subject and Gloucester finally turns away in desperation; become a vagrant over the desolate meaninglessness moors of uncertainty, where the lunacy of the king seems to have taken control of nature herself, driving him towards the cliffs at Dover, with suicidal decision.

The great pike sadly, had no such recourse.

The wide sky of Castile had cleared and the sun shone as I pedalled my way homeward along the canal path. The air was still and pure, diaphanous, such as to reveal the furthest details of the landscape. From some higher point, a promontory among the hills of Valdecastro, a hiker could surely see the distant snows of the Guadarrama.

* * *

Dead baiting, groundbaiting, night fishing and camping (except in designated areas) are all illegal in Spain and can be tremendous frustrations to the visiting British angler, accustomed to other freedoms and, of course, bivvying up for the night. It is all doubly frustrating, since some of the locations in inland Spain are so remote and apparently unfrequented. The ban on night fishing basically stems from legislation to control poaching, and the bans on live and dead baits, an attempt to control the introduction of alien species. The universality of the bans includes sardines, of course, that dead bait so favoured by pike anglers and indeed the pike themselves.

The subject of the sardine in Spanish culture, curiously, has one particularly entertaining dimension, namely the ritualistic burying of them. This unusual ceremony takes place every year and is called *El Entierro de la Sardina*, i.e. Sardine Burying. It is an essentially satirical ceremony which parodies a funeral procession, in which a real or artificial sardine is solemnly paraded around the streets in a coffin. Men and women dress up in period mourning attire; women have their heads covered with the traditional black Spanish lace veil, and some men even dress up as weeping widows. Burying the sardine symbolises the end of the festive Carnival weekend and the beginning of the traditional religious fasting period.

In Spain as well as many places in Latin America, most famously Rio de Janeiro, February, or occasionally early March, is the month for Carnival, according to the phases of the moon in the ecclesiastical calendar. The word comes down to us from mediaeval Latin, where *carnelevamen* or *carnelevarium* referred to the 'putting aside of meat' in the pre-Easter period of self denial. The Spaniards, who always love dressing up and partying, celebrate their most famous 'Carnavales' in Tenerife and in Cádiz, while other cities and towns celebrate too, each with traditional, unique twists of their own. The same is true with regard to the celebration of Easter itself, where Andalusia sees Seville and Malaga holding the most extravagant and colourful street celebrations. Meanwhile, in Valladolid there are very sombre processions with painted and somewhat gory wooden representations of saints and Christ figures, carried by members of special Easter brotherhoods, looking for all the world like members of the Klu Klux Klan, in long gowns and conical pointed hoods which cover their faces and have spooky holes cut for their eyes. But prior to all this, Carnival festivities take place about six weeks earlier, usually occupying most of the weekend prior to Shrove Tuesday, i.e. '*Mardi Gras*' (literally Fat Tuesday) which is really the big day or night of feasting and fancy dress. The next day is *Miércoles de Ceniza*, or Ash Wednesday, when pancakes are eaten traditionally in the UK and when in Spain, the sardine burying takes place, being the first day of the Catholic 40 day fast and abstinence season known as *Cuaresma* or Lent.

In Madrid's charming Real Academia Museum, the full name of which is the

Real Academia de Bellas Artes de San Fernando, there is a famous visual record of the event in Goya's painting of the same name, '*El Entierro de la Sardina*', dated between 1812 and 1819. The scene depicted is full of colour, costume, dance and spectacle, in which many of the traditional dignitaries can be identified. The funeral procession is usually headed by someone pretending to be a public prosecutor, whose role consists of clearing the streets ahead of the procession to allow the passing of the ceremonial carriage. He is followed by someone dressed as a priest, his assistants and those in charge of driving the funeral cortège. The carriage is adorned with palms, flowers and other offerings to the sardine inside the hearse. The widows follow, confessing their 'sins' to the false priest and lamenting the death of the sardine with melodramatic weeping and wailing. A devil figure usually appears and tries to prevent the passage of the sardine by abducting it, but a group of supposed policemen scare the devil away and restore order among the outraged mourners. When the sardine procession reaches its final destination, the funeral clamour intensifies prior to the ceremonial burial, which may take place on the beach or the banks of a river. Cities not on the sea or by the banks of a river do not usually bury their sardine but burn it in a symbolic cremation. Cremation also takes place at other locations around the country, and in some places the sardine's ashes are scattered into the sea, or are taken out on to the open ocean on a boat, symbolising the sardine's return home and the close of the Carnival festivities.

In a slight local variant, in the small town of Cervera de Pisuerga the annual event celebrates the ritual cremation of a trout. The town, to the north of Castile, in the province of Palencia, lies close to the banks of two trout rivers, the upper Pisuerga and the Carrión.

There are at least two different stories regarding the origins of all these fishy traditions, but it is far from certain which, if any, is true. The first dates back to the seventeenth century, when Charles III of Spain supposedly condescended to celebrate the end of the festivities with his humblest subjects and ordered quantities of sardines and wine to be served at a countryside picnic. The weather that day was hot, not at all typical for the time of year, and the sardines had begun to spoil in the heat. The common people, almost overcome by the stench, resolved on burying the now offensive sardines, to which the king consented. Following the interment it is said that the poor people began to lament their loss, weeping openly at the thought of no longer being able to enjoy the King's beneficence, on the eve of the year's longest period of abstinence. The trauma was such as never to be forgotten and so the annual ritual burial of the sardine was begun.

The other story, which seems altogether less likely, concerns a breed of pig called the 'sardine' variety, which was ritually killed and buried on the first day of Lent, in symbolic representation of the meat the people would have to forfeit during the period of religious observation. Apart from the fact that no 'sardine' variety of pig appears to have ever existed, it is surely unlikely that the common people would squanderingly kill and bury a pig, very probably their principal source of food and most valuable asset. However, another theory refers to the burial of a pig's skin, which would certainly seem more reasonable. As regards the so-called 'sardine' variety, the very common wild boar (*Sus scrofa*) has many sub-species, one of which is the Sardinian *Sus scrofa meridionalis*, a small, almost maneless boar, from Corsica, Sardinia and, notably, Andalusia. The animal is thought to be possibly extinct now in its original Corsican and Sardinia island range but survives in the south of Spain. It is at least possible that it was the skin of this animal that was ritually interred to mark the beginning of Lent but no hard evidence has come down to us.

In Old Castile, at the city of Salamanca, there is a slightly bizarre variant on the Lenten abstinence theme. Tradition here, and indeed throughout the Catholic world, dictates that during Lent, the abandonment of meat also included restraint from indulgence in other pleasures of the flesh. All the city's prostitutes were expelled over the 40 day period and the river Tormes, which flows below the city walls, was considered the boundary they were not permitted to cross. Doubtless, nocturnal masculine traffic in the opposite direction increased somewhat at this time but the ban on ladies crossing the bridge into the city held sway until the Monday following Lent, which became known as *lunes de aguas*. On this day, the prostitutes were joyfully and rapturously welcomed back home, and part of the ritual was their crossing of the river by boat, reportedly a highly colourful spectacle of flamboyant dresses and elaborate make-up. What the city's wives made of the event has not come down to us.

* * *

When I first arrived in Spain, I was just as blissfully ignorant of the rules and regulations that governed fishing, as I was of the language. Moreover, I knew no one who fished, and my earliest city friends and acquaintances thought angling was some bizarre countryside activity carried on by persons that should probably be best locked away in asylums. This meant that I went off into the countryside and did what I had always done. I know now how lucky I was to get away with it. Camping in non-designated areas, groundbaiting of any kind, live-baiting, dead-baiting, the returning of certain species to the water, even actually sitting beyond arm's length of your rods, all these things were illegal under the law. I fished in sublime oblivion.

Running through Valladolid was the river Pisuerga, not a pretty name but a formidable waterway, considerably bigger than the Duero at their point of union just south of the city. If it weren't for the fact that the Duero had covered many more kilometres up to this point, the Pisuerga would never have been obliged to give up its name to the lesser stream but simply accepted its waters and powered on through Portugal to the sea. The Canal de Castilla also emptied into the Pisuerga, near the city's Puente Mayor bridge, and it was this waterway, which seemed to stretch away into infinite distance, far from main roads, towns and villages, that really first attracted my attention.

The Canal runs a little over 200 kilometres south into Valladolid from the small town of Alar del Rey in the north of the province of Palencia, and along the way, there is a branch off to Medina de Ríoseco. It was originally built during the latter half of the eighteenth and the first half of the nineteenth centuries to transport wheat from Castile to northern market towns and on to the harbours of the north coast. There are very few navigable canals in Spain, due in part to the engineering challenges posed by the mountainous terrain but also because of the relative lack of water compared to the UK or France. The Canal never really became the great industrial artery its planners imagined, since almost as soon as it was completed, competition from the newly developing railway network effectively put it out of business. Since the Canal was fed by the crystalline upper reaches of the Pisuerga and the river Carrión, which both contained wild brown trout as well as barbel, the fishing must have been good almost from the beginning. In recent years the Medina de Ríoseco branch has been populated with tench; news, I recall, which I received with considerable delight. Just exactly when the pike appeared no one seems to know but that they were there as long ago as the 1920s is certain, since there were stories told at that time of washerwomen having had their arms bitten off to the elbow by marauding toothy monsters in the Canal.

Very early one morning, back in 1988, I remember waking to the sound of bird song. It was really loud, not that I felt any desire to reach out and turn it off. I just lay there for a while and listened. The nearest was a blackbird, then a black redstart, and further off, the hooting of a hoopoe. Then came a syncopation, with every tone of finches and every shade of warblers. It still wasn't dawn yet, a rich dark morning by the side of the Canal de Castilla, about 25 miles north of Valladolid. The flat canal side was ideal for my two-man igloo, which I had erected in the early evening of the previous day. I had arrived after not too strenuous a cycle following the canal path from the city. The last village I had passed through was Dueñas and I had stopped there to get water and a few other supplies.

I was fond of Dueñas and have often stopped there since on my cycling excursions north of the big city. There was a bar I liked too, along one of its dusty narrow streets, which had a partial view of the old church. The previous evening, I had sat outside a while with a glass of wine, a superb dark bodied red, and a *pincho de tortilla*. Nowadays, I have been living in Spain long enough to wonder what life could possibly be like without this marvellously thick potato and onion omelette, not to mention the wine. Having asked what it was, since I had only ordered '*un tinto*', the barman produced the bottle. It was from the area of the Ribera de Duero but didn't have the Denominación de Origen. The name on the bottle was Alta Pavina and I decided to buy a bottle to take with me. Time had been getting on, so I had continued my cycling, just reaching the spot I had decided to fish before dark.

It had been a very mild night, for which I was grateful, as I had already learnt that temperatures could plummet here in October. I lay there in the condensation and body warmth, enjoying the sense of peace. The weather report had been promising, although a lifetime's angling experience had taught me to rarely take them seriously. I watched the TV weather spot here recently with a stopwatch in my hand. The whole slot lasted seven minutes. The first three were dedicated to yesterday's weather, and the next minute covered the overnight temperatures. I suppose this ensures that the information contained in every bulletin is at least 50% statistically correct. The final three minutes covered the country's likely weather prospects region by region. The bit I was waiting for lasted 27 seconds. And I wonder why I invariably get angry, never seeming to obtain any satisfaction from the weather forecast. If I had blinked I would have missed it. Spain's weather forecasters, even so, hadn't yet reached the court jester status of the British, such as Michael Fish (what a great name) nor yet the dolly bird version, entirely prevalent in the UK. Spain's forecasters were serious looking, formally dressed chaps who never cracked jokes or referred to weather systems 'bubbling up' or to the likelihood of a 'sprinkling of showers'. There was something odd though, the expression '*intervalos nubosos*' always puzzled me, indeed it still does, cloudy intervals . . . it transpired that these were not intervals in an otherwise sunny day, of moments of cloud, but rather sunny intervals, in an otherwise cloudy day.

Old Castile's northern plateau, the meseta, is often radically different meteorologically from the overall predicted weather patterns for the area, so I tended then as now not to listen but just look at the satellite picture instead, and draw my own conclusions.

I poked my head out of the tent and breathed deeply, the air was quite still, seemingly scented with the imminent sunrise, and there was a slight mist hanging over the water. The eastern sky was glowing and the birds were quite ecstatic about it. Might I sing and dance around too, I wondered. It was tempting. There wouldn't be anyone to see me, that was for sure. I pulled myself out of the tent and creaked into upright mode. I then fumbled about just inside the flaps for my shoes and jacket and wandered over to where I had made a small fire the evening before. Next to a great fallen tree trunk, convenient as a back rest, the ashes and the circle of rocks were still warm, so I sprinkled on a few twigs and little bundles of dry grass which smoked almost immediately and promised well. I placed a couple of bigger sticks on top, I'd found plenty in the scattered bushes the last evening as well as rather a nice rod-rest. Filling up with water, the old enamel pot I used on these occasions, its deep browny orange exterior somewhat blackened, I balanced it among the twigs. One of these days, I thought, I would get myself a proper Kelly kettle. I blew on the kindling and the fire burst into life. The water would boil in no time, so I went back to the tent to find the coffee and breakfast things. I loved camping but it was always best with the prospect of a day's fishing to give it some sense of purpose.

The fire's heat made my face glow and as I sipped my coffee and watched the sunrise, it was such a beautiful morning that I thought of an occasion when Bertie Wooster was similarly moved.

What's all that about larks and thorns, Jeeves?
The poet Browning, Sir:
'The lark's on the wing, the snail's on the thorn,
God's in his heaven, and all's right with the world.'

Breakfast! What a treat! I soon had a piece of bread pierced on the end of a green prong and toasting away. I had butter with me, salted at that (a rarer treat than you might expect) and some marvellous lemon marmalade, made in a place called Moron of the frontier, near Seville. I remembered seeing a boat once, in Mallorca, called Moron 11. One of these days I really had to find out what the word meant in Spanish.

On the previous evening, I had set up a rod even before getting the tent erected, a strategy which would have been called into question by anyone who had seen my subsequent antics in the failing light. Things had worked out tolerably well though and at least now I had everything ready. I had brought an array of baits, since I didn't really know what to expect in the way of fish. Much further down the canal, near the city, I had caught very little and other anglers I had seen there seemed to have no better luck. The canal was reputed to contain pike and I remember one newspaper report a year or so back featuring a 9kg fish, a 20-pounder. It was caught near the Tafisa wood-processing factory. I had fished the same stretch a few times after that but never saw scale nor fin of such a fish. Local anglers kill everything they catch, unfortunately, which was true all over the country in my first years but which has begun to change a little in more recent times. Since I first wrote this, another brace of monsters have been taken from the same place on the canal, one of 9kg, the other reportedly 17kg, that was 37lb!

On that lovely morning, now so many years ago, there had begun to be light enough at last, and so I had stealthily approached the water and my chosen swim, armed with maggots, brandlings, bread, corn and Spam. I had not been able to get any luncheon-meat. I had groundbaited a bit too, the previous evening when it was already dark. A skulking coot hadn't taken the showering with maggots all that well, nearly scaring me to death with its indignation. I had scattered a few maggots and some bread paste all along the edge of the reeds upstream from the point I most liked the look of. Now I was ready, nicely positioned in a gap in the reeds. Some way downstream an old stone bridge was materialising from the mist and dark, tall reeds at each side hiding its ancient foundations. Odd stones were missing, doubtless fallen into the canal, making it look for all the world like a grotto from some eighteenth century English garden.

The flow of the water wasn't too strong so I had tackled up with a light balsa bodied float, the hook was 14 and my first cast was with a worm. All fish love worms . . . I trotted the float along the edge, letting it drift out a little where the current dictated. The turquoise- and orange-blurred streak of a kingfisher flashed by, right under my rod tip. The float wavered. A green woodpecker laughed its socks off behind me, just a few yards away, in the ruins of an old poplar. The float trundled on a way, then I tried again. A few casts later and there was a slight touch, my heart jumped a beat and the woodpecker fell out of the tree cackling. It undulated away, high overhead and across the open country opposite, clearly unable to take any more of this angler's antics. The float dipped a fraction and I gave a quick strike and began battling with some little fish. It was a short-lived skirmish and I soon brought a small chub up to my hand. I was delighted, a *cacho* as they were known locally and just big enough to go into the keepnet.

I'm not entirely in favour of keepnets but provided they are large and never overcrowded their use can perhaps be justified. Those anglers that crush dozens of fish together are really the problem. I sometimes keep a few fish for a group photograph or to avoid scaring off other members of a shoal, but if ever their use came to be banned I would definitely support the decision. I threw out the full length of my own net, nearly 20 foot of it, there at my feet, and popped the fish in. It would be able to swim up and down there happily enough until I found him some companions.

I put a fresh worm on and let my float wander off down the same stretch once more. I fished on for a good while and was rewarded with two more little chub. I couldn't help wondering if there might be anything else about, something bigger perhaps. I wound in and leaving the rod on the bank started to set up another, with a ledger. I thought I would try leaving a bait out nearer the other side where it might be deeper. There was a very nice space, nearly opposite, where the reed growth was thinner, making a small bay. 'A very fishy looking spot indeed,' I fancied I heard Mr Crabtree saying, 'positively carpy'.

I passed the line through a drilled bullet lead and pinched a shot on at the loop, then a quick hook to nylon size 10 and several small wiggly worms. Now, that ought to generate a bit of interest. The rod was my trusty old split-cane carper, complimented by a nice wooden starback loaded with 8lb line. It was all rather heavier than the other rod I was using, but then my hopes were high. I pulled out a few loops from between the rod eyes and cast straight into the reeds. A quick reflex tug and to my surprise the lead jumped out from among the thick green stems and plopped into the water only inches from their bases. I wondered whether to leave it there. I thought I had seen the bait still on and allowing for the trace length, I was quite nicely placed in the little cove. I lay the rod down and took up the slack, then clicked on the ratchet. It was always marvellous to hear a single click of contact from that old reel, or better still when it sang out to a fish running off with the bait. I clipped a little springy bell on to my new hedgerow rod rest and passed the line carefully through the little slit in the metal. Primed and sensitive, I'd hear the slightest movement on that line.

Happy with the set up I returned to my other rod. Sitting down on the lush grassy bank I let the float slip off, finding its way along the reeds as before. I noticed the hoopoe again, calling somewhere behind the poplars, and another replying at a distance. It was such a characteristic sound throughout the Castilian summer, though it wouldn't be long before they headed south. Then I would only hear them on TV, a background sound on the Serengeti, while in the foreground lions would be busy. Meanwhile, here they were and this nearly African morning was coming on very nicely. I rubbed some factor 12 over any exposed areas as the sun climbed rapidly. It was getting lovely and warm, I would be changing into shorts soon. And someone else had woken up, by the sound of it. There was movement in the reeds, a water vole perhaps, scurrying about and champing periodically at the succulent stems.

Another bite! I struck and again felt the spirited tugging of another small chub as it turned to go with the stream. It was a good fight on the lightweight rod but suddenly it doubled over dramatically and much heavier pulls yanked line off the old Mitchell fixed spool. I held on and thrilled at the heavy lunging feel of a pike, sure that was what it was. Then, just as suddenly, it was gone. The line slackened, though I could still feel the little chub kicking faintly. I wound in and there it was, rather bedraggled and bleeding from a bite mark across the tail end. I slipped the hook out and filling a biggish spare bait box with water, popped the little fellow in to see if it would recover.

I decided to set up another rod. Optimistically enough, I had brought plenty of pike tackle with me, plugs, snap tackle and an old cork bung. With an eye on the chub, which had turned belly up, gills flapping his last, I decided to set up the bung and snap tackle. If the pike was still anywhere around, I had no doubt at all that it would pounce on the same prey it had nearly got away with earlier. I soon had the chub out of the box and I slipped the barbless trebles into its upper lip and dorsal before casting a short distance upstream. I ran quickly and as lightly as possible the few yards necessary to get above the float, as it slowly drifted with the current towards where my ledger line lay. It bobbed lightly and came to a stop there in a slow eddy, before moving again, passing under the other line. It was the work of a moment to pass one rod under the other, checking as I did so that the bell was still in position.

The bung swung out across the stream and hesitated, close now to where the attack had come. The float stopped dead. The stream built up a ripple against its rounded bulk. The pike was certainly there. The float bobbed once, registering doubtless the knock of an inquisitive snout. Then it bobbed again, twice, and went under, sucking down a little surface tension with it. I took up the line and struck; the float flew over my head, bare hooks flailing, and into the bushes behind. I muttered curses to myself with exemplary self-control. I couldn't believe it. As my disappointment flooded in and I cast up my eyes in despair, unexpectedly, there in the overhead branches, I spotted something . . .

My exclamation hung on the air, a loud vibration, an affront, then the diminishing waves fled into the overhead, over-arching shade. The branches fanned out from the main tree and met others from the tall bushes below. Framed there in a little ring of broken light, a tiny bedraggled silhouette dangled by a fine thread. There were miniscule dots on the thread; lead shot, or lead free, it made no difference. The thing was the right way up, its little clawed legs outstretched, with summer blue and cumulus behind. One wing was tied up over its head, the other positioned normally. A small black muddled shape. I stepped along the bank and the sunlight fell on the colours of a robin. It looked as though it had gorged itself on the bait and the hook. I reached up with the pike rod and, twirling the line around the tip, easily pulled the whole bundle free. The hook had been swallowed completely, the line knotted round one wing and a leg. I cut the line away, popping the strands in my pocket, and threw the lifeless, weightless corpse into the bushes.

I then recovered my tackle. Accidents happened of course but I found myself thinking that all anglers should always go to any lengths possible to retrieve lost gear. I recall wading across rivers, scrambling up trees, delving into bushes, whatever was required, in order not to leave any such death traps in the wild. I had lost track over the years of the number of seagulls or swans I had seen with line trailing from their limbs or beaks. Even lost fish were worth keeping an eye open for, absurd as it may seem.

The robin brought another incident to mind which had played out in my old stamping grounds on the Kentish Stour. It had been a bright day, the river streaming by, crystal clear, as I crept along looking for Lilliput specimens of dace or roach. I'd had no luck and was approaching a gloomy damp place under ancient trees, where I was almost sure to be able to spy on a pike. No sooner had I approached when I spotted a large, dead perch, almost white and horribly inflated. I then noticed a spinner dangling from its jaws, tangled in a mass of twigs and weed. I felt angered at whoever was responsible, and yet just as soon recalled how many fish I had lost myself over the years, that had gone off with a hook at the very least. However, there was no doubt that well thought out end tackle would save an awful lot of fish, not to mention anglers' disappointments. I remembered having read a first rate article on the subject, by David Yates in *Carp Fisher* magazine, about what he very accurately referred to as 'death rigs'.

In such cases, the end tackle is stout enough but it is the main line that invariably breaks above the joining knot. With pike gear, it might be at the swivel at the top of a live bait rig, or at the snap ring of a steel trace. Perhaps the culprits were merely young lads or other inexperienced anglers. In any case the tragedy would be far greater than the loss of their tackle, since it probably led to the death of the fish.

Remembering that day, I was still sitting looking at the water, pensively sipping at a cup of coffee, when to my surprise another victim appeared, this time on the water. It was another small chub, swimming fitfully in circles, which I realised Mr Pike would certainly have in a flash. I jumped up, determined to be there first. Pulling out the landing-net to its full length, I was delighted to just reach it. On the bank I saw it had been hit, a hole clean through the back half of the body, the work of a heron perhaps. It was excellent bait, I had no doubt about that. I tidied up the snap tackle after its encounter with the branches and freshly baited, swung out the bung, to pass where I was hopeful the pike might be still lurking.

The bung vanished almost immediately, but I hesitated. It had to have a good hold. I struck just as the float reappeared, careering across towards the far side. The pike rocketed off, heading into the reeds. I kept the line tight, side-straining persuasively to get it back to open water. Up it came suddenly to the surface. A great green bony brow with angry eyes veered round on the water and plunged back down, coming my way. I recovered line rapidly keeping firmly in touch but I certainly wasn't going to tighten the drag; this was nothing but a sham charge. No sooner had I thought so when the pike turned 120 degrees and picking up speed tore away downstream using the current well. I scampered off after it, just managing to grab the landing-net. It had turned again now, holding its own against the flow. I tightened the line and pulled ever so slightly. I felt the fish bore down deep and push against the current solidly, inch by inch making upstream as though pondering its next move. A seven- or eight-pounder I thought with a lot of fight in him. The pike thundered ahead several yards, ripping through weed and sending a ghastly snagging sensation down the line. It was tiring though, staying down, but almost imperceptibly it was coming nearer to my side.

I moved along the bank a bit, looking for a likely landing spot. There were small breaks in the reeds here and there that would do nicely. My fish was close now and I increased the pressure, bringing it up to the surface. As soon as it appeared, it thrashed about dangerously and made a final dash for freedom but soon drifted up once more, breaking the surface and turning over on one side. Only one of the trebles was in, the other had slid up to the top of the wire trace. The pike came quietly over the edge of the net but then suddenly leapt away sideways and, with all the power it could muster, shot out into midstream, pulling line off the reel. I slid unceremoniously down the bank and in up to my knees in water. I kept the rod high somehow, a nice bouncing curve maintaining pressure on my runaway pike. I caught hold of the net, which I had dropped in the fall, and brought it round in front of me. I settled down to play the fish back to me, the muddy sense of cold in my legs gradually wearing off. The fish was back up on the surface and lolling over from one side to the other in the ripples. I brought it to the net and finally, with considerable difficulty, got back up the bank, rod, net, pike and all.

What a tremendous fish it was, in immaculate glossy green condition. I turned it over and soon had the treble out. The other was embedded in the net, but that too would be easy to deal with. A hook with a barb is a plague forever . . . I thought to myself. Then I slipped my first ever Spanish pike into a bag and held up my old Farlows brass scales to see 8lb 12oz, or 4kg registered. I took the required photos and then walked away downstream to release it. I held the fish there in the water a while, letting his gills work and asking him to be so kind as to shove off downstream and not interfere further with my fishing. Finally, with a kick of its splendidly red tinted tail, it disappeared into the greeny brown water.

Watching it go, I was reminded once again of the Stour back in Kent, where the water wasn't at all like this. There it was crystal clear and rather faster running, but it was there that I had most fished for pike. They were rarely very big, a maximum of around ten pounds, but they were great sport. You would know as soon as one entered your swim, where you might be happily catching small roach, dace or beautiful young perch, not because of any let up in bites but because you would see it. Out of the corner of your eye, usually, you would see a dark shape sliding under the trailing water crowsfoot. You would always look twice in case it were the advance guard of a shy shoal of bream. They would often appear in twos or threes, great burnt sienna dinner plates that required extreme caution if you were to catch one of them.

With the pike it was altogether different. Out would go the old faithful

Tadpolly, across the stream. Then, having let it float to the desired point, a slight tightening of the line and it would dive inelegantly from its bobbing position on the surface. If you got it to do that within, say, six or eight feet of Mr Lucius then wham! The pike would hit like a mini great white shark and the battle would be on. In the beautiful clear water you would see the big red gills open and the jaws chomping at the bait in an attempt to mash it to a pulp. Surge after surge would come, up and down and across the stream before, finally succumbing, the pike would come to the net.

My great friend and fellow angler Chris Ryan and I had caught many pike there but our most enduring memory, and one we have often recalled, was a day when they just seemed to go berserk, and we caught 18 in a single afternoon. They ranged from 2lb jacks to several good fish of 8 to 10lb. We actually kept them in three keepnets until the close of the day, and, having caught nothing else of any consequence or worthy of a picture, finally got a snap of that incredible haul of pike laid out on the bankside grass, before slipping them all back into the river.

I was still remembering the Stour as I strolled back along the canal. Before coming out to live in Spain, I had spent many marvellous summer days on its banks, within easy walking distance from home. The atmosphere of both these places had something fundamental in common. I lay the pike rod aside and had a look to see if the ledger line was OK, and as nothing seemed to have happened there, my mind ran on to another extraordinary moment back on the Stour while I placed the float rod carefully on its rest, which had the keepnet string looped round it.

That day on the Stour, I had been fishing one morning, quite early. It had rained overnight and the water was just slightly coloured. It was next to impossible to see anything in the muddied water but the fishing had been good, and I had caught a good number of small roach. There must have been a dozen of them up to maybe half a pound in the net as well as an odd dace, when all of a sudden a tremendous commotion started up in the keepnet. I jumped up to look and immediately saw a good-sized pike, up on the surface, smashing into the far end of the net, clearly trying to get at the fish inside.

I stumbled and slid down the bank and waved my arms in a bid to scare it off but the pike was having none of it and continued hammering away at the mesh. I started to heave in the net and it was then I realised what the problem really was. The pike was caught, and was none to happy about it. Its teeth and snout were all wrapped round with mesh and I was actually able to lift the whole thing completely out of the water, with the pike hanging on to the net like a ferret on to an incautious finger. It would have made a great photo, if only I had been able to take it. I laid the fish down in the shallows and had quite a difficult job getting the net free from its jaws. Eventually, I sent the doubtless hungry double-figure Esox on his way, hoping it would think twice in future before ploughing headlong into a keepnet again.

Back in the present, at the canal, I baited up afresh and cast back into the swim where hopefully the chub had not all been scared off by the pike. It was a delightful day. Even after half a lifetime of fishing, it was marvellous how the magic of the waterside was never diminished. Full of hope, I trotted the swim once more, and began to feel that focus of energy, of anticipation and concentration, all centred in some quasi mystical way on the tiny bright red float tip as it moved away, seemingly for ever, on the infinite stream, like the river of emotion and sensation that runs through every day of our lives. Acting as some greater power, it was as though I were able to halt its progress, whisk it back and start the illusion all over again.

And that is what I did, trotting the float a little closer still to the edge of the reeds. I was sure it was the perfect lie for a fish. I watched the float inch its way along several times more, but it seemed my feeling was wrong. I wasn't going to give up though; if the fish was there it might just get fed up with seeing the same worm trundling by and have a snap at it. Suddenly, the little bell on the other line made me jump. I stared hard back at the ledger rod, the bell was tense on its little spring, the rod tip perfectly still. I wound in the float and lay the rod on the rest. Then I crept up the bank the few yards and knelt poised by the old split cane. The line relaxed a fraction as I watched, the bell spring pointing down once more. I was quite certain that that wasn't going to be the end of it.

I trembled with nervous anticipation, my hand over the cork, not actually daring to touch it. The rod tip tapped very slightly and the bell moved again causing the little ball inside to roll. 'Tink' was the sound, exactly as before. Then, in a sudden pull, the bell tinkled properly and twanged free, the rod tip dipped and the old ratchet sounded. I had the rod and struck against a good run. It felt heavy and was ploughing deep. Could it be a carp? It felt like one certainly. I went off upstream after it, picking up the net, my fish pulling steadily against me and the current. It came to an abrupt stop and seconds passed before it allowed itself to drift back towards where I had stationed myself at a reasonable landing point.

The fish surfaced out in midstream. It was indeed a carp. Only a small one and done for by the look of it. The fish came over the net a minute later and up on to the bank; only a couple of pounds, no more, but a very nice bit of excitement for mid morning. I got down again to the water and slipped the carp into the muddied water. I watched with pleasure as his big fins sped him away quickly out of sight.

Maybe it was time to try scattering a little groundbait. I went for the bait boxes and flung out a few maggots and grains of corn as offerings. Returning to my pitch, I decided to change the float line over to a ledger too, partly inspired by laziness but mainly hunger. I sorted out another lead, a tiny Arlesey bomb, and soon had both lines back out, sticking to worms on one and with corn on the other. I had made rather a better job of loop casting this time and the little splash sent rings out from the centre of the eddy, between the reed shoulders opposite. The other line I had placed downstream a way, a much easier cast since I had left it to go pretty well where it wanted, trusting merely to Izaac. The business of casting centre-pins was a time honoured art I was far from being master of. Something which was true no doubt for many anglers, judging by the responses to an apparently serious item that once appeared in *Waterlog* magazine, which purported to instruct readers into the intricacies of the Nottingham style cast. One reader called the magazine offices to complain that the instructions were impossible to follow. The Editor asked if the reader had counted the fingers on the angler's hands in the illustrations. "Ah," said the caller, "I've been had haven't I?"

Once again I set up the bell arrangement on the old rod and on the other, a couple of eyes up from the reel, I put one of those dangly luminescent bite detectors that wouldn't look out of place on a Christmas tree. A big fluorescent pink and green (that surely should never be seen) bauble of a thing that I had bought at Eastertime that year on a trip to Prague. There was surely nothing like foreign travel for broadening the tackle collection.

With both rods set up nicely, I carefully got down the bank and fished out from the watery reeds a bottle of Rueda Verdejo, an excellent white wine from vineyards about as far south of the city as I was to the north. It had cooled perfectly over night and I pulled the cork in confident anticipation of a delicious accompaniment to my lunch. I took a glass and my tuck box from behind the tent and settled down to some well-deserved rest after the arduous morning's angling. *Empanadas* . . . the individual sized ones were definitely best. Light flaky pastry filled with tuna, tomato and egg, they are a real masterpiece of Iberian pie making. Curiously, they are almost the only kind of pies available in mainland Spain, particularly the huge flat ones, which are sold in large chunks and by weight. All the myriad English savoury pie variations are pretty much unheard of.

I held one up to my mouth and waited a second, my taste buds going berserk in an agony of anticipation. It was the exact moment for a bite. Enough food had been dropped and wine spilt over the years in reacting to inconsiderate fish that such caution was always more than warranted. I bit. The fish didn't. The moment of trial passed. I had the upturned lid of my food container to hand, ready for the next stage. Once the fish had lulled the unsuspecting angler into a false sense of security, dining with impunity, it would approach the bait. It was no good putting down your wine and food hurriedly into the grass at the sign of a bite, since a while later, when the invariably false alarm had passed, you would return to find both teeming with ants. I was sure that it was an example of interdependent co-operative relationship behaviour between disparate species in the animal kingdom, quite unknown to science.

Naturally, with these precautions there was not the least chance of a bite; this was the down-side of an otherwise highly satisfactory arrangement. The lines remained still and having wolfed down the *empanadas*, I began to think about sandwiches. I had plenty of them and began to unwrap one, all the while with half an eye and half an ear on the rods.

I took a sip from my wine and looked out over the landscape. Across the canal to the east swept the empty plains of Castilla, the fields hazy in the heat. Behind me the sun was high but past its zenith, I would have to be careful not to burn my neck and ears. It was pretty hot really, though there was a little shade from the spindly poplars at my back. I glanced again at the rods; still nothing doing there. It was odd they weren't being bothered by those small chub, really. Perhaps the pike was back. I decided I would wait and see. I heard a carp suck something off the surface downstream among the reeds. There were crows cronking away out in the fields opposite, upset about something, a kite probably or a buzzard. I couldn't see anything though. Oh, yes I could, there it was, cruising close above a line of pollarded trees. It was being mobbed by one of the crows, two others in hot pursuit, and I could see there wasn't really much difference in their respective size. I reached over to my bag, pulled out the binoculars, and watched the skirmish. The raptor was a marsh harrier, beautifully coloured, catching the sunlight on its grey wing and tail markings, its black wing tips upturned. Leaving the trees it whirled round and started to climb, finally annoyed into ascent by the clamorous crows.

I was startled back to matters in hand by the soft click of the ratchet on the fixed-spool's drag. The bite detector was up off the ground at the rod eye, the line tight but for the moment, quite still. I unclipped the bauble, watching the rod tip just like a hawk. I had left the drag loose but the spool had barely turned. The rod tip dipped slightly. It was a strange sort of bite, nondescript, non-committal. The tip righted itself and pulled down again fractionally.

I knocked back the wine in my glass and glanced up. There was no sign of the harrier now. Back at the rod I wasn't sure if the line was pulling tight again or not. Something was going on and I would just have to hang on. Suddenly, there were several quick knocks and I had struck before they stopped, but there was nothing there. I wound in to find the bait gone. What had all that been about, I wondered. Then, all the fish in the keepnet splashed up to the near end before falling quiet again. There was almost certainly another pike out there. Maybe it had been after the fish at my bait; I decided to try and find out.

Once again I went for the pike rod but this time I nipped through the line above the snap tackle and tied a new loop. Then I attached an ultra light wire trace and my trusty Tadpolly. I wondered where to try a cast. Leaving the other ledger line out, I opted for a short throw downstream. The lure floated away, as I let out plenty of line, to a point a little beyond where that last bite had come. I stopped the line and a few seconds later the Tadpolly blooped out of sight like a startled frog. I could feel its wobbly motion as it dived, and with occasional checks to halt its descent I avoided getting too close to the bottom, in case there were snags there. I kept the retrieve slow, imitating a sickly fish struggling against the current, tempting any pike to take a closer look. I repeated the operation, covering the ground as thoroughly as I could, but it was looking as though I would have to try upstream. I decided on one more cast to the near side. About half way in, the lure making a little for midstream, there was a thud on the line, but if it was a fish, it left it. I jerked the Tadpolly, making it jump forward and dive again and there was a further hit, much more decided this time. I immediately felt the heavy back and forth lunges as the fish fought to rid itself of this unexpectedly troublesome mouthful. It was a tremendous scrap. These Spanish pike seemed to be rather more feisty than their northern cousins. I had hoped for, but I certainly had not really expected, a day's pike fishing. This one felt quite heavy in the canal's midstream flow and I moved down the bank, keeping a good tight line on my fish as I went. Having cottoned on to what was happening, the pike too was off downstream and I quickly found myself trotting along the bank after it. Then came a sudden furious splashing and it broke the surface. I couldn't actually see it, the brilliance of the reflected sun on the water making me squint blindly. It pulled and pulled with the current. I pursued, recovering some distance and line until I caught up. We were level now but the fish was well down and I thought I could feel weed accumulating on the line. I played on as the pike resisted magnificently in the deeper water towards the far side. It had turned and was holding its own now against the current.

It was just then that I first doubted that I would be able to land it. The line sang in the breeze, there was no give from the other end. I pulled tentatively but it felt solid, it was deadlock and, what was more, I hadn't got the landing-net with me either. It was a good 20 yards back up the bank. I felt that lunging again, deep down, and I applied as much pressure as I dared. That did something, and the fish was off, speeding upstream like a torpedo. At least it was the right direction, but as I hastened to follow, it came straight into the near bank and embedded itself in the reeds. Now I was sure I would lose it.

I took up the line and getting to the same spot, held the rod out full length over the reeds. Again I applied pressure, the rod bending down to the water, in an effort to bring the fish back out into open water. Again the lunging, the reeds jerking this way and that. I backed downstream a little and pulled again. The pike was wild now. I could almost see it smashing and twisting deeper into those reeds. The sensations coming down the line were ghastly. And then, miraculously, it came out. A length of reed stem caught in the line as the fish came up to the surface once more. It was big enough, a ten-pounder maybe. I began to concentrate harder than ever, I had to get this fish. It was clearly tired now and swimming slowly upstream, high in the water. I let it do so, keeping the rod up and myself low, as much out of sight as possible behind the reeds. Only a short way to go before the net. It dived again and moved heavily across the other side. I made a run for the net, keeping up the tension, breathing out a great sigh of relief once I had it in my hand.

The pike was still battling steadily, trying to get into the reed beds opposite but I was sure it wouldn't make it. The fight went on valiantly but I was feeling more and more confident that the fish was mine. It was back in midstream and on the surface, looking angry but also looking tired. I made a play to bring the fish towards the net and it reeled over, churning up the water madly. It went for the reeds to the right. I got down to the water's edge and steered those last lunges to my favour. It came up as I tightened the line and lurched towards the net and, as it came over the rim, the pike made a last wild bid for freedom, and was nearly away again. With its head in, the lure's trebles dangerously tangled in the mesh, I dragged the rim up and over the bulk of the pike's powerful flanks and brought it somewhat unceremoniously to my feet. I pushed the rod up the bank behind me and heaved the fish and the net out ahead of me, up on to the flat.

Holding on tight to tufts of grass, I clambered up myself and then carried the net over to the tent. What a fabulous animal, truly worthy of its old appellation of freshwater shark. Its name in Spanish is *lucio*, directly from the Latin, and it is one of this country's numerous, and frequently controversial, introduced species. I couldn't help admire its superb lines. Slim, streamlined, camouflaged, designed to wait under trailing weeds or in the slipstream of some obstacle, in ambush. Then, with that powerful tail, they surge forward to capture some ailing or injured fish, or maybe one merely careless enough to come too close. A perfectly evolved hunter in its environment, a vital part of the natural selection process at work. So excellent an example set me thinking, and as all anglers know, there's nowhere quite like the waterside, for contemplation.

While my mind wandered, I got the camera and focussed on my pike, the rod and the Tadpolly alongside. It took only a few moments and then into a plastic bag, which I had cut open at both ends, for weighing - 12lb 12oz. It was really quite a fish. All too soon, for such a remarkable new acquaintance, I was down the bank and holding it in the water for release. I stroked the bony snout with wet fingers and marvelled at its form and colouring. Its bright chestnut eyes seemed fixed on me as the fish recovered his breathing. Then it slipped away, back into his own element, single minded and ruthless. It would go straight back to work, I was sure of that. I was thankful that I was not one of those little chub out there.

I felt quite exhausted and went back down the bank to get the wine bottle from the cooling reeds. My mind had turned meanwhile to TV nature documentaries and the times we are told how a given creature has adapted to its environment, in order to survive. The pike was certainly an excellent example, mottled green camouflage, well-armed front end, and powerful propulsion system. How the processes of evolution and natural selection work occupied my thoughts for the rest of the day. Interrupted by the appearance of occasional practical examples of the fish eat fish variety, I also amused myself by imagining some 'Great moments in Evolution', with apologies to the American cartoonist Larsen.

The way a creature's adaptation is described sometimes gives rise to the notion that the animal itself has played some consciously active part in the process; as if it said, 'Hmm, I'd better do something here or else I'll end up extinct.' Active participation undeniably occurs. For example the marine iguana of the Galapagos is quite clearly a land animal, which has developed an ability to swim extremely well in the turbulent sea where it once decided to go in search of food, the marine algae. It also evolved very strong claws to hold on to the volcanic lava shoreline in the tidal swell and thereby avoid being washed out to sea or smashed on the rocks. At some stage in the proceedings we can happily imagine an iguana or two, imitated by various others, trying the water with a claw or a nose as the tide rose, in order to get to get a bit of weed which in a few moments would disappear below the waves. To that extent the animal participated but the development of claws and swimming ability were clearly another, rather more complicated story.

We can imagine that these developments will have come about by constant returning to the water, and repeated training like going to a gym. Then, one day, in a rising tide, a group of these daring animals struggled to get that last mouthful of sustenance when suddenly things got difficult. There were stronger currents in a spring tide perhaps and many animals lost their lives, unable to swim strongly enough to reach the shore, or had claws that were not sufficiently powerful either to hang on while feeding or to scramble up the rocks out of the murderous tide once they reached the rocks. Others were 'lucky' we might say, they were stronger clawed, better swimmers, and their genes led to succeeding generations of similarly adapted animals.

Physical and behavioural adaptations as a general rule seem to have very much more to do with sheer chance than any active effort on behalf of the animal. Such extraordinary luck seems hard to believe however, until we remember the millions of species that became extinct along the way. One case which interests me greatly, is that of the viperine snake *Natrix maura*. This is a very common animal in my part of Spain, its distribution being restricted principally to Iberia and southern France. The Natrix species of grass and water snakes are given to quite elaborate defence behaviour. They will turn upside down and play dead, they may void the foul smelling contents of anal glands or feign apparently dangerous hisses and strikes.

This latter behaviour is remarkably developed in *Natrix maura*. When threatened, this completely harmless creature will flatten its head, exaggerating the triangular shape of its skull and jaws, inflate its body just sufficiently to create the impression of the shorter, thicker-set viper species and prepare itself to strike. This strike, when it comes, is completely ineffective, since the animal has no fangs and doesn't even open its mouth. The most dramatic aspect however, is that the viperine snake has an alternating pattern of smallish dark squares along its back and when the animal swells its body, these marks look exactly like the warning zigzag of the adder. It effectively copies the defence strategy of the Vipera species in every detail. We surely have to discount the possibility of learnt behaviour, not least because any *N. maura* that got close enough to witness Vipera behaviour would probably not live to tell the tale. We might rail too at the idea of pure coincidence and therefore are left with plain old chance and consequent natural selection.

All this talk about snakes reminds me of an incident which occurred in Galicia back in Spain's north-west some years ago, when hill walking with a teaching colleague, Tony Bonfield, from the west of Ireland. What Tony'd had in mind was a hike more than anything else and it was me that had suggested taking along a couple of fishing rods. It is great country for walking and for Tony it served as a kind of annual cure after the Irish winter, back in wet County Clare. Tony is actually from Limerick, where what is described as a 'soft morning' is one upon which there is only the slightest drizzle. For most of the year, Tony assures me, the only real solace is to be found in porter, or in the eyes of an Irish lass or 'colleen'.

On the day in question, we had set off after lunch on a Saturday afternoon and wound our way out of the part of the village of Mondoñedo known as Portugalete, where a new main road - yet another Germanic autobahn - bound for the coast, hacked through the quiet landscape. As we left the houses behind, a stream ran alongside the road, straddled at the last, by a huge *hórreo*, a time honoured corn store on stilts. It looked truly ancient, its wooden structure covered on one side with dozens of carefully constructed pigeonholes. Several were occupied by identical white doves, doubtless the pride and joy of their keeper. Our road led to Recadieira, a tiny hamlet on a hill, consisting of a single street, cut off from the world by another recent EU road development. Recadieira's isolation made it a peaceful place, much as it must have been half a century before. Life didn't appear to have changed much for many more generations. In the heat of the day, the place seemed abandoned and still, but there was an occasional bent-over figure working in the cornfields. Our '*¡Buenas tardes!*' were always returned with a laconic but nevertheless well-intentioned '*¡Buenas!*' invariably accompanied by the barking of a half asleep dog, startled from his siesta.

The old village had at least one *pallazo*, a kind of stone dwelling, circular in shape, with a low thatched roof that had a smoke hole, and a rudimentary doorway, unchanged in its design since the Stone Age. On a roadside hillock, next to a heavy Celtic cross, one of these *pallazos* dominated the narrow road. It appeared to be home now to a number of hens, several smaller ones bustling away into its dark interior as we passed. A line of picturesque cottages led away from us with huge blooms of hydrangeas at their fronts. One of the houses was abandoned, its windows and door completely hidden by these spectacular flower heads in pink and blue.

A footpath I knew led from alongside the cottages down past allotments to the road below. We followed it until we reached a fountain and then stopped to drink and wet our heads. The sun was burning and I suggested we head into the cover of the woods. A short way up the road was another footpath, the same one in fact, that, I remembered, had been sliced in half by the new road. A few minutes later we were into the crowded shade of tall sapling eucalyptus. The disrupted path quickly recovered its ancient character there under the rocky hillside. Dark with mosses and lichens, it led through the gorse and ferns towards the river. This would be the Tronceda, the river we would probably be fishing later on, in some of its higher reaches.

The roar of the water soon came loud through the undergrowth and I slowed our progress.

"Watch your step here, Tony," I said over my shoulder, "this gets a little tricky."

Ahead of us, the sun broke through and the path came to a sudden halt.

"The river looks a long way down."

"Yes, the point up ahead there is amazing, a sheer drop. Mind how you go."

To our right, the ground quickly began to drop away and the path became the very edge of a steep slope, thick with deciduous trees. Several green mossy trunks lay rotting, their roots having given way and stopped from further descent by the precariously angled trunks of others. Extravagant funguses grew in undulating discs in the decomposing bark and there were tiny yellowish toadstools everywhere. The air was heavy and still with mildew scents until at last we came out into the warm light. We put our bags down and approached the grassy edge. The drop was impressive. The river ran directly below us, the sunlight just reaching its smooth rock pools.

"It must be fifty feet," Tony said, half under his breath.

We got down on all fours and crept forward, then lay there watching.

"Look, there's a fish."

We watched a small trout darting between pools, then disappear into the blackness of deeper water below the main cascade. There were two superb waterfalls and several trickles amongst the thick vegetation covering the opposite walls. Spray blew up to us, filling the air a second, wafted on the occasional updraught, then clearing again, giving us a wonderful view. Below, the delicate fronds of a mimosa, or silver wattle, waved on the warm air. The tree was right down near the water, its thin branches stretched out over the river in their search for light. The upper foliage almost reached up as far as us, with its curious fern like leaves, silvery on the underside. It was presumably an escapee, I couldn't believe anyone could have gone to the trouble of planting so exotic and decorative a tree where no one was likely to see it.

"Do you fancy a beer?"

"Excellent idea!"

Tony produced a couple of bottles of '*Estrella de Galicia*' and we sat safely back from the precipice to enjoy them.

"We'll have to back-track from here," I said, "and carry on down the road to the bridge."

"Isn't there any way down?"

"Well, there is actually, though it's a bit tricky."

"I'd rather try it than retrace our steps though, wouldn't you ?"

It was true. We were always disinclined to go back the same way we had gone, on our walks, if there were any means of avoiding it. So, having finished our beers, we set off, continuing our climb. Though it seemed illogical, we had to go up quite a way in order to get down from the cliff edge. Right below where we walked, the rock had fallen away, creating a huge overhang. Leading the way up through the gorse, I told Tony about the way down. We had to follow the ravine back away from the rocks to where the sides were thickly matted topsoil once more. Amongst the tall trees were new skinny eucalyptus saplings that hadn't yet mastered the terrain. One or two had fallen and provided ladders down the bankside.

We soon reached the place where I knew we could get down. We skidded and slid in the soft earth, hanging on to the saplings for dear life. It was very nearly vertical in places and a long way down. Eventually, we thudded up against an immense oak that stood guard at the bottom, shading a good bit of the river. The noise now was deafening, the biggest of the waterfalls only yards away. Everything was wet. The oak trunk was inches thick with moss on its river side, and on all the lower branches too. We followed the water along until we got to the huge overhanging cliff. It, too, was literally dripping wet, its surfaces black and green with trickling water.

The place was extraordinary, like a mini rainforest. The ravine walls and crowded trees made it virtually impossible to fish, though I had tried. A bubble, and a worm on a tiny hook had brought me several of the small local trout, though they were much too small to fish for really.

"Hey! There's a snake!"

Tony visibly jumped.

"It's OK, it's over there, look, in the water."

Tony wasn't much of a fan of snakes, but provided they were at a safe distance, they weren't so bad.

This one was a grass snake, and was swimming along the far edge, clearly looking for a way out. It may well have been washed down the waterfall, since above this point it was all sheer rock faces into the water. It swam into a little inlet and beached itself at last, looking quite exhausted, its tongue flicking languidly, and just stayed there, its head on the grass, the rest of its body in the water. It was too far away to get a photo, and anyway the light was very poor under the trees. We watched it for a while; then with only the slightest movement, it was gone, safe and sound into the undergrowth.

We pressed on and eventually came out of the trees along with the river, into the still quite steep-sided valley that lead down to the old bridge. We continued along at the water's edge, able to hear each other once more.

"The bridge is just there."

Tony pointed ahead where the trees gathered once more along the bankside.

"We can get to it this way I think," I said, "better than cutting up to the road."

The slope beside us was all close-mown grass, worked by people from Recadieira. It was beautifully kept pasture and we didn't feel like tramping across it. The village was way above us on the high ground between this valley and that of the little river Cesuras, which we had seen back in Portugalete. From there it wandered in an enormous curve round to where it joined the Tronceda, just below the bridge, which was just coming into view.

It was a years old tradition, to pause on this old bridge and gaze down at the huge trout that held court there below, a good group of other fine fish always in attendance. The sign, '*Vedado de Pesca*', prohibited interference in this fellow's lordly lifestyle and well he knew it. We crossed the bridge and followed the tumbling adjacent stream. Just a few hundred yards up, was a point under the arching pines and giant eucalyptus, where a narrow path led down again to a waterfall. The cascade thundered into a deep pool, from where the waters spread out invitingly on hot days, to form a sizeable, triangular swimming hole, with a couple of massive boulders here and there, ideal for leaping from. There was good fishing too, though the trout were very small. The best method was a tiny black Mepps with a smaller than standard treble, in place of the original. Creeping up on the pool on most weekdays, when there were rarely any bathers, and zigzagging your lure over the gravel and around the boulders, often yielded good results.

The burbling water rushed out of this pool, between descending ranks of rocks, before following its course into deepish water with several more pools, all the way back to the bridge. Tony said he would have a bash here with the Mepps and I thought I would try the downstream stretch with a wet fly. I had brought along a small telescopic spinning rod, which I gave, already set up, to Tony, and an old cane fly rod for myself. I had loaded an ancient starback with brand new 4-weight line and after tying on my leader, selected a funny looking thing, not unlike a Bloody Butcher, said to be deadly in Mondoñedo's cathedral square corner shop.

I left Tony spinning, and keeping low, I crept off around the mossy boulders and out of sight. I passed through a heavily scented eucalyptus glade and under another dark, dripping, overhanging cliff, down past the pool's perimeter, to where the river rippled promisingly. It was very warm and humid as I waded out quietly into the cooling current and tried a few casts downstream. The line hissed snake like through the air, between me and the overarch of trees, carrying the fly to its destination. Apart from some brief encounters with jack in the box bushes and a few slippy wading moments, nothing much happened. Then I had a tug from behind a boulder 20-odd yards away. The fly may have just snagged a touch of weed but it had felt fishy. I inched my way forward and crossed precariously to the far side. A cast from there might be easier, a better shot at covering the tail of the pool beyond. I cast past the boulder with unexpected accuracy, and brought the fly by in short jerks towards me, and it was suddenly taken! A terrific little fight ensued in the thrashing stream and I brought a well-fed little trout up to my hand for unhooking. At about 6oz it was a big one, beautifully marked with black and red spots, golden fins and a white belly. I slipped the fly out and away the little fellow went. I fished on a while and although I had one or two more touches, I caught no more fish. I had got a fair way down and thought I ought to be getting back to see how Tony was managing.

I pushed against the current and eventually got out on to the bank, where I had left my bag. Clambering up some boulders and on to a fallen tree, I had a good view back up the river. Tony was casting, looking pretty at ease in the river. I got back down and retraced my steps along the waterside to the swimming hole. As I got nearer I could see Tony looking decidedly concentrated and determined in his movements. I wondered if he was having any better luck than myself. I waved and whistled from another boulder but there was no way he could possibly have heard me over the noise.

"How's it going?" I said, once I was within earshot.

"I've had one," he said, "a pretty little fish of maybe half a pound."

"Me too," I said, "a bit smaller."

"I put mine in that small pool over there, but he was out of it a minute later! I haven't seen a fish since."

We decided to try another, much smaller pool a short walk downstream and as we made our way past where I had been fishing earlier, I told the tale of my own capture. We agreed it was a splendid day's fishing so far. The next spot was tricky, at least half the pool was overhung with very low branches from the far side. I had seen biggish fish here over the years, but had never caught anything there at all. The lies were impossible to reach. I had tried a spinner all over the clear water and even tumbled a worm under the trees, as far as the current would take it. At the head of the pool was a light gravel patch where the water washed in, and I had seen the shape of a good fish against the bottom a number of times but it would always vanish at the slightest move.

I had never tried a fly though and so my hopes were high, inexplicably enough, since there was hardly any water that could be easily covered. Tony said he would leave me to it and take the spinner downstream. I told him that a hundred yards or so down, the river ran deep and narrow against an irregular wall of boulders on the other side, and might produce something. Tony slipped away, out of sight, only to appear again seconds later, crouched low. His whistle attracted my attention and in a hoarse whisper his voice came over the water.

"Will you look at yer man!"

I looked where he was pointing but could see nothing, the light reflecting too much on the water.

"There, ten yards back from the light patch."

I crept slowly along the bank and then saw a big wavering shadow and ducked down in the hope that the fish hadn't seen me. We were both in the shadows and the sunlight played on the ripples out where the fish was, making it hard to see well and with any luck, equally difficult for the trout to spot us.

We exchanged thumbs up signs and whispering each other good luck, set about our respective goals. Tony had disappeared again as I unhooked my fly from the cork. I held my breath as I got into position and tried a sideways cast. The only clear area was over the water and between the boulders behind me. The water at my feet was too deep to wade, the bottom then rising several feet further on to where the trout lay. The cast was not great but at least the fly reached the water. It had landed and sunk some half dozen yards beyond my fish, which appeared not to have moved. I retrieved carefully and again held my breath as suddenly the trout vanished, having shot off in the direction of my fly. It was a terrific take, the line jerked tight and snaked away, up went the rod and the trout headed away across the pool towards the outlet. Just then, Tony reappeared.

"He's on!" I called.

"I had a feeling," he said, "I just had to come up and check on you."

The trout reeled round and thrashed on to the surface. I had to pull hard against a dive to the far side, where the long sunken trunk of a eucalyptus lay shining white near the bottom. It doubtless looked an attractive refuge to 'yer man'. Tony was alongside by now and had the net ready when, with a sickening jerk the trout leapt, threw the hook and the line dropped on to the water, suddenly slack and lifeless. I wound up and both Tony and I looked at the leader as though to find some fault there, but everything was intact.

"Oh well," we said in unison, "that's the way it goes."

We decided on a breather. There was fruit in our bags from the kitchen and as we swigged on our beers, munched on pears and oranges, our spirits seemed to improve.

"Will we take a walk up to the wooden bridge?" Tony suggested.

It was another favourite walk of ours and besides, there was another pool up there, where Tony had caught his first ever trout, just the year before.

"Great idea!" I said. "We might get a bite up there."

A little while later, we set off, making our way to the woodman's path that wound up through the tall slender trees whose scent filled the air and whose bark and leaves littered every space and crammed themselves into every crevice on the rocky hillside. Once on the path it was easier going, though the baked earth reflected the ever increasing heat.

"Look out, John, there's another snake!"

Tony was definitely not a great fan of the limbless reptile, or any other reptiles for that matter, and this one was just a little too close for comfort.

"Don't worry," I said, "'it's only a viperine snake, totally harmless."

"Hmmm . . ." Tony observed, unconvinced.

"Their only system of defence is to imitate an adder," I went on, reaching down to pick him up.

What happened next remains fixed in my memory as though in slow motion. I had continued explaining *Natrix maura's* curious viper-like defence strategies. My hand at this point was still some distance from the snake, which was turning to defend itself. The dark zigzag was just like that of an adder. Its eyes didn't have the round pupils I expected, they were like those of a cat, wicked vertical slits. By way of cautionary advice to students on the English course, I had often said that if you could see their pupils you were already too close. I honestly think, I had actually begun to withdraw my hand, or at least the signals from my brain were on their way, but with lightning speed the adder struck.

I held my arm to my chest gently squeezing just above the wrist with my other hand, to slow the blood flow a little.

"I think we had better go back down to the village," I said. "I'm afraid this could be a bit of a problem."

I was doing my best to imitate a Captain Kirk calmness of voice in adversity.

Tony meanwhile was white as a sheet, a good deal more worried than I was, after all there were no snakes in Ireland!

The adder's fangs had hit my thumb, one in the fleshy part to the side of the nail and the other in the nail itself, where it had left a yellowy teardrop of venom. The pain was already remarkable as we walked steadily, though not too quickly back down the hill. Any panic or energetic movement had to be avoided even though it was still a fair walk to the village. Tony had all the fishing gear and I kept talking away to assure him I was fine as we reached the main path down to the bridge where the lord trout lived.

By the time we got there, my whole hand had become inflated like a rubber glove and the thudding pain from my thumb was considerable. For once I didn't stop to look down into the water.

During a lifetime's fascination with wildlife, and especially with Ophidia, I can honestly say that I had always wondered what it would be like to be bitten by a poisonous snake. After all, I had caught and photographed adders many times. What a foolish mistake to make. The viperine snake is ever so common in Castile, but *Vipera berus*, the adder, is unknown. The local viper in Castile is the nose-horned variety and is not at all common. However, the situation is quite different in Galicia, where the common adder occurs frequently and the viperine snake is rare. Moreover, the adder is much feared, being responsible mainly for frightening people working in the fields but also for the occasional deaths of livestock.

Down at the road, we managed to hitch a lift on a tractor into the village and we soon got to the clinic there. As I was walking to the ambulance, I began to feel quite dizzy and was glad at last to lie down. The swelling had spread considerably - my hand, forearm and up to my shoulder. I was beginning to look quite grotesque, not unlike the elephant man. Acute pains started in my abdomen, whether caused by nerves or some effect of the venom I wasn't sure. I felt cheerful enough, however, during the long journey to the nearest hospital. It was only about 25 miles, but they were narrow winding roads for the most part, through quite mountainous country.

What with the medication and so on, enormous doses of morphine and antihistamine among other things, I don't remember much of the succeeding night. I spent 36 hours in an intensive care unit, connected to all kinds of machines and with an uncomfortable tube in the corner of my mouth and running down my throat, providing oxygen, since my tongue had swollen to two or three times its normal size and I was in danger of suffocation.

My most dramatic recollection of the intensive care unit was waking up at some unearthly hour during my first night, at two or four in the morning, unable to really feel anything, not knowing where I was and yet feeling oddly calm and collected. I could see an array of screens reflected in the glass some feet beyond the bottom of my bed: pulse, blood pressure, breathing, all softly bleeping and wiggling in lines and lights as I gazed at them trying to tell one from another. I began breathing more quickly at one point and was greatly satisfied to see one monitor respond with an increase in the rhythm of its display. I played around in this way for a while and then, doubtless moved by some Dennis the Menace kind of influence, I breathed in deeply and held my breath. Suddenly alarms sounded, some kind of siren wailed and I heard the patter of several pairs of feet approaching. Three nurses burst into my little unit to find me staring wildly about me as the lights flickered into brilliance, but yet with such a mute, inane grin illuminating my countenance that they immediately started shouting at me, telling me off in no uncertain terms. A doctor then appeared and was apparently none too pleased either to find that I was still alive and evidently in such playful mood. I was, in actual fact, rather woozy on morphine, slightly drunk on antihistamine and altogether muddled by the cocktail of whatever other medication had been pumped and dripped into me, not to mention the contained excitement of being the cause of such consternation and unwanted nocturnal activity without being able to move a muscle or utter a word myself.

I could make no intelligible sound at all, since my tongue was still a horrible size and my breathing, despite my antics, was slow and painful. The swelling, which had spread all the way up my right arm and shoulder the last time that I had been properly aware of anything, had now extended down my right side to my waist, and came to an end finally in my right thigh. I looked something like the Michelin man and in the days to come the whole bloated mass of my right side would wobble like blancmange as I walked up and down the ward. I also had an ice pack around the inflated forearm and some days later it was a red patched pattern of black and blue from the consequent bruising. I learnt later that it was actually this tremendous swelling that was the most common cause of death resulting from viper bite, among animals particularly. A cow in Mondoñedo had died from asphyxia only a week or so before my own experience, its throat and tongue swollen after being bitten on the hoof. The poor old thing had simply keeled over and not been found until the evening, by which time it had been long beyond the need of a vet.

I was in the hospital at Burela on the Galician coast, for ten days altogether. All of which rather put an end to my trout fishing in Galicia that summer.

As far as the snakebite is concerned, I really would not repeat the experience or recommend it, but I wouldn't have missed it for the world. Tony on the other hand, said he wasn't sure he would ever step out of Ireland again, where St Patrick was famously and thankfully responsible for ridding the country of serpents.

Whether by divine intervention or the almost random twists and turns of evolution and natural selection, the world's wildlife today is an extraordinary testament to Mother Nature. The Galapagos iguanas with weaker claws and poor swimming ability were selected out by the rising tide, the Natrix family, with its curious tendency to elaborate defence behaviour, must have undergone a rather more complex process. *N. maura*, by chance, had begun behaving like an adder where numerous other, now lost, members of the species were perhaps behaving like other creatures, or like none, and therefore were not successful in deterring predators. Another series of Larsen-like cartoons springs to mind, which might chronicle the prehistoric age of imitators and impersonators. It would be a relatively short period in evolutionary terms, during which we might imagine *Natrix nitwitus* perhaps, in some way copying the house sparrow, or perhaps an early *Cyprinus* incautiously imitating the eating habits of the black bass, with all too small a mouth. All doomed to extinction.

After these not entirely scientific speculations, back on the bank of the Canal de Castilla, mixed with the capture of a couple more little chub, I felt ready for some tea. Some excellent Assam tea bags shipped out from England and a few left over sandwiches were very welcome. I sat back on the bank in the soft late afternoon light, having re-cast, and watched the mesmerising water run. I closed my eyes and listened to birds, near and distant, to the breeze in the trees and the ripple of the water. I drifted off. The Spanish siesta, though it may exist under other names and be practised in other cultures, was surely charmingly idiosyncratic of the Iberian way of life.

Not far downstream something big making a violent incursion into the reeds made me jump up and I saw the surface break with the shimmering flight of small fish. The tall green stems ripped from side to side and a sudden gloop nearby sucked down water, as though something very big had abandoned the chase and pulled back into the main flow. It was a pike, almost certainly, maybe the same one. Just as suddenly, stillness and quiet returned, I dropped back into my dream-like state and let my mind wander.

Monster pike, I thought. I was over the moon with the day's fish but I would doubtless return once my imagination had had time to work on that last sighting. There's nothing quite as exciting as the rumoured presence of a monster pike. I seemed to recall a story of a lady walking her dog around a lakeside in county Durham, throwing in a rubber ball from time to time for her Jack Russell to retrieve. There had been a sudden violent thrashing and the little dog had disappeared. It was found the next day along the shore, drowned and with some very nasty gouges in one of its rear legs. Fishing literature of course abounds with many and more fantastical stories about pike. The combination of human ignorance and imagination can work wonders. In European literature there are stories too of gigantic footprints left across the countryside by the devil. It wasn't until I went on a trip recently here in Spain to the provinces of Soria and La Rioja that I found the most likely explanation. In the 1970s, palaeontologists there discovered hundreds of ichnites, the fossilised footprints of dinosaurs, incredibly well-preserved and striding across the terrain. They are mostly bipeds, ornithopods, two legged animals with three- or four-toed feet, like birds. One I measured was 18 inches wide and was so perfectly intact that it appeared that the mud had squeezed up between those huge scaly toes only the day before, or, more thrillingly, during the previous night. This impression was considerably reinforced when, a few paces further along, I came across droppings, coprolites, or dinosaur excrement, fossilised and more than sufficiently real to be a little unnerving.

My afternoon reverie was finally interrupted by a hearty ring from the bell on the one rod I had left out. I jumped up and struck. A frenetic little battle ensued, albeit short-lived, and I soon slid the net under another small chub. I popped it into the net and before baiting up decided on some dessert. There was only a mouthful of wine left I was rather surprised to see, since I only have a glass or two usually. So, I finished it off and opened a tupperware box to reveal some homemade fruitcake. There was also a bottle of homemade *sidra*, a cider from my neighbour's village in Asturias, which I had quite forgotten about. The cake wasn't made by me I hasten to add, but by a very nice lady whom I'd become friends with after having explained to her one morning why I was such an early (and noisy) weekend riser. It was a fact that had quickly come to her attention after my moving in. Unfortunately this meant that she was forever and a day importuning me for fish. She flatly refused to believe that I returned them to the water, being convinced instead that I never caught anything. The same old story.

The cake went down very well indeed, helped along by the very dry, strongly flavoured cider. It is completely flat in the bottle and I had a hilarious time pouring it from as great a height as I could into my glass, just as they do in the *sidrerías* of Asturias. Suddenly, the reeds below were being hammered into yet again by a pike. This time I jumped up and grabbing the spinning rod, aimed my cast to land beyond the point in question, with a view to Tadpollying gently past, as close to the reed stems as I could. The lure flew majestically through the air, the light twinkling on its silvery flanks, way over the still attacking pike and into the far bankside trees. I ran off down the bank uttering various expletives, keeping the line high and tight, towards the bridge. I scampered across and, there being various other obstacles along the bank, propped the rod up with the line going directly into the offending branches.

Getting to the bushes, I fought my way into the brambles, which formed the trees' lower defences. One or two of the larger thorns embedded themselves in my hands. One bled profusely and hurt like mad but I could think only of getting to my Tadpolly. With my legs still under attack from below, I clambered up into the young willow, the branches of which began to give gently under my weight. A few moments later, my right foot slowly entered the water, the wet sensation causing me to inch my way a little further along the branch. Below it, the water looked deep and most uninviting, despite the agreeable late afternoon temperature.

The line passed overhead quite close and then dropped out of sight, somewhere in front of me, into the water. As I myself headed waterward, the lure suddenly pulled up out of the water and dangled before my eyes. I swung back and forth making the lure do the same until it bumped into my T-shirt a few times, finally catching there. As a resounding crack sounded from lower down the tree, I held on for dear life. With my heart in my throat, I rivalled any contortionist that ever existed until I got the line before me into my mouth. I bit through the nylon just above the wire trace and hung there watching the now free monofilament pull free and drift off on the slight breeze.

It was at this point I think, that I realised I was just a little drunk. A whole bottle of wine plus the cider was more, by more than double, than I ever usually drank. One thing was certain, I had absolutely forgotten about the pike. I was completely unable to move and my grip was failing. The feeling of tipsiness passed in practically the same instant that I had become aware of it. My foot was still in the water, and the tree, barely more than a sapling, was far from pleased with my antics. The rest is a bit of a blur, but I managed somehow to get back on to terra firma and to my tent, albeit bleeding profusely from arm and leg, and with both shoes full of water.

No sooner had I regained my little camp, than I decided that some coffee would be the thing and that the fire would help matters no end. It took only a minute to get it going again, with the wrapping paper from the *empanadas*, and the pot soon emitted a plume of steam which wound up into the clear blue sky along with the wisps of wood smoke. I poured myself some strong coffee to accompany the remaining slices of cake and made a mental note to show my kind neighbour the photo of today's pike. The sun was low now and would be setting in an hour at the most. I would have to get away just after dark as it was quite a long cycle back to the city with the tent and everything else. I sipped the coffee and leant back against the old trunk enjoying a renewed sense of safety and peace. The canal waters drifted by gently, various bird melodies still filling the air, and somewhere a big pike lay quietly in ambush.

A while later, I collected up my gear, de-tackled the rods and after dismantling the tent, loaded up my poor old bike. It was a fine machine, though rather past its best even back then. The Conquest model in its day had actually held the world record for altitude mountain biking, on Kilimanjaro, if I remember correctly. One thing was for sure, it was amazing what it could carry.

I had left the old rod until last, but to no avail, I didn't get another bite. The light was fading fast as I made my way, rather precariously, along the mile or so of canal side path before I could take a track, which led to the nearest road. The air was warm, and the main road deserted, just as they had been, my father often remarked, back in the 1950s in England. I soon settled into an easy rhythm that would have me home in a couple of hours at the most. That night I recall, I slept as I had rarely slept ever before in my life.

Chapter Six

The Ebro (Aragón)

Where the author discovers an angling Mecca, over Halloween and the Day of the Dead.
Monster carp and catfish are conjured up, following a long bus journey, and more language curiosities
arise before a Spanish breakfast. The Ebro ecosystem is examined, where carp and a catfish thrive,
and the author makes a catfish film, as well as considering many catfish legends.

Into which airport does a visitor to Spain usually enter the country? You might
fly into Málaga from any of a dozen UK airports, particularly if you are after
the sun and a beach holiday; or you might fly into Madrid for a more cultural
break, or into Barcelona, from where you might choose culture or beach, or
both. There are numerous other airports too around the Iberian Peninsula,
inland or away in the islands, served generally by various budget airlines with,
of course, amazingly low fares, making Spain one of Europe's most accessible
and economical tourist destinations. For the angler, Reus airport (Tarragona)
to the south-west of Barcelona, is perhaps the most frequent point of entry,
especially for those who have been lured abroad by the opportunity of wrestling
with the giant wels catfish of the Ebro. Actual statistics are a little difficult to pin
down but somewhere between 8,000 and 15,000 anglers travel to the Ebro
every year from the UK alone, with considerable numbers of Germans coming
a close second.

Anglers coming from abroad have invariably contracted an angling package,
including accommodation, airport transfers, tackle, bait and the all important
local angling guide service. Once collected from the airport, there is a drive
of around 140km to the river, to any one of a number of small waterside
towns, where the various angling businesses have their cabins and apartments,

dedicated shops and bars etc. The airport and the drive to the river are in Catalonia but the most popular side of the river is actually in Aragón, where, by the way, the licence required is from the Government of Aragon's Environment Agency. If you are going to fish on the Catalonian side you will need a different licence, issued by the Generalitat de Catalunya. There is nothing to worry about here, however, since all this will be dealt with by the angling services contracted before coming out, one of the many reasons why they are such a good idea. Nevertheless, details of how to obtain these licences can be found in the Appendix.

My own first trip to the Ebro was rather different. I travelled 420 miles overland from Valladolid and I remember very well it was the long weekend following Halloween, that international night of demons and witches, succeeded immediately by the rather more Latin world celebration of the Day of the Dead, when the deceased are remembered and honoured. Anyone who has read Malcolm Lowry's *Under the Volcano*, or remembers the John Houston film with Albert Finney, will recall the wildly colourful, demonic atmosphere. Lowry's story took place in Mexico, where the festival of painted skulls and dancing skeletons is rather more elaborate than in Spain, where tradition finds families simply visiting cemeteries with wreathes and garlands of flowers. There is one further local custom, however. Many theatres across the country stage a production of José Zorrilla's play *Don Juan Tenorio*. The climax of the story takes place, of course, in a cemetery, where Don Juan has been led by the ghost of the murdered Don Gonzalo, the father of Doña Inés, one of Don Juan's conquests. Don Gonzalo's tomb opens and reveals an hourglass that represents the dregs of Don Juan's rapidly passing life. The sand is about to run out and as the ghostly Don Gonzalo pulls Don Juan by the arm in order to consign him to Hell, the Don calls out for mercy and, somewhat disappointingly for those of us with a gothic turn of mind, ascends into Heaven with Doña Inés and is forgiven. The libretto for Mozart's famous operatic version, *Don Giovanni*, replaces this scene with the much more darkly dramatic arrival of a living statue, and the subsequent dragging down into the Eternal Inferno of a determinedly unrepentant Don.

As part of the traditions of the Day of the Dead, the Zorrilla play has been performed widely at least once every year for over a century. In fact it had already been a considerable success prior to the advent of this tradition but unfortunately the author, who hailed from Valladolid, did not benefit from his play's success, since shortly after its completion, he sold all the rights. Zorrilla had mistakenly expected little to come of his version of the old myth, originally made famous by Tirso de Molina in his *The Seducer of Seville* of 1630. Zorrilla even attempted to discredit his own play as time went on, hoping to be able to have it discontinued long enough for him to write and produce a revised version, but to no avail.

On this most lugubrious of holidays, it always seemed there was something special in the chill air as the '*Día de los muertos*' came nearer. I was not planning to visit the cemeteries or to go to the theatre, nor was I thinking of dressing up as a warlock or meditating upon how I might entertain or scare my intensely sceptical Castilian friends with ghostly tales from Old England. Rather, my thoughts as an inveterate angler were running fancifully upon other ancient myths, tales of towering giants: the Colossus, Gargantua or the Titans . . . the reason being that on the very weekend of these spooky fiestas, I intended to travel across country to the ancient kingdom of Aragón, there to spend the funereal day confronting phantasms of my own invention and doing battle with Spain's largest and hardest fighting carp. Home to these fish was the river Ebro and its vast reservoir system, known as the Sea of Aragón. In these waters, there was a chance too that I might encounter what for me, at the time, was a new colossus: the giant European catfish.

There is something great indeed about the sound of Aragón, a name which has a familiar enough ring to it in Britain. Many will recall from their school-days and television history series that Catherine of Aragón became Queen of England, when she married Henry VIII in 1509, and remained queen until 1533. She herself had previously been Princess of Aragón, then an ancient kingdom of the Iberian Peninsula, existing in various forms from the mid eighth century. Aragón reached its peak of power and considerable geographical extension in 1250, when it covered the modern day regions of Aragón, La Rioja, Catalunya, Valencia and the Balearic Islands. The kingdom finally came to an end with the marriage of Ferdinand V of Aragón to Isabella I of Castile, and the consequent unification of Spain as a single kingdom, in 1469.

Then there was the river Ebro itself, also a giant, of nearly 1000 kilometres or 600 miles in length, the largest river completely within the borders of Spain, and indeed within the Iberian Peninsula. In ancient times the Ebro was the Iberus, which gave its name both to the early Iberian peoples and to the penin-sula itself. Iberus is the Roman Latin denomination but the word Ebro, as is also the case with the Duero of Castile, is almost certainly Celtic, these ancient peoples being known to have inhabited the area long before Roman times. We find *dwr* (water) still in modern Welsh and the Celtic root word is understood to be *dubro*.

The Ebro rises in Cantabria, just over the mountains inland from Santander, and flows south and east to empty at last into the Mediterranean, south-west of Tarragona. Throughout its length there is excellent fishing, from wild brown trout in its heady highland waters to the many varieties of sea bream, bass and even tuna occurring in its estuary. It is in its magnificent middle course reservoirs where we find altogether darker monsters.

An all important consideration before planning the trip and having, equally, a bearing on final preparations before setting off, was the question of the weather. All anglers have their special relationship with the extraordinary world of meteorological phenomena and those proverbial signs of Mother Nature's intentions, from a red sky at night to cows lying down in their pastures. I myself place my greatest confidence in the gently shifting needle of an old pocket barometer, in preference to the vagaries of the official forecasts. I had been observing the rising tenths over a number of days and had smiled at seeing its prophecy confirmed on the TV's Meteosat images, and the stealthy approach across the Atlantic of a high pressure system. The old instrument, made in London by Negretti & Zambra in 1905, was a treasure found many years ago down Portobello Road and has never failed me. Trusting implicitly in its auguries, I had donned and packed plenty of warm clothing and spurned the cagoule and waterproof trousers that lived behind the kitchen door.

Long before these final preparations, it had been necessary to sort out the equally important business of licences and day tickets in order to fish the waters of Aragón. My projected excursion was to fish those banks of the Ebro which fall under the jurisdiction and authority of the INAGA, the Instituto Aragonés de Gestión Ambiental, the Environment Agency of the Government of Aragón. (Further details of how to obtain licences are given in the Appendix.)

As a Spanish resident, I have a few, albeit relatively minor, advantages. I receive a licence every year from INAGA automatically, which saves having to re-apply and I only have to take to the road to get to the magnificent Ebro valley. It's a long trip, far beyond my bicycle radius, and so I trust to the services of ALSA, Spain's largest national coach network, nowadays part of the UK's National Express.

On the fairly long bus journey, leaving Valladolid at 21.30 and arriving at 06.00 the following morning, I generally pass the time napping or jotting down a few notes in my angling notebook or diary, a veritable *Piscatoribus Vade-mecum*, recording not only my experiences but also ever more extravagant hopes and expectations. I like to think of it almost as the journal of a Victorian adventurer, like those of Burton or Speke, a personal record of the exploits of a foreign, undeniably eccentric (at least from a Spanish perspective) and certainly obsessed, rod and line angler in the Iberian Peninsula.

On this particular expedition I was not taking along the minimal, lightweight gear and tackle which I normally carry everywhere by bike, details of which appear at the back of my diary as a check list against forgetting anything. There is more than one list there in fact, since each is governed by whichever species is to be pursued and at what time of year. Glancing at the winter list we naturally find all the necessaries for harrying the pike, since the bitter Castilian winter offers little else to pursue. There I have detailed a range of spinners, plugs and wire traces, snap tackle, sardines (pure fantasy, since live- and dead-bait fishing is illegal almost everywhere in Spain, although catfishing on the Ebro is an exception), rods, reels and rod-rests, landing-net, binoculars, etc., but below these we also find the following essentials:

- thick woollen fingerless gloves
- hand warmer, and fuel sticks
- hip flask (wi' a dram o' Talisker whisky)
- balaclava, scarf
- thermos flask
- big bar of 'El Gorriaga' chocolate
- 'Fisherman's Friend' lozenges

Although it was too late then to put right any omission or run back and fetch anything forgotten, the long-distance coach having already pulled out of the bus station, I had to just re-check everything to assure myself that all was in order. Reading down the list of the basic tackle items, I could not help but smiling, since those simple rods and reels, those neatly cut hedgerow rod-rests, from wild cherry or holm oak, and so on, most certainly did not form a part of the equipment for this particular adventure.

On this occasion everything had been replaced by the absolute latest in carp fishing technology . . . Greys 'X flite' rods, not with the standard carp rod action of say 50 to 150gm but rather of an extraordinary 1.5 kilos. Rods like these are capable of chucking out tremendous 'heaps of scrap metal', as is occasionally observed by certain unsympathetic members of the fly fishing fraternity. Such rods would probably not flinch at having to grapple with a 1000lb blue marlin on the high sea off La Habana. Then there are the reels: tremendous big pit fixed-spools with a line capacity of over 500m of 0.35mm (15lb, 6.5kg). Even the landing-net is of astonishingly giant size, with arms nearly a metre in length, a two-metre handle and net itself, a doubled, re-inforced mesh, capacious enough to receive fish near on 100lb. Then there is the rod-pod, a full metal jacket apparatus not only designed to hold the rods in position but equipped with the most advanced of bite alarm devices, capable of detecting the minimum of movement in the line, where it passes over the sensors. Moreover, practically every element of this formidable gear comes in duplicate, to the great delight of specialist fishing tackle manufacturers around the world, since the really dedicated big carp angler absolutely must have two of everything if he is to be taken seriously.

Half hypnotised by the purring rhythm of the coach's wheels over the horizon-to-horizon tarmac of the motorways, I wondered whether I would really have need of all this specialist tackle. But I quickly realised that fishing at fairly considerable distances and taking into account the weight of the combined ledger and bait and, above all, the renowned size and strength of the Ebro carp, far from being encumbered, I would be quite simply, well prepared and equipped, I hoped.

The time skipped by surprisingly quickly, despite the many hours on board, and occasional service area breaks in the small hours of the night. Time spent mostly dozing off and starting suddenly awake from dreams that seemed more like nightmares, imagining tremendous arm-wrenching bites and rods hooped over, quite wrecking any real hope of a good night's rest. It was a southern *valpurgisnacht* after all.

The final stage was by local bus from the city of Lérida or Lleida, back across the border from Catalonia and down the C-1310, along the Aragonese sides of the river Cinca to Mequinenza, on the banks of the great reservoir. The angler cannot but feel the impact of such a vast expanse of fresh water upon all his senses. Standing at the water's edge, the surrounding high hills seemed great mountains, lit by the first rose-toned hints of the new day. A speck in the pale blue was suddenly recognised as a vulture and as my eyes focussed I spotted several others. The huge birds, seemingly impassioned by simple aerial geometry, quartered the firmament and traced their ascending circles as they rose ever higher on the dawning thermal currents. There was every chance of seeing a black vulture among them, perhaps even a stray lammergeier. Nearer to, great dark clusters of huge *cañaveral*, reeds, were silhouetted at intervals against the water. The long, pointed leaves glistened with frosty dew and the waving seed fronds seemed lacquered with the crisp silver of a winter dawn. A fitful breeze caused the great stems to wave, and from deep among them came those creaking sounds so familiar to fields of late season maize and yet always disquieting, as though something unspeakable was awaking therein.

Then came the extraordinary clatter of as many as a thousand cormorants, a vast dusky mass that extended low over the surface like a disembodied shroud, constantly changing its shape, searching for signs of the huge shoals of bleak that might suddenly glitter through the ripples where they attempted to escape the marauding jaws of the numerous zander hunting below them. Wild life around the Sea of Aragón was every bit a match for the wide Masai Mara or the Serengeti on the Discovery channel.

Before actually getting to the water I stopped at the old Bar Sport, to purchase the day ticket. The bar opened early and was already buzzing with local life. Truck drivers, bakers, road sweepers and delivery men were all roaring at each other along the length of the disappointingly modern, shiny aluminium bar. All manner of breakfast combinations were on offer. Spicy chorizo sausage, large wedges of tortilla, the great Spanish omelette, with crisp fresh bread and accompanied by beer, orange juice and coffee, or just plain croissants might be leisurely enjoyed during the process of the bar woman's writing out the details of your '*permiso*', with your name, your licence number etc., frequently interrupted by the more important demands of her other customers.

Most of the language the visitor will hear among the locals is Catalonian, in fact, and not Spanish, or Castilian, at all. This language is the mother tongue of Catalonia but is spoken not only there and in Andorra but also across the border west into parts of Zaragoza, including Mequinenza. It is, moreover, the language all the way down the Mediterranean coast, the famous '*costas*' - Costa Blanca, Brava or Dorada, etc. In the region of Valencia, this same language is known as Valenciano, and out on the Balearic Islands, it is Mallorquín. This can be confusing, not to say frustrating, for many visitors to Spain, including the angler who has spent some months acquiring the basics of Spanish before coming out to fish the Ebro. Spanish will always be understood, of course, but Catalonian is what he will mostly hear spoken and, as often as not, fail to understand: '*bon día*' instead of *buenos días*, '*mol bé*' instead of *muy bien*, or '*deu*' instead of *adiós*.

Unlike some other bars in Mequinenza, where the sheer number of foreign anglers means you will experience a real linguistic melting pot, in the Bar Sport there is a much more local mix of predominantly Catalonian and some Spanish.

While I was waiting, conversation turned from local politics, and the shenanigans of the mayor, to the efficacy of the so-called truck drivers' breakfast. This classic of old-time Spanish culture, not so commonly seen now in these days of thoroughly modern European rules, regulations and police traffic controls, is the '*sol y sombra*'. A heavy set, powerful-armed old man at the bar is loudly bemoaning the fact of its passing. The transport fraternity was not what it once was, he lamented. Retired ten years since from long-distance truck driving, Pau was telling the younger men how he thought nothing years ago of knocking back a couple of *sol y sombras* along with his strong black coffee, before climbing into his cab and heading for Athens or Tangiers. He drove all the better for it, he assured the smiling sceptics, and promptly called for another. We all look on as the chubby, chuckling lady behind the bar poured another huge measure of cheap brandy into old Pau's glass, followed by the same quantity of Anis del Mono, something like Pernod, and the two spirits mix uneasily together in a swirl of glistening sunshine (*sol*) and cloudy shade (*sombra*). By old British standards this amounted to about eight or ten gills, which, I thought quietly to myself, was also a way to distinguish certain varieties of huge deep water shark. In fact, I suddenly realised, the measures would be eight or ten eighths or tenths of a gill not whole gills, perhaps half a pint in total, but the shark-like devouring effects on mind and body still rang true.

Once I had my ticket, I was soon back outside and strolling, albeit rather heavily laden, along the riverside road and out of the village. I felt like a walk;

my chosen swim was at no great distance and in fifteen minutes or so I would be there. The early chill morning air blew softly off the reservoir and carried a particular aroma, a pungent smell more associated with the sea than with the riverside. It was not only the densely ionised atmosphere of so vast an expanse of water but that this was overladen with the heavy scent of the most popular bait among anglers there, the 'halibut pellet'. In modern carp angling on the Ebro and elsewhere, this processed fish feed pellet produced for farmed halibut, very rich in fish oils and proteins, had become almost ubiquitous.

I suddenly shivered with the cold and decided to indulge in the soothing effects of a further aroma, that of hot coffee. The effects of the tiny *'café solo'* in the bar had already worn off and so I set my gear down and poured a steaming cupful from my flask. Amazing things these modern flasks, I thought, as I raised the mug in a toast to the glorious surroundings. Sipping the warming black liquid, I pondered the prospect and the prospects before me, becoming wrapped at the same time in the billowing clouds of steamy vapour, as though I had become, after all, a wizard busily concocting a magic fish-entrancing potion.

Far below the surface of the great lake-like river lay the tumbled brick and adobe walls, the blank staring window frames and collapsed, sodden beams and rafters, of all that remained of old Mequinenza. There were odd telegraph poles that strode into the water and vanished, and even a whole football pitch, with its surrounding walls and buildings, great boards plastered with layer upon layer of mushy posters announcing once in a lifetime matches, the greatest games ever, and unforgettable classics. All were submerged and long lost to time, on what were the outskirts of the original riverside village. All this hidden topography, needless to say, could cause serious problems for the angler. Beneath the apparently quiet and steady ripples there were enormous snags and all manner of endless obstacles across the river bed where tackle might be lost and where the wily carp could seek refuge, wrapping the line around old stonework, door posts or mangled rust-eaten machinery. It was yet a further reason why the tackle had to be up to the task. I stumped on a little further and at last reached my goal, the Telegraph Pole Swim. I started to set up my gear, to make ready all and every preparation for the long campaign, while the temperature, even though the day was now well under way, continued to fall ever lower.

'What on earth . . .' we might well ask, 'was this man doing, setting up to fish for carp on such a bitterly cold, soul-less winter morning? The carp is a summer fish, anyone could tell you that!'

Even the most fervent believer might be prone to doubt. I could not help casting my mind back to that old standby from years ago, BB's *Confessions of a Carp Fisher*, where the author once observed that 'Carp fishers disappear in autumn and are not seen until the following midsummer . . .' Although modern carp fishing certainly may lay claim to a good number of celebrated winter catches for many anglers around the world, for most there is still little to be done over the winter period except perhaps clean and repair their carp tackle, or more likely, invent ever more ingenious new rigs and baits in anticipation of the new season. But on the river Ebro, despite temperatures being at least as low and often a good deal lower than in England, things were different.

Bankside paths and tracks or roads trace the immensity of the Embalse de Ribarroja, with its 280 kilometres of dramatically irregular coastline, its tremendous depth and wealth of vegetation and animal life, where the carp live a somewhat altered natural cycle as compared with most populations of *Cyprinus carpio* in the rest of Europe. The reasons for this are both varied and curious and, indeed, extend back through many hundreds of years of Spanish history.

The carp was introduced into the Iberian Peninsula towards the end of the sixteenth century from fish farms in France, which had in turn been supplied by other specialist fish keepers and breeders in Eastern Europe. The fish introduced were already heavier bodied, more sedentary creatures than their ancestors, natives of the waters of the greater Danube basin. These carp were very much accustomed to the good life, well adapted to the sluggish waters of large lakes and reservoirs and yet they conserved, somewhere deep in their genetic make-up, their ancient migratory instinct. Finding themselves once more in a vast river system, for the Sea of Aragón is fed by the Ebro, the Cinca and the Segre rivers and their tributaries, the arrival of spring triggered their hereditary impulse to set off in search of new feeding grounds or spawning areas. Once temperatures dipped the carp would return to deeper water, towards the great dams, where they would be safe from the severe cold of winter.

From the 1970s onwards, Ebro carp have been obliged to share their environment with Europe's if not the world's, largest freshwater predator, *Silurus glanis*, the giant European catfish. This formidable and very long-lived creature is rumoured in its native territory to attain weights in excess of 200 or even 400 kilos, perhaps 500 to 1000lb, the truth of which will undoubtedly be seen in the highly propitious environment of the Ebro. These silurian monsters have only been in the Ebro for 30-odd years, after being surreptitiously, and indeed illegally, introduced by a German angler with a vision for the future of great sport for his countrymen on their Spanish holidays. Verified specimens have recently been caught in excess of 200lb, fish that are still mere youngsters, so that in a further 50 years they may attain double or three times that weight, even, conceivably, an imperial three figures.

It so happens that the giant European catfish and the carp, despite finding themselves artificially thrust together in the waters of the Ebro valley, through the agency of man, are in fact natural co-habitants, having shared their original native habitat in the greater Danube region as predator and prey for many thousands of years. In consequence of their long association, mutual success of each species depended upon a certain behavioural equilibrium. The carp, for example, was always primarily a species most active in the daytime, where the catfish was largely nocturnal. Further elements in this relationship concern the seasons, as we shall see shortly.

The appearance of the catfish in the Ebro system led, not surprisingly, to the decimation of native fish species but the carp continued to thrive; indeed the rapidly growing population of catfish is having a positive effect on carp from the angler's perspective, since many small, as well as weaker or diseased individuals, succumb to the predator and the main carp population is of ever bigger and stronger fish.

Returning to the matter of winter carp fishing, it is significant that where the catfish becomes progressively less active as temperatures fall and eventually seeks out holes and hollows in which to virtually hibernate, the carp has not only altered its behaviour and become more active in the colder months but also, to the great satisfaction of anglers, tends to group together in various areas of the immense reservoir system, areas which carp specialists have made it their business to identify. This might be yet a further reason for contracting the services of fishing guides, since fish location in an area of around five million hectares, or 12.5 million acres, is an incredibly daunting prospect. So, why had I not done so? Well, in fact, I had, in a manner of speaking. I had done my homework and been in touch with an old friend of mine, who lived in Barcelona, Pau Castells, a railway engineer and fly fisherman, who had taken a purely academic interest in this stretch of the Ebro. He usually fished the upper reaches of the Segre for trout, but had a small summer apartment for several years in Mequinenza. During his evening strolls along the waterside, he had stood by to observe many encounters between anglers and 'the most extraordinary monsters'. After witnessing innumerable captures, he wrote to me with details of how and when and where these contests took place. It was Pau also who first suggested I came to give it a try but I had taken far too long about it. By the time I had got around to making this trip he had long left the village, his work had taken him abroad, but I would certainly be letting him know how it went.

It had again been Pau, I recalled, that had first told me about the earliest Spanish angling books, known as the *Dialogue* and the *Astorga Manuscript*. We had been waiting on one occasion for a Madrid friend of Pau's, ahead of a mountain biking trip up into the hills outside Vic, a small town on the edge of the Pyrenees. Pau was a thorough Catalonian and as such, rather impatient with Castilian punctuality, or more correctly speaking, their entire lack of it. It was already fifteen minutes after the time we had agreed to meet and by way of diversion I mentioned Anthony Trollope's somewhat disparaging remarks about Spanish time keeping, namely that 'Men have no idea of Time in any country that is or has been connected with Spain'. This remark had appeared in the 1830s and the truth was that nothing much had changed since, although Pau vehemently averred that such was not the case in Catalonia.

While we continued to wait, our conversation turned to fishing books and Pau told me about a sixteenth century soldier by the name of Fernando Basurto, who had written an intriguing little book known as the *Dialogue between a Hunter and an Angler*, originally published in 1539, just forty years after Dame Juliana's famous *Treatise*. The Spanish tract, according to its prologue, was directed at the type of humble fisherman that goes down to the river in search of cyprinids, as against the more aristocratic folk, who, during the non-hunting season, sought exclusively the nobler salmonids.

The author names his angler's preferred species, which included barbel, Iberian chub, nase, eels and tench; fish, which he remarks, are generally pursued for their eating qualities but also for simple sport and entertainment value, surely one of literature's earliest references to the pure art of coarse fishing, not to say pleasure angling. Basurto's 'Old Fisherman' defends his art before the arguments of his antagonist, a 'Knightly Hunting Gentleman' and speaks persuasively in favour of the humbler species, which he fishes for with just the same enthusiasm as for the trout, remarking most particularly the sporting value of the barbel. Pau already knew about Dame Juliana but then asked me if I knew about the Spanish equivalent. Around one hundred years after the *Dialogue* came the rather more famous *Astorga Manuscript*, or 'The Book of How to Manufacture and Prepare feathers for Trout Fishing', published in 1624 by the nobleman Juan de Bergara, whose dominions extended around the town of Astorga in Castile, where the trout streams were strictly controlled by the church, particularly the old town's bishops. Bergara's piscatorial interests were focussed entirely on the brown trout and fly fishing for them. The book was full of wonderfully detailed descriptions of flies as well as the frequent remark for each pattern, '*mata bien*', i.e. kills well.

Just then, Pau's rather tardy friend arrived, profuse with apologies, which we both rather laughed at, it has to be said, before setting off at last for the Pyrenean hills. Nowadays, I have facsimile versions of both the old Spanish manuscripts and even pdfs of them on my Kindle, which are absolutely ideal for whiling away the time when waiting for the least punctual of people to turn up. I wonder what Basurto's old man would have made of the carp, especially the huge fish in the country today, or the giant catfish come to that. Carp were not introduced into Spain until around a hundred years after the *Dialogue* appeared, and the catfish, of course was a much more recent development.

The loss of virtually all the originally native species to the central area of the Ebro, particularly some of the Iberian barbel, might reasonably be considered an ecological disaster, however, the Sea of Aragón, principally the Embalse de Ribarroja, is in reality a vast, extraordinarily complex and totally new, man-made natural phenomenon. Apart from the carp and the catfish there are abundant populations of other foreign species such as the zander, *Lucioperca lucioperca,* the perch, *Perca fluvialis* and the black bass, *Micropterus salmoides,* as well as bait fish including bleak, *Alburnus alburnus,* rudd *Scardinius erythrophthalmus* and roach *Rutilus rutilus,* none of which are native to any part of the Iberian Peninsula.

While I continued to ponder the wonders of my special Halloween weekend environment, I had also set up my formidable battery of rods and lines, positioned the rod-pod and was now ready to drill a few 22mm pellets, which I then mounted on a handful of hair rigs, so as to have plenty readily to hand and save time later on. I also tied a handful of water soluble PVA web-bags, packed with 5mm turbot pellets, which I would tie to the ledger with PVA string. Once this payload reached the riverbed, the bag would quickly dissolve and all the highly proteinated little pellets would spread out to form a patch of attractive flavours around the hook bait. Part of this strategy concerned the nature of the riverbed itself, which was for the most part a mass of crumbling mud brick and stone work. The tiny pellets would slip into all the cracks and crevices and so, when the fish approached, attracted by the pervading essences of fish oils, it would commence nosing the riverbed in search of the food itself, bubbling and clouding the water. Amid the billows of sediment and the inevitable reduced visibility, the carp was likely to locate the larger, hair-rigged pellet and hopefully not detect the hook.

This whole system of carp baiting and fishing is well known nowadays but it caused something of a revolution on the Ebro not so many years ago when it was found that the formidable, predatory giant catfish was to be equally seduced by the same method. A local carp and catfishing specialist and angling guide, who I later discovered was Colin Bunn of Catmaster, was already well-aware of the effectiveness of halibut pellets for carp and suddenly found that his clients were repeatedly suffering bites, hook ups and, all too frequently, tackle breakages as the result of the interest in the baits shown by the giant catfish. It was a most surprising circumstance, given that the catfish was a predator; the ideal bait locally, as well as elsewhere, being live fish, particularly eels, or deadbaits. The experience led him to experiment with large strings of hair-rigged pellets on the larger style catfish hooks, in combination with the much heavier rod and tackle combinations appropriate to the species, and before long his anglers were catching more and larger specimens of catfish than those local, longer established experts in catfish with their live or dead fish baits.

With my own gear organised at long last, I was ready to cast out to the two most promising points I could see from my chosen spot at the water's edge. Being able to handle the rods well and cast the combined bait, web-bag and lead, 80 or 100 metres, with the confidence that nothing would go wrong in mid-air, was essential. Many anglers nowadays are able to achieve this extraordinary feat, to yet greater distances, of 150 or 180 metres or even more. It must be said, however, that the truly advanced, expert angler is he who is able to guarantee the perfect positioning of his combined terminal tackle and baits to 200 or 300 metres without the least skill or effort on his own part. This method requires the services of a fishing guide or ghillie, an adept, moreover, with a small motor boat, dinghy or inflatable. Being afloat, the guide is not only able to position bait and tackle perfectly but may then freely and accurately ground-bait the immediate area with further quantities of pellets.

On that early winter's day, however, I did not have these excellent services to hand but cast my lines as best I could, keeping the rod high each time, and letting the line run smoothly through the rings as the bait dropped through the water. The tackle touched bottom at a depth of about 10 metres with that pleasingly gentle thud, which is transmitted to the angler through the line and the rod tip. Once the lead had settled, I took up the slack and set the rod in the rests of the rod-pod. I then connected the backbiter counterweights, adjusted the Delkims' sensitivity, tone and volume, and all was in readiness. Before settling down for what might well be a long wait, I catapulted out a few more free offerings of the 22mm pellets, as near as possible to each of the baits, in the hope of encouraging the carp to consider starting their early morning feed.

The Telegraph Pole swim was justly named, and had a good number of troublesome characteristics. Curiously enough the most significant of these was not the very evident pole with its tangle of broken wires and insulators immediately in front of me, some five or six metres out. There was something rather worse. At a distance of around 20 metres from the bank, below the surface, there was a very sudden vertical drop of three metres, formed by a brick wall, which ran for more than the full length of the old football pitch, almost parallel with the bank for 100 metres or so, gradually becoming lower, downriver. This phenomenon, needless to say, could prove a considerable difficulty to the angler when trying to bring in his fish safely from deep water. It was of the utmost importance that the angler tire the fish and bring it close to surface while still at a good distance from the bank before attempting to bring it in to the waiting net.

Should the angler not adhere to these tactics, the consequence, and sadly a frequent enough occurrence in this swim, was the appalling and all too brief rasp of the line over the top of the wall, before it broke and the fish and tackle were all lost. A further precaution I had taken had been to attach 20 or so metres of highly abrasion-resistant braid to the end of the lines, which then took the terminal tackle. The braid was surprisingly thin, 0.33mm, but had a breaking strain of around 80lb or 36kg, where the main line was only 15lb 0.35mm nylon monofilament.

Satisfied that all was as it should be, I settled back with that special patience peculiar to carp specialists, to await the first contact of the day. Almost curled up in my collapsible bankside chair I poured another coffee, since the air temperature was still irremediably falling. Pale sunlight gradually illuminated the great cliffs and high above Mequinenza town, the thirteenth century, seven towered castle had begun to glow a shimmering gold against the deepening blue sky.

Out of the corner of my eye, I suddenly caught sight of a curious object bumping on the ripples at the water's edge and so I jumped up to investigate. It turned out to be a broken and discarded, brightly coloured plastic toy, which seemed to have originally contained sweets of some kind. It was in fact the head of a comical punky red-haired penguin with yellow eyebrows, and a little further along the bank I noticed the lower half, complete with its fluorescent orange feet. I took up both parts and wandered back to my seat to see if they would fit together, which, with a firm twist of the head, they did, with a satisfying 'click' that resounded loudly in the serene morning air. It seemed a most appropriate good luck charm for the Day of the Dead

At that precise moment one of the electronic alarms suddenly emitted a sharp bleep before launching into a sustained scream as the line was wrenched into movement, the baitrunner spool humming its lower tone in accompaniment. I dropped the little penguin on to the seat, grabbed the rod and leant into a firm strike that was met by thrillingly powerful resistance. The rod hooped over and the reel groaned as the clutch reluctantly gave metre after metre more of line. I fought to control this initial run, keeping the rod high in order to take full advantage of its four metres of extra height. The carp eventually slowed and a rapid glance down at the reel showed that the fish has taken around 80 metres off the spool. At the other end of the line, the carp was heaving thunderously this way and that, attempting to rid itself of this sudden check to its freedom. Luckily, on its first tremendous run, the carp had not managed to get into a weed-bed or around any other deep water snags and so hopefully the battle could take place in open water. Only moments later the fish ripped off another 30 or 40 metres in the very same number of seconds, reaching somewhere around 25mph or 40kmh, which, curiously, I had noticed was the maximum speed permitted within the limits of the town. Fortunately, the carp's repeated charges soon lessened in violence and duration, and so began a rather more sluggish tug-o-war.

Time passed as I slowly and heavily gave or recovered line, the fish staying deep down and continuing strong against the steady resistance of both tackle and my own strength. Little by little, my arms and shoulders began to ache and a dull pain started in my wrists. Breathing deeply, and keeping the rod high, I shifted the strain from one hand to the other and back again, careful to maintain the pressure. The sun climbed higher and the carp continued to wrench the occasional metre of line, yet, as it seemed to me, with gradually decreasing power and impetus.

The carp had so positioned itself as to gain some advantage from a slight increase in the flow of the water. Some of the sluice gates down at the dam must have been opened and I noticed that the fish was now a good bit further to the right, further too, luckily, from the possible dangers of the telegraph pole. The main problem, however, continued to be the submerged wall, and the fish was still well down. My eye was suddenly drawn to my watch, which I had left by the side of the chair. Forty minutes had already passed and the fish was still a very long way out, 200 metres or more, and still felt immensely strong.

Just at that same moment I noticed a slight change in the angle of the line where it entered the water, a point which was gradually moving further away, cutting a vee across the placid surface. The great carp was coming up. Occasional thrusts and lunges still registered at the rod tip but as I obstinately hung on, I realised the fish was no longer taking line. A huge length of monofilament now extended across the water, singing its tension in the slight upstream breeze.

With consummate caution I began to exert a little more pressure and, still keeping the rod high, very gradually started to recover precious metres of line. I felt the advantage was swinging my way, yet I dared not pull too hard in case the fish should dive. The carp kited to one side then the other, only a metre or so below the surface but continued, albeit marginally, to approach the bank. Nearly an hour had passed since the strike and despite feeling more in charge, I still sensed the tremendous power of the fish as it repeatedly pulled and turned, staying obstinately some 30 metres out.

On such occasions, many a carp angler must have asked himself whether the roach man, the pike enthusiast or particularly the trout fisher, those so often his most vehement critics, had ever even imagined such an adversary as this, whether they had the least idea what such a battle might be like. The trout may tug and jump around a bit but, pound for pound, it has not even a tenth of a carp's strength and endurance, and all that without the assistance of running water. Furthermore, though we may regret the fact, there has never yet been a trout of 30 or 40 kilos.

I remained engaged in uneasy deadlock, my back and shoulders stiff and aching with the extending dull pain but yet I was still gaining precious lengths of line. This was a big fish, a very, very big fish. I hardly dared think about it, not before I had got it to the net. A sudden arm wrenching lurch and the fish plunged down towards the submerged wall. Risking everything, I had to keep the carp's head up, the rod hooped over spectacularly, the clutch tightened down as far as I dared, the line emitting a high pitched wail, but the fish was held, forced up to the surface and so came over. I suddenly spotted the knot between the braid and the main line and breathed with relief, now I had one further ally. Just as the braid reached the reel, the carp exploded through the surface and wrenched off a few metres, the knot slipping back through the rod eyes, but the fish was tired, it rolled over; huge, absolutely huge shimmering flanks of scales like ancient armour.

I slid down the bank, dragging the net into position, and inched into the water, my feet finding secure hold, the wide gape of the mesh at the ready. The sheer bulk and weight of the carp were now the main difficulty in the rock infested shallows. The fish was exhausted and yet still more than capable of one final surging tumble, which could yet spell disaster. Vast golden flanks glistened in the sunlight and the carp's eye seemed to fix the angler with a stare of incredulity, its great fleshy lips mouthing the cold morning air. 'How could such an ungainly creature on two legs have beaten me!' The huge fish at long last slid over the rim of the net and was trapped. The carp then became calm, not deigning to thrash about as perhaps a smaller specimen might have done, as I eased the large barbless hook from its hold. Leaving the rod to one side, I dismantled the arms of the net, trembling with a mixture of nervous relief and sheer excitement, and struggled slowly up the crude remnants of steps some other angler had once cut into the bank. Folded into the unhooking mat, the fish remained impassive while I set up the weighing frame and grabbed the all-important camera. Taking the weight of the fish in the sling I heaved the handles up and on to the hook of the scales and let out an involuntary whoop of joy and surprise . . . 15kg 750g! Subtracting 600g for the sling, the carp was a colossal 15kg 150g, around 33lb 4oz in old money, a positively fantastic fish!

Another angler, just setting up his gear several hundred metres upstream, came running along the bank to get a closer look at the formidable capture and after some hearty congratulations, kindly played the part of official photographer. Details of the magnificent specimen, a personal best, would have to be written up later, first the fish had to be carried back down to the water and carefully released. Getting down the bank seemed more of a struggle than carrying the fish up had been but soon I was holding the tremendous bulk in the water once more. With a couple of great sweeps of its tail and a sudden splash, which left me delighted and dripping from head to toe, the carp glided back into the depths of the Sea of Aragón.

The other angler, who turned out to be a carp enthusiast from Barcelona called Jordi, was something of a rarity among those fishing at Ribarroja, where the majority are usually British or German. Odd though it may seem, Spanish anglers are very much the minority and those who do come are usually merely holiday makers with unpretentious tackle, who cast out their floats into the margins after small fish and occasionally get a tremendous shock, especially those who manage a rather longer cast. A rod seen leaping off the bank and disappearing into the lake was not an infrequent occurrence. Jordi was of quite another breed, as I found out later, a veritable Señor Gadget, as he was equipped with all the latest and most spectacular tackle money could buy, including a remote digital receiver alarm device which he carried in the breast pocket of his shirt, something of a novelty at the time. As Jordi headed back to start fishing himself, I rebaited and made ready for a new cast.

Looking out over the water, I noticed the very slow progress of a broad curve of coloured water coming downstream, washing into the main river from the Cinca and the Segre, and decided to cast to the furthest point of its outer edge. With both rods on duty once again, deceptively at rest on the pod but ever alert, my mind turned to thoughts of breakfast. I knew from what Pau had told me that bites on this stretch of the embalse were at best infrequent, there was always time to sit back and relax, jot down a few ideas and observations into my notebook, details of that superb first fish, weather conditions, bait, etc., and of course, there was ample time for breakfast. Guided fishing trips scored well here too, since they usually included the services of a driver, who would head off into the town and return with the Full Monty, should such be the demand, or else bacon rolls, or croissants and coffee.

Since I had so little time on this occasion and Pau had given enough information for at least a single day's fishing, I had decided to make a go of it alone but this had meant rather meagre self-catering. Consequently, that day's particular repast was limited but the sandwiches had survived the journey well enough and the second flask of coffee was still hot. Sitting back and gazing over the glorious view, my attention was drawn once again to the little penguin, a veritable talisman of good fortune, which had toppled over on to its side. I set it upright and placed it under the rods, there to stand vigilant until the next moment of action.

The day slipped by gently and without further event. Fishing for really big carp was surely the gentlest and most contemplative recreation, interrupted very occasionally by bursts of frantically wild and strength sapping activity. The hours drifted, the air was becalmed. The sun idled and the world seemed antediluvian in its quiet perfection. From far away, the angler might hear an odd shout sound across the great water, a sign of joy at the capture of a fine carp, or sometimes an anguished moan, heralding the loss, most surely following a long and finely balanced contest, of some great fish, perhaps the biggest that poor angler had ever seen or at least felt at the end of his line. I enjoyed my breakfast and my lunch, and late in the short afternoon, resolved to join in on that splendid Spanish tradition, the siesta. The temperature had risen softly and I felt warm in my chair. A few minutes, a quarter of an hour of oblivion, a chance to recapture some of the sleep filched from me on board the night bus.

Since the capture of the fish, I let an hour or ninety minutes pass before winding in and checking and replacing the baits. In the intervening periods I tied up a couple more web-bags, drilled more pellets and prepared replacement rigs. Each re-bait consisted merely of snipping off the previous rig and tying on the new one; the simple objective being to reduce to an absolute minimum the time a line spends out of the water. Late in the afternoon I had another carp, of around 25lb. 'A small one,' I laughed to myself, 'If I'd caught that in my local river, it would have warranted a real celebration!'

At 6pm the sun had dropped behind the high cliffs and both light and warmth were lost in a matter of seconds. With barely half an hour of daylight remaining, I packed up most of my gear, slipped on my head torch, but left the rods, as always, to the last minute. I recalled how as a small boy, it was next to impossible to abandon the water at the close of the day. There was always that last hope, that highly propitious last cast. I sat again and looked at the rods. Despite all the technology, the sensors, the alarms, backbiters and so on, I try to never really take my eye off the rod tips. From my seat on the bankside I can observe all the extraordinary flora and fauna of Ribarroja all through the day but at the same time I will see the slightest increase in tension, the merest movement of the top ring. The sensitivity of the alarms is such that a slight puff of wind might cause a bleep to sound and then I would remain staring at the rods just in case the false alarm turned out to be something other than a quirk of nature.

Biting off a piece of chocolate to accompany the last of the coffee I suddenly shivered as a slight chill clawed up from the water, like the malevolent spirit of a drowned man. At the self same moment one of the rod tips pulled slightly, almost imperceptively, to one side, marking the merest tightening of the line. The little penguin tipped over backwards and lay staring straight up the same rod. The movement at the tip was very slow, the line over the sensors did not move. Nevertheless, the nylon relaxed the same fraction and tightened again. I jumped up and struck hard, to be immediately met with a very dull, heavy resistance which moved off powerfully through the depths.

"That's no carp," I suddenly said out loud. The movement was slowly relentless with heavy intermittent thuds that came bumping down the line. The powerful rod was curved steadily over, the spool of the reel turning slowly as the great fish took line. It was still very early into this winter; the great swathes of Siberian cold had not yet penetrated the Ebro valley, indeed, it was still a mild day in a so far mild season. Those creatures accustomed to seek their winter refuges may not yet have done so. The fish continued its weighty progress towards the centre of the great lake; at least that was how it seemed, and the mind of the angler recalled the old Spanish refrain: *¡Al pez grande, darle cuerda!* Something like, 'Always give a big fish plenty of line!'

The constant pressure kept up but the fish was clearly tiring and slowly rising through the water. Half an hour passed as I gradually pressured harder and harder but the fish was stubbornly holding the midwater and kiting round alarmingly close to the sunken wall. Once again I felt as though my arms would be pulled from their sockets; the sheer weight and persistence of this fish were considerable but the tackle was strong, time would surely tell in my favour. Suddenly the fish switched tactics and rose quickly, pulling steadily and started off downstream. On tiptoe and holding the rod as high as I could, I wound furiously, determined to keep the fish up, when I suddenly felt the agonising scrape of the line over the stonework. I realised, though, that it was not the wall; the fish was already over it and powering through the rocks in the margins downstream. Letting my head hang back I revolved my shoulders in an attempt to alleviate the increasing pain. The braid was on the reel, the banging head movements of the fish felt much harder, transmitted through the ungiving line, so different from the sensations received through nylon. The line cut the surface very near the bank and the water boiled, with foam and small stones being kicked up by the thrashing tail of the fish. The cloudy, troubled surface suddenly broke open to reveal a broad greenish head with wide gaping, whiskered jaws and tiny eyes, followed by the long, heavy serpentine body, twisting and turning through the shallows. The extraordinary creature suddenly vaulted, seeming to turn full circle in the air, before crashing down into the water once more. It was as though it were a dance of death, singularly appropriate to the day. The creature, of course, had no way of knowing I would release it. Then, the fish became calm, as though resigned to its fate, and rolled over the rim of the net. It was a catfish of course, around 20 kilos of muscle and purblind power. Not the desired species on this trip but a formidable opponent and a thoroughly good test of the rod and reel, the tackle and the angler.

It took a good while to settle the wrenching mesh in the failing light but eventually it was done and then I sat back on my haunches quite fairly exhausted, the extraordinary Silurus at my feet, still twisting slightly within the confines of the net. Switching on the head torch, I trained the light on to the great primitive head of the catfish and eased out the hook from the thick, heavy, velcro-toothed jaws. The fish was so ungainly and heavy I could barely lift it and so I shinned up the bank for the camera and weighing kit. With considerable difficulty, I set up the weigh frame with two legs in the water and after subtracting the weight of the net, the fish proved to be over the 20kg mark at exactly 22kg (48lb 6oz). It made for an extraordinary day; having never fished for these creatures before, this fish was in fact the largest of any species of fish I had ever caught. It would not be long, however, before I would look back on this day with a wry smile. This fish would be small fry compared with those taken on my first real catfish expedition on the Ebro, over a few days the following summer. Heaving the great head back into the water, I watched the broad, sinewy, mottled back disappear below the muddy ripples. Away to grow and to fight another day. Packing up, I felt privileged to have been able to spend a day on this water, surely one of the most extraordinary angling venues anywhere in the world.

It had been, merely, another day's fishing, another day to be recorded in my angling diary, but, what a day, and what fish! A day that had meant an entire night's journey coming and another to return but which was not the first or the last I would spend at the Sea of Aragón. Later, dinner in the Bar Ebro, with its huge brightly lit sculptures of giant carp and catfish on the walls, provided a great opportunity to exchange stories in a mixture of English, German and Spanish, with a further added layer of cosmopolitan accents: Dutch, French, Polish and even Russian. Jordi had had one good fish of 30lb and had also lost some tackle to a seemingly huge catfish that he had struggled with for nearly three hours. It had finally taken all the line off his reel, a cool 500 metres, before shattering the tip of his rod and snapping the nylon at the reel. It was a pretty good fishing river story by any standards but nothing out of the ordinary on the Ebro. There were of course many more tales told, though the exact locations where the action took place were most jealously and quite naturally guarded.

One angler, the youngest of a bunch of lads from Sheffield, told how he had lost a carp that he swore was over six feet long, and was thoroughly, laughingly ridiculed in consequence, but the eyes of the men round about told a different story. Who could be sure, 40 and 50lb carp are caught frequently enough and the odd 60-pounder too. Perhaps that lad really did have on an 80-pounder or a 90, or was it perhaps that he had been seduced earlier in the day by an invitation to a truck drivers' breakfast and had dreamt the whole thing.

So, a couple of hours in the Bar Ebro meant a chance to wind down, to recover from the long day, to tell a fishy tale or two and to listen to all the saturnalia of others' angling yarns. There was a chance, too, to choose from an international range of bar snacks and meals before calling it a day and turning in. Or, as in my case, before travelling up to Lérida and catching the bus back to Valladolid. I still had a little while to wait before I had to get going, when, unbeknownst to me, the owner of the bar came in. He was chatting to some of his clients and his guides and since I was sitting alongside, I found myself drawn into conversation. Colin Bunn turned out to be great company, and tremendously knowledgeable as regards the local fishing, which, admittedly, had been his line of business for many years. Hailing originally from Birmingham, he had been a keen carp angler all his life and was also an obsessive collector of Lambrettas. We kept in touch after that meeting and met again at a UK angling fair when conversation turned to a future project I had in mind with Spanish television . . . but more about that in due course. For the moment, I had to leave Mequinenza and get back to Lérida. It didn't take long but the wait at the bus station seemed interminable, not least because late night buses left from a stop out in the street and it was bitterly cold. It was no longer the day but rather the night of the dead, there wasn't a soul to be seen. Odd scraps of litter, an empty can and a page from a newspaper gambolled about at the mercy of steely sharp gusts of wind, and I stamped my feet. No traffic, no cafés or bars anywhere within sight. I eventually heard the bus long before I saw it and it seemed like forever before it finally appeared. Once aboard the long distance coach, a little before one o'clock on Sunday morning, I was, once again, scribbling away in my notebook, and particularly remembered the curious little penguin and its intriguing gestures of good luck. I had it packed safely away and suspect that, like many a lucky, cork-bodied float in my boyhood, it would act as a charm for some time to come.

I also jotted a paragraph or two on the remarkable prowess of *Silurus glanis*, the giant European catfish, a veritable champion among the fish fauna of Spain and of the world. Despite its undeniably ugly appearance it was a formidable opponent and could certainly be caught here at weights well over 100kg. Then and there I resolved that I would set out to capture a really fine specimen. At least once in his life, the angler, whether living or just travelling in Spain, should face the ultimate challenge offered by the greatest of her resident species. It is a gauntlet thrown down by Nature herself that must surely be taken up.

I was feeling thoroughly well satisfied with the trip. A weekend at the start of November that had encompassed the festivals of Halloween and the Day of the Dead but would be remembered more for my encounters with more earthly, or rather aquatic giants, the great catfish on the one hand but, what was still more, it had been the weekend when I caught my biggest ever common carp, its weight signalled in my diary, not with a skull and crossed bones but with a large star in red biro.

* * *

'*Tres ingleses y un destino*' or, 'Three Englishmen, One Destiny', was the title given by the Spanish television company Caza y Pesca (Hunting & Fishing), to the video report we shot on the Ebro in June 2006. Something which is lost in translation, however, is that the Spanish title somewhat amusingly echoes that of the classic western movie *Butch Cassidy and the Sundance Kid*, which is known in

Spain as 'Two Men, One Destiny'. Needless to say, I hoped we wouldn't end up as those two did.

The original idea was to film a couple of days' fishing for the giant wels catfish in company with Colin Bunn of Catmaster, back in Mequinenza. When setting out to tackle the catfish, once again the need to contract guided fishing services cannot be stressed enough, whether making a film or not. Apart from obvious difficulties, like the location of the fish at a venue such as the immense Ebro reservoir system, there are numerous other conveniences which quickly become apparent, not least among which are the highly specialised tackle and the very particular catfish angling procedures. It was going to be quite an adventure, and our greatest hope was to be able to capture all the details on film.

It was to be my first return to the Ebro after my carp fishing trip the previous winter. My appetite had been whetted then by a chance encounter with a small wels of just 40 odd pounds, which had given my carp gear quite a hard time, and so this new venture was conceived with rather bigger catfish in mind. As plans moved ahead, it transpired that Norman and Maureen Smith, a well-known couple of expatriate, not to say mildly eccentric, anglers based in Málaga, would be fishing the Ebro at the same time. I knew they had never tackled the giant wels catfish before, since Norman and I had been correspondents for more than 12 years. Courtesy of the Spanish Correos postal service, we had exchanged letters over that period, across the 400 miles that separate our respective homes, at opposite ends of the Iberian Peninsula, but, we had never actually met. It was decided that our first meeting would make good television. Needless to say, our first encounters with really big *Silurus glanis* would too.

We were at the waterside early the first morning, with the film crew phoning me every half hour or so, as they drove up from Valencia, to clarify directions, since we were fishing at a location well off the beaten track. They also wanted to check on how things were going, since the appearance of a television camera on the scene was as often as not the kiss of death to any hope of actually catching something. Each time they called I told them the same thing, "Yes! The fishing's really great, we've just put another one back!" Their response was more incredulous every time and by the fifth or sixth call they were desperately trying to convince us to keep hold of the next capture so they could film it when they arrived. I told them not to worry, the cats were coming every half an hour or so. They clearly thought I was a lunatic, suffering from ichthyological or even feline hallucinations.

At 10 o'clock the film crew's van came trundling slowly along the track and eventually pulled up under the trees, near where we were sitting in the shade, keeping out of the already considerable heat. We all shook hands - Franjo and

José Miguel, freelance reporters and camera men, and the modern day Wild Bunch or Hole-in-the-Wall Gang: Norman and Maureen Smith, renowned carp experts, Colin, Head of Catmaster Tours, his top guide John Deakin, and myself.

With the formalities over, I suggested to the crew that they had better get the gear ready as quickly as possible as the next catfish bite was imminent. My fellow anglers were equally insistent but the crew looked at us awry, evidently doubting our veracity, or perhaps our sanity; nevertheless, they began unloading the van in some haste. They became practically distraught when we informed them that we had released yet another catfish since their last call, a 70-pounder, just moments before they had pulled up. I was just beginning to explain that we were fishing rotation style, taking it in turns to rush down to the water and strike whenever a bite came, when the furthest right of the rods' alarms started screeching.

Norman set off across the pebbles as elegantly as his sandals, or his knees, would allow and grabbed the rod.

"Don't forget . . ." John yelled after him, "Don't strike!"

Norman soon had hold of the rod and he leant back, asserting his body weight steadily against the run, with the rod doubled over as the catfish made its first concerted bid for freedom. This dramatic meeting of forces was enough to set the hook. Striking a running catfish was, to say the very least of it, ill-advised. The tremendous power of these creatures, their sheer size and weight, could wrench the rod off you or, if you managed to keep hold, drag you into the water more easily than might be imagined. The rods were hugely powerful, the reels heavy duty multipliers, and the line was 130lb braid, but even so, the violence of the catfish's reaction to a strike could be enough to shatter the rod, snap the line or at the very least rip the hook from its hold. Needless to say, many an unsuspecting angler had come to grief. Having someone like Colin or John on hand was a must.

Meanwhile, the cameraman had everything organised and was making his way down to where Norman was locked in combat with Europe's, if not the world's, largest freshwater fish. It transpired that this particular specimen was not a really big one, perhaps 50 or 60lb, but what was rather more interesting was that the TV crew had never filmed the species before and indeed, neither of them had ever seen one. Colin and I were standing a little back from the action and cast a glance at each other, as if to say, 'This is going to be fun!' Moreover, I suddenly remembered a moment from the western when Butch Cassidy is asked if he knows what he is doing with the explosives. And he responds with, 'Theoretically'. Unbeknownst to them, this camera crew was dealing with piscatorial dynamite.

The Ebro water was richly coloured with sediment in suspension, as it is most of the year, and so you could see nothing beyond the surface of the water. John was already in the shallows, a chinning glove on his right hand, and taking a loose hold of the line with the other, in order to guide the catfish to the bank. The cameraman was down on his haunches focussing his lens on the point where the line entered the water, hoping to get some good footage of the fish breaking the surface. He was expecting to see a fish, moreover a freshwater fish, usually a not particularly large member of the world's finny tribes. What exactly were the cameraman's expectations it is hard to divine - something like a trout, perhaps or a carp.

Suddenly, in a tremendous swirl, the broad head of the catfish, its great gaping maw and enormous whiskers, crashed through an eruption of muddy spray, straight at the camera.

"Woah!" cried José Miguel as he tipped over backwards, legs kicking in the air, one arm flailing but the other still holding the camera, and still filming, albeit capturing nothing more than a broad sweep of brilliant blue sky.

The rest of us burst into laughter. It was rather like the somewhat exaggerated blowing up of the train and Sundance's query: "Think you used enough dynamite there, Butch?" The film crew were more than a little disconcerted, particularly José Miguel, who had clearly seen his life flash before his eyes.

Very soon, though, we were all back concentrating on the fish. Colin and I dragged over the sling and unhooking mat ready for John as he heaved the fish out of the water and on to the green padded material. He slipped the huge size 10/0 circle hook free and no sooner had he done so than the massive jaws snapped shut with a lunge that suggested an attempt at biting him. José Miguel was impressed and had been alert enough to catch the moment on film just before we hoisted the fish up and read off the figure indicated by the Reuben Heaton 'Specimen Hunter' scales, at 64lb 8oz.

"Only a nipper," Norman remarked. "Let's see if we can't hook a nice big one next, and get the whole thing on film."

Franjo and José Miguel looked at each other.

"Oh yes," Colin added, "they get a hell of a lot bigger than that you know!"

"Don't sugarcoat it, Kid," I laughed. "Tell 'em straight!"

Lowering the sling once more, John splashed water from a bucket over the great long sinuous creature and flapped a corner of the sling over its head to keep it from thrashing around. As is the case with many fish species, covering their eyes will calm them considerably, often making them completely passive. Next, we quickly got a few trophy photos before returning the tremendous creature to the river.

Following the capture of our first catfish on film, we were soon all for relaxing back in the shade with a few early *cervezas*. Well, not quite all, both Colin and John wanted to get the line back out. It was an opportunity too, to film the whole process, from baiting up the rig to John rowing out the inflatable with the hookbait, dropping it into a likely spot and following up with a good quantity of free offerings.

The rig comprises a 3- to 5-foot length of the same braid as on the reel, tied below a free-running conical lead of 10 or 12oz. The hook is whipped with an enormous 8- to 10-inch hair of lighter braid ending, ideally, in a very large loop. As many as five or six of the largest size (22mm) drilled halibut pellets are then threaded on to the hair, with the aid of an enormous baiting needle. The last pellet then has the loop passed over it, the simplest imaginable trick to fix it in position and thereby have it act as a stop for the others.

The curious story of how these fish feed pellets came to be used as bait for such a formidable predator as the giant wels catfish has already been mentioned above. The pellets, produced originally for the fish farming industry, are a protein and fish oil rich food, ubiquitous in carp fishing nowadays, and consequently, over recent years, they had become the bait par excellence among the Ebro's carp anglers. Colin Bunn, realised that with adequate tackle these huge cats could be caught using the pellets, thereby avoiding the time consuming, messy, and even ethically unsound practice of live-baiting, which was usually done with small carp or eels.

Once adopted, the new catfish angling method quickly caught on and nowadays the largest specimens, over 200lb in weight, are frequently caught on the pellets.

An alarm suddenly sounded and it was my turn. I was off across the bumpy beach before Franjo and José Miguel could say, 'Action!' Taking a firm hold on the rod, I leant back, just as we had all been instructed, into the immense, juggernaut counterweight of my running catfish. The 'Awesome Wels'. It was a good name, it really was. A full-scale tug-o-war then commenced, during which I was dragged more than once to the water's edge. I had no real frame of reference for the sheer strength of these creatures but one thing was clear, the more I battled, the stronger the catfish fought back. Never in my life had I been pulled step after step, against all the resistance I could muster, against my very will, down the bank of a river and all but into the water. If I relaxed, or just simply weakened momentarily, the fish slowed too, which was certainly rather generous spirited behaviour, since, had it not done so, I would have been in the river. However, as soon as I recovered and winched in some line the catfish would pull away again with seemingly inexorable power. Experimenting at one point, albeit somewhat foolhardily, I really wound down hard and pumped the rod back as strongly as I could but the ferocity of the response was staggering and inevitably I was dragged from my position of relative safety, way up the bank, to near disaster. A wet foot was a small price to pay for my audacity.

Power, that is the word - dogged, heavy, ineluctable power. The relatively slow, yet ponderously determined resistance of a huge creature to escape capture was staggering. The sun was merciless, there was not the merest breath of air. I was soaked in sweat and my eyes burned as I blinked repeatedly through the stinging sensation in order to see where the line was going. My mouth meanwhile was dry, my tongue like leather, stuck to the roof of my mouth, while my back ached and my arms seemed about to be pulled from their sockets. Nevertheless, I began to win the battle. The powerweave of the carbon fibre, the torque of the multiplier and the incredible strength of the braid had begun to tell, and the great fish was at last approaching our media reception committee at the water's edge.

This time it was essential that the crew got the whole sequence of bringing the fish to land. The business of landing a giant catfish, however, is no easy matter. Landing-nets, even those spectacular specimen hunters' carp nets with a gape of 52 inches and more, are simply not enough. Moreover, landing a big cat is not really a one man affair. We all appreciate a hand when landing a good fish but in the case of catfish it could be sheer lunacy to attempt it on your own. Fishing with a guide has this yet further advantage. While you are struggling with possibly the biggest fish you'll ever catch in your life, your guide will be dragging out an enormous landing mat and donning a thick protective glove with a view to 'chinning' the catfish once it is played out.

The process is alarming to witness. While you are still, hopefully, on dry land and finally subduing your catch in the shallows, the guide steps into the water and takes hold of the line, while you maintain the pressure. The water around the guide is in violent torment with bow-waves and swirls huge enough to herald the coming of the Cracken. As the animal's great broad head thrashes the surface, sending water crashing up the bank like the aftermath of an ocean breaker, the guide's gloved hand plunges straight into the widening maw and grabs hold of the lower jaw. A fair bit of strength is needed at this critical juncture, since the creature's innate response is to twist itself like a crocodile tearing the hind leg from a hapless wildebeest. The guide then employs his own body weight, very likely a good deal less than that of the fish itself, along with every ounce of strength he has, to drag the catfish out of the water.

This cat was not only my personal best for the species but my biggest fish ever, at 105lb, and so it warranted a few good photos, some holding the great fish in the river as well as a few of the ritual dousing with water, a special treat for any angler who lands a catfish over 100lb. On this occasion enthusiasm ran high and Norman, Colin and John all had their buckets ready, buckets ostensibly kept to hand for wetting down the unhooking mat and the fish itself, the latter to avoid dehydration under the tremendous Aragonese sun. While I posed, still grinning like a Cheshire feline into the lens of Franjo's stills camera, I was most thoroughly drenched. Moments later, while I was dripping dry under the happily burning sunshine I noticed that my cat was a semi-albino, with a good part of its flanks a very pale cream in colour and flecked with shimmering pinkish silver. Upon my commenting on the fact, everyone's response was somewhat derisive, since they had all noticed this long before. I suppose I had been too busy with the excitement of the whole thing. To make matters worse I remarked:

"I thought there weren't any albinos along this stretch . . ."

"You just keep thinking, Butch. That's what you're good at!" laughed Colin.

"They can move about just about as much as they like you know," Norman added. "This side of the dam, anyway."

I thought it best to change the subject.

"Well, let's get him back in the water."

This time we also filmed the release sequence, getting some great footage of the creature's long body snaking past the angler's legs and disappearing among the bankside ripples. The fish obligingly lifted its tail at the last moment and gave a final flourish before vanishing below the surface. With that bit of film in the can, it was time to re-bait and take the line out once again, all of which was soon accomplished and filmed a second time, as the lowering, golden light was particularly good.

At this stage it was thought that we ought to film the positioning of the rods. These were mounted in a near vertical position using the kind of forged iron rod-rests beach anglers would be familiar with and which I remember spending some weeks making in Metalwork classes at school. Each licensed angler is entitled to fish with two rods and so we had six set up, in two groups of three, the first to the right and the other in the middle along the edge of our little beach area. Once John had rowed out and dropped the bait, he would raise an arm as a signal to the angler to take up the slack, place the rod in the rest and switch on the alarm, which was clipped to the rest itself.

With the rod in position, it was important to tighten down the drag. I thought I had done this well enough but when John was back on the bank, he thought it advisable to check, since a novice catfish angler such as myself was not to be trusted. And indeed so it proved. For a moment I imagined I heard the voice of the Sundance Kid: "The total tonnage of what you don't know is enough to shatter . . ." a splendid, custom built Eurocat rod, at the very least.

John was able to pull line off rather too easily and so tightened the multiplier's star drag down until he could no longer do so, at least not with his bare hands. I was invited to test the result and very nearly cut my palms to shreds trying. It seemed excessive, even dangerous, to leave the reel like this but I was assured that such resistance would be needed. It wasn't long before I was able to see this for myself. The third catfish to take since the crew had arrived, picked up the bait on that self-same line. The alarm sounded and the rod doubled over incredibly and fairly bounced as the fish ran. More incredible, however, was the fact that the line was pulling off the reel fast, as though the drag were barely set at all.

This was Maureen's fish and Norman happening to be nearer to the rod, he rushed for it, leaned back to set the hook and moments later handed it over to her. Despite the rod's repeated thudding with the movement of the fish, the handover was slick enough to be the envy of Olympic relay runners. Once having hold of the rod, Maureen staggered at first, with a startled glance at the camera, but quickly recovered. It made a great shot and it looked as though this fish might be the big one. We all gathered round, the crew filming, Norman and myself getting pictures with our own cameras and John giving important advice as poor Maureen held on for dear life. But there was no doubting her angling skill, and much to Norman's chagrin, it seemed she was about to out-fish him again. History might well have been about to repeat itself but there was no hurry, Maureen's fish having run into a distant channel, out in the deep water, where, by the looks of things, it was decidedly intending to stay.

Suddenly, one of the other alarms rang out and Norman was again sprinting off across the beach. A few moments later, I left Colin, John and the crew with Maureen and ran across to where Norman was busy battling. His didn't seem to be much of a contest, however.

"Another small one," Norman sighed, and with a glance over towards his better half, "I think Maureen's is bigger than mine . . ."

There was little doubt about the truth of this observation. Maureen continued to be engaged in a serious wrangle, her rod doubled over and the line singing across the slight off-water breeze that had thankfully sprung up to aid her. John came over to attend to the landing of Norman's fish, which turned out to be a tiddler of around 40lb.

"That would have been something on your carp rod," he said.

Norman agreed and glanced again over towards Maureen, with an expression that revealed rather more than a touch of envy. His catch was a good-looking, well-proportioned fish, however, shimmering green in colour and just exactly like my first ever, from the dreaded Telegraph Pole swim. In one of those coincidences, which always seem to occur in angling, Norman's catfish turned out to weigh 48.4lb, exactly the weight of my fish on that previous occasion. We noticed that this fish was very muddy under the belly and John observed that it had doubtless been laying up somewhere on the bottom and not actively feeding, perhaps because of a recent snap of chilly, wet weather. He had seen a number of fish like this over the past week but now that the temperature was soaring it certainly seemed they were back looking for food. We took a couple of pictures, returned the fish and got the line out again before strolling back across the beach to see how Maureen was getting on. She had been wrestling with her cat for nearly an hour by this time and was most certainly winning, despite having had to follow the fish to the far end of the beach. Her line now entered the water around 20 or so yards out but the cat was staying down, still stubbornly resisting. Nevertheless, John ambled over, donning the glove as he went, a sure sign that the fish was almost ready for landing. Once again José Miguel was at the water's edge and managed to film a magical moment when the catfish surfaced, its full length seeming to dwarf the six-foot tall figure of John Deakin, knee deep in the same area of water.

This catch made for the best footage of the whole report, most of the fight having been recorded and now the landing, unhooking and weighing. At 168lb, it was the best fish of the day and indeed of the whole session, over two metres long and in solidly superb condition. The ensuing photographs featured a slightly bedraggled but triumphant lady angler sitting with the enormous creature across her lap. With Colin, Norman, John and myself alongside her, the fish still took up the greater part of the frame. Maureen soon also had the pleasure of receiving her buckets of congratulatory water, before the beast was released back into its murky home, to grow even larger and to fight another day.

Later in the afternoon, Norman finally got his hundred too and the film of that dousing proved to the best of all, water pouring down his cheeks and dripping copiously from the ends of his beard, entertaining enough to be included finally in the finished film.

Our intrepid angling team fished on till late but there was little further action worthy of comment, a few incautious cyprinids of around 20lb coming to our carp rods last thing and seeming almost insignificant after such a day's fishing. Eventually we retired to the Bar Ebro, where Colin oversaw the provision of splendid dinners and drinks before we all retired ahead of an early start next day.

The following morning, we all met early to film the arrival of the leading characters in our story into Mequinenza and, of course, to shoot the spontaneous and dramatic first meeting (particularly good by the third take) of myself with Norman and Maureen.

Also to be filmed on the second day were some conversations between the various members of the Wild Bunch, which would provide a little biographical information, some history and local knowledge, with expert input from Colin, as well as a few more scenes of the '*tres ingleses*' struggling with giant catfish.

Back at the riverside, we began as we had done early the previous day with some fine carp, which this time we were able to see filmed, but soon enough the catfish moved in once again. Catching and shooting were fast and furious until José Miguel suddenly announced that they were running out of film. What remained would have to be kept for the interviews and we half hoped, admittedly with some reluctance, that this second day would not produce any bigger fish than Maureen's 168-pounder, which otherwise would absolutely have to be filmed. In the end, there was no need for concern. The fish stayed obstinately below the 150lb mark for the rest of the session.

During a lull in the action that afternoon, Franjo organised the interviewing sequences, each of us giving our various angles on the catfish. The real specialist, of course was Colin. He told the story of how he had come out to the Ebro back in the 1990s to fish for carp and had quickly seen the potential for business as a carp angling guide and then his move on to the catfish. He now has hundreds of clients a year and employs three full-time guides, fishing for carp during the winter months when the cats are in semi or total hibernation and then during the warmer months everything is almost exclusively dedicated to the giant catfish. While he runs the practical side of the operation, his mother Kate does all the paperwork back at the family home, now become 'Siluro House', in Birmingham.

Next, Norman was able to plug the British Carp Study Group, he being that excellent institution's regional organiser for Spain. For carp fishing he was using a pair of rather fine rods, issued exclusively for members of the BCSG to commemorate 30 years of the group's existence in the year 2000. Norman went on to praise enthusiastically the Ebro's carp, that species being his first love, and pointed out that here 20-pounders were nothing at all to write home about; 30s, 40s and even 50s were to be expected but there was every chance of a 60, and nowadays it seems only a 60 is something really special.

For my own part, I was able to talk about the fact that it really was no surprise that so many of the world's carp anglers made a beeline for the Ebro, with such spectacular specimens to fish for. Moreover, these fish are wild, not pets with names and pedigree kept in little French or English waters, fed up to size and then pulled out periodically to claim a national or even a world record. The vast Sea of Aragón, though man-made, is wild too. The old river course, the flooded irregular terrain, including whole towns and villages along with their hazardous walls, abandoned machinery and telegraph poles, the pumping stations at irrigation extraction points, the estuaries of tributary rivers, all combine to form an exceptional environment. There are no specially constructed artificial underwater features here, and no conveniently landscaped swims and approach points. On the Ebro, the specialist carp men and the guides have to do their homework and know their angling.

Coming to catfish, the Ebro experience was a vital part of my research for *The Complete Book of the Giant Catfish*, the book I was writing on the species for Medlar Press at the time, and later published in 2009. I duly plugged this as much as I could, although the book of course was not really destined for a Spanish audience. I also went on to praise the skill and hard work of both Colin and John, without whom our adventure would never have succeeded, and the enthusiasm of Norman and Maureen, who made the report all the more entertaining.

Once the interviews were over, we all sat back and relaxed in the shade, as the evening sun was still very warm, perhaps not too concerned whether the catfish continued to be active or no. Needless to say, our conversation waxed piscatorial. My research for the catfish book had already led me to uncover some startling information, not least the following yarn from Russia:

One of European Russia's largest lakes is Kuybyshev Reservoir, an immense water with an extension of 6,450 square kilometres, larger still than the Sea of Aragón. The reservoir is contained between dams on the great Volga river, which is native territory to *Silurus glanis*. As is the way with legendary waters, among many of the townsfolk and villagers of the region, Kuybyshev is rumoured to be bottomless. Many vessels ply their trade across the reservoir and the number that have vanished without trace over the years is startling. Lurking in the depths, even before the river's waters were contained, there was said to be a colossal beast, a catfish, known to have pulled ships under and swallowed all hands. Its huge whiskers acted like tentacles and enveloped the stricken craft causing it to capsize. All manner of ships have been lost but fishermen, trawling the waters with their deep nets, tell the most frequent stories of the monster catfish, which will seize the netfuls of fish as they are being brought up and drag the hapless vessel under. Though precious few have lived to tell the tale, there is one man, old Viktor, from the town of Saratov on the Kuybyshev waterside, who has sworn never to go aboard ship again. He was a fisherman, the only survivor of the sinking of his vessel *Babuchkin*, and he claims to have seen the monster catfish alongside his trawler: 'A huge grey beast, the same length as my ship and at the head it was just as wide!'

According to his story, the monster upset the trawler, tipping all the crew into the water. Viktor became tangled in flailing ropes as the vessel went over and swears he saw the beast swimming round and round the ship like Moby Dick gulping down each and every man where they thrashed about on the surface. Eventually the great catfish sunk from view and Viktor managed to escape, set adrift on a shattered spar and halyard, as his old trawler went down. He was finally rescued after drifting to shore on the tangle of ship's rigging that had saved his life.

Such tales were good entertainment as we sat under the trees ostensibly waiting for a bite and Colin had one which was rather more local. Only a few years before, stonework on one of the dams which contain the waters of the Ebro, was found to be in need of superficial repair below the water line. In due course a team of frogmen were sent down to carry out the repairs but very shortly afterwards they reportedly ran screaming from the water because they were allegedly being nibbled at by huge underwater monsters. The chief of works was not impressed, claiming that it was merely a ruse to support a demand for a higher rate of pay for the job. The frogmen, however, refused to go back into the water until the matter was investigated. They testified at a formal enquiry that jaws a metre wide would loom at them out of the murky darkness and bite at their arms and legs It was soon discovered that the monsters were peckish or perhaps just curious giant wels catfish and that they were indeed approaching and nipping at anyone daring to be busy at work in their element.

In the end, reinforced steel cages, of the sort used by Pacific Ocean divers wishing to feed and film great white sharks, were brought in for the men to be submersed in and they resumed work, at a higher hourly rate after all, given the added labour risk attached to being observed by tiny eyes in the gloom and see-ing the bars of their cages chewed by leviathan jaws while they were busy with the masonry.

We then moved on to consider how curious it was that anglers from the world over came to Spain to fish for the catfish when it wasn't a native species to the Iberian Peninsula and had only been established in the country for 30-odd years. The simple reason why the Ebro had become the world's most impor-tant wels fishery was in part because anglers were virtually guaranteed an encounter with what would probably be the biggest fish of their lives. The cat-fishing was exceptional and word had got around. Colin's Catmaster Tours business had had customers from 27 different countries over the past ten or so years, including anglers from as far afield as New Zealand and the USA.

When I had asked him early on the first day how he viewed our chances of getting a good catfish on film, he had smiled and quite casually remarked that we would probably pick up a carp or two early on but by mid-morning the cat-fish would most likely move in on the feeding carp, in the hope of picking off a sick or weaker one. Having our baits at different distances all along the gently shelving riverbed that led down to the deeper, main channel of the river, there was every chance we would start catching them. The fact of the matter was, that this was exactly what happened. It was as though Colin had been out there day after day in a submersible observing exactly what the fish were up to and working out his strategy. It was really impressive. There was no doubt that local knowledge combined with many years of experience was everything.

But what was the wels doing in Spain in the first place? The wels or giant European catfish is well known to be a native of the Danube region river sys-tems and its original natural distribution in Europe extended north as far as southern parts of Scandinavia but the species did not occur in other areas of Western Europe until introduced there through the agency of man. Natural distribution east of the Danube includes rivers draining into the Caspian, Black, Aral, Aegean and Eastern Mediterranean Seas, some Baltic Sea tributaries as well as the Upper Rhine and rivers entering the Persian Gulf, such as the

Euphrates, and on into Asia. The wels occurs mainly in large lakes and the lower reaches of rivers, though occasionally enters brackish water, notably around the Aral, Baltic and Black Seas. Scientists have recorded that wels have even spawned at Kulandy, in the salt water of the Aral Sea. This salt water resistance has enabled the catfish to skirt the Black, Caspian and Aral Seas in the evolutionary growth of its geographical extension and ascend the large rivers that drain central and Eastern Europe as well as further east into central Asia. The creature's ideal habitat, however, is found in the deep waters of the middle and lower reaches of large rivers and, in modern times, most especially where dams have been constructed. The vast Ebro water system of huge dams and reservoirs, the Sea of Aragón, is the perfect wels habitat.

It was not until the 1970s, however, that *Silurus glanis* was introduced into Spain. In 1974 a German biologist and keen angler, Roland Lorkowski, released a mere 32 small catfish into the river Ebro, just above the bridge at Mequinenza. Those yearling fish were between 12 and 18 inches in length, each weighing approximately ten to 12 ounces, and came from a small pond in the Cologne region of Lorkowski's native Germany. Since then, there have been a number of further introductions but the biggest and oldest fish in the Ebro system, those currently being landed at over 200lb, date almost certainly from 1974.

Next, there is the question of just how big would or could *Silurus glanis* grow. It is said that those original 1970s fish were of genetically poor stock, being siblings, the offspring of a single pairing. This means that growth rate and maximum potential size of future generations would be far from optimum. However, subsequent stockings have enriched the gene pool and the population is now thought to have reached a conservative minimum of 30,000 individuals, which means that giant catfish outnumber the human inhabitants of Mequinenza and Caspe combined by three to one.

The species is, moreover, long-lived, possibly very long-lived indeed and specimens reaching 50 or 70 years of age could quite reasonably be expected to attain weights in the region of 500lb or even twice that. The largest specimen ever recorded was reputedly caught in the river Oder, the major Eastern European waterway that runs from Poland through Germany and into the Baltic. The fish was taken by net in 1761 and, after it had been gutted for market, weighed an incredible 375kg, a cool 825lb. When the fish was alive it would certainly have weighed closer to 1000lb. The most important factor to be considered with regard to those waters where the wels is native is simply that they are and have been heavily fished commercially for centuries. The chances of any given species reaching advanced age and considerable size are very much reduced. In Spain, the wels is subject merely to some sport fishing, the great majority of which is guided catch and release angling, where the captures are treated with considerable care. It would be something to be able to return with our film crew some years from now, perhaps another 30 or so, and really see what size of fish will then be found in the Ebro. As the Sundance Kid once said: 'I have vision, and the rest of the world wears bifocals.'

And so our catfish filming expedition drew to a close. The crew packed up early that evening and the rest of us were not far behind. Despite the documentary film's focus on the three Englishmen and their destiny, we all knew that the real star of the piece was Maureen, a great character and an angling force to be reckoned with. A special mention too, must of course be given to *Silurus glanis*, the giant European wels catfish - maybe not the most beautiful or endearing of fishes but certainly one of the most powerful and challenging opponents any sporting angler could wish for.

Chapter Seven

Extremadura

*Where the author looks into a region's history and biodiversity plus the country's sport of
bullfighting and animal welfare in general. A cycling and fishing film is made, with bleak,
carp and black bass and many famous British travellers in Spain are recalled as well as their
writings before going afloat on Alcántara Reservoir and zandering from a boat.*

Extremadura is an entirely landlocked autonomous community, covering over
40,000 square kilometres, close to four times the size of Yorkshire, and more
than ten times that of Kent. The name itself means something like a very hard,
extreme place, and its climate is therefore unsurprisingly severe, with very hot,
dry summers, with extended periods of drought, and very long, albeit relatively
mild winters, due to the Atlantic oceanic influence which extends across
Extremadura from the coast from Portugal.

Glancing back through the mists of time, Extremadura was once part of the
ancient Roman province of Lusitania, which also included most of present day
Portugal with Mérida (Emerita Augusta) as its capital, one of the most important cities in the Roman Empire. Today, Mérida continues to be the capital city
of Extremadura and boasts some spectacular Roman architectural remains,
principally the incredible and almost completely intact Roman theatre, constructed in the years 16 and 15 BC under the auspices of the consul Vipsanius
Agrippa. The theatre has, of course, subsequently undergone several periods of
additional construction and renovation work, particularly between the first and
mid fourth centuries, during the reigns of Emperor Trajan and Constantine I.
Later, the theatre was gradually abandoned and eventually became almost
completely covered in earth, with, at one time, only the upper levels of the

amphitheatre of seats remaining visible. This oddly isolated stone work became known as 'The Seven Chairs', particularly during the Moorish occupation of Spain, when, according to legend, several kings successively took possession of these grandiose Roman 'chairs' to sit in state, from whence to rule their dominions.

The theatre is today the city's most visited architectural site, and, since it continues to be in such excellent condition, it is actually still used to stage theatre productions in the city. Since 1933 it has been home to the Mérida Classical Theatre Festival and it really is an extraordinary experience to enjoy a play there today, which may well have been enjoyed by theatre goers sitting in the very same seats over 2000 years ago.

Extremadura was also the homeland of many of the most famous Spanish conquistadors of South America; Hernán Cortés, Francisco Pizarro, Francisco de Orellana and many others were born in Extremadura and many towns and cities in America carry a name from their homeland, such as Guadalupe, Trujillo, Cáceres etc.; and the administrative capital of Mexico's Yucatan state is named Mérida.

Returning to the present, Extremadura is, because of its low population, extremely rich in wildlife and features, above all, the Montfragüe national park as well as the newly designated Tagus River Natural Park. I remember once in my early years in Spain, being taken on a long weekend trip south to Monfragüe, parking just off the road near the entrance to a huge high sided gorge and looking up at the deep blue sky. There were hundreds of huge birds circling overhead, really huge birds with immense wingspans and small heads, which my companions told me were vultures. I remember being amazed. I hadn't known then that Spain was home to vast numbers of these birds. Following their drifting cycles through binoculars we were able to pick out a few black vultures, and just two pairs of Egyptians, among the great majority, which were gryphons. I remember the country suddenly feeling even more exotic to me, as though I were somewhere in Africa, a sensation which has often returned to me since.

The considerable biodiversity of Spain is extraordinary, and likewise, what I might perhaps call its bioanimosity. I once read in an old travelogue, written by an anonymous early Victorian, that, 'Your Spaniard is no great Lover of Animals'. The *corrida de toros*, i.e. bullfighting, would appear to demonstrate that little has changed in this respect in modern Spain. Whenever the subject of a ban on sport fishing is debated anywhere in Europe, it tends to provoke a sardonic smile on the part of many anglers and the invariable averment that those campaigning for it, would do better to turn their attentions to other rather bloodier pursuits, among which tauromachy is surely king. The ban on bullfighting, incidentally, that has been in place in the Spanish Autonomous

Community, Catalunya, since 2011, has nothing whatsoever to do with any ethical standpoint but is merely a political manoeuvre, part of that region's desire to distance itself from the Spanish state in any way that it can.

Bullfighting is, beyond doubt, an extremely popular, colourful and musical spectacle, which is also well liked in Portugal, much of Latin America and a few areas in southern France. For those who are unfamiliar with it, it is a confrontation between men and fighting bulls, an outstanding and magnificent species, for the purposes of public entertainment, and has much in common with the world of the ancient Roman coliseum.

Bullfighting is consummately ritualistic, held by the aficionados, or bullfighting experts and fans, to be highly aesthetic and sublimely artistic. The fight is principally understood to be a demonstration, amid pomp and pageantry, of extravagant individual style, complex technique and supposed macho courage, in which the bull is not a sacrificial victim but a worthy adversary, deserving of respect in its own right. Ernest Hemingway brought the event to international attention in the 1930s, particularly in his *Death in the Afternoon* of 1932, wherein he stated that: 'Bullfighting is the only art in which the artist is in danger of death and in which the degree of brilliance in the performance is left to the fighter's honour.'

Indeed, the truth is, that very occasionally a bullfighter is injured or even killed. A moment of carelessness or an unusually intelligent bull could lead to such a crisis, but these moments are rare enough. Some of these incidents, nowadays, have been uploaded to YouTube and often have titles like, 'The bull doesn't always lose'. I am not sure I would recommend actually viewing any of them but cannot help recalling a particularly horrific example, which was shown in the fullest graphic and slow-motion detail on Spanish national television, in every news bulletin for a week at least. My memory of the scene focusses principally on the attitude of the bull at the moment when it succeeds in catching the point of one horn in the man's tight trouser leg and flips him into the air like a coin. The animal then appears to follow the hapless chappie's trajectory quite carefully and as the man descends, the bull puts forward its right horn and impales him. Through a combination of the violence of the animal's upward thrust and the weight and velocity of the falling man, the horn rips into the solar plexus area, shatters the rib cage and reportedly tears the matador's heart in two. The death of the bullfighter in question was an occasion for national mourning.

The words of another twentieth century writer come to mind. Although he never visited Spain, James Joyce's heroine Molly Bloom in the immortal *Ulysses* was born and raised in Gibraltar. In reference to the Spanish, at one point Joyce remarked that 'All are washed in the blood of the sun', a singularly appropriate observation in any appreciation of the national blood sport.

What exactly goes on in the arena should perhaps be explained. In the traditional Spanish *corrida*, there will be three matadors, each facing two bulls, between four and six years old, and weighing a minimum 460kg, or 1014lb, and a maximum of around 700kg, which is an incredible 1540lb. A ton and a half . . . they really are huge animals. The matadors each have six sidekicks: two mounted picadors, effectively lancers on horseback; three *banderilleros* (who, along with the matadors are collectively known as *toreros*); and a sort of squire, the *mozo de espadas*, or sword page. This group comprises the *cuadrilla*, or bullfighting entourage. The word 'matador' is commonly used in English for any of the individuals in the ring but in Spanish, the more general term '*torero*' applies. The matador, or more accurately the *matador de toros*, is specifically the main bullfighter in each encounter.

The modern *corrida* event has three distinct and intricately choreographed stages, *tercios*, or thirds, the start of each being announced by a bugle fanfare. The participants first enter the arena in a parade, called the *paseíllo*, which is accompanied by traditional band music, and they approach and salute the presiding dignitary, the local mayor for example, the effective equivalent of the classical Roman emperor. The salute, however, no longer contains the ancient words, 'Those who about to die etc.', which should perhaps be pronounced on behalf of the animals. The remarkable traditional costumes worn by the *toreros* have their origins in seventeenth century Andalusia, and matador outfits are particularly extravagant. The bullfight proper then begins with the entrance of the bull, and the *tercio de varas*, or the lancing stage. The animal, usually a glossy black, muscle bound and spectacularly horned mass of agitation and apparent fury, is then tested for ferocity by the matador and the *banderilleros*, who flourish their very large magenta and gold *capotes*, or capes. The matador himself plays a prominent part in this first stage, confronting the bull with his cape and performing a series of complex 'passes', each having a particular name, such as the *verónica*, taking note all the while of the animal's strength and of any idiosyncratic behavioural characteristics.

Next, the *picadors* enter the arena on horseback, armed with their very long *varas*, or lances. To shield the horse from the bull's horns, the horse is skirted with a protective, padded leather covering called a *peto*. This measure was introduced in the 1930s, prior to which the horses were not protected and would frequently be horrifically injured during the encounter; the number of horses killed during a bullfight was actually greater in those days, than the number of bulls.

The picador has to ram his lance into the *morrillo*, the powerful mound of muscle immediately behind the neck of the bull, attempting the maximum possible damage and leading to the first loss of blood. In consequence, the bull will be unable to hold its head up properly or buck its head and horns throughout the remainder of the fight, and, ultimately, this will enable the matador to deliver the killing thrust later in the performance. The encounter with the picadors often radically changes the behaviour of the bull, which becomes bewildered and distracted, less wildly aggressive and frequently less able or less inclined to charge indiscriminately, becoming more likely to focus on a single target.

In the next stage, the *tercio de banderillas*, the three banderilleros each attempt to plant two *banderillas*, which are long, very sharp, barbed steel rods, into the same muscle area. They will then remain hanging in place, continuing to tear the muscle, through the remainder of the creature's doomed existence. These men and their torture instruments drive the animal wild with helpless fury and, of course, further weaken the muscle driving the only real defence it has.

The final stage is known, graphically enough, as the *tercio de muerte*, or death stage. The now unaccompanied matador re-enters the ring with a small red cape, or muleta, and a long sword. The colour red is pure tradition, since, contrary to popular belief, red has no particular effect on the bull, which is completely colour-blind. The matador uses the movement of the cape to attract the bull and perform a series of passes designed to wear the animal down for the kill and also form the highlight of the show, the *faena*, the skill of which is highly valued by the aficionados. He may also demonstrate his supposed dominion over the bull by making it pass very close to his body or even kneeling disdainfully in front of the crippled animal. The *faena* is itself divided into *tandas*, or series, of specially composed passes. The *faena* ends with a final range of passes in which the matador manoeuvres the bull into the required position to allow him to plunge the sword between the animal's shoulder blades and through the heart. The sword is called an *estoque* and the final act is known as the *estocada*. Up to this point, by the way, the *estoque* has in fact been a fake, usually made of wood and much lighter and easier to manage, not to mention safer for the matador, than the real sword. However, at the end of the *tercio de muerte*, the matador receives the real sword from the *mozo de espadas* in order to perform the *estocada*. If the matador has performed particularly well, the crowd may petition the presiding dignitary to reward the matador with one or both of the bull's ears, even occasionally the tail, too by waving white handkerchiefs. A matador that the crowd considers ineffectual or inelegant may find himself being pelted with seat cushions and verbal abuse. On very rare occasions, during the fight, the public or the matador himself may appeal to the presiding dignitary on behalf of the bull for a pardon, or *indulto*, and if granted, the bull is spared and allowed to leave the ring to return to the ranch, where it will become a stud animal for the rest of its life.

I have only been to two *corridas de toros* in my time in Spain, in part because I felt I had to actually witness the thing I felt more than ready to condemn out of hand before actually ever having seen it. On the first of those occasions, in

May 1992, tickets were in tremendous demand for seating in the magnificent brick-built bullring in Valladolid. Dating from 1888, it is a splendid, steeply graded, classically circular amphitheatre, with beautiful painted ironwork forming its upper spectator galleries. The little box offices, three small windows in the whitewashed wall outside, had signs over them in large letters, '*Sol*', '*Sombra*' or '*Sol y Sombra*', Sun, Shade or Sun and Shade. Seats in that part of the interior which received the full force of the sun all through the afternoon were markedly cheaper, with those in continual shade, much more expensive.

As an Englishman, with the genes undoubtedly of a mad dog, I chose the cheaper option, thinking I would be able to get nicely suntanned without having to go to the city beach on the river. It was a mistake. The summer sun of inland Spain is not to be trifled with.

Six bulls were on the agenda. The first animal, announced as being bred by an illustrious family, from a prestigious ranch near Seville, and weighing 550kg (well over a ton) thundered into the ring, seething in taurean glory, as though imbued with pride, arrogance and very real brute superiority, but which was soon mercilessly plagued, degraded, exhausted, severely injured in joint and sinew, and debilitated by a handful of harlequin individuals that ran around like cowards as soon as the creature approached them, and frequently hid behind special screens at the edges of the arena. I was reminded of nothing more than circus clowns and buffoons, but things soon took a much more serious turn. The three individuals were in tight-fitting and sequined fancy dress; outfits known as *trajes de luces* or suits of light, and had very large colourful capes which they swung and waved around to attract the attention of the bull and make it charge as much as possible one way and the other, with damagingly abrupt and violent turns.

Next, the mounted riders, the picadors, alternately plunged their very long lance-like spears into the large hump behind the head, rising in their saddles and exerting their full force and that of their mounts, finally leaving that muscle area absolutely pouring with blood, quivering with palpable pain, and causing the animal to become evidently dazed and disorientated. Though I may do so imaginatively, I feel I am the last person to seriously anthropomorphise or empathise with any animal, yet, in this creature's staring eyes I swear I read absolute fear, horror and panic, as clearly as in the eyes of any human sufferer.

Later, a couple of men, the *banderilleros*, came running in with their weapons, which were decorated with colourful baubles and streamers, and stabbed them into the same hump. These men have to get very close and exhibited the only element approaching any real bravery, and indeed some acrobatic skill, that I witnessed in the whole afternoon.

Once this last, atrocious process had been brought to its desired conclusion, with the bull staggering, its tongue protruding from its mouth, and blood pouring from its shoulders, in came the hero of the event, the *torero* 'matador' or killer, who would demonstrate his talent and valour by further torturing the beast and forcing it, skilfully enough, through a series of entertaining manoeuvres, until the animal could barely stand, at which point, he thrust his sword into the shoulder of bull, supposedly with the intention of bringing the creature's sufferings to an end. The razor edged sword rarely if ever penetrates the heart, the supposed object of the thrust. The bull is then harried and harassed by the other two of the same cowardly clowns who started the whole event, forcing the animal to lunge one way and another, so that the long sword, embedded in the animal to the hilt, will cut left and right inside the bull's body until the internal bleeding effectively drowns the beast from the inside and it falls finally to the ground to tremble and gasp, to vomit blood and bellow in asphyxiated agony, to agonise and effectively bleed to death. The hero then steps in to deliver the *coup de grâce* and plunges a dagger into the top of the creature's skull.

Since the crowd plainly considered this matador's ignominious performance to have been praiseworthy, as exhibited by the frantic waving of handkerchiefs and cheers of '*ole, ole*' around the arena, he was presented with both of the bull's ears, which were hacked off for the purpose from the still shuddering corpse, and he was then carried from the arena in glory, high on the shoulders of the other *toreros*. The carcass of the bull was roped around the horns and dragged off by a team of horses, to be butchered.

I had tears running down my face, felt physically sick and would probably have left altogether had it been practicable to do so through the pressing crowd. And this was only the first of six for the afternoon. However, with the second bull, things began unexpectedly to go somewhat awry. The animal, curiously, did not look like the typical fighting bull; it was even bigger than its predecessor, a shade under 700kg, not black but rather a patchwork of black, brown and white, and with horns that seemed rather wider, at least four feet from point to point, but none of this caused any reaction in the spectators, which led me to assume that such bulls were not particularly unusual.

The spineless *toreros* ran this way and that with their capes but curiously, the bull did not seem to react as the previous one had done, but trotted around immensely, with occasional apparently feigned menaces, as though it refused to tire itself without purpose. The crowd reacted. There were gibes, insults and a great deal of noise, all deriding the animal but not the errant fools that continued running at and away from the bull ineffectively. Once in a while, the animal saw an opportunity and very nearly impaled one of the *toreros* against the boards of his hiding place. I found all this decidedly entertaining but the crowd continued with boos and howls of derision. To my eyes, the animal seemed just too clever for them, but the crowd continued to deride *el toro* as useless rubbish. When the *picadors* entered the arena, the bull seemed to measure both his time and the distances, repeatedly avoiding the blades of the spears. I heard shouts and complaints all around me that this bull was no good, that it was stupid, and that it needed to be taken away. I was absolutely fascinated. Then, with a swiftness which froze the audience to a man, the bull suddenly charged and slammed into the flanks of one of the horses, getting under the protective *peto*, both horns tearing into that animal's underside. The bull actually lifted the horse and rider off the ground and threw both into a grotesque and twisted heap, while the crowd erupted with shock and, above all, sheer fury. The horse's entrails poured out on to the sand, in a disgusting purple and red steaming heap of quite literally visceral horror, and the rider was yelling, screaming for help, half crushed under his mount. The horse had emitted no sound of agony whatsoever and I later learnt that their vocal chords are cut so that they always remain silent, no matter what their sufferings in the arena.

Once the *picador* was stretchered off and away to a casualty department somewhere, with both legs broken and several ribs too it later transpired, but otherwise unhurt, except, perhaps in his pride and sense of honour, I was next surprised to see a group of four very large and dewy eyed cows brought into the ring, which had a remarkably calming effect on the bull which had, meanwhile, continued patrolling the arena, as though looking for his next chance to do some serious damage to his tormentors. Eventually subdued, the bull was led from the arena, applauded and with shouts of '*bravo, bravo*' from my lips alone, which caused something of a stir, briefly.

I stayed to see the start of the third bull's opening period of senseless Calvary, which appeared to return to the expected series of events as far as the public was concerned, and amid general hubbub and restlessness I attempted to leave, but once I had had a drink in the bar downstairs, a shot of Soberano brandy, I returned to the fray, feeling that I had to finish what I had started. The archways leading to the seating area are known as *vomitorios*, from the Latin *vomitorium*, which I thought singulary appropriate. I then witnessed the massacre of the rest of the day's victims and left the bullring, swearing I would never enter one again as long as I lived.

I did in fact go again, to a much more rural version of the spectacle, in which young bulls were tackled by unarmed antagonists in a small village arena made from large lorry tyres. It was very amusing and entertaining, and mercifully with no 'death in the afternoon', as Hemingway had styled it. This relatively harmless event is known as '*novillos*' or '*la novillada*', and usually sees young men challenging the bull with a *capea* or small cape. There are no particular rules or regulations and it is a common enough summer pastime in smaller towns and villages all over the country. I recall one occasion, when fishing some gravel pits near Villanueva del Duero, when a young black bull came trundling along the unmade road that ran through the pit heading for the pine woods beyond. It saw me as I stood up, perhaps somewhat unadvisedly, but took little notice and continued on its way. Some time later a gaggle of noisily vociferating villagers appeared, running back and forth, up and down banks, searching clearly for their lost star of the *novillos*. They came across and told me that the very dangerous animal had escaped and that if I were to see it, I would do well to jump on my bike and clear out as quickly as possible. I told them it had just trotted past and that it was now doubtless chomping the sweet grasses beneath the pine trees a little further on. To my great surprise, I was hailed as a *'gran hombre'*, steadfast and brave in the face of untold dangers, before, with many shouts of *'muchas gracias'* they headed off with their lassoes and ropes, to cordon and capture the renegade.

Like that anonymous Victorian I quoted earlier, I too have come to the realisation that animal life is not generally very highly valued in this country. I have often been surprised, particularly by the reaction of youngsters, when the subject comes up. I have heard young people and adults alike say, quite simply, 'I don't like animals,' often with something of a sneer. I have never attempted to record the percentage of persons holding this view but I am sure it is much higher, as a general rule, than we might expect to find in the north of Europe. This would appear to be the consequence of education. It might equally be argued that we, the British, swing rather too far in the opposite direction, attributing almost human status, not to say empathies or emotions, to creatures, which in the end are killed and packaged and offered up for sale as food in our supermarkets.

Aside from the 'don't like animals' phenomenon, however, there exists a far uglier dimension. There are so many cases in which the abuse of animals is a factor that it is perfectly clear that in a large part of Spanish society, it is the norm, or at least has been until recently; the sheer number of abandoned cats you'll find in almost any city might attest to the fact. But the worst examples of this abuse are those, like bullfighting, which fall into the highly dubious category of 'tradition'. There has even been an attempt to have UNESCO declare bullfighting an event of International Social, Historic and Cultural Heritage . . . may the gods forbid. This policy is, of course, merely a manoeuvre designed to protect bullfighting from those attempting to have it banned and perhaps even more so, to protect the highly lucrative breeding industry behind it.

Tradition lies equally insidiously behind the mutilation and murder of albino children in Africa or the sexual mutilation of women in different parts of the world. But returning to animals, in rural areas of Spain, primarily although not exclusively, it is entirely normal that, once a dog has reached the end of its useful life, it be hanged by the neck until it is dead. If the animal has been a good dog, a good working animal as a hunting companion for example, it will be hanged from the branch of a tree to agonise relatively briefly until it dies. If the animal has not been such a good dog, it is common practice to hang the poor thing by the neck with the tips of the claws of its hind legs just touching the ground, so that it may kick and jump and strangle itself for several hours. Sometimes, the dog is starved beforehand and food and water is left nearby to drive the wretched animal to distractions in its last hours.

These practices have come to attention of the international press more than once, but public memory is lamentably short. We have seen the headlines, 'Dogs left to die after they "humiliated" their masters', and 'Animal rights campaigners claim Spanish hunters hang, drown and poison 50,000 greyhounds every year', in *The Observer*, Sunday 1st January 2006, and earlier in *The Independent*, Sunday 16th February 1997, 'Briton fights to end Spanish dog hangings', and 'A London nurse is saving old greyhounds from a "traditional" cruel death'.

Other Spanish traditions include the public torture or destruction of animals as part of some ludicrous festival, such as a one time well-known event in which a rope was extended across a village square and a device on a roller attached, from which a large white goose was tied by the legs and hung head down, wings flapping wildly. The participants in the event then saw how far they could ride swinging across the square holding on to the live goose by the neck, until it finally stretched and broke; when the individual landed, he held up the bleeding head to the delighted crowd.

This particular event, or one very like it, also took place in Lekeitio, or Lequeiti, in the Basque Country, where the *Fiesta de los Gansos*, or Goose Festival, sees a goose hung in much the same way, from a rope that crosses the harbour. Men jump from small boats to catch hold of it, in an attempt to see who can hold on for the longest, finally tearing its head off. International animal rights activists have managed to put a stop to this particular barbarity, since the geese used in the spectacle nowadays are dead, which was certainly not the case a few years ago.

Another appalling and very well-known event is the *Cabra del Campanario*, or the Goat in the Tower Festival, which took place in the small town of Maganenses de la Polverosa in the province of Zamora, in Old Castile. So infamous was the event that it has now been banned following public outrage throughout the region when the festival became more widely publicised some years ago. Tradition in Maganenses demanded that a goat be taken up to the top of the church tower, from whence it was cast from the belfry, in honour of the patron Saint Vincent, and landed a bloody and broken mass of flesh and bone in the square below. Such was the indignation of the townsfolk in the year that their tradition was banned by law that there was a popular revolt, and two goats were sacrificed in this traditional manner to commemorate the passing of the high point of their festival. Whether the law is properly respected nowadays, I cannot say.

Continuing with this catalogue of horrors, there are many other small towns and villages that indulge in the decapitation of live birds in their annual festivals. Pigeons, chickens, ducks or geese are hung by their legs from ropes across the streets. It is common for young men to then ride their horses through the streets in a race with each other and when passing under them, grab the heads, ripping them from the bodies of the unfortunate birds, which then stream their blood into the street below. These events have always been popular in Extremadura particularly, and in La Rioja. There are many similarly barbarous events around the country, some with birds buried in the ground with only their heads visible, which are then decapitated by enthusiasts armed with shovels and spades. In the village of Robledo de Chavela near Madrid, similar celebrations feature the capture of wild squirrels, which are then stoned to death or decapitated in the village square.

In other festivals bulls or goats are made to run around the towns or villages with fireworks, such as rockets or bangers, tied to their heads, to the great amusement of all and sundry. I think it would be fair to say that nowadays a good many of these traditions have been banned or are dropping away. Younger people are more aware of international sensibilities and education is moving towards a better understanding of animals in general. Bullfighting, and the agricultural and business empire behind it, continues to be a huge commercial and financial affair, unlikely to be seriously affected by any social or political circumstances for a long time to come, but it is my hope that it will eventually come to an end.

Such extremes, of an abundance of wildlife on the one hand, and of frequently anti-animal perspectives on the other, are perhaps merely part of the remarkable diversity that is Spain today. The extremes suggested by the sound of the name of Extremadura, perhaps, which, although lying at no great distance to the south of where I have lived for many years, is nevertheless a somehow more remote and wilder place.

I had not been south over the border from Castile for several years, when, in 2008 I had the chance to join the crew of Spanish television's *Caza y Pesca* (Hunting & Fishing) programme, on a cycling and fishing trip to Extremadura. The plan this time was to cycle some of the newly opened network of converted railway lines, the *vías verdes*, and stop off at the Ruecas, Sierra Brava and possibly Orellana reservoirs to fish for pike, black bass, bleak and carp with fly, spinners and boilies. Moreover, it was spring time and the rains, the proverbial '*aguas mil*' of the month of April, had filled the rivers and reservoirs of one of Spain's most beautiful and, certainly as far as foreigners were concerned, least explored regions. It was the final weekend of the month and I had to get myself and the bike to Madrid, where I would be picked up for the long drive down to the Sierra de Guadalupe, in the province of Cáceres.

The excellent ALSA coach company is both efficient and economical but they require bicycles to be broken down and packed in order to be transported in the hold. This needed some thought since I would be cycling to the bus station, panniers fully loaded with all my fishing gear: four rods and reels, fly boxes, quantities of bait, spinners, rod pod, alarms, as well as all the essential paraphernalia of flasks and mugs for tea making. My bike, the old 1980s Saracen Conquest, has always been known among my friends in Valladolid as '*El Toro*', the bull, since it is black, a good deal larger than modern mountain bikes and has wide steer horns. The whole machine and particularly these latter features were a remarkable novelty when I first arrived in the city many years ago. In those days, whenever I left it chained up in the street, a crowd would gather to look at it. True, it was distinctly heavy and old-fashioned but as a one time world mountain biking altitude holder it was still a formidable ATB, as they used to be known.

Making sure I had the necessary tools in the panniers, I rolled up a few metres of bubble pack and wedged it like a sleeping bag into the top of my rucksack and set off, wobbling slightly under the weight, for an early bus to Madrid. Some while later, the bus driver was delighted to find I not only had a ticket, which included the minimal supplement for carrying a cycle, but also to see the bike with its front wheel removed, the handlebars swivelled round and the whole machine bound up in bubble pack. Doubtless he had had cyclists turn up with none of these prerequisites and had been involved in the inevitable wrangle and frayed tempers. Though *El Toro* made a formidable bundle, it slid into the hold easily enough and in no time I was on my way to the capital.

Reading for the journey was Jan Morris's *The Presence of Spain*. It was a re-read, in fact, since it was one of those books I had read when I first moved from Britain, to help orientate myself in the Iberian Peninsula. This was before learning any Spanish, when all my reading about Spain was done in English, and written by English writers, a curiously one-dimensional introduction, as I discovered in due course, to the country and its culture.

In those days, and as continues to be the case today, Spain has more of absolutely everything, and particularly more fish and fishing than most of its millions of UK visitors ever realise. Back in the 1960s, when *The Presence of Spain* was first published, I recalled the author observing that:

> It was in Spain that Charles I of England was given trout, out of the Segovia hill streams, so big that he actually took the trouble to write home about them - '*certaine troute of extraordinary greatnesse*'.

It was as little a known fact then as now, and Morris continued:

> Throughout the mountain masses of Spain delectable unfrequented trout streams abound, and the fjordlike estuaries of the northwest are full of salmon. Nothing is better organized, in the whole gamut of Spanish life, than the system by which the fish of the Atlantic and Mediterranean coasts are hurtled across Spain to the capital: a tragic sense of urgency informs the process, from the swift silent loading of the iceboxes at Valencia or San Sebastian to the pounding of the big trucks through the night ensuring that whatever else may happen in the world, whatever strikes or outrages may mortify Spain, still there will be red mullet, lobster, oysters, and spidercrabs for lunch in Madrid tomorrow. There are always fish about in Spain: fish in the stream beside the road, fish glistening in the huge markets, dried fillets of fish in boxes on grocers' counters, trapped fish leaping helplessly in the saltpans of Cadiz, fish brought by mule or truck to the remotest mountain village, or if they count as fish - those little wisps of elvers, hardly old enough to be animate, which are offered to you like dishes of some fine-spun pasta in every Valencian eatinghouse.

Little has changed in the succeeding half century, there are still fish everywhere. A notable exception is the elver which, along with its parent, is on the verge of extinction. In the 1980s it was not unusual to be served your grilled salmon with a garnish of elvers but nowadays the real thing is rarely seen; a sprinkling of 24 carat gold dust would be cheaper, and elvers have been replaced by a fish-factory, crab-stick style grey imitation. Salmon have also declined somewhat since Morris's day but there are still rivers, mainly in Asturias, where they are caught. There have been other changes too, but they, in contrast, have brought even more fish into the country. Among these, the giant catfish looms exceptionally large but there are also the rainbow trout, the zander, and of course the black bass, and there are plenty of these latter species to be found in Extremadura.

A couple of hours after leaving Valladolid, I arrived at Madrid, where I was met by Pepe, from the TV channel, and Alfonso the cameraman and we soon loaded the re-assembled bike into an enormous van and headed off to pick up the others. First was Benjamin, a Madrid dentist, originally from Santiago de Compostela in Galicia, and Juan, the director of the TV channel. My companions were all consummate all-round anglers but particularly expert with the fly and so I had packed my fly gear too, in part hoping to pick up a few hints, since I never do as much fly fishing as I should like.

Getting a licence for Extremadura is not as easy as in some Spanish regions, simply because you have to apply by post or go in person to a Caja de Extremadura, which is a regional bank. There is no Caja de Extremadura in Valladolid but there is more than one in Madrid and once located, actually getting the licence could not be easier, or at least a receipt which proves you have applied for one, valid for 60 days which serves until the actual licence arrives by post. You fill out a form issued by the Junta de Extremadura headed Tasas Licencias de Caza/Pesca 50 and pay out the princely sum of €4.85 for a one year licence. Licences can also be obtained which are valid for up to five years. My own licence for Extremadura had lapsed some years before and so Pepe had kindly got me a new one, which I determined to maintain in future. In the event my pink cover note substitute for a licence ran out long before the licence arrived, due to a major administrative overhaul in Extremaduran Local Government. My actual licence finally arrived eight months later, in January 2009.

The Autonomous Community of Extremadura is, I believe, unique in Spain in having a close season for coarse fish. The calendar month of April is off-limits to the angler; this is the period when the very popular black bass are nest building, spawning and defending their progeny. As a consequence of this prohibition, Pepe had been in touch with the Junta de Extremadura and had obtained a special permit which allowed us to fish, with the proviso that the fishing must be catch and release. Needless to say, this was no inconvenience at all. The existence and enforcement of this close season seemed to me a most enlightened policy and one which would do well to be adopted elsewhere in the Iberian Peninsula. We also praised heartily the decision to allow us to fish the dates we had elected, since the following weekend was a four-day-long 1st of May bank holiday period, when the watersides of Extremadura would doubtless be lined with anglers and holiday makers.

Having got ourselves and the transport thoroughly organised, we were at last on the road heading south-west on the N-V motorway, a fairly long haul of three hours, which would take us through New Castile by way of Talavera and then on towards Trujillo in Extremadura. The ancient walled town of Trujillo is a charming pile perched on a small hill, its main square full of house martins and its church tower crowded with lesser kestrels. Historically, it is famous above all as the birthplace of the most renowned conquistadores of the New World, particularly Pizarro, who with less than two hundred men conquered the Inca Empire and took Peru, and Orellana, the first European to sail up the Amazon. Another remarkable citizen of Trujillo was 'The Samson of Extremadura', a reputedly huge man, as strong as an ox, who founded the new town of Trujillo in Venezuela. Many of Trujillo's most adventuring sons returned from the Americas very wealthy men and the town boasts several splendid palaces, monuments to their memory. It was a delightful place, which I had been to a number of times over the years, but we wouldn't be visiting the town on this trip, since just before it, we turned off on to the C-524, which was the road for Zorita and then Logrosan. Here we had booked into a *casa rural*, the Spanish equivalent of a small countryside hotel or bed and breakfast. These are often beautiful old houses, fully equipped and modernised, which offer either self-catering or B&B accommodation. No sooner had we arrived when suddenly everything was accelerated. We dropped things off in our rooms, hurriedly got our bikes sorted out, with Alfonso filming our antics, and in no time cycled or rather wobbled up hill out of the village. Our plan was to fish the Embalse de Ruecas, at no great distance, and so were soon pedalling feverishly along small country roads and finally dirt tracks in search of the water, without a map. Miraculously, coming over a rise we spotted it, a great glistening extension of blue, which looked really beautiful in the late afternoon light. Full to the brim and beyond, there were feverfew, daisies and buttercups submerged in the shallows and little fish rising in every direction. We all had our rods set up in record time and Alfonso was already busy setting the scene, filming the landscape.

My role in the proceedings was to represent the modern carp fisher, a part I rather doubted I would be able to fulfill. Even so, I set my pod in a likely looking spot and put out two lines, fishing to the deeper water side of a distant ridge which appeared to mark a drop off from the flooded shallows. Pepe, Juan and Benjamin went off around the margins stalking with their fly rods. We fished hard until nightfall but with little success; only Benjamin managed to hoodwink a small bass before a general feeling of thirst and hunger dragged us away from the waterside in the failing twilight. We cycled back to Logrosan, getting pretty well lost in the dark, but luckily arriving near the right village, albeit a couple of kilometres above. We flew away down hill and were soon back at the *casa rural*, where, since it was already 11pm and too late to find anywhere to eat, our hosts offered us some traditional *embutidos*, cold meats, cheese and crisp country bread along with a few beers, sitting out on the patio. We laughed and told fishing yarns under the stars, breathing in the balmy night air, full of the scents of flowers. The eves of the old house were visited by an occasional bat and not far away we could here the piping note of a scops owl.

We did not make a late night of it, however, since at eight the following morning we were to meet for breakfast. Before nine we were back on our bikes and on the *via verde* peddling south for Madrigalejo through the tremendous sweeping valley of the river Ruecas, the mountains of the Sierra de Guadalupe to our left. We stopped to take photographs and for Alfonso to film the wonderful panorama, including a charming mediaeval bridge spanning a pool in the river, and, of course, to get plenty of footage of the intrepid cyclists.

At one point we arrived at an old railway station and while everyone was dismounting to get more footage and commentary, I cycled on a short distance to a bridge I had descried while we were approaching the station. There were lizards everywhere amongst the brick work: Iberian wall lizards, spiny-footed lizards, one juvenile with a bright red tail, a couple of Spanish psammodromus and one enormous green ocellated lizard. I climbed up on to the bridge and looked down the track that lay before us, stretching seemingly into infinity. It would be a daunting prospect to walk, especially now that the sun was high but cycling it would be a breeze. All the countryside was brilliant green, flecked with the myriad colours of wild flowers, the sierra de Guadalupe a shadowy deep purple and blue under brilliant skies and the old railway track a shimmering streak of ochre. On the distant horizon to the south there was an oddly symmetrical high hill, smoothly conical and, apart from the mountains, looking almost like an enormous sponge pudding. Notwithstanding the delights of this spring morning, the region, it should be said, was famous for its inhospitable climate, torrid summers and bitter winters. George Borrow, travelling here on horseback in the winter of 1835, wasn't particularly enamoured:

> When the sun rose, which it did gloomily and amidst threatening rain-clouds, we found ourselves in the neighbourhood of a range of mountains which lay on our left . . . our route, however, lay over wide plains, scantily clothed with brushwood, with here and there a melancholy village . . . Towards evening we reached a moor, a wild place enough, strewn with enormous stones and rocks. Before us at some distance, rose a strange conical hill, rough and shaggy, which appeared to be neither more nor less than an immense assemblage of the same rocks . . . a strong wind rose and howled at our backs.

Along the path which led to the bridge across the fields, I suddenly noticed a wizen faced old man approaching, whose ancient wrinkles immediately put me in mind of another British visitor to these parts, S. F. A. Coles, whose *Spain Everlasting* appeared one hundred years after Borrow:

> In a rail coach ambling southwards sat a hard-bitten old Estremenean farmer, with a head like Albrecht Durer's 'Hans Imhof', covered by a wide black hat . . . His face was seamed, pock-marked, as if by acid . . . His voice was rugged in tone, Rabelasian, as he argued testily about the parlous state of the country, 'there is no honour in the world. Food is unwarrantably dear, and a man has enemies all around him. Ha, fortunate indeed is he whose own woman is honest.'
>
> "*¡Buenos días!*" beamed this modern extremeño, as he approached me on the bridge and I saluted him likewise.
>
> He certainly had the weathered and wrinkled features of Dürer's portrait but appeared to have quite another temperament from that old farmer.

"How beautifully they have tidied up this old line," he continued, "and what a fine day! Are you cycling? Oh, yes, I see your bike. A serious looking machine, and well loaded!"

"Yes, indeed," I replied, and I went on to say I was waiting for my companions who were a little way behind at the station.

"How far are you going?" he enquired.

"Not far, we are going fishing," I explained, "to the Sierra Brava reservoir."

"Oh! There are huge fish there!" he said as he resumed his walk, "Monster carp, they say. Have a good day and welcome to Extremadura!"

"*¡Adiós!*" I called after him, "*y muchas gracias!*"

It rather seemed as if the people had changed since Coles's day and the country too, since Borrow, or perhaps it was that the spring brought out the best in everything.

Back in the nineteenth century, British tourists had been travelling through Europe in ever-increasing numbers and the need for guidebooks had grown rapidly. The demand was soon supplied, though, by a number of publishers, the most famous of all, of course, being the German Karl Baedeker, who effectively pioneered the concept of the international travel guidebook. Known simply as Baedekers, these books contained maps, travel routes and other useful information, as well as entertainingly written descriptions of all the most notable sights. Baedeker's *Spain & Portugal* was first published in English by Charles Scribner in London in 1898 and contained a useful phrases section, where the legendary, albeit possibly apocryphal, words, 'My postilion has been struck by lightning', may have had their origin, since the Baedeker section contained the following gems: 'Postilion, stop; we wish to get down', 'a spoke of one of the wheels is broken', and, 'Are the drivers insolent?', 'Lightning has struck' and 'the coachman is drunk'.

Meanwhile, the British publisher John Murray, whose most famous authors included Jane Austen and Lord Byron, began a series of Handbooks for Travellers, which constituted a defining moment in British travel literature. In 1845 Richard Ford, who, like George Borrow, had gained intimate knowledge of Spain by touring the peninsula on horseback, published his excellent *Handbook for Travellers in Spain*, a charmingly written and fascinating read, even today. Some moments, indeed, are quite frankly superb:

Aragon is a disagreeable province, inhabited by a disagreeable people. Obstinacy, indeed, is the characteristic of the *testarudo* [obstinate] natives, who are said to drive nails into walls with their heads . . . [however,] they are fine vigorous, active men, warlike, courageous and enduring to the last.

This last remark doubtless has in mind the Peninsular War, 20-odd years before, when Great Britain and Portugal had aided the Spanish in a long campaign against Napoleonic France's occupation of the country, eventually driving the Gallic enemy out in 1814.

Another remark from the *Handbook* was still charmingly true when I first came to Spain in the 1980s but is, perhaps sadly, no longer the case, as a consequence of the mass modernisation carried out by the European Community: 'The roads in the Asturias, much like those of Galicia, savour more of the age of Adam than of Macadam.'

Travelling around the highways and byways of Spain today, we will all come across cities, towns, seaside settlements and even the smallest of highland villages, where some local individual will inform you that their bread or cakes, their main square or principal street, their church or cathedral, their women, their fish, their nightlife, their lace or their decorative tiles are unrivalled, the very best in the country or even in the entire world, comparable with anything in Madrid, New York, Beijing, Sydney, London or Rome, without the least hint of self-effacement, humility or embarrassment. George Borrow had already remarked the fact in the 1830s when he stated that: '. . . the spirit of localism so prevalent in Spain, [makes locals] boast that their town contains a better public walk than Madrid.'

Richard Ford, following on the success of his *Handbook*, published a further volume, entitled *Gatherings from Spain*, which appeared in 1846, the consequence of a second period in the country. He also reflected on the Spaniard's tendency to locally limited ideas:

> From the earliest period down to the present all observers have been struck with this localism as a salient feature in the character of the Iberians. Spain is today, as it has always been, a bundle of small bodies held together by a rope of sand.

For the angler, as well as the huntsman and ultimately the conservationist, there were of course, among the many writers on Spain, Messrs Chapman and Buck. However, the country's sporting characteristics had also been acknowledged rather earlier, with a certain Henry O'Shea, whose *A Guide to Spain & Portugal*, first published in 1838, contained the remark that, 'Spain is the land of the man, of the gun and of the rod.'

Nevertheless, it was Richard Ford, along with the eccentric Bible peddling George Borrow, who had begun generating a greater, literary interest in Spain that would continue on into the twentieth century, leading to some remarkable works by several British writers, including Gerald Brenan's *South from Granada*, Rose Macaulay's *Fabled Shore*, Norman Lewis's *Voices of the Old Sea* and George

Orwell's *Homage to Catalonia*, where he captures the essence of what, perhaps, we are all searching for in Iberia:

> For almost the first time I felt that I was really in Spain, a country that I had longed all my life to visit. In the quiet backstreets of Lerida, and Barbastro, I seemed to catch a momentary glimpse, a sort of far-off rumour of the Spain that dwells in everyone's imagination. White sierras, goatherds, dungeons of the Inquisition, Moorish palaces, black winding trains of mules, grey olive trees and groves of lemons, girls in black mantillas, the wines of Malaga and Alicante, cathedrals, cardinals, bull-fights, gypsies, serenades - in short, Spain. Of all Europe it was the country that had had most hold upon my imagination.

Meanwhile, my thoughts had wandered considerably, I realised. The long hot cycle path, the spring air of Extremadura and the friendly old man's remarks had combined to beguile my senses. Looking back down the old railway line I saw my friends approaching and so I scrambled back down to my bike and got ready to join them.

After some kilometres we left the track and followed another, which was rather ugly, being really a service road running the length of a steep sided concrete irrigation canal which led to the dam of the Sierra Brava reservoir. About halfway along this road, we came across a lost sheep wandering forlorn at the bottom. It had plainly fallen into the trench and there was no possible way out. The shiny smooth concrete sides of the canal intensified the heat of the sun and were far too high for us to be able to get down or back up again. The sheep was in dire straits, its spindly legs and sheered flanks a pathetic sight indeed as it stopped every few moments to drink from the very low stream of water. Pepe took a few pictures and said he would post the images along with some comments online, as part of an ongoing campaign to have some access points built along these canals, which would allow lost livestock and other animals to escape, should they fall into them. There was nothing else we could do and so we cycled on hoping that someone would come looking for their missing sheep before too long.

We reached the lake perhaps half an hour later and immediately saw dozens of large carp thrashing around the surface, a pair of males chasing females and competing for their ladies' attentions. My heart sank rather, since my chances of encouraging a carp to get its snout down to the bottom bait were somewhat slim when the fish were frenetically spawning. We moved around the rocky shore and found a spot far enough away from the dam to film without its great mass of concrete dominating the skyline.

While we were organising our gear we suddenly heard some positively indignant yelling coming from far away and training our ears and eyes we eventually spotted two gesticulating figures on the walkway of the dam. With tremendous bellowing and arm-waving they were performing their duty as good law abiding citizens of Extremadura and informing us that no fishing was allowed: it wasn't yet the date; the cheek of some people, what a scandal! Doubtless their observations were sprinkled with illuminating decorations and colourful epithets but these did not reach us. In our turn we bellowed back, in five part harmony, that we had special permits. Yet greater consternation and indignation was certainly produced by this information, especially if they were anglers, but it was kept *sotto voce* and after a while they moved off rather disconsolately.

Following this interlude, I set up all my carp gear and soon had the baits out along with PVA bags stuffed with all kinds of aromatic goodies. As hook baits I had opted for a halibut pellet, dipped in halibut N-Butyric, on one line and a tutti-frutti boilie, flavoured with sesame oil, a few drops of pilchard essence and a little Magic X extract, on the other. Luckily, Alfonso didn't spot me doing all this, otherwise I would have had to explain the unexplainable to the camera, since I had little idea what half these things really were or what they might do. I would catapult a few more offerings of the various boilies and pellets I had brought along during the day. Meanwhile Pepe, Juan and Benjamin had set up their fly rods and were about to set off to stalk the margins. There were a few sunken trees just a couple of yards out with large bass lurking in their shadows and the margins were teeming with bleak, some of which looked like record breakers. To my right were half a dozen even bigger bass guarding nests, which could be seen clearly scooped out of the bottom. I set up a spinning rod and my fly rod too, choosing a small silvery streamer. The bass treated all my various attempts to entice them with considerable disdain but the bleak chased everything that went by, their mouths too tiny to be hooked.

A lovely little fish the bleak, once farmed around Europe for a pearl essence which was obtained from the guanine crystals found in their scales. Between four and five thousand fish were needed in order to obtain 100g of this pearly material which was then used to coat artificial pearls. A fish of 20cm and around 40g would be a whopper, and the UK record was only 4 to 5oz, but, the fact was I had other fish, if not to fry, at least to angle for.

I set up the landing-net. I had brought the big one, designed for monster carp and catching sight of it, Alfonso almost fell over laughing, in part perhaps because the only fish in sight at that moment were the bleak. Such crackpot optimism clearly had to be filmed and so I dismantled the arms and collapsed the telescopic pole until he was ready and then talked through the process of setting it up as well as explaining the need for such outlandish measures. After all, a 33kg carp had recently been caught from the Orellana reservoir, just a few miles further south, and there were certainly carp that size here in Sierra Brava. The scene was finished off with the remark that such a net was good enough for almost anything, even a cameraman, and swishing the net over I enveloped the man, the fluffy microphone, the camera, the tripod and all.

Some hours later, not a twitch having been registered by my Delkims, nor a bass lured to my Rapalas or streamers, I decided to tie a miniscule black gnat and commenced to angle for the bleak, for which my landing-net was most certainly superfluous to requirements. In ten minutes or so I had caught a dozen and was enjoying myself enormously, much to the amusement of Alfonso, who was staying with me all day. Juan had taken his TV camera with him, so all the possible angles could be covered. By early afternoon I felt it was most certainly tea time and so I pulled a flask from my panniers along with an excellent Wedgewood fisherman's mug. This business of tea time is always a great source of amusement to the Spanish, who view it rather as Asterix and Obelix did during the Roman invasion of England. Alfonso was no exception and so had to film the whole proceeding, which terminated in a toast to the viewers and the scene of a thoroughly contented angler and cameraman enjoying English tea and digestive biscuits on the shores of a great Spanish lake.

There was only one other event worth filming and by chance Alfonso had been in position when I was casting to a large, patrolling bass, which had appeared some yards out. First cast, the fish had hit the little minnow lure and leapt spectacularly, dived and leapt again, almost before I could react. I tightened down but it was too late. In one final eruption from the water, the fish tail-walked away from me and threw the hook, but Alfonso had the whole sequence on film, which made it all more than worthwhile.

As we sat down to review the sequence, the sun was lowering and thin layers of high cloud were forming, which led to the appearance of a curious meteorological phenomenon. The sun itself had converted into a huge hazy disc behind the swathes of cirrus and some distance to the south, at the same elevation, a breach in the cloud cover was filled with an oddly truncated rainbow. I snapped a couple of photos and Alfonso also caught the moment on film.

It was several hours before the others returned and, moreover, announcing rather greater success. I had no doubt caught more fish with my bag of bleak but Benjamin had had a good bass, Pepe too, and Juan had caught a 5lb pike as well as another bass, all on the fly. Most exciting though was Juan's having hooked a very large carp which had stripped off his fly line plus almost 120m of backing. Just as the battle seemed to be turning in Juan's favour, the fly had pulled free but it had been a great fight and demonstrated above all that the carp here could be taken on a fly. They had done really well, all things considered, but the general complaint remained that by far the majority of the fish, the carp and bass, were in far too romantic a frame of mind to be caught and so we thought we would try different territory the next day; perhaps the tail of the reservoir, where there were many more trees in the water and both good carp and bass were said to abound.

We were by this time unanimously hungry, since, in our excitement of the morning we had brought very few provisions. There were perhaps two hours of light remaining and Alfonso volunteered to speed cycle back to Logrosan and return with the van so that we could get to the restaurant we had been recommended by the people at the *casa rural*. This outstanding manifestation of heroics would later be toasted with an aperitif and again with the dinner's accompanying wines. Not least because when he returned, Alfonso brought with him a bag full of ice cubes with chilled cans of drink among them, which were very welcome indeed. These were guzzled down in no time and then we got all our gear together and made our way back to the van which Alfonso had managed to bring really close to the dam.

Back at Logrosan we stopped briefly at a bar in the village and sipped cooling shandies at a terrace on the street before the drive to the restaurant. Juan and Pepe arranged with the woman in the bar to provide us with food and water early the following morning. She turned out to be the queen of a real treasure house. There was nothing she couldn't provide in the way of food, drink, local news and even angling advice. When our companions returned to our table they had even acquired a few cans of corn, which I thought might tempt the carp, where my other offerings had so far failed. Perhaps I could float fish for some of the fish that moved close in.

We sat together a short while longer, speculating on what the restaurant might be like and indeed, just how far away it was, since the various people we had consulted, between the *casa rural* and the bar, had offered anything between one and eight kilometres. There had been a further contradiction, moreover. The place was said to be hard against the road and could not be missed, yet another man had said it was set well back and we were likely to drive straight past it. As we speculated, we became progressively more vociferous. Since Benjamin was originally from Galicia, and retained a tinge of that delightful, musical accent, so different from Castilian Spanish, all through the trip the rest of us had adopted the characteristic 'O' which frequently ends any utterance in the Galician language.

"Another shandy,O?" Pepe asked.

"Yes, O!" we all responded in unison.

From the only other occupied table, where a few local villagers were sitting, we suddenly heard a voice enquire: "Are you all from Galicia?"

"Yes, well, more or less," Juan replied. "I'm half Galician, from Valla DO lid!"

Valladolid, it has to be said, is certainly very much nearer Galicia in the far north-west, than any part of Extremadura, and Juan, though long resident in Madrid, was originally from there.

"Me too," I piped up. "I am half Galician too. I'm from England but I live in Valladolid." There was much laughter all round and as it subsided we bade them farewell, got into the van and headed at last for the restaurant.

In an amusing sequel to this story, I went to see the new Wayne Wang film, *A Thousand Years of Prayers*, some days later in Valladolid, and the main actor's name was Henry O. I emailed Benjamin the following day to say I had never seen a man from Galicia who looked so Chinese.

The restaurant turned out to be set well back from the road and we sailed right past it before seeing its lights behind us, between the trees. In order to turn round we had to follow the narrow road for some way, which, we decided, explained the bizarre variation in distances offered from Logrosan. After a series of remarkable manoeuvres we at last drove on to the track leading to the restaurant.

The long day finally ended with a superb if slightly late meal, including a seafood salad, deliciously tender cuts of venison, and Extremeñan wine, all in what turned out to be a really first-class place. There was a large bar as well as the restaurant in a complex which comprised a beautiful group of old buildings, including several circular *chozos*, or traditional shepherds' dwellings, converted and modernised into self-catering or B&B style accommodation. The owner of the business told us he also had a large tench pool, tench being something of a gastronomical delicacy in Extremadura, and that holiday-makers staying at the *chozos* would be welcome to fish for them. Not that anyone had ever done so. The pool had been stocked some years before and as yet, no fish had been taken from it, since he'd preferred the pool and its fish to become settled first. We would be welcome to angle for them, he said, if we so wished. It was a tempting prospect, the accommodation, the food, the tench . . . but it would have to be on some future occasion. We made our farewells and leaving there we found several large rhinoceros beetles humming around a streetlamp in the parking area. We were too tired to try to catch or film them and so after the short drive back to Logrosan, we turned in.

The next day, we agreed we needed all the hours possible in order to improve our number of captures, particularly my own. We drove out early with the van still loaded to the gills with all the gear from the evening before. We took the road for Zorita in search of a turning off to the left which would take us down to the tail-end of the reservoir. After a few kilometres following a dirt track, we were remarkably lucky to arrive within sight of the water, after the path had bifurcated and trifurcated a number of times along the way. The view which opened up before us was superb; the shore was an irregular series of promontories and inlets, the latter with numerous sunken holm oak trees showing at various distances from the bank. Benjamin immediately spotted fish moving in one of the inlets and we took turns to peer though his binoculars. There were bleak certainly but there were also some rather bigger shapes lurking there, whether carp or pike we couldn't be sure.

Leaving the van on high ground we unloaded our bikes and Alfonso sped off with the camera gear to film us descending the broad sweep of undulating ground between us and the largest of the promontories, on the bikes. On the higher part of the promontory, half a dozen ancient holm oaks provided a welcome area of shade from the already burning heat of the sun. Once again Juan, Pepe and Benjamin set up their fly rods and prepared to stalk the shallows around the bank to the left, covering the numerous inlets. I set up my pod and rods on the point, fishing one line to deep water and the other in the shallows daringly or perhaps foolhardily close to a number of the sunken trees, where a running carp would have to be firmly steered away.

The shallows fairly teemed with bleak and there were many more bass among the boughs of the sunken trees, although much smaller fish than those we had seen the day before. Again, Alfonso stayed with me but had to run off occasionally, while the others were still within cameraman sprinting distance, to film the capture of a bass.

All through the long day, the pod, the rods and the lines remained mute and still, locked in expectant concentration which gradually lapsed into fatigue if not despair. I re-baited and re-cast at intervals, loaded web bags, catapulted out boilies and pellets, all to no avail. Once again I turned to the bass and the bleak for entertainment and caught a good number of both on the fly as well as with small Rapalas. All my bass, oddly, came from the same spot. Although several bass chased my lures elsewhere, the only point where I was able to hook and land fish was among a dense group of oaks a short distance to the right of my carp rods. Each take came at exactly the same spot, very close to one of the submerged trunks. The fish varied in size, half a pound to perhaps a pound, and were great fun to catch, as were the bleak. The day wore on and the heat eventually began to subside but not a single carp came anywhere near. I thought more than once of packing up the pod and taking just one rod off stalking, but we had all our gear nearby, under the trees and both Alfonso and I were a little concerned about leaving it. Not that we had seen another soul anywhere near the waterside but there was valuable camera gear as well as fishing tackle and we thought best to stay put. Nevertheless, I was determined to change tactics once the light began to fade and the others came back to base.

The return of the intrepid fly anglers, late in the afternoon, brought even better news than the day before. Both Juan and Benjamin had caught carp, and Juan's fish was a very fat 15-pounder, definitely spawn laden, which he had spotted amidst a cloud of silt and bubbles in one of the more distant inlets. He had cast an olive green mini-nobbler to this fish and tweaking it close under the feeding snout, had suddenly felt it picked up and he struck. The carp sped or rather wobbled heavily off and had put up a brave resistance on the light tackle. Benjamin's fish wasn't as big but had been in powerful aquadynamic condition, giving run after run of thrilling fight. They had both enticed other carp during the day but they had either escaped hooking or the fly had pulled free. One really big one had pulled so hard before being lost that Juan had assumed the hook to have opened or the leader to have broken but everything had been intact when he wound in. The hook must have pulled free despite seeming so firmly hooked during the first couple of runs. The fish had picked up his fly near the tip of a spit of land all the way back down near the dam, where the deep canal we had seen the lost sheep in, emptied into the reservoir.

All three intrepid anglers had caught numerous bass and Juan had also landed another pike, of 3 or 4lb, demonstrating that all the lake's species could most certainly be caught on the fly. And, moreover, fly fishing was producing even carp, where my own almost infinitely patient and distinctly frustrating and more conventional carp angler's approach was failing completely. I told them I had not had the least twitch all day, just as the day before, and here we were, arrived at injury time, perhaps two hours before we would have to start the long drive back to Madrid, if we were to arrive there at anything near a reasonable time.

Needless to say there was much ribbing at this stage. All my tackle, all the bait, *El Toro*, everything . . . and not a carp to show for it! We all agreed that the best would be to load up the van and drive the length of the reservoir back to the dam, where we had seen some superb fish on Saturday morning and where Juan had lost his big carp. We accomplished the drive in Paris-Dakar record time and as we drove on to the dam itself, Juan and I decided we should take a look down from the top to see what fish were moving. Pepe and Benjamin immediately followed, leaving Alfonso at the wheel. He drove on at walking pace while we gazed over the edge like schoolboys at their local bridge in the close season. In the shade of the dam wall there were thousands of bleak in huge shimmering shoals and the occasional large carp. We had not been looking more than a few moments when I spotted a vast pale shape deep down, approaching the dam.

"It looks like a manatee!" Juan said.

"It's a carp . . ." I stammered, "a huge carp. It must be fifty pounds!"

I had said fifty but surely that fish could have been nearly double that weight. It slowly submerged again and our attention was then drawn once more to the bleak. A great hole had suddenly appeared in their formation and a huge pike came up vertically through the water, in no apparent hurry, and stopped, pointing at the bulk of the shoal like some huge compass needle, a good five feet long.

"That's a record pike!" Juan exclaimed.

"You can't cast from here," Benjamin said. "'No Fishing', see?"

There were signs prohibiting any angling from the dam.

"Come on," I said, "let's get going."

We scampered along the dam walkway seeing more and more carp until we overlooked the point Juan had talked about, where the canal water gushed into the lake. There were numerous large carp milling about, occasionally feeding, it seemed, off bits of silkweed washing into the water from the canal; 20- and 30-pounders most of them but at least three that looked like high 40s or 50s. I had to catch one, any one would do.

We ran on and caught up with the van, piled back in and quickly drove round to where we had arrived at the water the previous day on our bikes.

This time though I set up just one of my carp rods, with a float and a few shot; then, grabbing a tin of corn, we all hot footed it around the bank towards the dam. Juan and Pepe brought their fly rods too but by mutual accord, the ground was to be mine, at least for a few casts. With a tremendous swing I launched the little float into the ruffled water coming from the canal and squinted at its progress into the reflection of the falling sun. I let it drift some way until it eventually became wrapped up in a drifting clump of weed. I re-cast and was again watching its erratic progress, when suddenly it vanished. I was more than ready and my strike was met with a scorching run, the fish kiting fast away from the dam. The power of the ensuing fight combined with the relative lack of any sense of real weight made me suspect something was not right, and as it approached the bank, I saw that it was foul hooked in the dorsal.

"*Robada!*" I cried out, despondently.

Robbed, or stolen, was the very appropriate Spanish term for a foul-hooked fish and as soon as we had released it, a beautiful common of around 12lb, I was back casting anew. A couple of casts later my float again became bound up in surface weed and as I gave the line a slight tug to free it, the reel was suddenly screaming as line tore off in response to a tremendous run. In a matter of seconds the fish seemed to be well on its way to the horizon and from the way the bite had come, I feared it was again foul-hooked. Twenty-seven miles per hour Richard Walker had calculated to be the maximum speed of a running carp. I looked at the spool. In a matter of seconds this fish had taken a good hundred yards. I managed to brake the run at last and then began a really good battle, which Alfonso had been filming from the moment of the cast. The fish felt heavy this time and despite being convinced that I had again robbed the water, something in the feel and movement of the fish gave me a glimmer of hope. And so it proved. Perhaps ten minutes later, the fish was at last tired and came towards the bank where Juan was poised to lift it from the water. It had indeed been properly hooked, something I had quite quickly become sure of as the battle progressed. The superb looking, deep golden scaled common carp was now almost mine but the great landing-net, needless to say, was still in the van.

Luckily, Juan's ghillying was perfect and moments later I was at last able to hold up a decent capture to the TV camera. A 25-pounder was more than good enough but deep inside I was vowing to myself that I would have to come back to this water as soon as I possibly could. There were truly tremendous fish to be caught at Sierra Brava.

After the comparative slow motion of the long fight with the carp, everything once again sped suddenly into fast-forward mode. We packed up almost immediately after photographing and then releasing the carp and, after spending a little while arranging all our kit, the bicycles and the camera gear, we were on our way to Madrid. The weekend now seemed to have flashed by. We all felt as though we had only arrived a few hours before, but the job was most certainly done; there was more than enough film in the can for the report. All that remained was to wait to see the finished product, probably to be broadcast in September.

* * *

Looking back at my notes on Extremadura, I find that an earlier, indeed my first ever fishing trip there, had been a novelty in more ways than one. The idea back then of going fishing exclusively for the zander had been an extraordinary one. I knew practically nothing about the fish beyond the legends of my boyhood: not a proper fish at all it was said, an unnatural hybrid, a cross between a pike and a perch, terrifyingly voracious and damaging to the inhabitants of all watery environments. Over the years, I had of course learnt that it was in fact a proper fish and was native to the more eastern part of mainland Europe. Like the wels, the pike, and the large-mouth black bass, it was yet another introduced predator species into Spain, existing exclusively for the purposes of sport. Much has been said elsewhere about the catastrophic effects of such imported predators on indigenous species and their habitats. There are beyond doubt some man-made waters where the fish population has been established and manipulated by water authority managers without these detrimental consequences to the environment. Such waters and their fish species had never held any particular attraction for me, but the suggestion was made and at the very least it would be an opportunity to see for myself.

The Alcántara reservoir was to be the venue and my occasional fishing companion Antonio was going to pick me up early for the long drive down to Extremadura. The opportunity had come about through a friend of ours, Chema, a forest ranger in Valladolid province, who had recently been down to Alcántara on a field trip related to his work. On his return he had told us of the marvellous fishing, particularly for zander, to be had there, over a few Guinnesses in the 'Seamrog', our local Irish bar. Whether it was the way he told us, or the effect of the porter, I'm not sure, but we planned our trip there and then.

The truth is I had already heard of the place, not because of its locally very popular black bass fishing, nor its monster pike and zander but via some carp fishing friends back in England. Over the years I had lived in Spain, I had often been asked what I knew about Alcántara and its 50lb-plus carp, not to mention 20lb barbel. I had never been able to answer these queries with anything more than what appeared in the Spanish angling press. Twenty and thirty pound carp were caught every five minutes throughout the year and monsters in excess of 50lb were definitely out there, if they could only be found. Barbel over 20lb were common and decidedly carnivorous. Local anglers there said they could be taken on crayfish baits put out for carp and pike as well as any lures used for black bass, pike or zander. It had all seemed rather a long chalk from those few grains of corn, which were more than adequate for a specimen barbel back in the UK.

All in all it sounded like a very interesting experience. The Alcántara is an immense expanse of water and not particularly inviting to look at. It lies in wide open, bleached and deserted country at a point twenty odd miles north of Cáceres, on the river Tajo. Local fishing methods also left something to be desired. It was somewhat Rambo style, all science and technology with nothing of the art or sensitivity of good old traditional angling. I had recorded a Spanish TV programme, only a few months before, an item from the series *Jara y Sedal*, a fishing and hunting programme, which had featured zander, or *lucioperca*, fishing from Alcántara. The real star, I remembered, had been a powerful inboard motor launch, equipped with sonar, radar and underwater cameras for locating the fish. That done, hefty lures were trolled up and down over the fish which, when they took, were wrenched up to the surface by the velocity of the passing motorboat. Within a very few moments, stunned into near unconsciousness, they were alongside, hoisted aboard and thrown into special boxes in the deck of the boat. The voice-over informed us that despite their fame as sporting fish, they offered surprisingly little resistance to the angler.

Our trip, I felt sure, would be something completely different. I sat down with a few books and watched the video again the evening before by way of a little preparation. The film, I felt, would serve as a model for exactly what not to do. The fish in the programme seemed to bunch together in little hollows on the reservoir bed, which appeared to be devoid of vegetation. The fish looked lean and pale, and I felt sure they didn't get anything like enough to eat. They launched themselves suicidally at the passing lures and never knew what happened next. All the fish taken, at least 20, were killed and taken away, presumably for the table. It is certainly a much appreciated food fish in its native areas of Europe, and Muus & Dahlström's book *Freshwater Fish of Europe* emphasises the 'usefulness of the zander in converting large quantities of small valueless fish into delicious flesh'. It was not difficult, however, to see why it is not popular with traditional anglers and many fishery managers in the rest of Europe.

Antonio and I, needless to say, were much more interested in the sporting element and what might be done with a more sensitive approach. As we loaded up the car, at some unthinkable hour the next morning, I rattled on enthusiastically about the various new lures I had bought for the occasion. Antonio, rightly enough, concentrated on sorting out the map and getting me, as a non-driver and navigator of doubtful ability, on to the right page. It was still dark as we set off out of the city and after half an hour or so we were on the *Nacional* 620 heading south for Salamanca. From there it was the N 630, all the way to the lake, about 20 miles north of Cáceres. Even I could manage that.

We had the classical music station on the radio and amused ourselves trying to 'name that tune'. Something always seemed to distract our attention, both from hearing the pieces introduced and then, after considering and offering all kinds of excellently reasoned opinions, we would, inexplicably, also miss having our decisions confirmed or refuted by the announcer. As often as not we were completely foxed. An exquisite violin concerto suddenly filled the car, just after we had driven over a bridge where we had seen a very inviting stretch of river, glistening down a green and lush little valley. We were all speculation and erudition for the duration of its three movements.

"C major," Antonio affirmed.

"Later eighteenth century," I offered.

"A contemporary of Mozart," added Antonio.

Very lyrical, and very Mozartian it was too. But we had absolutely no idea who it was. Things didn't improve much when, for once, we actually managed to catch the announcer telling us that we had just been listening to Shizuka Ishikawa and the Dvořák Chamber Orchestra's interpretation of the violin concerto in C major by Josef Myslivecek. Antonio looked puzzled.

"Miss who?" he said.

"Miss Liver Check," I hazarded. "Never heard of her."

We both burst out laughing and needless to say missed the next introduction.

"Ah! Schubert," said Antonio.

The melody was so familiar, I immediately agreed and opening up the map was delighted to discover we were only about 20 minutes from the turning for Portezuelo.

"I think we should leave the main road just after Cañaveral," I said, "and follow the reservoir a while."

"Speaking of Schubert," I said, suddenly remembering some CD/LP cover liner note I had read, "you know the text was a poem or something, I forget who by."

"Yes, 'Die Forelle'," Antonio said.

"Well, I was very amused to read that before setting it to music, Schubert had stripped out some tendentious line, about the need for young girls to avoid 'fishy' men."

"Very sound," Antonio laughed. "Never have anything to do with a fisherman, good advice, unless of course the lady fishes too."

"A Miss Ballantine would do me nicely," I said.

"Are we anywhere near yet?"

"I think so, let me look at the map."

Chema had told us that there were several places along this road where paths and tracks led off to the water.

"We must keep a look out for likely spots for getting the trailer down to the water," said Antonio.

"According to Chema, some of the tracks are reasonable enough to get a car down," I said. "We should find something OK."

We had a little dinghy with us, which we had been lent by a friend of Antonio's, and were both rather excited about this opportunity to use it. The business of getting the permits both for fishing and embarkation had been horrendous. If it hadn't been for the help of the boat's owner and that of Chema himself, I rather doubt we would ever have managed it.

We reached the turning and leaving the *Nacional*, we found ourselves on a narrow B road, as yet, rather attractively, unimproved by EU money. After about ten minutes we saw the great blue-green expanse of the reservoir. Its yellowish white, sun bleached, gently sloping sides spread away into the surrounding, sparsely vegetated, desert looking country. It was not an attractive landscape in the traditional sense, but it had a certain stark beauty of its own. Summer temperatures here often got to 50°C, a murderous 122°F, definitely not for unprotected paleskins or the faint hearted.

We stopped at various points along the road and walked down towards the water. In the distance, occasional patches of chequered hillside were easily identified as vineyards, or were they mirages? Nearer to, the odd shrub or outcrop of grassy or prickly vegetation would be frazzled into nothing as soon as the summer got underway. For the moment though, they were little twisted clumps of grey-green struggling to extract some nutrition from the impoverished soil. But the lake was stunning, a tremendous extension of turquoise for all the world like the very Mediterranean, reflecting a spotless blue sky. Along its zigzagging irregular banks there were bays and inlets, invariably marking where small rivers and streams lost themselves in the immensity of this vast body of water. Many of these points certainly made life easy as regards getting down to the water with a small boat, but we decided to carry on looking.

We had eventually obtained our permits by post from the local Club Nautico some weeks before, after having spent a small fortune in telephone calls. Boating was an extremely popular pursuit on the lake and much promoted as part of the local tourist industry. However, we had been assured that by being far away from the club's lakeside buildings we would not come into conflict with the interests of other users. There were a number of designated fishing areas on the map they supplied us with, several of which were very popular with waterborne anglers. However, we thought we would investigate some of the less visited places. There was no doubt that the place was big enough for all.

We continued on our way, marvelling at the sheer size of this water. No wonder it held such huge fish. Alcántara is over 55 miles long, though rarely more than a mile wide. Its colossal 35,000 acres are retained by a dam at a town of the same name, 20 miles or so further west, almost at the border with Portugal. It is the fifth in a series of reservoirs on the river Tajo before it passes into Portugal. In fact, it is the border for a few miles, then it runs on unobstructed to the Atlantic as the Tejo, better known in England by the classical appellation Tagus.

The road suddenly veered away from the water and we lost sight of it for a few miles until after we had passed through the village of Portezuelo. When it reappeared we decided we were far enough off the beaten track, as far as other visitors to the lake were concerned, and we started looking in earnest for a suitable embarkation point. The road soon reached a small bridge over a minor tributary and we pulled off into a dusty layby. A roughish track led down to the lake over good solid looking ground. Antonio manoeuvred the car so that we could easily get the trailer to the water. After the three hours it had taken us to finally get here, being out in the boat was a very attractive prospect. It was a lovely still day, quite warm already, the air dry and scented with wild thyme.

We unhitched the little trailer and managed its heavier than expected weight down the slight slope to the water's edge. As we did so we noticed a whitened margin of bare ground with a line like a tide mark a couple of yards up the bank. The water level was clearly quite well down, though I imagined it was insignificant on a reservoir of this capacity. Having got the trailer into the water, we collected our gear, and while I sorted it out, Antonio parked the car. We hadn't got too much stuff, for a change; just a rod each, my old creel full of tackle and a couple of bags of provisions. I loaded it all into the boat. We had suncream and hats too, as it was sure to be a scorcher. I already had on a pair of old plimsolls, which would be fine in the water. We both quickly changed into shorts in order to get the dinghy underway. The water felt quite cold. Antonio unwinched while I got in a bit deeper and steadied her progress into the water. *El Torbellino*, it was a bit of a grand name for such a little boat,

'Whirlwind'! I unhooked the winch cable and throwing the mooring rope up on to the land, went up to secure her to a convenient boulder. Then, Antonio and I hauled the trailer back up to the car and re-attached it for safety's sake. Not that anything was likely to happen to it, but it wasn't ours, after all.

A few moments later, we were both in the slightly chilly water briefly, before clambering aboard. I had the rope with me and I coiled it up on the prow as my father had taught me years before. It had been when we used to go dinghy fishing for bass in the Medway estuary, off Kingsnorth power station. I had some great memories of those days, and made a mental note to persuade Dad to take the old boat out one day that coming summer.

Since Antonio had done all the driving, the least I could do now was to take over the oars and give him a bit of a breather. We pushed out on to the still water, but before moving, we got a couple of rods tackled up. This enabled me to show off the dazzling array of lures I had brought along in the hope of tempting the infamous pikeperch or at the very least a black bass. It was all a bit mind-boggling. There were a couple of super modern Rapalas (made in Galway, I noticed), a squashy green, yellow spotted frog, and some furry, rubber tailed imitation mice (with and without weedguards). Then another box with buzzers, poppers, chuggers, rattling bugs, creepers, trailers, jerkbaits, and Texas twisters. I had some spoon type spinners too, one I'd had since my childhood, an ancient Mepps with a nice red fluffy tail concealing the treble.

But there was more of the weird and wonderful! I had gone a bit mad during the previous summer in England, and this was going to be my first chance to try them out. I had bought some of those then quite new rubbery vinyl lures; worms in fluorescent colours, glossy wet black leeches and a natural tone crayfish, apparently in drag, with silver, pink and gold lamé tassels.

I had some flies too, really big ones. There were some streamers, one of which was a rather comical effort I had made following the illustrated instructions in a fishing magazine. It was supposedly an 'Eelworm streamer', and I was really rather fond of it. As if all these weren't enough, I had also brought along my old faithful pike lure, a silver floating 'Tadpolly' and a handful of traditional lures including jointed plugs and two flying Cs.

"Which are we going to try?" Antonio asked, looking somewhat bemused by this harlequin collection.

"I haven't a clue," I said.

"What ever happened to the Toby and Devon minnow?"

"Oh yes," I said, "I've got plenty of both, but I think we should try something as exotic as the fish we're after."

"Hmm, OK, come on then."

"What about this?" I said and held out my eelworm.

"It looks as though it should be on someone's hat at Ascot," Antonio said with that characteristic chuckle of his that I find I've adopted myself since knowing him.

"Give it a try," I said, "you never know. I'm going for one of these fancy new Japanese diving plugs."

Appropriately, since we were in Spain, these superbly crafted baits were called Marías; I wondered how they hit upon that. They were metallic blue and silver over a finish like ultra-fine chain mail and all the hooks were barbless. The Virgin Mary was usually dressed in blue and white, perhaps that was it. They were very impressive looking lures but I would have to be careful near the snags. We set up our lines, taking the precaution of adding in 12-inch wire traces, just in case a monster put in an appearance.

"I think we'll just let it drift a bit, once we are out a little way," I said, as I rowed out into the inlet, which joined the main lake about another hundred yards down. There was no detectable flow from this side stream, which was just as well since the zander was known for not liking any hint of current. If there were any here or in the main water up ahead, then the point where the banks of the inlet jutted out into the lake would provide excellent barriers. We decided we would fish our way there and then swing round and fish into the leeward sides of one, then the other. We were a good way off shore, in deeper water, but how deep I had no idea. Visibility down there was poor, which was a good thing on such a bright day. The water was an opaque turquoise, in which the zander would be happily oblivious to the sunshine and able to hunt easily. According to what I had read, they were well adapted to these conditions in which the pike, for example, could not compete.

I lowered my line into the water, about a yard at a time.

"We've about twenty odd feet of water here," I said. 'I suggest we try here, casting as far as we fancy."

"That won't be far in my case," Antonio laughed.

"It doesn't have to be far at all," I said, "but try different depths too, we'll search this area as thoroughly as we can."

Antonio always underestimates his skill as a fisherman, where my own tendency is quite the reverse. He's always convinced he's never going to catch anything, but I have a number of photographs of him with some superb fish. He's not as bad as my dad, however, who seems to go to quite extraordinary lengths not to catch a fish. I thought again of that little boat of his, upside down in the back garden. It was nearly ten years since we had last taken it out into the immense Medway estuary. The memory was so strong suddenly, I started to tell Antonio the story while we made a few exploratory first casts.

"It had been pretty hair raising that day really. Even though we were miles from the sea, the river was about five miles across at high tide and it could get surprisingly rough out there."

That last trip I remembered had been in September; we had heard that there were bass in the river, or rather I had. Dad never believed such news.

"They just make it up," he would say, "to get us poor fools buying bait and tackle, throwing our money away on all the latest bass gear. How's the fish going to know we've got all this gear? All he sees is a worm and he thinks 'Oh lord what fools these fishers be!'"

The gentle lapping of the waves under our boat brought to mind that long row out towards the huge power station jetty, the wind whistling round our ears. We had anchored not far off and fished towards the pylons of the pier, letting the tide drag our lines as close as we dared. I had the odd bite which Dad was convinced were nothing but pure fantasy. Then came the magic moment. The dinghy swung round in the wind and I had to swivel round on my seat and fish out of the back. Dad was holding his rod up high to avoid wrapping his line round my ears when I was suddenly nearly yanked out of the back of the boat. I had a fish on! A terrific fighting sea bass weaving through the powerful current that ran into the pylons.

Dad was absolutely amazed. He had barely had time to finish complaining about the wind, the size of the boat, my tangling position changes and the lack of fish when he had to switch tack and moan about some people's unbelievable luck. It took a while but eventually we got the fish alongside and up into our little boat. As it leapt about in the bottom we realised that we were being tossed about rather alarmingly too. The fish was a beauty, about 4lb and we both felt jolly pleased with ourselves. But it was to be the only one that day. The water was dropping fast and the wind was thrashing up-river against the tide. We had to get back, or else we would end up in Sheerness. It was hellishly hard work rowing right across to the Rainham side, but we had bass for tea. Not that Dad would eat it of course. He can't stand fish.

"He can't stand fishing either, if I recall correctly," Antonio laughed.

"Very true," I said, "he told Chris that I had cured him of 'the fishing lark' last summer when we had taken him down to fish Dover Admiralty in a Force 8."

I had dragged Dad out on several fishing trips when visiting me in Spain, but he only really came along because the weather was good.

Today was certainly glorious. I had been casting and recovering, searching the water at various depths and Antonio had been doing the same. Though I rather think that neither of us was quite with it yet. After so long in the car, and so much music, our minds were slow in adjusting to the business of fishing. The boat had drifted quite a bit, so I dipped in the oars and moved us out a little further.

"There is some current here you know," said Antonio, "the lure drifts slightly when I cast to the other side of the inlet."

"I think you're right, we'll do just a bit more here and then swing round into what should be slack water, off one of the points there behind us."

We fished on and I tried another, longer cast back towards the bank. The lure was quite heavy and I let it touch bottom before starting to recover in not too violent upward jerks. I could feel it wiggle and fall, wiggle and fall and as it did so it was definitely drifting, albeit slightly, round to the right. A sudden thud on the line made me strike and I was snagged. Luckily, after a few tugs it came free and a moment later I pulled it in to find a couple of little chunks of rotten wood on the rear treble.

"There's a tree or something down there," I warned, "near the centre of the channel."

I re-cast, again towards the bank, but this time further down the inlet, and let the lure go a little with the current. The wiggle felt more pronounced, the rod tip bouncing in time as the *María* skipped along down the side of the gulley heading towards the deep water and the stronger current of the feeder stream. The bait was well down now and making, in fits and starts, against the flow, towards where I judged the snags to be. I had a sudden, definite and I must admit very unexpected hit. It hooked itself and made off up the fairly steep side of the inlet into shallower water, my rod arching over wonderfully.

"I've got one!" I called out in surprise.

"Well done! I'll bring mine in and get the net."

My fish was pulling hard, already well away from where he'd taken. Zanders are shoaling fish and I was sure there were more down there, probably in the lee of that submerged tree. All of a sudden it splashed up to the surface, a fair way off and I caught sight of what I thought was a big triangular dorsal.

"That's not a zander!" I said, more surprised than ever. "Or a black bass either, it looked for all the world like a barbel!"

The fish battled on valiantly for a good while, tremendously strong but eventually just had to give against what was, after all, pike tackle. It approached the boat at last and Antonio leant over and netted what was indeed a barbel, a comizo, and quite a good one too. It was hooked on the front treble, having made its attack square on, unlike our intended quarry which, I had read, always took from the rear, usually after following a while through the murky water. A barbel on a pike lure was amazing; I don't think I had really believed it possible before. It weighed a fraction under 10lb, a personal best. Its mouth being relatively small, compared with a pike, I was doubly glad the trebles had no barbs, otherwise it would have been difficult. As it was, it took only a moment, but just before I extracted the hooks I got Antonio to take a picture of the unlikely combination of barbel and crankbait.

We slipped the fish over the side and got on with our supposed zander fishing. Suddenly, we were more attuned and Antonio had a touch almost straight away, but whatever it was, it eluded us. His lure had been passing close to where the snags were. We tried a few more casts to either side of them but to no avail, so getting back to the oars I took us out into the mouth of the inlet. We decided to have a try there before tucking in behind one of the promontories, into what we were beginning to feel sure would be very quiet water, where a shoal of zander would surely be lying in wait. It was curious how their behaviour was really a pikeperch mixture. They are basically shoaling fish, like perch, but the really big ones tended to become solitary, like pike.

With our first casts we both fell foul of some more submerged trees and after a moment or two of our expecting the worst, we managed to recover our lures. This time it was Antonio's that had its hooks embedded in sodden lumps of dark bark. Taking note of the spot, we fished with great care towards and around them, avoiding any casts directly over the top. We both snagged a couple of times more and were undeniably lucky not to lose our lures. The rear treble on mine had its hooks pretty well opened out though and I had to bend them back with the aid of forceps. We did, however, manage to establish exactly where the snags were and fished on without any further problems. There was, unfortunately, no sign of fish either. Not a touch, and so I took the oars once more and we floated gently round the promontory, which marked all that remained visible of the side stream's little valley.

A hush had fallen over us; there were fish here, we could sense it. The sun was high and the land temperature would be tremendous, 'cracking the flags' as Chris Ryan would say. On the water, despite the reflected sun, the air was cool. We were more silent and stealthy in our movements than ever, we had high hopes of this spot as a zander producer.

"Do you think we should try those squeaky voices Bob James and Chris Yates used at Redmire?"

"You can if you like," Antonio whispered, "I've got a respectable reputation to maintain."

We both nearly rolled over backwards in silent laughter. I imagined I could hear Bernard Cribbins narrating:

'For those of you who think that all anglers need certifying . . .'

Antonio was first to cast while I was sorting out the bit of a muddle my line had managed to get itself into. Honestly . . . you only have to turn your back for a minute and a fish will leap out of the water, grab any bit of loose line you happen to have left unattended and wrap it appallingly around everything in sight, including the rowlock on my side. But, on returning to his hiding place, this particularly villainous fish had caught sight of Antonio's dubious looking eelworm lure and taken a contemptuous snap at it. Antonio nearly jumped overboard with the surprise of the take, only a few feet from the boat. I had just about got my line sorted out so I hooked the lure on to the bottom eye and placing the rod out of harm's way, grabbed the net.

The fish was fighting away from the spot where it had taken, out into open water. It was a tremendous run, arching Antonio's rod over and causing our free-floating boat to swing around in the water. Line was still pulling off to the wailing accompaniment of a high note from the reel. It was a terrific fight out in deep water. While Antonio battled on I sculled the boat out little by little, stopping finally about 50 yards off. The fish was more or less under control after a good ten minutes of hard runs into the depths, and began its approach to the boat. I got into position with the net ready. Then came a tricky moment, where our fish made a concerted dash right underneath us. It was fortunate we had no anchor line out and Antonio was able to swivel round on the bench, stopping the run before the fish had made any headway back to where his companions probably were. Though supposedly not as renowned for its fighting abilities as the pike, this zander was proving a formidable opponent. Suddenly, it was all over. I switched sides and brought the net under the first of what we hoped might be several *luciopercas*.

This one was a beauty, much better looking than those I had seen on TV. More than just a cross between a pike and a perch, it looked more like some other exotic predator like a barracuda with large eyes, adapted to murky conditions. It had shining silver, metallic blue tinted flanks, which were darker above and then the characteristic bands inherited from the perch. The elongated, well-fed body was certainly pike like, though not the fin arrangement which was clearly perchy. Most notably the double dorsal, the first with its magnificent spikes, just like the perch in shape, but in the zander it is much more marked with dark decorative blotches and spots. Its other fins are transparent, unlike the autumnal red of the perch. Speaking of spikes, the most striking feature of all was the prominent array of needle sharp teeth.

We extracted the treble with great care; the fish had only been hooked on the rear set demonstrating nicely the zander's attacking approach. We sorted out the scales and I got a quick picture of Antonio with his first ever zander, which weighed in at 3lb 9oz. Then we held it in the water a moment, while it got his breath back and then catapulted away into the depths.

I rowed us back to our spot and after only a couple more passes with our lures, Antonio suddenly struck and the rod hooped over in response to the tearing run of another zander. They were out there all right and I decided to change my lure before casting again. Meanwhile, I had more ghillying to do. Antonio had to sidestrain pretty hard to keep the fish away from where the others were certainly lying. Every chance it could get, this fish made a furious run back in that direction but it was a losing battle until suddenly it broke surface in a half hearted sort of leap and threw the lure. Oh, that sinking feeling. We both sat back with mutual sighs of disappointment. Well . . . it wasn't the first fish we had ever lost, and it certainly wouldn't be the last.

We decided to commiserate over a bit of lunch and a rather fine bottle from the Ribera del Duero, called 'Moro'. There was every chance anyway, that our fish had shot straight back to the shoal to warn them there were anglers about. So, it was time for bread, cheese and some excellent serrano ham.

"Cheers!"

We toasted the great Alcántara reservoir and wished for more of its remarkable fish. A warm breeze had sprung up, coming from off the land and bringing with it the combined scents of thyme and rosemary. The wind gently buffeted against our boat and so we lowered the anchor to keep us within reach of the shoal, if they were still there.

After lunch I switched to a more brightly coloured lure, another of the Japanese Marías, this time red turning to yellow along the back, and we were soon casting once more into the deepish water on the protected side of the promontory. We fished every square inch of the water over the ensuing hour but had no more takes. We thought we would move round to the other side of the inlet and try the slack water there. From what we could see of the bank, which was steeper and appeared to have been terraced at some point in its history, there was probably even deeper water there. Antonio said he would get the anchor and steer us a bit in that direction, the breeze would get us there quickly enough. I threw out my lure deciding to troll it along in the meantime. I cast quite a way off, towards the near bank, the far side of the little backwater we had been fishing. Near the bank at that point, the odd stumps of branches showed and so I would have to keep the bait high in the water for fear of getting it snagged. Seconds after hitting the water there was a commotion on the surface and something rose to make a snatch at the lure. I thought I had seen an odd rise there earlier in the day, though I had decided it was probably a little grebe which I had spotted nearby. The hit came only moments later, good and hard, and almost immediately the hooked fish leapt and showed itself spectacularly. It was dark green, almost black, stocky bodied and at least 50% mouth. It went absolutely berserk, seeming to spend as much time out of the water as in it. I couldn't help wondering what it must be like to hook a big one, what they call a lunker in the US. This wasn't a big one though and it wasn't long before it was beside the boat, still thrashing about wildly. Antonio got the net to it and it was soon in the bottom of the boat, looking rather fierce, its great gaping jaws making the lure look quite small. The very aptly named largemouth black bass, known in Spain as the *perca americana* or *blas*, was about as popular with traditional anglers as the zander. This one was easily a couple of pounds but we didn't bother to weigh it. After I had slipped out the hooks, away it went, back to its preferred haunts around sunken trees at the edge of the water.

We were still drifting and steering towards our next pitch and with any luck a shoal of what for me at least was a very elusive fish. I threw out my line again to troll the few yards that remained but there were no takers this time. We dropped anchor once more and settled down to fish. The breeze was hot now, the afternoon temperature around 40°C already. We were glad of our hats and suncream. We cast to either side of the bay ahead of us; it was much wider and allowed plenty of scope for casting. It looked ideal, even better than where we had been. There didn't seem to be any obstacles either in this definitely deeper water, which I guess was something of a mixed blessing. We weren't in danger of snagging but then maybe there were no little hides for a nice group of zanders to skulk around in, just waiting for our lures to come by.

The sound of a motor some way off across the lake caught our ears and we looked up to see. It was an impressive looking launch, powering through the water, but it was too far away to see very well. I brought my bait alongside and got the binoculars. I could just see well enough to make out a fishing party. It looked as though they had all the gear, like in the video. They roared nearer, passing a little too close for comfort, heading for their chosen swim bristling with aerials and antennae. There was also a thing like a satellite dish spinning around at the top of a mast. I counted nearly a dozen figures on board and an amazing number of rods. There seemed to be special seats on pedestals too. It all looked somehow unsporting to me, too technological altogether. They would have looked less out of place somewhere out in the Pacific after blue marlin. I suppose it's just a different kind of fishing - each to their own - but it wasn't for me. I would always prefer the out of the way backwater, the unfrequented stream or pool, even if the fish were smaller. In the present case though I rather hoped we would do better than them.

"Another glass of wine, Antonio?"

"No thanks," he said, "I've got to watch my daily allowance, I'll have one more a bit later. It's all right for you, you're not driving."

"I'll have yours for you then," I said laughing.

Pouring myself a drop, I thought again of the polemic in the angling world over indigenous and introduced species, the worst situation being where local fish were all but wiped out by the introduction of predatory sporting species. Fish like the zander and the black bass attracted plenty of anglers and made the water a lot of money but with irreversible consequences for the habitat and its native bio-diversity. Alcántara though was fine, it was a man-made ecosystem in the first place and its residents were almost all introduced. Although the original river species - gudgeon, nases, wild carp and the small Iberian chub - may survive in some parts of the lake, I imagined they had mostly fled into other courses of the river. The exceptions are the larger carp and barbel, which, finding themselves converted into lake species, grew accordingly. The balance of power between the huge number of predators is controlled, I imagine, by the water managers through their stocking programmes to ensure healthy co-existence and first class fishing, among the lake's other leisure activities.

Back in Valladolid at the time, interestingly enough, attitudes were very different. The zander was considered a dangerous threat to the province's waters and any fish taken had to be killed by order of the local authority. They were under no circumstances to be returned to the water, the optimistic object being to avoid the spread of this species throughout the waters of Castile. The same rules apply to the sunfish (*Lepomis gibbosus*), the little catfish (*Ictalurus melas*) and even the rainbow trout (*Oncorhynchus mykiss*). With regard to the zander, the attitude of anglers particularly has changed spectaculary nowadays, with huge specimens being caught, particularly in the Duero, near Valladolid, but the law regarding the non return of these fish remains unchanged: they must be killed.

Moreover, under a new directive from the European Community, drawn up as usual by persons with little or no idea of what they are doing, *cotos* or controlled fishing waters, which specialise in catch and release of any of the so-called noxious species, including the wels catfish and the rainbow trout, have been banned. Although authorities will be obliged to accept and adopt this ruling, I do not imagine that anglers will pay it any heed whatsoever.

It is quite clear that responsible management of fisheries means good fishing for all and no fatal side effects for the environment. The most irresponsible aspect undeniably is the releasing of exotic species into any water without permission or without a proper study being undertaken into the consequences. Over-population too is irresponsible. I'm quite sure from the film I watched that there are areas of even this vast water that are overcrowded with zander. I was interested to read in Muus and Dahlström that there are both sedentary and migratory tendencies in these fish. The former have certainly stayed in and around the Club Nautico release points, hence the angling hot-spots, whereas the latter have extended into the lake. These fish, though fewer and farther between, were certainly the magnificent, healthy looking fish we had encountered.

By way of illustration, Antonio called out suddenly that he had another fish on. I put down my now empty wine glass and moved over to him, landing-net in hand. The rod was jerking like mad.

"It's a good one!"

"I should say so," I said, "it's going like a rocket."

Antonio's reel had just screamed impressively as his fish sped out to my right, the line whistling over my head. We both moved round and the dinghy did too. Then at last we had a clear field in which to play our fish.

"They certainly do go," Antonio commented, half to himself, as he began to recover a little line.

The fish had taken a good 20 yards off, surfacing in a series of splashes in the brilliant sunlight, sending turquoise glittering spray everywhere. Antonio was getting it nearer though.

"I think it's tiring."

He had the rod up high, the drag loose, keeping light careful control over his fish's approach; it could make another run for it at any moment. We didn't want to lose it now. Gradually the fish came nearer, staying up on the surface, rolling from one silvery, black mottled side to the other. It was a big one, 6 or 7lb or so. Its gaping jaws and oddly separated canines looked decidedly menacing as he slid finally over the rim of the net. There in the bottom of the boat, the two dorsals stood up magnificently, the golden eye glistening. It was in superb condition, all the fins intact, no marks of any kind. I pulled out the weighing bag and watched the scale register 7lb 11oz, a specimen surely. Definitely worth a picture.

"They seem to like this lure," Antonio observed, and I agreed, adding that I thought I would change again since he'd had three zander takes and I still hadn't even had one.

So, while Antonio got back to the angling, I carefully released the fish, with some gentle advice that he should buzz off lakeward and not alarm his chums. Then I rummaged around among the myriad lures and selected another streamer, a bought one, similar to the one I had made but with a bit more red chenille and tinsel in the body and big golden beads for eyes. That should do the trick.

The sun was notably easier on us now, the light more diffused, as though through a heat haze, streaming in across the water from the south-west. In the turbid turquoise conditions down below, visibility would be dropping off even more dramatically. The brilliant colours of these eelworm streamers ought to serve us well. In my preparatory reading, I had also discovered that the zander's eyesight is aided by a substance called *tapetum lucidum* in the retina giving them superb vision, especially at night. Night fishing is prohibited by Spanish law, although in some places special permits can be obtained. As for us, we had only these few hours of daylight left, then we would leave our finny friends in peace. It was just after 5 and we expected it to be getting dark at 8. We would pack up before then though so as to be able to get back to the shore reasonably safely. I began to wonder if we should try another spot. We had tried a number of casts more with no response; maybe that last fish had not heeded my warning.

"What about shifting back to the other side of the inlet," Antonio suddenly suggested.

"OK," I replied. "We've got about two hours left I guess and we'd be closer to our landing point there."

Antonio glanced at his watch.

"It's 5.15 now, let's give it another 15 minutes here and then move."

"Right," I said.

I made a long cast right to the tip of the promontory to my right and brought the streamer along the bottom fitfully towards deeper water. As has often been said, there's always a spot in your swim where you expect to get a bite - a point perhaps where the float wavers, where a side current meets the main flow, or where a light ball ledger rolls under an overhang, or in this bay, where the lure, after touching bottom softly several times at each careful pull, suddenly doesn't. You see it in your mind's eye embark on a precarious journey over a hollow in the lakebed, a perfect resting place for a whole shoal of hungry zander.

The expected unexpected take was massive. Just like that bass when I was out with my dad. It pulled the rod round 45°, the drag wrenched and I brought the rod up into a quick strike.

"Do you know," said Antonio, "I just knew you were going to get a fish before we moved."

The rod was bent right over as the fish steadfastly stayed down.

"It feels like a good one too, though it's not moving about much."

My drag whined as the fish pulled steadily, taking another yard or so. The line began to emit a shrill note, I loosened the drag and it sang out suddenly into the evening light.

"This feels very interesting," I murmured. "I think we're into something special here."

There was nothing like it. A big fish, an early summer, late afternoon on an exotic water in Extremadura, western Spain; I felt sure that some day I would be writing all this down.

Unexpectedly, I was recovering line, but the fish was still on, on a power drive towards the boat, but diving at the same time. I got ready to swing round. Antonio had his line in, the net in hand, and had moved to the middle of the boat in readiness. My fish had changed course a little but still came very close as it passed us making for open water. I wondered how big it was. It felt heavy, fast and powerful. It hadn't come up a single inch in the water. They reputedly got to 15kg in this reservoir . . . that's 33lb! This one felt like maybe half that, but I hardly dared think any more about it. The persistent pulling was taking off more line than I had just recovered and it was well down, deeper than ever and about 30 yards out. Our dinghy had swung round on the anchor rope and was acting as the more powerful team member in a tug-o-war. The drag continued giving little by little, with just the odd moment of recovery, but the balance was shifting. The fish would have to tire quickly at that rate and I suddenly felt it coming up and found myself recovering line very quickly. There it was!

"Wow!"

He looked big all right. Great flashing silver flanks in the reflecting ripples. He made just one leap, silhouetted black against the glistening waves, the splash refracting in the diamond studded air. Then, in no time at all, it was alongside.

"There are others with him," Antonio called out, "look at that one."

Incredibly, there were two other zander weaving around our fish and one of them was huge, double the size even.

"That could be a 20-pounder," I exclaimed, hardly believing my eyes, just as it and the other vanished under the boat. Antonio had the net to their erstwhile companion in seconds and hoisted him into the dinghy. The hook was embedded in the fellow's snout, the barb showing through. A spot of blood appeared and trickled under its left eye. Not quite sure why, I wiped it away as though it were a tear and held him up for Antonio to get the picture. What a fish! I pinched the barb flat and slipped out the steel splinter. Then I fumbled around in my bag and found a bottle of 'Medicarp' waterproof antiseptic to dab the little hole, which was no longer bleeding, I was pleased to see. A moment later I had the fish in the weigh bag: 11lb 14oz , two personal bests in one day!

Slipping the zander back into the water I leant over the side, both hands under its belly and waited for its complete recovery. It was a spectacular animal, for all their bad fame. I held on to its tail end as the pectoral fins stabilised and its muscles started to shift. Any second now and it would be gone. It was a moment to savour. Then the zander pulled away and dived out of sight.

The streamer was in a bit of a sorry state, with only one or two of the Flashabou saltwater holographic tail strands left.

Feeling sure that there would be no more fish where that one had come from, we upped anchor and started back for the other side of the inlet. I stowed the rods while Antonio took the oars and rowed us into the rising breeze, the water lapping rhythmically under the bow. Once we were back in the other little bay we got ready to try our luck. It had been remarkably active earlier, so there was a good chance that with the setting sun, we might see a little more. We soon had our streamers out and were fishing hard, searching every part of the water. After my first cast, however, my mind wandered to the leftovers of our lunch and so I laid out a few bits of bread and cheese and filled our glasses with the last of the wine.

We took a bite and sipped our excellent Moro between casts and were lucky enough not to be interrupted by a bite. As I was finishing my wine I had a slight touch and nearly sent the glass overboard with the enthusiasm of my strike. I think it was the thought of that 20-pounder.

Reeling in I found the poor old lure even more bedraggled than ever. I would have to spend an evening soon tackle tinkering, and tying in some new tails.

Antonio suddenly had another hit and his line ripped off dramatically as his fish made a run for the shallows. Luckily it headed parallel with the shoreline toward the promontory, leaving behind the deeper water and a possible shoal of companions. It was quickly subdued and having stowed my rod out of harm's way, I was soon leaning over to net our fifth zander of the day. This one was darker than those we had seen so far and about 2 or 3lb. It was unhooked and slipped back in record time, sensing that we had little time left to us. The sun was low over the lake and to the west was an immense shimmering mass of light. I felt I could have sat back and watched it forever. Away in the distance a silhouetted yacht's sail was the only moving thing discernible. This was in its way a very beautiful place. I then noticed a bird coming towards us, still some way off. We both stopped to watch. It was an osprey and was quite clearly searching the water for fish, with a view to using pretty well the same number of hooks as us. It was a magnificent bird and through the binoculars we had a good view as it gradually came closer. We were almost holding our breaths in anticipation at seeing it stoop and take a fish. It had drifted landward and appeared to be following the shoreline, when suddenly came a quick change of direction and we watched the bird disappear into the evanescence of water and sky.

Although the light was fading, visibility was still good and we had maybe half an hour at most before we would have to make our way back to the landing point and to the car. We cast out anew and began to cover our respective parts of the little bay. Time passed. Curiously enough, time only really passes at the close of a day's fishing, when packing up time approaches or it gets too dark for the particular kind of fishing in hand. Time doesn't pass in the conventional sense throughout the rest of the angler's day. As Chris Yates once observed, 'Time doesn't pass at all, it collects.' Great pools of time like Redmire or vaster reservoirs of time like Alcántara. 'It's just a matter of time' doesn't mean the same thing to the angler. He might well respond, 'Yes, like the universe.'

My reverie was broken by a vigorous tug on the line as my streamer busied itself near the bottom, off to my right. It had been a long cast, almost out of the protected water on the lakeward side. I had been just bringing it along with more or less random pauses, allowing it to sink slowly before giving it what I hoped were tempting flurries of activity. I carried on, alert in case another grab was made; it was going to end up with no tail at all at this rate. Another yard or so and there came a second tug, stronger than the first. I pulled in what was a lightish strike and bang; the fish was on. It immediately felt different though I had no idea what it was. It wasn't a big fish and was making hard short runs, punctuated by heavier sensations of tossing from side to side. I then suddenly saw Antonio strike too.

"I was just winding in to give you a hand," he announced, "and I got hit on the retrieve."

So there we were in the approaching twilight, battling with two fish simultaneously. Mine came up first, already quite near the boat, it was a pike! A jack of maybe a pound and a half.

"We might have to net them together," I said. "How far out is yours?"

"It's nearly in. It's a zander, another two- or three-pounder I should say. This is great isn't it?"

It certainly was. Both fish got it into their heads that it wasn't time to be landed and made good runs from right in near the boat. We were more than once in danger of getting our lines crossed but finally my pike was back in. It thrashed about wildly on the surface, twisting and turning so much that I thought I would lose it at the last. But in the end it came to the net fairly exhausted and rolled over on its back. I got the hooks out quickly and let it go just in time to slip the net under Antonio's fish. Seconds later it too was in the boat and having the hooks carefully extracted.

"That's six zanders," Antonio said, "and a great day's sport. I could get used to these fellows."

"I only had one," I laughed.

"It was a beauty though," Antonio went on, "and you had a pike, a black bass and a barbel too, all on the same bait!"

"'What a great day!" I inevitably agreed.

We got our gear packed away and I rowed us back into the inlet and up to the gentle slope where we'd cast off. We soon had all the gear in the car and *El Torbellino* back on the trailer. Swinging right on to the tarmac, Antonio leant forward and clicked on the radio. We sank into complete silence as the car was flooded with glorious music. It was sublime - shimmering tremolando strings and evanescent harmonies, an immense adagio, as massive as the great lake we were leaving behind us. The music shot through with the purple, pink and mauve of the sunset, the scale and range of its utterance having no equal in symphonic literature.

"Bruckner 8," we announced in unison.

Part Three

THE SOUTH AND SOUTH-EAST

Chapter Eight

The Ebro Delta, Tarragona, Catalunya

In which the author encounters the extraordinary leerfish in a Natural Park with horizon
to horizon rice paddies. Further language curiosities come to light, along with
giltheads, various sea bream and sea bass, which are caught on rubber lures.
A mystery fish appears, and the author stops at an old town.

The giant leerfish or *palometón* (*Lichia amia*) is among the numerous species that can be caught in the delta of the Ebro river, near Amposta in Catalonia. It is a truly stunning fish of up to six feet in length, weighing a maximum of 70 or 80 pounds and, most invitingly, the current International Game Fish Association world record of 61lb 4oz, was caught here, at L'Ampolla, in April 2000. The leerfish varies in colour from brownish bronze to golden green above with silvery, purple sheened sides, and a highly visible, wavy lateral line. All the fins are pointed and dark tipped, the dorsal is set well back and corresponds approximately with the position of the point of the anal fin below, both these fins then extend back to the tail, which is large, forked and with pointed lobes. The leerfish has a large, prominently lipped mouth with bands of numerous small sharp teeth. It is an inshore predator species, which has a particular preference for estuaries and occurs all round the Spanish coast but no further north in Europe than the Bay of Biscay. It is found throughout the Mediterranean as well as other parts of the world, including the West African coast and the Indian Ocean.

The Catalonian Delta de l'Ebre is a huge wetland area, which, at around 320 square kilometres, is the second only in national importance to the Doñana National Park near Seville. The delta has grown considerably and, indeed, rapidly over the centuries, as may be seen from the fact that the town of Amposta, which was a sea port in the fourth century, is now located 15 miles inland from the current Ebro river mouth. The adventuring English writer Rose Macaulay passed by here in 1947 and observed that it was:

> . . . an ancient town piled steeply, house on house, above the greatest river of Spain. Amposta was always, it seems, as hard to capture as it looks.

Amposta lies at the centre of the mainland abutting the delta wetlands and offers plenty of accommodation and information for tourists, birdwatchers and anglers alike. The companies offering chartered fishing trips are often run by Germans or British expatriates, making their webpages very easy to consult. Similar services are available in the towns of Ampolla, Deltebre in the delta itself, and at Tortosa, about 15km upriver.

Between here and the sea, as Rose Macaulay observed, 'spreads the marshy, lagoon-strewn delta of the Ebro, and the strange encircling hook, like a parrot's beak, of the punta del Calacho curls protectingly round the most enclosed harbour basin that for centuries was fought for by Romans, Carthaginians, Saracens, French and Spaniards. It is indeed a harbour, as Tortosa is a city and the Ebro a river, worth fighting for.'

The delta extends into the Mediterranean forming a dividing mass between the northerly Costa Dorada and the Costa de Azahar to the south. Its rounded shape and easterly progress attest to the continuing battle between sediment deposition from the great river and the moulding and removal of this material by wave erosion from the sea. There are two oddly hook shaped peninsulas, north and south, the Punta de la Banya and the Punta del Fangar. The northerly Fangar can be visited but the much larger Banya area to the south is closed to public access. The delta comprises largely intensively farmed agricultural land, producing mainly rice, fruit and vegetables, and its large areas of beach, marsh and salt pans, with their extensive networks of canals and irrigation ditches, provide excellent habitats for hundreds of bird species.

The Ebro delta area, part of which is a Natural Park, is also well known for its extraordinary piscatorial bio-diversity, with sea bream, bass, four species of tuna, albacore, dolphin fish, amberjacks, big rays and the leerfish being among the most sought after by anglers, along with any number of smaller species. Even an occasional wels catfish, the true freshwater giant of the lower Ebro, has fallen to a sea rod in the greater estuary area. Most fishing is done from boats but shore angling is a throughly exciting alternative, and one that I was keen to try for myself. The river itself and the numerous fresh or brackish water lagoons are full of fish. Mullet, mostly the thin lipped grey mullet, can be seen everywhere and are certainly a challenge for the angler. Then there are eels, gilthead bream, two or possibly three species of barbel, carp, black bass, zander and other smaller fish to be caught almost anywhere.

It was October 2011 when I chanced to have the opportunity to spend a long weekend investigating the famous angling possibilities of the delta. I had heard that weather factors were particularly important in this area, since the presence of strong winds not only affected those wanting to take a boat out but also made the estuary and delta water turbid and unproductive for lure fishing - spinning and jigging with vinyls and Rapalas, which were the prescribed methods it seemed for virtually all species. The number one tactic, moreover, was stalking, covering as much ground as possible in constant search of those tell-tale surface signs of predator activity, fleeing baitfish and swirling disturbances, often signalled by swooping noisy seagulls. All this sounds very easy, and it is certainly one of the most thrilling styles of fishing there are, but it is incredibly hard work, with or without a boat.

There was a weekend of gentle, blue-skied days in prospect, according to the Spanish Institute of Meteorology website, with light winds from the Levant. The news reminded me of Francisco Suay's delightful little book *The Gilthead Sea Bream*, a Spanish addition to the famous How to Catch Them series published in the Fifties. He knew this coast well and observed that:

> The very best wind, however, the wind most favourable when fishing . . . is that which springs from the sea itself, namely the Levante. Just so long as it does not blow with too great an intensity . . . An ideal wind will bring merely a steady ripple or a light swell to the water.

My first view across the immense expanse of the Delta de l'Ebre was on a pre-breakfast stroll from my *casa rural* south of the town of Amposta, actually in the delta area itself. Rice paddies, rutted and watery, glistened under the early silvery rays of a misty sun which had risen far out at sea. It no longer felt like Spain, nor even Europe, it was as though I had suddenly woken up among the rice fields of the Far East. There were clouds of beautifully fluttering white birds in the distance and as I walked closer I could see they were mostly little egrets and seagulls, with a couple of great white egrets and a glossy ibis stalking the muddy borders a few yards further off. The main undulating flock was following the progress of an extraordinarily bizarre tractor. The machine itself was a muddy blur, a cloth covered cabin hiding its driver under a maelstrom of black rain. Its front wheels were shiny thin discs like saw blades but the rear wheels were more like huge baskets, or over-wide water wheels from some mediaeval mill. Quite what the tractor was doing I could not fathom but whatever it was, the bird life was delighted with the whole proceeding.

After snapping a couple of photos, I was drawn away by the sound of rushing water and soon came upon a concrete sided canal. The delta area was criss-crossed by hundreds of these water ways, which kept the paddies (*arrossars*) inundated all the year round. Some of the canals were ancient stone and brick-work structures with the occasional remains of lock gates and sluices but most were modern like this one. Peering into the deep water torrent issuing from one narrow sluice, I saw hundreds of small fish tumbling in the flow. The water was crystal clear but still very much in shadow. I think the small fish were mullet fry but at the bottom, hugging the steep sides of the canal walls were some larger specimens, a shoal of darker bodied and noticeably scaly fish I could not iden-tify. They were very easily spooked and quickly vanished downstream almost as soon as I appeared. I decided I would return when there was more light. Crossing a tarmac road I could see another canal a little way off, with grassy banks running by large fields of cabbages and brussel sprouts, but between the road and the canal there ran a line of stunted palm trees, looking for all the world like huge pineapples. My *casa rural* was surrounded by acres and acres of mandarin trees and the rising sun was now picking out the bright orange fruit and dark green leaves on the far side of this little canal. The variety of plant life was most peculiar, with the distinct scent of wet cabbage leaves mix-ing in the vaguely salt air with the heady perfume of citrus groves.

As every angler will do, I crept up upon the edge of the water in the hope of seeing some finny denizen or other. The water was sluggish, green and weedy, and I imagined it full of eels, just like a spot I had fished as a boy in wildest Kent. Suddenly, my heart almost stopped as a huge fish drifted by, just a few feet from me. Silvery flanks with dark bars, double dorsals, it was a big fish, as much as 15lb; it saw me and vanished instantly into the depths. A pretty fine zander, in a stretch of water which looked as if it had never been fished. No one had even strolled its banks; the wet grass was lush and untrodden, only the cab-bage fields showed signs of any human presence. It was another spot I would have to return to.

I went back for breakfast feeling oddly leisurely, given the staggering prospects for an angler that seemed to be presented everywhere around me. Olga, the lady who ran the *casa rural* on a bed and breakfast, and, if required, evening meal, basis was a wizard with conserves and preserves of every kind. Breakfast included home made bread, cakes and sweet preserves made from figs, red peppers, pumpkin, aubergine etc., as well as superb coffee and a vari-ety of ham, cheese and tomatoes.

Olga had a broad Catalán accent, a much stronger emphasis on the L sound and a little more musicality than in standard Spanish. Many tourists coming to Spain to the coasts of Catalunya, Valencia or the Balearic Islands find them-selves bemused by the local language they hear, so different from that they had been attempting to learn something of before travelling. There is a much stronger connection with French; anyone knowing Spanish and French would undoubtedly find these Catalán variants very much easier. Word endings were invariably more French in style than Spanish, *'buenos días'* is *'bon día'*, *'adiós'* is *'deu'*, and *'campos'* (fields) would be *'camps'*. With verbs you will find that the Catalán equivalent, for example, of the Spanish verb *'comer'*, to eat, is *'manjar'*, much closer to the French *'manger'*.

I took my time over breakfast and it was almost 10 o'clock before I set off with a small rucksack of provisions, the heaviest items among which by far were two rather cumbersome 1.5 litre bottles of water. I also had a salmon angler's collapsible aluminium landing-net poked horizontally in the top and held in place by the flap, which I had buckled down as tightly as possible, thinking I might find myself in uncertain shallows.

In my lightweight waders I felt I looked uncharacteristically like a proper angler, a sophisticated game fish angler or fly-fisherman at least, with my short waistcoat jacket, its myriad pockets stuffed with lure boxes, steel traces and other tackle, then decorated with zingers, from which dangled forceps, snips, hook sharpeners and who knows what else. Then there was my peaked cap with the cloth neck protector behind. All that was needed was a few flashy American style sportfishing logos and I would have been a credit to Bass Pro Shops or even Farlows of Pall Mall.

Getting to the water and to promising swims anywhere in the delta requires some research, as there are areas which are closed to the public and others where there is a need to negotiate difficult and decidedly soggy terrain. More than once, I perched my rucksack on a bit of higher ground and slung the landing-net on to my back, before setting off to search for likely spots across marshy expanses rich with the smell of the sea, which was entirely invisible behind a barrier of three-metre-high reeds and grasses.

Having found myself a likely spot, I hurled out my heavy headed vinyl shad a satisfyingly long distance, the very light spiderwire style braid curving in a high arc through the bright morning air. I began the recovery almost immediately and made a series of casts covering the entire area before me in the classic fan shape recommended in all the books on spinning techniques I had ever seen, from as far back as my boyhood.

Since I had not yet started on my intended stalking, I hardly deserved to make contact. I was just enjoying playing at chuck-it-and-chance-it, something many modern anglers seem to have forgotten the simple pleasure of. To my great surprise and delight, after a dozen or so casts, something was happening. The sensation coming down the line was just like that experienced in freshwater, from the attacks of hordes of small black bass, their mouths snapping at the tail of the lure and not becoming hooked. It happened for two or three successive casts and so I quickly wound in and swapped the quite large, wiggly tailed vinyl for a much smaller one, about three inches long and, though it would not fly as far, I found I was able to cast it beyond the point from where the nibbles had come. A couple more casts and I had just begun to think that I had been touching bottom or snagging weed tops after all, when a positive hit lead to the jagging fight of some small but undoubtedly keen antagonist. Moments later, up to my hand came the prettiest imaginable little fish, a *lírio* in Spanish, a charming name, taken from the word for a flower, the iris or fleur-de-lis. The English name for the little fellow did not sound English in the least, it was either a 'vadigo' or a 'derbio', two distinct species in fact, *Campogramma glaycos* and *Trachinotus ovatus* respectively. Francis Day's *The Fishes of Great Britain and Ireland* (1880-1884) gives the likely origin for the English words when the author observes that 'Derbio is a local term employed at Montpellier'. The language there is the Langue d'oc (Occitan) variant of standard French. Day goes on to suggest perhaps a similar etymological origin for the vadigo.

In overall shape and fin arrangement both these fish resemble the very much larger leerfish and might easily be thought to be juveniles of that species, but perhaps for the relative straightness of the lateral line. The two smaller species were virtually indistinguishable in shape and size, although the mouth of the vadigo was in fact a good deal larger. The derbio, however, was the more colourful, a metallic turquoise green above running into silver below, with a yellowish tinge and with between four and six distinct, dark, near vertical dashes in the middle of the flanks. My fish, however, was a vadigo, duller in colour overall and with some 15 dark, near vertical bars along the length of the body, from the top of the back to halfway down the flank.

My fish was about ten inches long and I seemed to recall the guidebooks saying they got to at least double that and could weigh as much as 5lb. I popped the fish back into the water and continued casting, delighted to have found something to catch so early on, and I managed to hoodwink half a dozen more of these pleasing little predators over the following hour or so. Soon, however, the novelty wore off and I began to feel the need of some motion, not to mention a chance to catch or at least locate bigger fish. I moved around the bank, squeezing between trees and clumps of undergrowth and wading through the shallows.

I cast periodically just to test the water but there was nothing doing. I followed a spit of land for some distance, which was somewhat treacherous underfoot, with tangled roots and scattered limbs of bleached white driftwood, and eventually came to an opening. My heart leapt as I saw a swirl some 30 yards out and a spray of fry scattering in all directions. I cast the small vinyl and immediately had a hit from a larger fish. Some moments battling soon led to a scramble to get the landing-net ready while keeping the fish under control and out of the thick border of flotsam and jetsam in the margins. Soon enough a fine school bass of 2lb or so slid over the rim and lay glistening like a precious silver sculpture under the mesh. I had the hooks freed in a moment - my having pinched all the barbs flat when I bought these lures had been a decidedly good idea. I slipped the fish back and scanned the water for any continuing signs of action.

Disappointed, I ventured into the shallows and skirted the driftwood, watching all the surface ripples the while. A couple of gulls started to screech somewhere behind me so I doubled back and made my way through the undergrowth to a point on the other side of the isthmus. With a tree to my right I had barely room to cast but there was a commotion going on at no great distance and the circling gulls were increasing in number. One suddenly stooped and I cast a little wildly, my lure almost colliding with the bird at the surface. I retrieved quickly and again it was hit but my strike met with no resistance and I wound down and continued the retrieve. The water fairly boiled now, as hundreds of fry fled from marauding jaws, and I cast again and again into the mêlée, expecting a hit at any moment.

Quite a few casts later, I was at last rewarded and the fish felt bigger this time. Another bass, and I quickly saw that I was going to have difficulty landing him. I managed to get across the branches at my feet and into the water. There was a steep drop off and I couldn't advance. My boots sank into the sand and silt under my feet and while the rod bounced in response to the runs and dives of my fish, I gradually began to lose balance and felt that helpless sensation a wader sometimes experiences, of being washed away by the current. There was no current here, to speak of, yet I was sliding down a sandbank unable to get a sound footing and my fish was pulling the rod round to the far side of the tree, causing me very nearly to topple over altogether. The water was now just six inches from washing over the top of my chest waders.

It was an oddly calm, potentially terrifying moment. I saw myself slipping away into the water, waders filling with brine and sediment, the weight dragging me down. I had drowned once before, as a boy of fourteen. No breathing, no pulse, sickly blue-white faced, I had been dragged out of the chalk pit by a school chum, who knew about life saving. The most extraordinary chance. It had clearly not been my time, but this, now, perhaps was. I closed my eyes a moment, almost as though enjoying the odd sensation of absolutely no control over my circumstances. The fish was still tugging at the end of my line like a soul in limbo.

Then my left foot came up against something solid, a rock or a mass of more substantial waterlogged timber, a trunk of a fallen tree perhaps. I manoeuvred the other foot so as to obtain some purchase and began to inch my way under the tree and on to more solid ground. The fish was still on and now I was able to bring him in. I had left the net behind but being in four feet of water, I was sure I would be able to get hold of him safely. I wound down and fought the bass hard, quickly tiring him and suddenly I was able to reach out and grab him behind the head. With the fish safe, I tucked the rod under my arm and struggled through the margins to a point beyond the tree where I could get back safely on to terra firma. I sat on a fallen bough and unhooked the fish. It was a good five-pounder and would have made a splendid supper but I dropped him back and breathed a sigh of relief after my ordeal, which, truth be known, was quickly forgotten. The fishing prospects were just too exiting. Nevertheless, I was tired and it was most certainly time for a bite to eat and a drink.

After a quick lunch I made my way slowly back down the long narrow spit of higher ground. Getting my bearings once more, I headed for the point where the Ebro finally met the open sea, which it took me some while to reach. Across the broad expanse of the sea I could see the coast and the small town of L'Ampolla.

I was now fishing directly into the open sea, albeit at the very point where the great river finally ended its course. The first breakers were a couple of hundred yards out but there were others, coming transversely where a deeper channel cut by the flow of the river itself, created a swell. The furthest of these broke no more than 50 yards out and was easily within casting range. I sent my surface lure, a large-ish white popper, out beyond this mark time and again as the evening came on, quite certain that there had to be hungry jaws nearby, or that there would be as the light failed. I varied the angle and waded up and down the same stretch of beach where I had enjoyed my early morning adventures with the bass, working the water again and again.

Not more than 20 feet from my rod tip, seconds before I was about to lift the popper and cast again, a silvery flash came from deep down in the water. Something had made a pass at the lure, something rather bigger than the fish I had seen up to now. "Palometón," I muttered to myself, under my breath, it had to have been a leerfish, and a good one at that. I cast again and worked the popper back across the same area, and then tried again but to no avail. I decided to cast as far as I could further to the left, over where the swell suggested there was deeper water. The lure absolutely flew, caught on an uplifting gust of sea breeze and splashed so far off, I barely caught the white fleck on the crest of a bulging distant wave. I yanked the popper into life, wound down and worked it across the surface in high hopes of a take. I was not disappointed. Maybe 60-odd yards off, the line gave a tremendous jerk as if suddenly snagged and then started tearing off the reel, the drag wailing dramatically. The fish ran for a minute or so, in towards the river mouth, with me pressing my thumb harder and harder on to the spool, trying to stop too much braid from being taken. It dawned on me that the spool capacity was not really sufficient for this, I would have to pump the fish on as hard as I dare as soon as the first run was over. The rod was arched over beautifully, its full action against the power of the run. This was a good fish all right, a leerfish at last, I was quite sure. I then had a chance to recover line before the fish set off again, this time out to sea. The change of angle allowed me to half fill the spool once more, which made me easier. This second run was dogged enough but it was definitely slower than the first. As the fish slowed further, I started a little pump action and, though it took time, I eventually had the fish fighting out its last stand in the deep gully where it had first hit the popper.

It felt heavy, like a 20 or 30lb carp, but the rolling swell made the weight come and go strangely, the rod pulling hard down one minute, line ripping off against the drag, and then nearly flailing in the air as I struggled to wind down once more. Deep silver flashes much nearer now and I could see the flanks of the fish just 20 yards out. It came to the surface and rolled over. It was done for, all of a sudden. I waded out and brought the fish round on its side into the shore. It was over three feet long and close on 30lb I guessed. I unhooked it and held it upright in the water. It was clearly exhausted. I had heard stories of these great fish dying when landed, whether from shock or heart failure, I knew not, but I didn't want it to happen to this fish. I let it go twice and both times it rolled over on its side on the surface and I was sure it was going to die. Its eye stared skyward but its gills still seemed to be working so I got the fish upright once again and gripping the tail wrist, forced it back and forth steadily, making the foaming brine rush through its gills until it gave a slight kick and I released it once again. This time it moved forward, lilting perceptively but attempting to swim. Then it was gone. I stood among the ripples watching, my thoughts lost in the absolute timelessness of the sea and of fishing. It was as though I were in part myself and at the same time I was Günter Grass's mythical fisherman in *The Flounder*, who on a day 'towards the end of the Stone Age. A day unnumbered. [When we] hadn't begun yet to make lines and notches'. . . on that day he caught the talking flounder, a fish that gave earth shattering enlightenment to its captor. Down the ages, it was as though fish and fishermen were immortal, and standing there on the edge of the land, on the edge of the sea, I felt the rush of that immortality as though I were on the edge of the world. It was something that fishing did. Being utterly alone here, breathing the salt air, it was matchless.

* * *

Next morning, I set out earlier and took a long walk in search of flamingoes, eventually finding them at the l'Alfacada lagoon, where I stopped to take pictures. Not far away was the Serrayo beach, a huge length of sand which leads to the Barra del Trabucador, the long narrow sandy isthmus which extends over 5km out into the sea and ends in the restricted Punta de la Banya, an area of dunes and salt pans kept as a wildlife sanctuary. I walked away almost the entire morning before coming to a spot where I thought I would rest beneath a eucalyptus tree and close to another of the modern canals I had seen everywhere, again with a sluice and a flurry of small fish in the fast water. I had not quite forgotten those other fish from the previous day but was certainly surprised to see them here, just as I had before. I still could not make out what they were. The water was again deep, and the fish, a shoal of perhaps 20, were dark bodied and scaly. They were just as jittery too but I could see they had not moved very far off. A darkish moving shadow gave them away, about ten yards or so downstream, in deep water below where the foot of a concrete ramp entered the water. I had no convenient bait, apart from the bread rolls in my lunch pack but I was tempted to go in search of a worm. It is a well known fact that no fish that swims can resist a worm and never in my life had I been surrounded by such wormy countryside. Keeping away from the canal, I soon found a few rocks nearby and, turning over a couple of them, I quickly located two or three of the desired invertebrates, the most delicious looking small red worms imaginable.

Creeping back to the water, I crossed the small bridge over the sluice and keeping back from the water, tackled up with a small ball ledger, a small hook and the choicest of the worms. I cast out gently and let the weight tumble along towards the fish. The shadow suddenly moved out, across the flow and tucked in under the wall opposite. They really were the spookiest fish, whatever they were. I kept quite still, some considerable time, and my patience was rewarded when the shoal, which had inched upstream towards the little bridge, gently swung away and returned to the foot of the ramp. My line trembled. The current, the flanks of several fish passing, all made the line jittery. No fish that swims can resist a worm . . . the line jerked and I upped the rod to feel a brief tug before whatever it was escaped. I recovered the line and watched the shoal dash out into the flow and away downstream. The worm had been devoured, the merest sliver only still on the shank of the hook.

I took a break, sitting a short distance off under the eucalyptus and had my lunch. I really needed to discover what those fish were. The day was warm, in the upper 20s centigrade and beyond the canal, the wide rice paddies were dotted with the ubiquitous white birds. Peering through my binoculars, I could see various egrets, gulls and herons. One purple heron kept an aloof distance and a little further off a small group of spoonbills was busy in the grey water. This really was a birdwatcher's paradise. I was perfectly able to identify the commonest species but I had no doubt that there were many I was missing.

Still crunching on an apple, I headed back to the water. Crouched on the far side of the bridge I could see there were fish back at the foot of the ramp. Inching the rod forward, I lowered the lead into the water over the edge of the bridge, avoiding a cast or any sound whatsoever. Letting the line run slowly through my fingers, I judged the position of the bait as best I could and, once again, allowed it to reach the shoal of mysterious fish. Everything was quiet. The only sound was the distant indignant squawk of an occasional grey heron and rush of the water through the sluice. The rod tip quivered as before but the shoal stayed where it was. I had laid the rod down but I still had my hand on the cork handle, almost desperately expectant. The line pulled tight and I struck very gently. This time the fish was on. A wildly jagged fight ensued, the fish boring downstream, tiring and swinging into the wall repeatedly before rolling over and allowing itself to be wound in. I ran round to the ramp and brought the fish to my hand. Even before doing so I had seen what it was. It was still a tremendous surprise, a small, perfect, glistening bronze golden common carp, with softly tangerine tinted fins.

I have no idea what my imaginings were, but a small carp, a little bigger than the palm of my hand, had not been among them. I dropped the little fellow back at the foot of the ramp and returned to the bridge. There was no sign of the shoal now but I cast back to the same spot and sitting across the bridge waited for confirmation that they were all little carplets. Despite their decidedly jumpy character, it wasn't long before I had another bite and another pretty little common carp came to my hand. Well, the mystery, such as it was, had been resolved and I pressed on along the road towards the lagoons at Els Calaixos at Buddha Island (*Illa de Buda*), with the hope of catching a gilthead sea bream. Access was difficult but I managed to reach a few spots and try my luck with float and ragworm, the method employed by the occasional local angler I had seen fishing more accessible stretches of water when I had first arrived.

One old fellow had been sitting on one of those tiny stretched canvas topped foldaway stools I hadn't seen for years. I was sure I still had one somewhere at home. He was fishing a slow flowing channel for '*doraditas*', or small giltheads, using ragworm which he said I could get from vending machines at various points in Deltebre, San Jaume or Amposta. This was great news, as it was a bank holiday weekend and all the tackle shops I had seen thus far were closed. The channel ran slowly from a completely concealed small lagoon, behind huge reeds and rushes, passing under the unmade road, which led to the Gola de Migjorn, and on across the wetlands to the sea. I watched him for a while and he pulled out three little giltheads, no bigger than my hand, which he dropped into a large bucket by his side. There were already half a dozen in there, all destined to make a fine supper he assured me, and I'm sure he was quite right about it.

It wasn't until my last night that I took a walk into Amposta and found one of the vending machines he'd told me about, with the words *Cebo Vivo*

(Live Bait) lit up in neon. There were several varieties of worm on offer, each with a small photo for identification: *gusano americano*, which were apparently conventional earthworms; *gusano coreano*, ragworms from Korea; *gusano de playa*, which I recognised as good old fashioned lugworm; *gusano de cerrín*, which I did not recognise, and *gambas* or shrimps, as well as *cangrejo ermitaño*, or hermit crabs.

I opted for '*Coreanos*'. I had never heard of Korean worms before but they were ragworms and I was sure they would do very well, and they were also the cheapest on offer. For the princely sum of €3.50 I obtained my little box jammed full of cool, very succulent and, if you prodded them with your finger, decidedly nippy ragworm. I recalled an old UK seaside guidebook telling me that the large ragworm *Nereis virens* could 'draw blood with its hard chitinous jaws', there was little doubt these fellows could do the same. They were *Paranereis acrata* I found out some time later, a *nereis* worm imported mainly from China but which had originally been imported from Korea, hence its common Spanish name.

Back at my lagoon, the float bobbed gently in the ripple as an evening breeze sprung up while I fished carefully along the margins I could reach but it was all to no avail, I could not find or tempt a *dorada* no matter how I tried. Becoming tired at last and seeing one of the delta's small towns not far off, I eventually strolled into its oddly North African style streets in search of a café. The old part seemed for all the world like a small town in Morocco, with its narrow streets and single storey buildings. Shortly afterwards, I was sitting in the tiny main square of Sant Jaume d'Enveja, sipping delicious coffee, with the pretty façade of the church of Sant Jaume totally concealed from view by a modern tent-like structure supported by ingenious steel work, presumably to keep the sun off in the height of summer. A good idea, I supposed, but rather spoiling the view. Suddenly, the bell tower started up an appalling racket, perhaps announcing evening mass, but which went on and on, so long as to become unbearable torture. It just did not stop. Neither was the call effective, as far as I could judge, since the only person to approach the church during the cacophony was a young woman dressed in somewhat erotically semi-transparent black attire. Ten minutes, and still the din continued. I was reminded of Rose Macaulay at Cadaqués, just up the coast in the 1940s. On being kept awake all night by a church clock she remarked: 'I began to understand the Spanish passion for church burning.'

The peace of the square having been utterly destroyed, I paid for my coffee and got away as quickly as I could. I could still hear the bells some distance away on the road to Els Muntells, where another lagoon had caught my eye on the map, a much smaller one called Bassa de la Platjola. Reaching the spot at last, the light was failing as I tried to find somewhere I could fish. It proved impossible, unfortunately, and so in the evening's half dark, I started the long walk back to the *casa rural*.

It had been a wonderful trip and I was convinced that I would return. There was so much fishing to be done in the delta, so many species to tempt and so much territory to explore but for now, what I had in mind was the evening meal I had requested from Olga. It proved to be very much based on the *plats tipics* of the delta, a wonderful paella style seafood rice dish, *arrós a banda* in which the rice is cooked in a fish broth, which Olga told me she had prepared with red gurnard, red mullet and monkfish. Later, when the rice was almost cooked, she added clams, prawns and crayfish. As a main course there was fried fish, some four or five different kinds of small fish, the size of sprats, battered and fried whitebait style, which were absolutely delicious. I thought I recognised some of the fish - one was the weever, not a fish I was accustomed to eating but I did notice there was no sign of the poisonous spike. There was also a streaked gurnard and a tiddler flatfish that I think was a megrim.

The label-less white wine accompaniment tasted more like amontillado sherry but was certainly excellent. I rounded off with figs, mandarins and coffee, which I was confident would not keep me awake, since I was fairly exhausted. And so it proved. I slept like the proverbial log and early next day started the long journey home.

Chapter Nine

The Gilthead Sea Bream, Alicante

Where the author fishes for gilthead sea bream, during his father's holiday in Dénia. They consider some local history and have a night fishing adventure. The British and Spanish How To Catch Them books are remembered, wrasse and painted combers, giltheads are caught in the dark.

"Larderarder?" Dad looked bemused. "Sounds more like a car. What on earth is it?"

"It's a kind of sea bream," I said, *"Sparus aurata.* In English it's called a 'Gilthead', much prized around here by the anglers and even more so as a fish for the table. Very expensive too."

"That's why it's called a guilt-head then," Dad laughed. "Gold value . . . or it feels bad about it!"

"Could be!" I agreed. "It's also got a gold band across the bridge of its nose, between its eyes, that's where it gets its Spanish name from, '*la dorada'*."

"Ah! Yes, I've got it, like 'El Dorado'. Makes sense, especially if they really are worth a few bob!"

"There's no doubt about that, maybe we could try selling a few to the hotel chef," I suggested.

"We won't catch anything," responded Dad with his usual only half joking pessimism.

"We'll see," I said, and off we set.

It was high summer and we were taking a coastal break, nearly 400 miles south-east of Valladolid and even further from the desert-like vernal plains of Old Castile. Dad was out for his usual annual visit, and finding myself with a few days free at the end of the June term, we had driven down to Dénia, near

Alicante, for some sightseeing, and a bit of fishing. It had been Dad's idea, as he had been there before, one Christmas on an organised package holiday. On that occasion, I had travelled down by train one weekend to visit him and we had investigated much of the nearby coast, especially the wilder stretch along to 'Barranc de la Racona' and 'Punta Negra'. The weather had been disappointing though and we hadn't been able to explore much further or go fishing. It hadn't been the best fishing season anyway, although there was always something to catch in the Mediterranean. Just before deciding on where to go as the term ended, we had seen on the TV news that the Costa Blanca was having really superb early summer weather, and so Dad was keen to return. The fishing, needless to say, had been rather more my own idea.

We had been suffocating under a sudden early heatwave in Valladolid, making the thought of the coast yet more attractive. It was definitely hot here too but a balmy sea breeze and the shade of few tall palms would protect us a good bit in our chosen spot along the Alicante coast. It was late afternoon as we drove off, leaving behind holiday makers and ice-cream sellers and eventually the crowded sandy beaches. We parked off the road and taking our gear from the back seat, followed a path down among the rocks we had found a couple of years before but hadn't really explored. Driving past here as we approached Dénia, we had both suddenly remembered having paused at this point that Christmas to watch an expert angler at work. There had been a brilliant white little egret snatching tiny fish from the crevices and gullies where the sea washed gently in and out, its yellow feet almost dancing from one vantage point to another. Further west, along the coast of Andalucia, you could see egrets all the year round but here they only wintered. There had been cormorants too, standing up on the rocks, wings outstretched, taking a rest from the arduous afternoon's fishing. Remembering all this, we had stopped, I jumped out and scampered down the pathway to investigate. I had run down and back, delighted with what I had found and had gone on about it so much that Dad had come round to the idea of its being worth coming back to. Now, there was no sign of any of the egrets or cormorants as we made our way down the rather precipitous and winding pathway.

It wasn't too long a walk, despite Dad's complaining and saying we were lost, and it took us past an exquisite old house, a long low single storey dwelling, painted bright white, the roof too, and with pale blue doors and windows. It was certainly a fisherman's house, for alongside, hanging from a motley array of coat hangers were the bleached tentacles of about a dozen octopuses, drying in the sun. I paused to get a picture while Dad remarked that we'd never get there at this rate.

At last we reached the remnants of some stone steps which survived somehow the ravages of excavating crabs, tangled crowds of mussels and rather more orderly limpets.

"Boring bi-valves!" Dad announced.

We both laughed. Looking at a guide book to the Alicante shore the previous afternoon, we had been highly amused to find a section headed 'Boring bi-valves'.

"Don't look very exciting, do they!" I said.

A few yards further we suddenly came upon a truly exquisite fishing spot. There were some smoothed surfaces among the craggy rocks, with a couple of tall thin palm trees gently waving their bright green fronds overhead and one of those funny looking stunted ones, more like an enormous pineapple, providing a convenient pool of shade.

Late afternoon and evening were thought to be the best times to try for *doradas* so we had really been able to enjoy the long, relaxed Spanish '*hora de comer*'. But instead of following up with a siesta, we had walked off our fine lunch of gazpacho, chicken salad and some delicious white Rioja, with a gentle stroll out on to the sea wall opposite the hotel. From there we had a tremendous view along the coast to one side, a popular beach known as the '*platja de la Marineta Cassiana*', with cliffs in the distance, and to the other, the port with its yacht club and the old castle occupying the whole of the hill behind. The thoroughly entertaining Rose Macaulay had passed through here in 1948:

> Of all the lovely places down the Iberian seaboard, I believe Denia (the Roman Dianium) to be the most attractive, and the one in which I would mostly gladly spend my days.

Tourism had grown massively here since then and, like so many places in the south of Spain, it was now overwhelmed with apartment blocks and hotels and tens of thousands of visitors, making it rather less a place to spend one's days. The angler was more fortunate. Here, among the crags of ancient yellow limestone along the coast, it seemed as if nothing had changed in centuries, or indeed millennia. The turquoise sea broke softly, foaming white over the rocks, silvery fish glistened over scattered pinkish pebbles and shiny green palm fronds waved under a brilliant blue sky, just as they had done when Cicero, Pliny and Strabo had first written of the beauty of Dianium.

Dad and I hadn't brought much gear with us, just a couple of light, convenient telescopic rods and some bits and bobs of tackle I had collected together back in Valladolid. I had taken the precaution, however, of selecting good long rods and loading up the reels with some reasonably sturdy line since I knew we would be fishing over rocks. We soon set up with large-ish floats, and, as I was sorting out hooks and things, Dad spotted the handful of little glow-in-the-dark tubes I had included for later on in the session.

"I'm not fishing in the dark!" he said. "You must be crackers! We'd break our necks climbing back up that path!"

He was probably right but then I had other things in my bag he didn't know about and I wasn't planning to enlighten him for a while either.

During the morning we had spent a good while searching around the harbour walls in Dénia and among nearby rocks for crabs and any other shellfish we could find. We had a fair collection, to which we added a few ragworm, in a little flat box from the local angling shop and even some bread smuggled out of the hotel dining room. I had thought that there might well be a few *Eatapus anythinses* about, not the wild coyote but grey mullet, which we might be able to catch, if nothing else.

The tackle shop had been of great interest, as usual, and while Dad observed sardonically that I already had enough gear to set up my own business, I had gone looking for curiosities. Mostly it was yachting supplies and fabulously expensive gear for game fishing. However, I did find some marvellous reels, clearly modern versions of an age old local design. Originally of wood I imagined, these were made of dark purple brown bakelite. They were simple centre-pins, but with no check or ratchet. The odd thing was that the rod mounting bracket was in the middle of the back, so that when fitted it was flush against the rod instead of standing away. The man in the shop told us they were called '*carruchas*' and to my great delight he produced a wooden one too. They weren't dear so I bought one to add to my collection. Dad said he couldn't see the point since I was never going to use it, but then that was before he had taken up collecting pewter. There wasn't a square inch back home now that wasn't graced with a tankard or hip-flask. And he doesn't even drink.

The curious reel was back in the hotel, of course, and not with us on our angling excursion, and some years after this discovery, on a subsequent visit to Valencia, I had come across a really old one in an antique shop. It was attached to a three piece, 12-foot cane rod with the line running via a little hole near the *carrucha* all through the length of the rod and emerging at the tip. It was fully set up with a float, some tiny pieces of lead pinched on to the line and a hook. It was a real treasure, which I had bought for the bargain price of £10.00.

Dad and I had set up our somewhat more modern rods but rather than having started fishing, we were actually just sitting back lapping up the sun. Our little cove was very quiet, the odd raucous gull and some equally noisy shearwaters being the only disturbances. I spent odd moments during the evening peering at the latter - they were biggish with their odd tube-nose beaks. When one came closer, heading for the cliffs, I could see that its beak was yellow and so my pocket guide told me it was a Cory's Shearwater. I was delighted about that, having never seen one before and immediately ticked it off as seen.

The cove really was idyllic, its protected waters moving very little and judging by the shadows and the reflecting colours of the water, it was quite deep in places. Rising up from the ripples, there were the remains of high stone walls and a bit of a jetty, off to the right, squared, rough hewn rocks piled one on another, gaping spaces between and some heavy rusted and green weedy metalwork going into the water on our left. It had clearly been some kind of small docking point years ago, long abandoned to nature and certainly seemed like a perfect habitat for the *dorada*. In the brilliant midday light of the previous afternoon I had been able to make out in the three or four metres of water, that the bottom was relatively flat, having probably been excavated at some stage, but was strewn with biggish rocks and stones doubtless tumbled into the sea during winter storms. The white rocks were dotted with sea urchins, those dark reddy black ones which bathers often find out about the hard way. Their needle sharp spikes break off, rather too easily, and become embedded in your foot. There were great clumps of sea grasses too, the sort that leave softish brown balls of what looks like horse hair washed up on the beach. All this vegetation and varied debris provided excellent homes for the crabs, while the rocks all around definitely provided good cover for the fish. The *dorada* was known for making powerful lunges for shelter into crevices and hollows, smashing many an inexperienced angler's tackle. They fed there principally too, slipping in and out to capture scuttling crabs or picking mussels and clams off the rocks with their specially adapted mouths prior to crushing them with their remarkable molars. One Spanish author has the following to say:

> As we know, the gilthead has very powerful teeth, capable of pulverising all manner of shellfish. The hook needed, therefore, should be of tempered steel and strong enough to withstand not only the crushing power of its teeth but also the violence of its fight when under pressure.

I had, therefore, brought very strong stainless steel hooks sufficient to resist the teeth of this curious fish.

"They are a bit over the top aren't they?" Dad said, on seeing them.

"They have teeth powerful enough to mash crabs and shellfish into Shippam's Paste in a single munch," I said.

My number one source of information on the gilthead was, surprisingly, the How to Catch Them book I mentioned earlier. A dozen or so of the original 1950s British series were translated and published in Spain very shortly after their publication in the UK but one volume, Francisco Suay's *La Dorada*, was specially commissioned in Spanish and added to the collection to give the series a more Iberian flavour. This was certainly necessary, since, among the other titles were a few which must have caused much consternation - *Chub* and *Barbel* for example, which concern totally different species from the *cachos* and *barbos* occurring in Spain. The commonest Spanish chub, the *cacho*, grows no larger than our English dace. Keen *cacho* anglers must have been disappointed with their results after following the advice offered by Michael Sheppard, which suggested using a whole frog for bait. The eel was also included in the series, a fish which, as far as I was aware, has never been angled for with a rod and line in Spain, either before or since.

Suay's book never existed in English and some years later, I translated it, with the consequence that *Gilthead Sea Bream* was eventually published, in Herbert Jenkins's original How to Catch Them style and format, by the Medlar Press in 2008. Despite being written in 1959 the book is still an excellent source of information on fishing for the gilthead.

Francisco Suay believed in the most thorough preparation:

> . . . the distribution of fish, their behaviour and habits, as well as the all important when and how to catch them, [are] all such things as a good angler needs to know. I would say that a knowledge of these things amounts to around 60% of what you need for success. The other 40% comprises, in equal parts, the angler's particular ability and his luck!

I had attempted to do my homework as best as possible, hoping to keep the luck element within these roughly 20% limits.

Dad and I put on a few non-lead swan shot to weight the floats well, making them as sensitive as possible to bites in the quiet water. Our river rods were light and would be pretty exciting against these hard fighting fellows. Dad said he couldn't understand what I was getting so worked up about, he was sure there wasn't a fish for miles around. I had made the mistake of telling him that I had been able to see clear to the bottom the day before and there hadn't been so much as a minnow in sight. But I pointed out that I had seen a couple of quite big fish just as we first got there.

"Pure invention!" he said predictably. "It was only bladder-wrack."

Dad, I think it's fair to say, is not inclined to look on the bright side. Long and bitter experience of blank days spent alongside his fanatical son, who would be pulling them out non-stop, rather tended to confirm him in his pessimism, seeming to delight, moreover, in being justified. Moreover, he would always forget completely those days when he actually caught any fish.

So, finally our first casts were made. We had both baited up with mussels, since we could see some on the old piles, just at the water line, and agreed to try different depths, in search of where the fish might be feeding. They had the habit of cruising back and forth over, or along the edges, of their hunting grounds at a particular depth. Once this level was exhausted of its food possibilities they would move up or down and so the process would begin over again.

The angler would have to try a likely depth and keep at it long enough for the passing fish to find the bait. Just how long would be a matter of intuition, patience, or luck.

My bait dragged a little on the bottom causing the float to lie and stand up in time with the gently undulating surface. Dad was fishing about three feet higher in the water, letting his float wander slowly with the slight current towards our left and the tangled rods of old iron. We made ourselves comfortable in the rocky hollows and waited. The air was warm, and an occasional drink from Dad's flask of iced orange juice was more than welcome. We couldn't see more than a few feet into the shaded water, where at the edges we had our attention distracted from time to time by the appearance of occasional crabs. Mostly they were very normal greeny coloured fellows like those we had collected for bait; however, once in a while a reddy orange hermit crab would materialise just below the surface.

Dad was re-casting, having reached the dangerous end of his swim, and I decided I should set up the landing-net.

"You won't be needing that!" he announced.

"I'm going to try for one of these crabs," I said, and keeping half an eye on my float I slid the net down, close to where the hermit had last shown himself, and let it rest there, the handle near to hand. I didn't have to wait long, as my moving about had caused it just to duck out of sight for a minute until the coast was clear but it was soon back. I slipped the rim of the net in behind the crab and brought it up on to the rocks. He was rather a strange looking chap with apparently two shells, or a sort of duplex arrangement. The shells were soft too, covered in anemones that seemed to release a stringy sort of protective substance. I got a photo of him as he inched slowly over the foreign green surface of the netting, his dark little stalk eyes peering at me suspiciously, and then I put him back. I looked out to my float, Dad was watching his intently, but there was no sign of any action. The hermit crab had popped back into view after having scuttled off rather indignantly and was busy feeding, carrying minuscule bits of food to its mouth parts with claws that seemed somehow too big for the job.

"Shall we try changing the depth, Dad?"

"You're too impatient!" he said. "You've got to be patient at this fishing game!"

"OK," I laughed back, "but I'm going to re-cast."

I pulled in and checked the bait. All being well, I tried again at the same distance but a little further over to the right. It just looked more promising somehow and a slight off-shore breeze had sprung up, bringing a dancing ripple into the cove, just the ingredient a venerable old angler had indicated to the young Francisco Suay as being highly favourable:

There's a fine breeze coming up from the Levant and any moment now this flat calm will ripple, which will spur the fish into action, to hunt for food. If the wind doesn't drop, later we'll have a bit of a swell, which is just perfect for some good fishing.

All of a sudden we were indeed getting bites, from small fish almost certainly but the atmosphere became instantly electric. We watched our floats like hawks and it wasn't long before Dad had a fish on. It took only a moment to get it in, a little saddled sea bream, the right family of fish at least. Dad unhooked it carefully and dropped it into the water where it vanished in a flash.

"There's nothing but tiddlers in here, we'd've done better in the harbour!"

I felt inclined to agree. We had seen some enormous mullet there the previous morning, one must have been nearly a yard long, a 15-pounder at least. That would be something. Anyway, we fished on, taking several more of the small bream. After releasing one of these, I set my bait higher, partly to avoid them but also hoping to locate the elusive giltheads. I had bites again straight away, especially near the rocks. I persevered against what I hoped would be only a temporary plague of tiddlers, as did Dad, though I rather think he was quite enjoying himself. It was rather fun in fact and, to add to the amusement as time drifted by, I pulled up the occasional Martian looking fish with frog eyes, big cheeks, bizarre antennae and rather over-elaborate fin arrangements. One such, with a dark brown lateral stripe, I had never seen before, turned out to be a long striped blenny. But they were mostly of another kind, marvellously camouflaged, bespeckled with pastel browns. 'Glory be to dappled things,' I thought, though Manley Hopkins's trout certainly didn't have such a gaping great mouth as these fellows. They were gobies of a kind familiar enough to anglers around the British coast, and pretty big really, one was a foot long. The giant goby, aptly enough named, was, according to my Spanish book *Peces de Mar*, a voracious taker of hook baits and, more surprisingly, its flesh was considered excellent eating. I rather thought I'd put him back.

I noticed Dad changing the depth he was fishing at, out of the corner of my eye, and he cast a little further out, probably fed up with pestering tiddlers or my pestering him to do so. I wound in to check my bait and then tried nearer the old tumbledown jetty. We had to make sure we covered the water, as I had no doubt the fish were there somewhere. The time was right, the light was changing, a rosy glow filtered into the evening. The sun was quite low already, creating an exquisite red sky at night across the glistening sea. It was beautiful, and it really is a pity that photos never do such scenes justice. My float was still continuing to register bite after bite when Dad suddenly said:

"You made me fish at this depth on purpose . . . There are no fish there!"

"These tiddlers are driving me crackers," I said. "I'm going to change again."

"Humph!" Dad observed, laconically.

There was still no sign of the much desired giltheads and after a while we moved our floats again and began to explore about 18 inches higher in the water. I had set mine a bit higher than Dad's and I soon had a couple more rock fish which brought him to the logical conclusion that I had tampered with his bait and not only that but I had told him to cast just exactly where I knew for a fact there wasn't a finny thing of any kind.

We switched places and popping on one of Dad's crabs I cast out a little off to the left and eased the float along the edge of an old crumbled bit of wall which vanished darkly down into the water. As usual, my attention was distracted by the visit of another curious creature. There is nothing in the world like fishing for encouraging these close encounters. This time it was a starfish, bright red, four proper legs and a fifth replacement limb about half the length of the others. I hadn't noticed it appear but there it was on a rock a few feet below the surface. I'd have to get a picture of him. Out of the corner of my eye I thought I glimpsed a movement and I paused for a second and watched Dad's float, just off where I had been fishing minutes before.

"You've got a bite there, Dad!"

"No I haven't! I've never known anyone with delusions like yours!"

The float suddenly dipped very convincingly, more so than any of the blenny nibbles we'd had previously, and a sudden hard tug nearly yanked the rod out of Dad's hand.

"Strike!!"

Dad's line, float and tackle leapt out of the water and sailed away behind us, landing on the rocks.

"Oh! If you hadn't distracted me I'd've had that one," he grumbled.

I burst out laughing, in fact we both did. We retrieved his tackle and got back to the fishing; perhaps there were bigger fish about at last.

I set my bait at the same depth as Dad's and re-cast, hoping for some action. Dad had his line back in the water after inspecting it for rock damage, and a soft silence fell in the diminishing golden light as we stared hard at our floats. I suddenly remembered the starfish, but there was now no sign of his ever having been there. Oh well . . . It was a shame though, I'd've loved to have got a picture of that orange red star in the crystal clear aquamarine tinted shallows.

We fished on and watched the sun set, the great disc looking like a huge Seville orange dipping into the Mediterranean horizon. It was delightfully warm, the light breeze sweet with the scent of palms and the salt sea.

"Where are those luminous gadgets?" Dad asked, "We'll be needing them shortly."

"I'll get them," I said. "They just shove into the float tops in place of the red and yellow stripy antennae, we can position them for our next casts."

The nibbles of the *blenniidae* and *gobiidae* seemed to have ceased, and an expectant quiet hung over the proceedings. My float was near the wall and the bait was catching against the rock below, making the float topple over on the surface and then right itself in the ripples. I was afraid of getting snagged there and more than once gave a tentative tug to the line to pull it slightly away. There was a sudden resistance and my heart dropped at the thought of being caught up there, then a solid thud came down the line and I struck. The rod bounced into action, it was something to battle with at last. A good fight ensued, around the rocks and weed clumps, dangerously close to razor sharp mussel colonies before a wrasse broke the surface, suddenly spent. A beautiful fish, a good pound in weight, speckled reddy brown and cream stripes, with a lovely blue patch just ahead of the anal fin. A painted comber is in fact what it was, and living in these transparent waters made it rather more brightly coloured than those I had caught off the British coast. I slipped it back while Dad was grumbling about some lucky devil jinxing another chap's fishing.

"You just watch your float!" I cajoled, and sure enough he had another impressive knock and this time the hefty tug-strike sequence led to his rod arching over and a desperate battle to keep the fish out of the rocks. Lunge after lunge down and to the right where cover was thick and dangerous showed that this fellow knew all about survival, but Dad fought on, equal to the task, and it wasn't long before I was leaning down with the landing-net. It was a smashing fish, just under 3lb of solid silver plated crab cruncher with that characteristic gold band between the eyes and a dark thumb print behind the gills. There were flecks of red and yellow on the gill covers too, and its long spikey dorsal stood up for the photo, the proud angler beaming behind, great red spots in his eyes as it later turned out.

Despite their being tremendously good eating, we slipped him back into the water a good bit off from our spot, just in case he might scare any others in the vicinity. Then we settled back down to fish once more, our floats barely visible in the gloaming. We'd have to get the luminous sticks on next cast but I couldn't bring myself to wind in just yet.

"What's that noise?"

Dad's query echoed back down the years of my childhood. I paused to listen.

"I don't know," I said.

He had always been able to hear funny noises, invariably from the car, from the engine, the brakes or something, that no one else could detect, always with the ominous idea that something was seriously amiss and that enormous expense or interminable hours in his workshop were inevitable! But this noise was definitely odd.

"It's the giltheads!" I cried. "They're feeding!"

The strange watery crunches were quite distinctly audible in the still evening air, coming at longish intervals from the depths, seemingly at our very feet.

I couldn't help remembering a lovely moment in W. A. Hunter's 1927 book, *Fisherman's Knots & Wrinkles*:

Hush, Hush.
Don't include cracker biscuits in your lunch packet;
the noise made in munching these may prevent you
hearing a fish rise.

You'd hardly expect it to be the fishes' munching that was audible. It was all beginning to make me feel a bit peckish.

"Do you fancy a sandwich, Dad?"

We took advantage of the last bit of daylight to tuck into some peanut butter rolls and hot tea from Dad's magically produced 'other flask'. He hadn't told me about the tea; he had used the kettle in his room and some full strength tea bags he had kept in the car for emergencies. I produced from a mini cool bag I had hidden in my rucksack some strong dark 'Elgorriaga' chocolate, which I had bought in Valladolid. If there was one thing guaranteed to get Dad into the best possible mood, it was a nice slab of plain chocolate. The peanut butter, and of course the tea, were special imports, courtesy of Dad, and what a treat they were. It's funny how you miss some things.

We finished our tea and reeled in to sort the floats out. I snapped the little glass tubes and pushed the phosphorescent lights into the slots on the float tops, and put the normal daylight tops back in the tackle box. I was most impressed with these modernisms particularly as, in those days, I had little time for most. If pressed, nevertheless, I would have had to admit to having all sorts of ghastly things in fact, telescopic rods for one, but as the years passed, I gradually succumbed to all manner of modern inventions, realising perhaps that virtually all of them were thoroughly good ideas. I sometimes wondered if it was the effect of English teaching. I had begun my career pedantically enough, always insisting on correct usage. In fact, this facet of my character had begun much earlier. My mother always recalled that my childhood was full of scenes in which I corrected or loftily informed someone or other in what I considered to be the correct use of language. On one such occasion, when I was about six, I apparently enlightened a neighbour, with the unlikely name of Mrs Upham, that the 'birdie' she had asked me to come and inspect, 'wasn't a birdie at all but a budgerigar!' As time had gone by, and my teaching years became decades, I found that I was less and less rigid and indeed became fascinated and fond of the organic development of language, away from rules, which were often entirely arbitrary in the first place.

A rather purist, musically minded friend back in England, an archetypal crashing pedant in many ways, was nevertheless extremely amusing and often said things like, 'There's been no serious music since 1750!' or, more radically, 'If it's not Bach, it's not music!' His most entertaining remark, perhaps, occurred once when Beethoven's late quartets were being announced on the radio: "Bah!" he said, turning it off. "Erudition for its own sake . . . besides, the man was deaf!"

On occasions, particularly as an angling youngster, I had felt much the same way: 'If it's not cane, it's not fishing!' or 'There have been no acceptable tackle advances since the Arlesey bomb!' And electronic bite alarms? 'Bah! Technology for its own sake, besides, the man was too clever by half!' In other situations, a rather nice tench pool for example, even today I wouldn't dare produce one of these glowing float tips, I'd be much happier slipping the quill end of a small white feather under the rubber float ring instead. They are well-known to be amazingly visible well into the night.

While these reflections tumbled through my thoughts, out went our glow-in-the-dark floats into the darkling waters and I had a bite almost immediately. The float jerked to the side and then disappeared. I struck pretty hard and started to hold against a very single-minded dive down towards the rocky niches below. The rod arched over wonderfully, soaking up the power of the thrusts and turns deep down in the water. There were plenty more dives but eventually the fish came higher, and broke the surface with a number of twists and rolls. It was tiring at last.

"Grab the net, Dad."

"I'm ready!" he said, "You just stop trying to make out it's bigger than mine and get him in here!"

Just to prove the point my fish made another tremendous lunge and I began to feel the line being rubbed and dragged horribly over a rough surface down there. I scuttled along the rocks a way, keeping the rod out as far as I could. The persistent tension started to tell though, and with a sudden rush, up came our fish. I went with the fish's every move, certain the line must be damaged. In an instant Dad had the net under him, and up on to the rocks came a plump solid looking gilthead, about the same weight as Dad's.

"That's one-all," he said. "Maybe we should be keeping them for the chef after all!"

It was tempting really. When we had mentioned our plans to one of the waiters we had got to know, he told us that if we had any luck, the chef would be delighted to cook them for us. '*Dorada a la sal*' was a great local speciality, the whole fish packed and baked in sea salt.

"They really are good looking fish, aren't they?"

Dad agreed and wondered if there would be many more about. As he took our capture along to the same spot where we'd released his earlier fish, just the other side of the jetty, I listened hard.

"They're still there," I said. "I can hear them."

"We might as well fish on a bit . . . Any tea left?"

The dusk was closing in and our little greenish float lights were transfixing in an inky Dylan Thomas-ish, 'sloeblack, slow, black, crowblack, fishingboat-bobbing sea'. I'd had to cut nearly ten yards of damaged line off and tackle up again prior to casting. Running those few yards through my fingers, it had felt more like sandpaper. It would never have held another fish with any punch in him, and these fellows were solid muscle.

I sipped my tea and a second later, just as Dad was taking a sip from his, down went the cup, up went the rod, but it was too late. The line went down into the dark, into the rocks, snagged. Dad said he couldn't feel any movement, it was held fast. Letting out the line, but keeping it tight for the moment, just in case, I clambered off over the rocks to the derelict jetty. I walked out the few feet it allowed, to get a better angle, wondering if the fish was still on there. I gave a few pulls, felt a quick tug which went through me like electricity and tugging in response, I felt the line suddenly come free. Oh well, never mind. I made my way back to where Dad was finishing what was left of his tea.

"Don't you find it uncanny that they know just exactly when you've got your tea up to your lips?"

"It's happened too often to be coincidence," I said. "Not only that but he's snapped the point off your hook."

Dad hoisted an old Tilley lamp out of his bag and in a moment had it lit, adjusted and bathing us in its lovely yellow light.

"We'll be needing this then, to see what we're doing," he beamed.

I had to laugh, he was even better prepared for this nocturnal escapade than I was, and I was supposed to have been the crazy one for suggesting it. I wondered if there would be any other surprises drawn out of that bag before the day was out.

As soon as we had replaced the hook, we were back being hypnotised by those little green dots. It was an odd experience, all the surrounding coastal features had gradually blended into dark masses, and these then fused into one opaque mass. There was no longer a divide between sea and sky. Above us the moon had appeared and its mirror image was trapped behind rippling bars out ahead of us. Our occasionally flickering pool of light cast imaginary shadows on the blackness and the sea itself seemed to have shapes lurking in it. All was quiet, a gentle lapping of waves, the muted hiss of the lamp and once in a while that faint, rather too distant, tell-tale munching sound. The last had seemed nearer though and we were both tense with expectation - there had to be some action any minute.

We were fishing the same area, our floats within a few yards of each other, and still at the same depth, having apparently located the fish. But as usual my patience was wearing thin.

"I'm going deeper," I announced and I jumped up and started winding in.

"Me too," said Dad, somewhat to my surprise. "I think they've got wise to us."

Dad was really a believer in presentation, getting the bait nicely placed in the most likely spot and waiting as long as it took for a fish to find it. I was far too impatient, as he often told me, and spent my time seeking out likely haunts, stalking, even if I couldn't see the fish. In fact, with the exception of carp perhaps, I preferred not to see my intended quarry. It added to the mystery. I suddenly recalled that marvellous moment in Ted Hughes's essay:

> You are aware, in a horizonless and slightly mesmerised way of the fish below there in the dark. At every moment your imagination is alarming itself with the size of the thing slowly leaving the weeds and approaching your bait.

I was trying in close again, not far off the old wall, and deep. The clownish lurching of my luminous float tip showed that my bait was hopping about on the bottom. My heart skipped a beat once or twice when the bait dragged, making the float vanish for a second but it bobbed quickly back into view. Stealing an odd glance over my shoulder, I saw that Dad's was back by the mangled iron, its pin-point glow showing up nicely against the twisted shadows. A bit of a wind was getting up, the waves lapping more noisily. My float vanished again, I took up the line tentatively and bang! A fish was on. Its frantic jagging immediately told me it wasn't any size and it was only a few minutes before I swung what I thought was another little saddled bream up to be unhooked. To my surprise it was a gilthead, but only about six inches long.

"I've got one!" Dad suddenly called out, his rod hooped dangerously over.

"Wow! that looks a better fish than this little fellow," I said popping him back in and getting over to Dad with the net.

"He's well out, and down deep," the reel suddenly screeched, "and still going!"

Dad's rod tip bounced as he held on as though for dear life, the reel shrieking in fits and starts, the drag giving occasional inches while Dad managed to recover a few feet at a time.

"He's coming."

Just then the water burst open, spraying salty droplets everywhere that glistened and fell like snowflakes in the lamp light.

"It's another larderarder I think," Dad called out. "Blimey! They really do go!"

It was a super fish, we got several more good looks at it between furious tail driven dives and bright silver flanked thrashings off across the surface. Our biggest gilthead so far, now rolling and edging nicely towards the net. We were both very prepared for a sudden last ditch bid for freedom, but it wasn't until he was safely over the rim that a last thrash came, too late to do him any good.

It felt jolly heavy in the net.

"What weight do you think?" I said. "He must go at least 5lb."

Leaving Dad to the unhooking, I went for my old Hardy brass scales. The Tilley lamp was marvellous, I would never have found them without it, perched on top of a rock near my bag where I'd left them after the first fish. I would have been very sad to lose them.

"Two-all!" I announced, absolutely delighted with how the fishing was going.

"What are you on about? It's two-one . . . to me! You're not going to count that last poor little thing, surely!"

"Ah . . . well, I suppose it was a bit on the tiddler side!" I admitted, rather reluctantly. "But it was a gilthead!"

"Hmm, well, you'll have to do better than that. Come on, time's getting on!"

I didn't know what time it could be and Dad had left his new watch back in the car for safety's sake. It had to be at least midnight, and I wasn't sure if I wasn't feeling peckish. The tell-tale signs were there: fantasising about hot-cross buns, melting buttered and smelling of nutmeg. Houmous and golden crispy Mexican style tacos! The hotel had some great food, too, especially those big buffet lunch-time specials. I recalled we had done justice to a great mountain of *langostinos* the previous evening.

"Do you fancy a biscuit?"

Dad was rummaging in that bag again.

"They're only ginger nuts," he added.

"Cor! Yes, please!" I could hardly contain my delight.

"I think there's a drop of tea left, too."

So saying, he dipped back into the bag and producing the No. 2 flask soon poured us enough to wash down the biscuits.

We were both feeling pretty tired and decided it was time we should think about getting back. I searched the bottom of my bag and produced a little head-torch which I had intended to surprise Dad with, along with the chocolate, with a view to convincing him to stay.

"Ah! that's a coincidence!" he said, dipping once again into his own bag. "I've got one of those, exactly the same!"

With the help of his own torch, Dad started to pack up after a minute or so but I insisted on the angler's ancient right to a last cast! A last cast was not a bit like a last drink, it was never just one more for the road, there was something almost mystical about it. The night air was deliciously fresh and richly sea scented, but from along the coast came wafts of warmth, laden with the oily aroma of oranges - '*Azahar*' in Spanish, a lovely sensual word, reminiscent of

Arabia. There was something heavier too, that smelt somehow green, and hung suspended on the perfumed breeze. I swung the rod and watched the little phosphorescent bauble fly into the darkness. I hoped I was back out over the stone strewn flat area straight ahead but the line had pulled round quite hard. I hadn't taken my eyes off the little green dot's erratic progress and it was now getting close to the end of the jetty once again.

"Come on!" Dad called out, snapping me out of my reverie.

He'd already been up to the car, now he was coming back down the steps of the old wharf, torch flashing, the thin yellowy beam playing over the rocks.

"I'm finishing up this drop of tea and we're off."

"OK," I said, my eyes fixed once more on the tiny dot of light. The truth is I could barely see it. Then I realised it was slightly beyond the old stonework, further off than I'd thought. It was too close to the jetty and started to blink in and out of sight. I tightened the line a little, which fortunately bowed out away from the wall, and felt nothing. But, I was uncertain if I could actually see it or not. I struck suddenly, recovering the line as rapidly as possible and immediately my action was met with pounding resistance.

"I've got one!" I called out.

"Typical!" Dad called back. "You always have to catch more than me!"

"Come on," I said. "It's not caught yet!"

Dad was soon on his way down the rocks and came alongside with the landing-net just as my reel let out a series of screams, the line stripping off in yards.

"This could be a goodie," he half whispered under his breath.

"I think you're right there, Dad, he's going like a rocket."

The rod was arched right over, the tip nearly in the sea, and the reel continued to sing out into the night. Luckily, the fish had gone straight out into open water, but a glance at my spool told me it was a long way off. I kept the rod high but I could feel the line getting heavier.

"It's in the weeds I reckon, but still there."

I could feel the repeated thudding of its manoeuvres coming down the line and I imagined its determined course through the waving 'posidonia' weeds, for which they were known to have a marked predilection. I only hoped it wouldn't be able to wrap itself round too many more of them, or get to the rocks. It felt big but I was determined the fish would not make it right across to the other side of the clearing. There were certainly other outcrops beyond those visible in the daylight, continuations of the edges of the cove. The same idea obviously passed through the fish's mind as it suddenly lunged forward and ran hard, ripping another few yards off my wailing reel. I applied more pressure, as much as I dared and to my relief found I was suddenly recovering line. I kept on winding, the fish's movements felt dulled, but the weight was incredible. It was a good job I had stripped off that damaged line.

Dad was down at the water's edge with the net and I struggled to play the occasionally fitful, dead weight away from the old rusty piles. There was determined strength down there still making the line sing as he turned into the breeze, swinging round and finally flagging, then briefly surging again, bound for the bottom. If it hadn't bolted initially for open water we would never have got it. Up it came at last, tired, and with a great wodge of sea grass wrapped around the line above him. It was a big fish and after such tremendous resistance, was finally ready for the net. As Dad slid the rim under him, he flashed in splashes of spectacular silver attempting one more dive but his stamina was gone and we had him.

"That's a real beauty," Dad said. "How big do they get?"

"According to the book," I said, "they grow to around 5kg, that's 11lb, but I don't know what the rod-caught record is, or even if there is one."

I fished around in my bag and found my scales and slipped the magnificent fish into a bag for weighing. The old spring balance stretched down and read 7lb exactly, 3.2kg. A tremendous fish to finish the night and to crown our visit to the coast of Alicante. We still had another day but we had decided to visit the castle and spend the day as idly as possible. So, we slipped our last *dorada* carefully back into the sea and grabbing our gear started up the rocks and back to the car, Dad leading the way with the Tilley lamp.

"So, it was two-all in the end after all!" we laughed.

Chapter Ten

Andalusia and the Gypsies

*The author travels south to celebrate Mr Smith's birthday. Gypsy culture, language and
Flamenco music loom large, as do bizarre holiday characters that have also flown south.
The two friends fish on gypsy rivers and catch their barbel on the fly. Bloomsbury then turns
up in Spain, before the author leaves Seville, and cycles to a secret lake after black
bass, crayfish and an encounter with the largest carp he has ever seen.*

Recently, it was my old friend Norman Smith's 70th birthday and so, after
many years of absence, I was returning to Andalusia, land of sun, sangría,
Flamenco music and gypsies, as well as being the aquatic home of the somewhat lesser known gypsy barbel. Andalucía is, of course, the ancestral
homeland of Spain's gypsies. Not exclusively, but it is there we find the true
culture of the south, the essence of this region's immense landscape, from the
smouldering coastline to the Alhambra's majesty, from often rather squalid
expatriate, beery fish and chip dens to the gleaming white hillside villages, all
permeated by the thrum of guitars, the clatter of castanets and the anguished
lament of '*el cante jondo*', the most profound style of Flamenco *cante*, or singing.

On an earlier visit to the south, to Seville, I remember drifting between bars and
cafés, each and every one of them pouring Manzanilla wine, laced with the tones
and shudders of Flamenco. It was overwhelming but I learnt to breathe the heady
atmosphere while watching the often extraordinary elegance of the gypsy listeners. Sharp suits, high heels, long hair behind earrings, and invariably a carnation
in the glistening black hair of the women. Spirited shouts of 'Óle' punctuated the
performances, as well as a continuous murmur among the listeners, the rising and
falling drone of an almost mystical special understanding of the cult.

Spain's gypsies, believed to have arrived from North Africa as early as 1425, are known as '*gitanos*' and have the same roots and origins as those ancient nomadic Romani peoples found elsewhere in Europe. Their most ancient origins lie in Northern India, from as far back as AD 1000, almost certainly from the Punjabi and Rajasthani regions, where the people today continue to be great travellers. I once encountered a colourful group arriving from Bikaner in Rajasthan at the Taj Mahal in Agra. These far from footsore pilgrims, I learned, had walked there, a mere 300 miles, and they told me they would be walking back again in a day or so.

The word '*gitanos*' in Spanish, like gypsies in English, or *gitanes* and *tsiganes* in French derives from 'Egyptian'. It is as though European memory or cognitive power had only been able to comprehend the latter half of these people's journey, fixing their roots arbitrarily enough in Egypt. The original Romani language must have been gradually diluted on the long journey west, surviving only in fragments throughout the continents' gypsy communities. In Spain it became Caló, a kind of creole of Spanish grammar and much Romani vocabulary, which brings us, unexpectedly, to an extraordinarily bizarre British character, George Borrow. Borrow, subsequently famous for his 1920s gypsy adventures around Britain, as revealed in *Romany Rye* (1851) and *Lavengro* (1857), became an undisputed expert in Romani culture and language. He travelled widely, and, in the politically and socially turbulent 1830s, rode his apparently magnificent thoroughbred Arab steed (he was also an expert in horseflesh) around the Iberian Peninsula on a mission to extend, or rather to sell, the word of God, that is, the word of God as interpreted by the British and Foreign Bible Society, in the form of Protestant Bibles in Spanish. It was an intrepid venture, hawking an alien gospel among Spain's fanatical Catholic clergy and almost entirely illiterate populace. Moreover, he even translated the Gospel of Saint Luke into gypsy Caló and, yet more extraordinarily, passed the same text into Euskera, the impenetrable language of the Basque Country. He must have been very nearly a linguistic genius. If my tone sounds a little derisive or uncomplimentary, I crave forgiveness, for, beyond doubt, Borrow was a most remarkable fellow, an adventurer, a thoroughly courageous chap and, by all accounts, a distinguished and noble gentleman. However, it seems that his imagination, to say the least of it, somewhat ran away with him in his accounts of his adventures generally, and specifically as published in *The Bible in Spain* of 1834. As the scholarly Margaret Drabble once observed, it seems that he 'exaggerated both his linguistic achievements and the extent of his travels'.

I was first alerted to his inaccuracies in a minor way when I dipped into the chapter in which he stops at Valladolid:

Valladolid is seated in the midst of an immense valley, or rather hollow, which seems to have been scooped by some mighty convulsion out of the plain ground of Castile. The eminences which appear in the neighbourhood are not properly high grounds, but are rather the sides of this hollow. They are jagged and precipitous, and exhibit a strange and uncouth appearance. Volcanic force seems at some distant period to have been busy in these districts.

At first this passage reads true. The whole Castilian region, including the city and province of Valladolid, actually appears almost entirely flat when viewed from the higher ground, but it does in fact have numerous valleys scooped out of it, in such a way that from the valley bottoms, as is the case from the city, the surrounding hills are seen as broad flat-topped plateaux, all the same height. The entire landscape is very smooth indeed, there is nothing jagged or precipitous, and even less is there any aspect which might be remotely considered of volcanic origin.

I was bound to reflect whether Borrow had actually passed through Valladolid at all, if his memory were unreliable or whether, which is the most likely, he had picked up information about many places from more or less reliable sources as he travelled. His information regarding the city centre, however, is perfectly accurate, The Trojan Horse restaurant is still here, as are the Philippine Mission Building and the English College, exactly as he describes them. These details of veracity, however, are really of relatively little significance, for the best of Borrow is beyond doubt the revelation of his own ebullient personality, his picaresque telling of wonderful tales and his vivid presentation of the larger than life characters he encountered along the way, whether really run into or no. The worst, for a modern reader at least, has to be his appalling religious bigotry and general pre-Victorian hypocrisy. It is nevertheless a great read and deserves a space in the rucksack of travellers to Spain today just as much as when it first appeared.

Returning to the gypsies now, the music and culture of the Spanish *gitanos*, based principally in Andalucía, was considerably influenced by the cultures they encountered throughout their epic migration, but most especially in the Al-Andalus region of northern Africa, a name almost mythical in Spanish gypsy culture today. Flamenco music and dance, famous the world over, lies at the heart of *gitano* culture. The word 'Flamenco' itself may derive from Andalusian Arabic *'fellah mengu'*, meaning something like 'escaped person', in the sense of refugee or emigrant. There are other etymological notions with regard to the origins of the word, which may relate to Flemish and Spain's rule of that country, and so to a general concept of 'foreigner', or, to old Spanish words for flame and fire, to convey the deep, flaming, passion expressed in Flamenco culture. Whatever the root of the word, Flamenco is clearly a melting pot of Greek, Persian, Arabic and Moorish, and perhaps most deeply, Indian musical, choreographic and poetic elements, with highly complex rhythms, the foot tapping, graceful arm movements and erect posture of Indian Kathak style dance, and wailing, impassioned semi-tonal singing. The sound is notably non Western, where music employs the conventional major and minor scales. To these, Flamenco adds something called the Phrygian scale that has its origins in an ancient region of Asia Minor, home to the golden King Midas, and nowadays part of modern Turkey.

The songs themselves (if that word can really be applied to the extraordinary utterance given to language by a Flamenco voice, inspired by '*El Duende*', the mysterious spirit of the art) conform to one of several classic Flamenco rhythm patterns: tangos, siguiriyas, bulerías, fandangos, tarantos, rumba, alegrías, soleá etc. Of these, tangos, rumba and fandangos will certainly sound familiar to those with any knowledge of Latin style dance. The words are never easy to follow, sung in the Andaluz accent, in which many of the sounds of standard Spanish are elided and, moreover, are often so distorted as to be beyond recognition, and invariably express pain, anguish, regret, bitterness or nostalgia for the past. We might be reminded of Mick Jagger's famous remark, something to the effect that, if 'you want to maintain the audience's interest, you should only let them understand half of what you are saying.'

There are so many great names in the history of Flamenco, such as the guitarist Paco de Lucía, but we might pause a moment to consider just one, the singer Camarón de la Isla, who was born in San Fernando, Cádiz in 1950. Towards the end of the 1960s, Camarón was already establishing himself as one of the most important new voices in Flamenco music. Between 1969 and 1977 he recorded several influential albums, accompanied by the legendary Paco de Lucía, before moving towards experimental fusions between Flamenco and elements of pop, rock and even classical music. In 1989 his CD *Soy gitano*, 'I am a Gypsy', was released and quickly became the biggest selling Flamenco album of all time. In 1991 he was diagnosed with lung cancer, the consequence of a long-term addiction to tobacco and hard drugs, and he died at the age of only 41 in July 1992. Camarón de la Isla was mourned nationally, with many banners and writings on the walls claiming 'Camarón Lives!' His coffin was wrapped in the gypsy flag, and he was buried in his native San Fernando.

The gypsy or Romani flag, by the way, first came into existence in 1933, and is clearly based on the design of that of India, where the three horizontal bands of orange, white and green become two, creating a background of blue and green, representing the sky over the heads of an eternally itinerant nation and the earth below their feet. In its centre, as in the case of India, there is a chakra, or spoked wheel, further representing the nomadic tradition of the Romani people.

Included in Camarón de la Isla's 1979 album *La Leyenda del Tiempo* (The Legend of Time) is a Flamenco lullaby entitled '*Nana del Caballo Grande*', highly evocative of those ancient Indian roots, in which the haunting, melancholic theme, with words from a poem by Federico García Lorca, the greatest Spanish poet of the twentieth century, is accompanied by an Indian sitar. Another Camarón performance, the legendary 'bulerías' '*Pasando el puente*', or 'Crossing the Bridge', performed live with Tomatito on the guitar, in Seville in 1986 is replete with all the symbols and metaphors of the Flamenco tradition, the gypsy bandana, the dark pearl, the black and white horse, tears of blood etc., and features the following lines, remembering times long passed, delivered with such tremendous power and emotion as to leave you breathless:

Eres aquel triste palacio, You are that tragic palace
Donde cien principes soñaron con la gloria Where a hundred princes dreamt of glory
Donde cien reyes soñaron con el amor Where a hundred kings dreamt of love
Y se despertaron llorando . . . And they awoke sobbing . . .

These lines could easily have come from Lorca, whose *Romancero Gitano*, or *Gypsy Ballad Book* contains many such lyrics, about which the author himself said that 'the gypsy is the most basic, most profound, the most aristocratic of my country, [the *Romancero* is] representative of their ways and of whoever keeps alive the flame, blood and the alphabet of universal Andalusian truth.'

In November 2010, UNESCO at last recognised Flamenco as one of the 'Masterpieces of the Oral and Intangible Heritage of Humanity'. The bitterness of the long gypsy memory has solid foundations all across Europe, and nowhere more so than in Spain. Following the Castilian re-conquest of Andalusia, after 700 years of Moorish occupation, the government expropriated lands formerly occupied by the Moors, giving them to the military men and mercenaries who had finally driven the invaders from Al-Andalus. The Spanish Crown then ordered the expulsion or forceful conversion to Catholicism of the Andalusian Moors, many of whom took refuge among the gypsies, becoming '*fellah mengu*' to avoid persecution or deportation. In 1492 gypsies were included in the list of peoples to be assimilated or driven out of Spain.

Over the succeeding three centuries, gypsies were subject to special laws and policies designed to effectively eliminate them: settlements were broken up and the people dispersed; they were coerced into marrying non-gypsies; their language and rituals were prohibited, and they were excluded from any public office. In the mid 1700s there was a concerted campaign to rid the country of gypsies, with indiscriminate arrests and internments in forced labour camps. Gypsies were seen not only in Spain but across Europe as an indolent people but also decidedly dangerous, prone to thieving and the kidnapping of children. Their customs and itinerant disposition were seen as alien, even as being in league with dark forces and magic, popularly evinced by their tradition of fortune-telling and palmistry.

Persecution of the gypsies continued through to the Civil War of the 1930s, when Republican forces killed many gypsy converts to Catholicism, and then Franco's ascendant cohorts killed many more, as supporters of the Republic. Under the ensuing dictatorship, gypsies were generally victimised or, in the case of those more fortunate, completely ignored, as effectively not forming part of the country's people.

Spanish government policy has been much more sympathetic since the transition of power following the death of Franco and the establishment of a parliamentary monarchy. Social welfare and services policy began to embrace the gypsy community, and in 1977, the last anti-gypsy laws were repealed. Since 1983, the government has operated a special education programme for the disadvantaged, including those in gypsy communities. Today, while the gypsy population remains largely outside mainstream social, economic and political life, it continues to be fundamental to Spain's cultural and linguistic heritage. The stereotype of a Spaniard throughout much of the world owes more to gypsy culture than anything else and the 2010 UNESCO declaration was embraced nationally, as though a credit to Spain rather than to the wider gypsy community.

Returning a moment to language, the word '*Caló*' actually means 'dark' and the Caló word for gypsies is *calé*, meaning 'the dark ones'. Something dark and indeed wild persists not only in the fact of their being a darker skinned race but in our concept of what it means to be a gypsy. A century before the cinematographic concept of Film Noir, with its darkly dangerous women characters, *Carmen* by Mérimée was published in 1845. Its protagonist is a dark-haired gypsy beauty, a *femme fatale*, ready to lie, to undermine or debase the lives of men, and subsequently made world famous through Bizet's opera of the same name.

The well-known music of that same opera's overture was ringing out over the PA as my plane taxied into Málaga airport, and a delicious wave of heat entered the cabin as soon as the doors opened and before the passengers had begun to disembark. Even though it was October, and the flight duration had been a mere 30 minutes, I was suddenly in a different world. From the chill high northern plateau of Old Castile I had descended to the warm coastal south, where the scent of ripening pomegranates and orange groves permeated the atmosphere.

The south of Spain is another country in more ways than one. In part it's an English or German or Dutch colony; there are supermarkets full of the sorts of things I would never find in Valladolid. There are even Sunday car-boot sales. The sense of the expatriate was everywhere, and particularly in the ways of life of ageing northern Europeans, oddly cut off from home and yet in some way still living there. There was a sense of British 1940s' cinema in the Berts and Lils or the Alecs and Dots. It was all endearing somehow, reminiscent of Ealing Comedy's *Passport to Pimlico*. While waiting by the luggage belt my mind suddenly flashed back to my first ever visit to Spain, and this very same airport. The name of the place I had been heading to on that occasion was the 'Bahía Dorada', the Golden Bay . . .

How I had first come to hear of the Bahía Dorada was all down to the inimitable 'T'. One afternoon in Rochester, a university friend of mine, James Gray, and myself had been visiting a friend of ours called Simon, and we had driven out to his parents' place to lend a hand with moving some furniture. Simon's father was always known quite simply as 'T' and was something of a legend. Mr and Mrs T were a remarkable couple in their vigorous seventies; they were always lively and busy at something, repairing this and tending that, dashing between the cottage and the village shops, keeping the garden and the allotment, campaigning for closing something or keeping something open, as well as running the local active retirement association and flying off to 'our marvellous little place in Spain' for holidays. T, furthermore, was an enthusiast at home improvements and even tried his hand at inventing, not always with the best results. He was hilarious to speak to, or rather listen to, since he only ever used two superlatives: 'marvellous' and 'ghastly'. Both words were pronounced with the most extraordinary and emphatic aspiration of the initial vowels: for Mr T all things of this world, or any other for that matter, were either ghAstly! or mArvellous! Occasionally and powerfully modified, when circumstances demanded, to Absolutely ghAstly! or Absolutely mArvellous!

Remembering the remarkable character that T most certainly was, I was then reminded of a very funny and characteristic story he used to tell concerning some coal, or anthracite as I believe he later called it, that he had bought on the cheap, 'off the back of a lorry'. One bitterly cold winter's evening, while his wife Betty was cooking their tea, T had piled up the bargain coal in his grate around a couple of Zipp firelighters. Soon there was a bright glow in the hearth and an Absolutely mArvellous measure of heat being given off, warming the room and toasting the elderly couple as they enjoyed their boiled eggs and soldiers. T continued to feed the fire enthusiastically, "MArvellous stuff this, Betty," he announced periodically, until Mrs T observed that the room was quite warm enough and pushed the living room door ajar. Soon, however, the heat became rather too much. Doors were opened fully and even the windows a crack, despite the sub-zero exterior chill factor. This was all the more remarkable since Mrs T was always able to detect the provenance of even the very slightest of draughts.

The glow of the coal in the grate, meanwhile, had intensified beyond red and orange, beyond yellow even, to a blinding white. The fireplace tiles and stonework were giving off such heat that Mr T thought it advisable to shift all the furniture away, indeed, he even rolled back the deep pile carpet. It transpired that these precautions were executed in the nick of time, since moments later, it was no longer possible to be within 15 feet of the fireplace, the underlay of the Axminster was scorched, an *objet d'art* on the mantelpiece had cracked and the varnish on the legs of a nearby occasional table had bubbled.

Next, the cast iron grate melted, spilling coals on to the tile catchment, which duly shattered, looking suddenly like Roman mosaic, but which event at least led to a dissipation of some of the heat, obviating the need, T had decided, for an emergency call to the fire brigade. The couple stayed up late into the night until the fireplace had calmed itself down, its clinker and ironwork by this time resembling, for all the world, the contorted maniacal features of some hideous monster, which even scared the cat. Enquiries made the following day led T to the discovery that old Skivvy Arnold, the village's notorious procurer of all and anything, had acquired the coal from a mate of his at a local factory, and that the consignment was, in fact, foundry furnace coke. "A ghAstly experience!" as T would sum up his account of the whole affair. "Never again," he promised his wife, but Betty knew better and just smiled and nodded. "There's never a dull moment with you dear," she added. T then headed down into the basement muttering 'Absolutely ghAstly!' to himself, doubtless already ruminating on possible uses for the two and a half tons of anthracite still in the bunker.

And so it was that James and I were offered the chance to go to Spain. "You must go down to our place in Andalusia, Jim," he had announced one day. "MArvellous fishing down there. George'll take care of you, absolutely mArvellous chap, keeps an eye on the place when we're back here." Everything T had to say about the villa, the coast, the local people, the food and the landscape inland was prefixed with the sonorous 'Absolutely mArvellous!' The only exception being the summer heat, so 'Absolutely ghAstly' that they never went there from June to September.

James and I decided it would be a great opportunity to see something of Spain, to fish a bit, to soak up the sun and generally avoid overtaxing ourselves in any way whatsoever. A few months later, the trip out unfortunately proved somewhat stressful, with a delayed flight and consequently unsociable arrival time, leading us to take a very expensive taxi from Málaga airport, which dropped us hours later in the pitch dark, on the coast road, in what seemed like the middle of nowhere. Across the road were the silhouettes of a scattering of low villas, some with small over-door lights. Before our eyes had properly adjusted to the night, a four-wheel-drive vehicle came tearing along the road causing us to jump backwards to avoid being killed. The vehicle screamed to a halt, reversed and seconds later we were accosted by Civil Guards pointing machine guns at us. Our Spanish was non-existent but luckily one of the guards understood some English. They didn't exactly treat us badly but 'civil' was certainly a misnomer. Eventually, they were satisfied with our story and cursorily directed us across the road before going back to their vehicle and driving off. We could, by this time, just about make out some footpaths and guessing our way, struggled and fumbled with cases and rods in search of our villa. Amazingly we found it, the keys worked and we were home. Once inside, we decided on bedrooms and, quite frankly exhausted, called it a night.

Next there was George. On our first morning at the villa, I had woken early and got up with the intention of seeking out Mr T's Absolutely mArvellous supermarket and getting in some breakfast provisions. After studying the sketch Mr T had made for us, I stepped out of the rear door and from the head of the few steps down to the coarse grass I saw a pronouncedly pot-bellied man watering his section of sward in a decidedly dejected manner. Momentarily, I thought he was standing there stark naked but then I saw he was wearing miniscule and not entirely flattering shorts, in faded and tatty condition. Over the succeeding fortnight, and indeed throughout our further visits to Bahía Dorada we made over two or three successive years, I never saw him wearing anything else.

"Morning!" I said.

"All right," he returned, somewhat dolefully. Then a sigh . . . "Never had to work like this back 'ome . . ."

He had a very slow and tired sounding manner of speaking, which I eventually realised was permanent, not just his morning tasks' voice.

"Watering the garden?" I said, unsure if there might not be some other labour afoot.

"Yeah," George admitted, sounding more depressed than ever. "'Er indoors, innit," he added.

Just then, the door of his villa burst open and out popped two women, one gabbling away ten to the dozen, the other, proving to be a teenage girl, responding just as chattily.

"God knows what they're on about," George observed, from the depths of his depression.

They were both clearly Spanish and called out cheerily "*Hasta luego!*" before disappearing round the side of the villa.

"*Logo*," George said, slightly louder. He had a gold medallion glowing among the thick grizzled hairs of his chest and more bulky gold rings on his fingers, all his fingers, than I'd ever seen anyone wearing before. He also had massive heavy gold chains round both wrists, at least three gold teeth and his suntan was so deeply ingrained that the wrinkles in his skin were completely black.

"*Logo* means, well, I don't really know what it means, but she always says it when she's going out," George explained. "Probably going down to Fingerola."

"Who is she?" I ventured.

"Me wife, Rosy, innit," he replied " . . . and Gloria, that's me daughter."

"Oh," I said.

"Never learnt nuffink of the lingo," George went on, in explanatory mode. "Nineteen years we been married . . . funny really, innit?"

'Fingerola' was George's understanding of Fuengirola, just along the coast, and the nearest important shopping place for Bahía Dorada. I didn't really know any Spanish myself back then but I had a notion of the basics of pronunciation. The same could not be said for George.

"You go down to Fingerola, you'll be all right," he said and sauntered miserably to another flowerbed. The one he had watered was utterly drowned, converted into an expanse of glistening and bubbling mud with a few green leaves and dirty red flowerheads sticking out of it.

I found that he often remarked, enigmatically, 'You go down to Fingerola, an' you'll be all right,' without ever revealing how it was that we would be all right. He never went there himself. In fact, apart from the morning watering of the flowers, he never did anything except lie in the sun and drink bottled beer, 'Mahoo' as he called it, or sometimes 'Sam Miggyouwell'.

"Cheap as water, this stuff," he'd say, raising the bottle with the nearest thing he could manage to a chuckle, if ever he spotted you during the day.

He took a step forward, sighed, and aimed the annihilating hose at yet another innocent flowerbed.

"You James then?"

"No - John. James is still asleep. I thought I'd nip down to the supermarket and get some things."

"Oh yeah, I went down there once. Years back, 'fore I got married, you know."

"Is it far?" I suddenly wondered aloud.

"Nah, down the path, cross the road, down the bank, can't miss it."

"Thanks. George, is it?"

"Yeah. Need anyfink, just let me know. You know, 'er indoors'll get it."

"OK, thanks, see you later then."

"Yeah. Not much round here really, you go down to Fingerola, you'll be all right."

With the intention of letting this parting shot sink in and perhaps thereby fathoming its meaning, I said cheerio and headed off.

I soon found the supermarket, bought various things, including some wonderfully fresh bread, and got back to find James up and complaining he'd been bitten by ants. Upon closer investigation we found quite a few ants in his bedroom and more ominously, little white rings of powder on the floor round the bottom of the iron bed posts. One of these rings had been broken and there were several ants running up and down the post, as well as a few more between the sheets. We checked in my room and found all four powdery rings intact.

James wasn't fond of ants. The Formicidae would soon be everywhere in the kitchen, their battalions converting to regiments, keeping perfect time with our acquisition of provisions. No cupboard was safe from them, above or below the work surfaces, where two-lane ant highways traced every edge and union with geometric precision. Nowhere was out of bounds, certainly not the fridge, and they even got themselves into the electric kettle. Days later, this proclivity proved James's chance for revenge. I remember hearing him yelling 'Die, die, die . . . !' from within the steam-enveloped kitchen and the rattling sound of the furiously boiling kettle.

I remembered I had run outside, my sides fit to burst with contained laughter. George was sitting in a deckchair, beer in hand.

"Going down to Fingerola?" he asked, sounding no more cheerful than before.

"No, not just now, anyway," I said. "You have trouble with ants?"

"Yeah . . . blimey, you gotta have powder down, they got it in the supermarket, I'll ger 'er to get some for yer."

Over the ensuing fortnight I found myself drawn into these occasional chats with George but there was little to be learnt of his life. 'Fingerola' seemed to represent his pre ''er indoors' days in some vague way and prior to that, he claimed he had been a taxi driver in London. Who knows, perhaps it was true, but I couldn't help wondering if he was really a retired Great Train Robber. Little by little, it became apparent that he had seemingly unlimited funds, keeping his wife and daughter in whatever luxury they wished for. For himself, aside from the old gold, his only requirement seemed to be innumerable boxes of the bottled beer. La señora and la señorita often went off on holidays, were forever struggling out of the car with armfuls of fancy looking clothes' store bags, and wore almost as much jewellery as George himself, albeit different sets every day. George just smiled and shrugged his shoulders, whenever they were around, as if to say 'God knows what they're on about now!'

For himself, all he seemed to wish for was peace and quiet and the beer, which he had, and yet I never saw him tipsy, let alone drunk. Rosy would come round once in a while and ask if we needed anything and on Fridays a little wizened cleaning lady appeared, sent by '*la señora*' to generally tidy up.

But I've digressed yet again . . . Back at Málaga airport my case and rod tubes came trundling along the belt almost last. I loaded up my trolley, pushed off towards the exit and moments later, I was met by Norman and Maureen. These two were far from typical of the southern expats - they lived a more bohemian, almost a hippy style life, in a single storey house far from the sea and its tourist attractions, which they had bought for a song 40 years before. They tended the *huerta* of fruit trees, did permanent battle with their irregular water supply, which depended on a natural spring, and fished and fished and fished. That evening and the following day we busied ourselves with errands and piscatorial reconnoitering. Whilst driving between suppliers of celebration knick-knackery, Norman was keen to show me as many as possible of the waters he and Maureen had fished over the more than three decades they had lived a short drive inland from Málaga city. It was a treat to see all those reservoirs, lakes and streams, with us stopping briefly to spot cruising carp, or barbel tumbling in the rills, until both of us were beginning to become somewhat desperate to wet a line, but, family obligations kept us from it. The birthday lunch was planned with a group of friends and there was much to do. However, on the morning of the day, Maureen, who, by the way, had a lifetime habit of putting her husband in the shade as an angler, wanted us out of the way while she and her daughter-in-law organised things at home. Receiving this news, Norman and I glanced at each other over our breakfasts with a mixture of surprise and barely-concealed delight. We would be able to nip down to the river after all, even if it were for only a couple of hours!

The river in question was the magnificently named río Grande, the slightest of tributary streams that ran into the Guadalhorce. The name of this river, like that of the famous Guadalquivir (water of life), to the west, derives from the Moorish, meaning, this time, something like 'forked water', with reference to its point of union with the río Grande. It was late in a year which had been decidedly short of rainfall, and although there had been years enough in which the stream didn't run at all, there was at least a flow, even if the level was now very low. The point at which we would try our luck was actually the confluence, where we had stopped only two days before to gaze longingly at a delightful ripple over gravel and small rocks, which was really very pretty indeed, equally charming to both eye and ear.

Moments later, we were out of the door and throwing tackle and things in to 'The Beast', Norman's four-wheel-drive monster, since the path down to the river was rutted and pot-holed to an alarming degree. Norman had recently acquired some fly fishing gear and, having never fly fished before, he was keen to give it a try and I had promised to show him the rudiments of how to cast, so we had put it in, along with a light ledgering rod and some corn.

It wasn't any time at all before we bumped over the riverside terrain and parked. The riverbed was a white expanse of small rocks and stones covering an area at least five times as broad as the river that snaked through the middle of it. I could not help wishing to see it in its bank-high glory but Norman reminded me that it had been many, many years since it had been anywhere near that level. In fact the last time he remembered well, since they had fished it one day from the spot where we were now standing and something quite bizarre had occurred. Both Norman and Maureen had spotted a large log or tree trunk washed into the opposite bank. They had thought nothing of it until they noticed that it had apparently moved, upstream. Looking more closely at it, they perceived that it was indeed drifting very slowly against the slight current in the margins. Perhaps there was a slight backwater flow there, yet there was no apparent feature near the spot to give rise to such a phenomenon. There was even the slight glisten of a ripple at the upstream end as if the log were indeed pushing against the current.

"It looks like a bloomin' crocodile!" Norman had laughed.

Then they had both stared hard at it anew. It *was* a bloomin' crocodile! Maureen suggested they packed up and got well away from there as soon as possible, which they duly did. Though no hard evidence or news ever came to light, the floodwaters had certainly inundated a number of gardens, including the grounds of some pretty fancy properties. It was well known that there were certainly those around Andalusia who were famed for keeping exotic animals, and there had been a clamp down not long since by the Guardia Civil on the illicit trade in tiger cubs or rare birds and reptiles. Norman and Maureen were only glad that this particular creature had chosen the far bank of the río Grande to investigate its new found liberty.

Norman and I opened up the back of 'The Beast' and began to set up our rods. I picked out a small red nymph-like bloodworm fly from Norman's box and a tapered leader which went down to almost invisibility at its finer end. I was certainly no expert but the fly rod was light to handle and seemed perfect for the little stream running by us. I said I would just try out its action and dashed off to the water. The rod cast easily and I tried a few throws across the shallows but I had only been there a moment before the ripple upstream, where the two rivers actually met, called out to me as a much more propitious spot. I almost ran up there, keeping well back from the bank, and tried a cast. Following a quick mend in the short line, I brought the fly round to where there absolutely had to be a fish. Instantly there was the tiniest tug and recovering my line I found I had actually caught something. It was a minuscule boga, a member of the nase family, probably *Chondrostoma willkommii*. This particular example was tiny, not two inches in length but clearly hungry enough to make a snatch at a nymph that was bigger than its head. Dropping the little fellow into the shallows at my feet, I rolled the line out once more, following the current round and soon felt a more definite tug and a quick battle ensued in the fast flowing water. I eased the little fish to the bank and held it up to Norman who had approached the water further down and had noticed the action. It was a small gypsy barbel, *Barbus sclateri*, the first of the species I had actually ever caught. I resumed my position and cast again. The catch was repeated exactly, and after releasing the fish, I ran down to Norman and told him to go and give it a bash. There was clearly a chance for his first ever fish on the fly. Going through the motions of fly casting with someone, when the supposed teacher has no real expertise to impart, nearly led to both of us literally having our ears pinned back. Had there been a dropper on the line it would certainly have happened. As it was, I left Norman to battle on alone at what the Irish riverside observer refers to 'bating the waater with a shtick'.

Downstream at the shallows, looking across the slower flowing water I saw the reflection of an egret over a narrow patch of deeper water. I settled on the folding seat Norman had positioned and baiting up with just half a grain of corn flicked my line out there. There were fish feeding in that very spot, I could see the occasional flash of their glistening flanks and no sooner had I registered the fact than I had a bite. Upping the rod, the tip rattled with the frantic flight of another small barbel. I looked up towards where Norman was fishing, about to show him the catch when I saw he was pulling in a fish. I released my little barbel, grabbed the camera and raced off to get a look.

"Don't bother, John!" he called out.

I looked and saw it was another tiddler boga.

"Come on," I said. "We've got to record your first ever fish on a fly!"

The picture caused great hilarity back home a little later, not least because the little fellow was a job to actually see, even when the picture was full screen. It was a fish at least and on the fly. I then said I'd had one of those bogas too before the barbel started so it was surely a sign of things to come. Norman cast again and sure enough had a take before his line had swung round into the current. Following a brief skirmish with the nearside reeds, the barbel came to our feet, was quickly unhooked, and another photo ensued.

For the rest of the brief time allowed us that morning we alternated between the fly rod and the ledgering, catching little barbel almost non stop. In the one real lull that did occur, I took the fly rod downstream and waded a short stretch where the river narrowed over smooth large pebbles. To the left was a shaded back water overhung by a straggling bush and I immediately spotted a group of larger fish. My first cast spooked them and I was about to give it up when I saw them re-group, so I tried again . . . with the same result. This tantalising situation kept me midwater for several minutes, the game hung in the balance while I began to wish I had the ledger rod, the slightest of lead weights and perhaps a worm. I could just imagine a worm dropped into the near end of that backwater where a sandbank lay between it and the main flow. All I would have had to do was tease the bait along the sandbank until it fell enticingly into that little area of shade.

Suddenly I heard Norman calling me; we had to shove off. As soon as I got back to the our vehicle, Norman was keen to recount his exploits with the gypsies; he had landed half a dozen of them and was over the moon. I congratulated him on his newly fledged fly fishing prowess and then told the story of the whoppers downstream. It was clear we would have to go back there, but exactly when, it was impossible to say. It would all have to wait now, until after the birthday weekend at least, and for myself, a good deal longer than that, since I would be flying home again on Monday morning. Norman promised he would report back on his next trip to the river and we drove off quickly to avoid the wrath indoors of 'she who must be obeyed'.

* * *

'Your bait of falsehood takes this carp of truth'
Hamlet Act 2, Scene 1

Even though I had been living in Spain for more than seven years, at the time of this last adventure, I had then only once been to Seville. I went one bank holiday and spent the long weekend there, sampling the famous street life, the superb food and drink, and reading Gerald Brenan's *South from Granada* of 1957, even though I was somewhat to the west of that town at the time. Brenan had come to Spain in the 1920s and wrote much on Spanish literature, but his most notable and entertaining work describes his life in the small village of Yegen, in the fertile Alpujarra, south of Granada. He was visited there by members of the extraordinary Bloomsbury group, most notably Virginia Woolf, who, I recall, did not much like the experience.

I read Brenan's delightful and insightful pages propped up against bars and café tables all over the city and, during the evenings, I remember noting the formality of many of those around me, particularly in contrast to my own, not entirely tidy appearance. It was a national characteristic, just as much so in Valladolid, where, during the traditional evening stroll or '*paseo*' it seemed to me in my early days that everyone was dressed as though going to a wedding. Brenan himself observed that, 'The Spanish pattern of culture is so right and rigid, and the need for keeping up appearances so strong . . .' The question of clothing and external physical appearance is a simple thing, yet it has great social ramifications, very similar in nature to those assumptions and prejudices still held in Britain with regard to accent and ways of speaking.

My attention was frequently distracted from my reading by other essentially Spanish phenomena, not least among which was the delicious and heady array of aromas coming from the kitchens. From that first bank holiday visit to Seville, I particularly remember a fish on many of the bar menus, mysteriously named 'japuta' or whore's daughter, which in fact turned out to be *Brama*

brama, one of the sea breams or pomfrets. Its English common name would seem to depend on the authority consulted, variously the Atlantic pomfret, the Black sea bream or Ray's bream, the latter deriving from the surname of the seventeenth century English naturalist John Ray. The bars of Seville also had on offer the most incredible variety of olives, from small, dark and wrinkly to huge pale-green and shiny, with mild, strong or frankly murderous flavours. Some left your mouth incapable of tasting anything else for hours. Everything was accompanied by the characteristic white *Manzanilla*. In other parts of Spain, ordering this you would get a little pot of camomile tea, but here it was the name of the local wine, closer to a sherry in taste.

On that trip, which didn't include any fishing, I strayed briefly into a map shop. The extraordinary allure of the map! I recall Chris Yates writing about something so many anglers find themselves doing, namely scouring Ordnance Surveys for the blue bits. I spent a while in the shop doing just this with a number of charts of the local area and, to my great delight, came across a small reservoir, well off the beaten track, part of an abandoned slate quarry in the north of the province of Huelva. I immediately bought the map, a 1:50000 scale military document dated 1976, fantastic value too, at less than a £1. During the succeeding year I pulled that map out from time to time and wondered how, or indeed if, I would ever get there, or whether the place still existed. I dreamt of it as a lost lake, quite different from many Spanish reservoirs, which were invariably bare banked, ugly places, as often as not teeming with holidaying visitors. Something about this place, principally its being some considerable way from any road and a long way from any significant towns, began to obsess me. I had to go there.

Eventually, when the Easter holidays came round more than a year later, it was 1996, I decided to escape, to disappear for just a few days. I didn't rush right off though. I had a few days with visiting friends watching the extraordinarily sinister processions of Valladolid's Easter days. I waited until the next week, which I had off, and left a message on my answerphone, saying 'Gone fishing, back Sunday'. It didn't quite have the effect of Bruce Chatwin's legendary 'Gone to Patagonia', but I felt rather pleased with myself none the less. My good friend Chris in London had done rather better a year or two before, I recalled. I had phoned him in March, to be greeted by the following message: "I've gone fishing," pause, "in Zimbabwe," pause, "I'll be back in June!" How I envied him that. My trip would be somewhat less grand, but to be going fishing for nearly a week to some unknown water was more than exciting enough.

So, I took the bicycle, fairly well loaded, and boarded the overnight train to Madrid. There, I took the early morning AVE (Alta Velocidad Española), the super high speed, no expense spared, train to Seville. The word 'Ave' also means bird, and so I chuckled to myself over the thought that it is the early bird that catches the worm. The journey flew away uneventfully in squeaky clean, clinical modernity and I almost wished I had taken the very slow, old-fashioned and much more entertaining regional train. Once in Seville, I stayed the night in a rather grubby *pensión* near the station, certainly cheap but so bad that it reminded me of Laurie Lee's experience in Valladolid in the 1930s:

> The narrow stairs dripped with greasy mysterious oils and a feverish rotten smell. They seemed specially designed to lead the visitor to some act of depressed or despairing madness . . . The bed . . . was the only piece of furniture in the room which otherwise seemed to have been devastated by violent tenants.

I was looked upon by the family that ran the establishment as an eccentricity indeed. In khaki shorts and T-shirt, with an overloaded mountain bike including a tent and fishing rods, along with a Neuchatel number plate from 1988, which I had never got around to removing: I was just about as foreign as I could be.

I had an easy start the next day, since the first bus didn't go until 9 o'clock, and I was on holiday, so I spent the afternoon and evening taking in the sights, strolling around the cathedral, climbing the 300 foot Giralda tower and discovering hidden corners of the fortress and gardens of the Alcázar. I returned to the *pensión* late and slept deeply. When morning came I had a leisurely breakfast in a nearby bar, of croissants and delicious strong coffee. Then, on my something of a struggle to the bus station, I stopped for bread, ham and tomatoes to make big sandwiches, Spanish style *bocadillos*, which would add nicely to my largely tinned provisions. The people at the shop were wonderfully friendly. In Andalucía, without doubt, the people have the most *joie de vivre* of all Spain. I did, however, have a great deal of bother getting myself and all my gear on to the bus out of Seville, which would take me on the Huelva road to San Juan del Puerto. The driver clearly thought I was '*loco*', crackers, even though he was well used to the antics of foreigners. Eventually though, I did get everything loaded and collapsed into my seat. I knew I would need to be as fresh as possible for the cycling as it was already getting very hot. I had an hour and a half to San Juan so I sat back to relax and enjoy the ride.

The country looked dry. There had been practically no rain in Castile in the first four months of the year but here it was virtually African style drought. I wondered what my lake would be like. Looking out of the window, things looked well enough. The great river Guadalquivir wasn't far off and the agricultural land was irrigated from there. Classical scholar and adventuress Rose Macaulay had come along this road, through 'the dull fertile plains of Baetica' in the 1940s, nearly at the end of her famous travels. At San Juan, however, she had gone south to Huelva, the capital of the province and I would be heading north. I had convinced the driver to let me off before San Juan, at the Valverde turning if possible. I think he agreed as much as anything to be rid of me before getting into the town. Despite quite a bit of traffic, including an accident, which tragically are so much a feature on Spain's bank holiday roads, we seemed to arrive in no time. The driver, suddenly turned friendly, gave me a hand with the bike at a convenient layby, and waved me off cheerily, wishing me luck.

Now my adventure was to really begin. The bus disappeared away down the road and I stood there with my bike in the heat and the dust. It was a nice round 40°C and the sun burned down with midday fury. I caked myself in total block and donned a headband to prevent my being blinded by stinging sun-cream and sweat. Tonto's Expanding Headband. That had been the name of an LSD permeated, surprisingly beautiful sounding, electronic music outfit in the Seventies. I hadn't lived in Spain for very long before I learnt that the word *'tonto'* meant stupid. *Kemo sabe*, on the other hand, which has long puzzled commentators and linguists alike, I'm sure comes from the Spanish too, from *'Quien lo sabe'*, which means 'He who knows' . . . the omniscient Lone Ranger and his Red Indian sidekick Tonto. Surely, they would never have got away with that? Perhaps it was me. Was I already suffering from the furiously intense heat. Frankly, I would think twice before recommending midday summer cycling in Andalusia to anyone!

According to my map I had a ride ahead of me of only 25 kilometres or so, to the turning off the Valverde road to Calañas. From there I would be following just a couple of kilometres of tracks and forest paths, which should be fun. The bike was a bit unstable so I spent a moment trying to redistribute the weight around the panniers. There was quite a lot of food and a small pot for boiling water; I never would have had room for a Kelly kettle. The lake water would be fine, I had decided, provided I boiled it. All in all the bike was seriously heavy and I started out at a snail's pace. I had not even packed that much fishing gear or bait. I had tins of corn and some breadcrumbs and I hoped to find a worm or two around the lakeside. I wondered if the lake would even be there, or if so, whether I might get any fishing in that same afternoon.

I crept along the burning tarmac for what seemed an eternity, and was delighted when the village of Trigueros came into view. It was already 1.30 and I resolved to stop and investigate what tapas might be available. I soon found a bar and sat outside under the shade of a fully loaded lemon tree, with a glass of *Manzanilla* and a little bottle of water. Neither lasted very long and I had to repeat the order. I had a plate of *boquerones* too, delicious vinegared white fleshy anchovies, and a dish of olives. With 20 kilometres to go I rather felt I could have stayed the rest of the afternoon quite happily under that tree. As time ticked on however, I felt well enough fuelled to continue my pedalling. I bought another bottle of water and with the sun high and still apparently very angry about something, I headed slowly north out of the village, my shadow almost immediately below me.

I continued on the Nacional 435 road, which was newly surfaced and very quiet after the Seville to Huelva motorway. With the appearance of a very slight tail breeze, I began to pick up a bit of speed and was making good headway at last. My mind ran on the solitary nature of the fisherman, the sense of retreat and freedom. I sailed along a while, cooled by the air, without paying much attention to anything when all of a sudden I heard the sound of an engine. It was an odd sound that I couldn't identify, high pitched and somehow powerful. Then I saw it. Up ahead there was a man and a young lad next to a big four-wheel-drive vehicle. They were using a remote control and up in the sky was a huge model aircraft. I had never been much of a model maker or enthusiast, except when a little boat might help with my fishing, but this machine was exceptional. I paused, as yet unseen, and watched its wheeling, its dives and roaring climbs. At one point it came quite close, it must have been over ten feet across and incredibly loud. I carried on towards them and a few moments later stopped to pass the time of day.

They didn't have local accents and it turned out they were from Madrid, a wealthy father and his teenage son down for the holidays to Valverde del Camino, which was the young lad's mother's village. They were even more interested in my origins and eccentric appearance, smeared as I was with total block and topped off with a flat canvas hat I had been meaning to throw away for more than ten years. I learnt, with some relief, that I was only a couple of kilometres short of the turning for Calañas. I enquired about the lake and the old slate quarry and the man told me that many years ago his brother- in-law had occasionally fished there, spinning, he vaguely recalled, for '*blas*'. Juanjo, the youngster, who had been fishing with him when he was younger, said that there were not only black bass, but *carpones* too. Big carp.

They took turns talking to me and flying the monster plane, he and his father both clearly very adept and experienced flyers. It was a German model apparently; the father went there frequently on business and it was a hereditary hobby. The field beyond was of rather dry closely cropped grass and served them well as a take off and landing strip. Handing the control over to his father the lad went on to tell me that his uncle had never fished for the carp but that he himself remembered seeing some of them; they were enormous. His hands indicated more than three feet and he added that his uncle said they used to feed on the lake's abundant freshwater crayfish. This was exciting news, on all counts. I was thrilled with making their acquaintance and after cheerful farewells, turned back on to the road. I pedalled on, fired with excitement and soon reached the fork and followed the direction for Calañas.

Alone once more, I suddenly remembered a reference to model-plane flyers, from Sven Berlin's 1964 publication *Jonah's Dream, A Meditation on Fishing*, that had been skulking in the back of my mind, from the moment I had heard the roaring and whining of the motor.

> There are few friends with whom I would angle - not chosen because I am considered rare company, but chosen because they too seem to understand that fishing is a kind of meditation. Only those who pretend but fail to understand this; those who have shown a perversity of nature or distention of themselves, like the model aircraft that fly incessantly round their owner's heads for their own amusement and satisfaction, but not understanding the stillness of the mind and the quest of fish, have I carefully eliminated as unsuitable; for like any adventure on the brink of the unknown wherein a dream may be caught, the true fisherman is on a search for wisdom - therein hides the meaning of his long vigil and the purpose of his understanding.

Yes, essentially a solitary occupation, angling. The path to wisdom, and to the lake, was only a couple of hundred metres from the junction and I was careful in case I should miss it. As it was, the slight gradient was more than enough to enforce the slowness of my progress and I easily spotted a battered old sign strung across the entrance to a track. I was delighted to read 'El Dique del Campanario'. That was the place. It also set the distance at four kilometres. The thin rusty chain and sign effectively barred the way to most vehicles but to one side was a gap. As I wheeled my bike round I noticed tracks, they looked like deer, doubled impressions of fore and hind feet. They weren't that clear though, since other feet or hooves had passed when the ground had dried, scuffing the earlier ones. Stretching away through the trees was an unmade track in pretty dire condition, rutted and furrowed where the odd vehicle, few enough by the look of it, had passed in rather wetter conditions. Now it was as dry and as hard as concrete and so, despite the bumps, I got along well enough. This is what mountain bikes are for I thought. Poor old thing, my Saracen had seen better days; at 15 years of age it was about ready for retirement but present day prices for the latest thing in all-terrain biking were rather alarming.

I was in deeply shaded woodland and suddenly noticed it was eucalyptus. After the bright light, I could barely see at first but the scent was unmistakable. The sandy ground was strewn with strips of bark, long scythe-like speckled leaves and here and there were pale turquoise, round leaved saplings. All the trees were young in fact, many springing from around the cut trunks of much bigger specimens. It was clearly forestry land, in constant cycle. These trees were just a few years old; I wondered if they went all the way down to the lake side. I felt thankful for the shade; back at the road the temperature had been nearly too much. Along the path there were lots of white flowers covering sturdy *jara* bushes. This was the more southern variety of rock rose, with big purple blotches at the bases of the petals and brilliant yellow anthers.

I came to a fork in the path where another sign would have been handy. Just as I was pondering the fact, I saw a rectangle of thin metal face down on the ground. It had the word *'embalse'* on it, reservoir or lake. I wondered which way it had indicated. If I was on the path that I thought I was, according to the map I would run more or less parallel to the water a while until I got to a fire break. I wondered just how many years it had been since Juanjo and his uncle had fished there. I looked again at the map, hoping once more that the lake would indeed still be there, then I decided to go straight on. Before the fire break there was a *cortijo*, a settlement of dwellings, almost certainly where workers in the old quarry had lived and I was keen to see it. The path rose and fell as did the vegetation, and it became softer under foot. Eventually, on leaving a few sparse trees behind, I came upon some old pines and the ruins I had been looking for. I was doubly pleased, since this also meant I was sure where the lake was.

Walls rose out of the thick brown grasses and eucalyptus branches projected from crumbling empty windows. It must have been a pretty place, it still was really. Lizards were the main residents, along with a good number of birds. Coming to the end of where the path led out from the *cortijo*, the land dropped away into a valley the far side of which was crowned with the ruin of a more imposing residence. White painted, it shone bright, framed by two huge palm trees. Below to the right wound the path, certainly to the lake, and on the slopes were dozens of ancient olive trees.

I couldn't help wondering what a paradise this had been or could be again. From my promontory there was nothing but wild open country and woodland in any direction. I pushed off after getting some pictures and clattered rather obtrusively into the silent valley. Bee-eaters complained overhead and several azure winged magpies flew up from the olive grove towards the house. Turning away, into the trees once more, the path meandered down, hopefully waterward. All was dusty and dry however; you would never have believed that there was water near. Maybe there wasn't. I began to doubt. The cicadas' shrill monotonous din was deafening, and it was a pleasure when my rattling bike startled the nearer ones into momentary silence. These enormous fly like insects were called *cigarras* or *chicharras* in Spanish. The latter name, in the verb a*chicharrarse*, also meant to be fried by the heat of the sun. Their sound was singularly appropriate in this arduous terrain and a few lines of T.S Eliot's poetry came suddenly to mind:

If there were the sound of water only
Not the cicada
And the dry grass singing
But sound of water over a rock.

As I trundled on, the path was cut across from time to time with what appeared to be the courses of winter spate streams. Dusty white rocks, baked, crumbled patches of clay and miniature dunes of large-grained sand marked what seemed ancient riverbeds. But there was no water.

I had gone rather further than what had perhaps been the most direct route to the lake and on this path I guessed I still had a kilometre to go. The trees were low, mixed pine and eucalyptus now and provided no shade to speak of. I paused under one of the taller trunks and took a drink. There were little psammodromus lizards scuttling all over the place; if only I had their energy. Up the next rise the trees were larger again, the shade extended, cooling to both mind and body, and I began to sense water. I walked the bike, not wishing to come upon the lake all of a rush. It would be something to savour, if indeed the place still existed.

A sparkle suddenly glinted through the foliage, a hint of reflected sky between the giant eucalyptus on the final slope. There it was. I slowed even further and tentatively approached, grinning to myself. I'm not sure I didn't actually laugh out loud from sheer delight.

I came into an angular bay, a recognisable part of the zigzag shape of the *embalse* on my map. It was more beautiful than I had dared imagine, the far side wild and overgrown, bathed in brilliant sunshine. From where I stood in the shade, I could see that the water was easily accessible, deep, green and clear. To my left and behind, the hills rose heavily wooded with eucalyptus but opposite there were old pines and holm oak. I leant my bike against a tree and walked down the bank. The water's edge was sandy, with pinky fine-rooted weed in the shallows. Further out though there were outcrops of dangerous looking slate that could present serious problems for the line of an unwary angler.

Then a movement, and I spotted my first fish, a black bass hovering in the midwater after a brisk movement of alarm. I stepped forward and one or two more darted and froze. They were small, half a pound the biggest. Great sport too, I thought, if there was nothing else doing. I would certainly have to take a leisurely stroll round to see if there were any other signs of life.

It wasn't a big stretch of water by Spanish standards; there are some truly vast reservoirs in this country. This one was 20-odd acres I guessed, maybe a kilometre and a half long, and an average width of perhaps 100 metres. According to where I thought I was on the map, this was the east end and the dam was nearby. I followed the bank, almost on tiptoe, although there was no sign of anyone. I hadn't really expected there would be. Then I saw the dam, a lovely rustic, old brick and stone double wall with a path between. Here I could see that occasional visitors had been and the area under the trees showed picnicker signs too. Camping anywhere in Spain, as I've mentioned before, is pretty much illegal, except in recognised sites, and night fishing is prohibited too. As a consequence, I would leave unpacking my gear till later. At dusk I could set up my igloo sharpish in a discreet spot ready for spending the night. As for fishing, I would certainly try a bit in the last hours of light at the very least. I felt extraordinarily excited, it was a real *Boy's Own* adventure.

A terrific rolling splash suddenly caught my ear and I scampered up the bank behind to see the remains of some ripples about 15 yards out. It had sounded like a very big fish. I could see a bit of activity near some reeds across the far side too, though it didn't look like carp. The word 'rise' seemed inadequate somehow for big carp, especially those resonant belly flops that so inspired the carp fisher; 'uprising' was more appropriate perhaps. This splash had sounded very carpy and the feeling was confirmed from right there, where I was standing. A fish of 15lb at least cruised past, near in, up tailed, swirled, sending muddy clouds in every direction, and vanished. I walked back down to the dam and crossed, looking over the wall every few minutes. It looked very deep, the bottom rising as it approached the old wall, with thick weed among large rocks and piles of slate. It had clearly been built up artificially, to alleviate pressure on the dam proper. I still couldn't see much of the rest of the lake though. Unless it were possible to reach a higher vantage point, I could see from the map that it wouldn't ever be possible to see as much as half of the surface extension from anywhere at the waterside.

The double wall soon met with an enormous natural barrier of rock. The top was quite flat and scattered with fragments of brown and grey slate. It was very exposed, and the few grasses that showed were frazzled yellow and brown. To the right was a rocky precipice with plenty of bushy vegetation dotted with wild oleander or adelfa blooms, which led down to the dry *arroyo* Pajarrón. Although the valley looked fertile, it seemed as if the river hadn't flowed down there for many years, perhaps since the dam had been built. There was what looked like an overflow and a narrow gulley but it all looked as dry as dry.

After another glance into the rocky depths on the lakeside, I walked on and soon reached the wilder looking banks opposite and for a short distance I followed more deer tracks. It seemed that they were by far the place's most frequent visitors. It was just after four o'clock and I turned back deciding to get my knife and baitbox and take advantage of my reconnoitre to search out a few worms. The knife was a great Rambo sort of thing which doubled as an axe for firewood and digging implement. I'd had it since first moving to Spain and bought it partly because of all the gadgets that came with it: a line, a float and hooks, a skinning knife (good for opening troublesome shot) with a can-opener bit, a compass and a catapult. The latter could send boilies an impressive distance. There was also a first aid kit and some odds and ends I had never figured out the use of. All in a snazzy leather sheath and holster. Whenever any of my friends saw it they would look at me as though expecting me to have human heads in the freezer. It was in fact one of the most useful bits of gear I had, incongruously perfect for the philanthropic, ecologically minded, pacifist angler.

So armed, I set off again in the other direction, pausing first for my camera and binoculars, to see what I could see. I took the map too and went partly in search of where various small rivers, the Pajarrón, Agua Agria and Beltrán, joined the lake; not least because they would probably be good spots to dig. I walked a long way, leaving behind the shady eucalyptus, to find the first, which proved to be the main river, and which at some point in many years, perhaps flowed on from the dam outlet. For the present though, it too was almost completely dry. I did manage to locate some worms, mainly by shifting rounded rocks which lay in the bleached riverbed. In the murky shallows, made cloudy I thought by ripples from the light wind, I spotted one or two crayfish, their reddish backs and claws breaking the surface. They might prove to be a bit of a plague on the bait, especially the worms.

Digging and upturning soon revealed plenty for my baitbox and I moved on round, following the irregular angles of this exquisite place. The banks became steep and difficult; I could see that only the deer ever came this way. The thin line of their tracks led between old pines and holm oak. Down at the water's edge *adelfas* (oleander) and *jara* grew in large bushes. I crept behind them to sneak a glance at the water on several occasions, frequently spooking small numbers of black bass. Coming down into a more heavily wooded corner, where the Beltrán stream was indicated on the map, I caught sight of a group of three carp. I froze in my tracks, half against the trunk of pine. Two were ten-pounders and they swam like escorts either side of a fish which I could hardly believe I was seeing. Easily three feet long, only inches down in the water. They turned away and dropped into the dark. How could I put a weight to this fish. It was double the size of any carp I had ever seen at that time, 40lb, or even 50, I didn't dare think any further.

I ascended, looking to get a vantage point, where the vegetation thinned out considerably. Copses of holm and gall oak made headway on the harder drier ground and there were a few acorns lying around, leftovers from the autumn, which I collected as I went, picking out those in better condition. Lizards were everywhere, mainly large psammodromus, but after following a crashing racket into one thicket I spotted a good sized ocellated lizard too. I was not really stalking, so they generally scampered off before I was close enough to see. Then, my ear caught a more constant rustling, quite distinct from the fitful erratic noise made by lizards or the dry crackly slide of a snake.

This was a vague, slow, almost bulky sound. After a lifetime of such attentive listening, I was surprised by not knowing what it was. When I had first come to

Spain I had been really foxed, I remembered, by the fractious micro-second twitch of a skink, not to mention its lightning fast disappearance. I moved cautiously towards the sound, which continued, unperturbed, then made a few quick strides forward and came upon a tortoise. A tortoise, that homely creature which ate lettuce and hibernated, so common as a pet back in the UK. I had never found a tortoise in the wild before. It was a big one too, nearly a foot long and continuing its determined journey, apparently oblivious to my presence.

I was suddenly reminded of a Mafalda cartoon by Quino, the pseudonym of the brilliant Argentinian artist Joaquín Lavado. In the first few frames, Mafalda, a little girl, who is remarkably socially and politically aware, is screaming, apparently declaiming, 'Democracy!' at the top of her voice. In the final frame a tortoise appears and she says, "Here's a little bit of lettuce for you."

There was a single large scale over the tail of this particular individual, which was the only way I could remember to tell that this was the Spur-thighed and not the Hermann's variety of tortoise. The carapace was quite smooth and flared at the edges which suggested an older animal, as did its size. I took a few photographs, and found myself referring to him as Lonesome George as I angled this way and that to get the best shots. He was all by himself but hardly in the same predicament as his namesake in the Galapagos. The final clack of the shutter scared him and he ducked his head back inside. I took one more picture with just his legs showing, really quite comical. I had more than enough snaps so I left him to his afternoon wandering.

Another great rolling splash had come from down at the lake and I hurried back and scoured the surface. Spotting the place from higher ground, I could see definite carpy movements. I focussed in with the binoculars and took a sudden deep breath as a humped back silently broke the surface - a long, lovely, tapering dorsal - then it vanished leaving no sign. Again it had looked like a very big fish. I trembled. Either it was pure excitement or the place was beginning to scare me.

I rambled on and noticed there were ever more crayfish in the now transparent shallows. The water, I realised, was turbid only at the feeder stream end. I guessed there had to be a slight subterranean flow into the lake. I sat a moment and watched the crays. They were doubtless easy and popular prey, a staple for the fish of the lake, both the black bass and the carp. I had read odd Spanish magazine articles about them as natural baits as well as soft plastic imitations as lures. Lure fishing for carp seemed ludicrous, but before coming to Spain I had thought the same about catching barbel on a plug, and I had already had experience of that. And I certainly knew of carp sometimes taking a lure or a fly.

Smaller tumbling splashes sounded over the water and I continued on my way, following deer tracks down. I soon reached a promontory, an area of lower ground nearly opposite where I had first arrived at the lake. Across the other side to my left was the dam. I had just traversed the steepest side of all and looking around I felt sure that the lake's deepest point was off there. There might easily be 40 feet of water . . . bottomless. From here I was able to see about as much of the lake as was possible. Reflecting blue, edged with red and white blossoms and ringing with bird song, it hid in its depths some remarkable fish. It was quite perfect. I took a few more pictures and sat down once again just to enjoy it. All that was missing was to have a line out.

I was about to get on with my surveillance when a large bird of prey appeared and dropped out of sight again, fluctuating on the tree line. Down at the water's edge, half hidden in a small inlet was more movement. They were egrets, four or five of them. Through the binoculars I could see their black beaks and legs; they were poking around in the shallow water between two reed beds. They took off in a flurry suddenly spooked and the bird of prey swooped in on them creating absolute havoc. It was hard to follow what was happening with or without the binoculars. The hunt, if that was what the attack had been, seemed to fail. I watched the great white shouldered eagle flapping massively and it soon gained altitude. I had seen some fragments of action really well, including a moment of flailing yellow talons as he cut into that sheltered corner.

It was an imperial eagle, something else I had never seen before. Not only that but by its conspicuous shoulder markings, it was almost certainly the rare Spanish variety *Aquila heliaca adalberti*. If only I could have got a picture. I wondered whether I might get another look at him at least. For the moment though he had disappeared and I started again towards the dam. In a tree near me, a serin (a type of finch) was jangling so noisily I could barely hear anything else. The drama seemed to have escaped his attention altogether. The egrets were long gone and would probably think twice before settling into that spot again. Was it normal, I wondered, for an imperial eagle to try for an egret for afternoon tea? It seemed unlikely to me; maybe there had been something else there, a rabbit or a hare.

It was after 5 and I began to think about the prospects for both tea and some late afternoon fishing. I remained alert and as stealthily as I could, being somewhat in the open, approached the scene of the skirmish. There were indeed rabbit droppings near, but then I had seen them almost everywhere. Otherwise there was no sign at all that anything had occurred. A few moments more and I found myself nearing the big eucalyptus where my bike was patiently leaning. About an hour and a half I had taken in going round the lake, and what with the heat, I was fairly tired.

There was no sign that anyone had been near and I felt sure that I would be able to pitch the tent without attracting attention. There was the chance that

Civil Guards or Forest Rangers might appear at some point over the coming day or two, so I had gone to the trouble of getting a regional licence to fish in Andalucía. Although I had known guards who would turn a blind eye to my pitching a tent, a licence was an essential. Here, since I knew no one, I would have to be discreet.

Another problem was night fishing, but having seen the size of the fish, I really doubted I would risk a nocturnal encounter. Alone with a 50lb carp in the dark; it didn't bear thinking about. I muttered my apologies to the frowning spirits of great past members of the Carp Catchers' Club, and hoped that no present day anglers would learn of my cowardice in the face of Campanario's giants.

I unloaded my gear and looked round for a good camp site. There was a nice shady nook a little way round the bank that I had seen earlier so I lugged the tent and the bags over. It was the shallow valley of a small cove where everything would be hidden from view and nearby was a spot I rather liked the look of for a first shot at the fishing. I carried the fishing gear over, stopping in my tracks at one stage as sounds of yet another commotion greeted my ears. I wasn't prepared for what I saw as I approached the spot I had chosen to fish - a massive dark shadow lurking in mud clouds a short way out. I ducked down and stayed still, watching. The rippled film above the fish shook occasionally. I fancied I saw a sort of Coriolis effect, the surface of the water turning in reaction to the tail's motion. Then the creature's aqueous element split open and the fish grew into the air, like a whale, turning midway and crashing down heavily. It was those numbers again, 50lb . . . 60? This one was bigger still, surely the biggest carp I had ever seen. A common at that, beautifully scaled, golden brown, green tinted, its tremendous dorsal erected like that of a sail fish briefly before impact. I too fell back, somewhat stunned. I fumbled in my bags until I found the sweetcorn and threw out a handful. Nothing happened and I felt an inexplicable sense of relief. Did I really want to catch a fish like that?

Time fluttered at the ends of the branches overhead. There was no further sign of my quarry. I inched backwards to the protection of a eucalyptus trunk and stood up in its lee. Looking cautiously out over the water I saw the fish again, just a surface lurch in fact, but it was there, and approaching. The upper fan of his tail slipped into view, undulating vertically, slowly, nose down, sending up billows. This huge creature was feeding, sucking up grains of corn. A surge of panic bolted through me. I could hook this fish. I could cast out just corn. He was only ten yards away. The line I had was new, 12lb breaking strain, along with traces of 8lb. What had my expectations been? I would see and feel the first rush after my strike had set the hook, the rod hooping over dangerously. A ten-pounder put a pretty drastic bend in that old rod. I felt I could hear the hissing, the singing monofilament, the shattering snap of line, of rod, of an angler's spirit. What on earth was I going to do?

As these ghastly premonitions churned through my mind I realised I was setting up my tackle, as though I were in auto-pilot mode. The old Milbro Perfect, Mitchell 330, a size 8 hook, three bits of corn, a swan shot . . . I paused again. I slid the landing-net handle out of a rod bag and screwed in the triangular frame net, the biggest I had. It wasn't even half big enough. I crept nearer the water and paused once more. I didn't feel as though I could do it. I hadn't the nerve to cast to a fish that size. I thought of Dick Walker, of Mr Crabtree. Then before me appeared the reproving spectres of Dame Juliana and of Izaak. 'Isaac' in old Cornish meant corn, that had to be a good omen.

The cast was poor. However, the line was out there, too far out in fact, lying across the dry dusty surface in the still evening. I watched the far end sinking gradually, my heart in my throat, as the bait made its way gently towards the bottom. I was crouching and scanning the water. Something was going on still. I tweaked the line a few times to bring it in, once it had all sunk. I managed to pull it nearer to where the great fish was still moving but finally I dared not bring it any further. I fanned out another handful of corn. I couldn't believe I was doing what I was doing. I held the rod and waited.

Time passed, behaving normally at first, then it began to mill around, finally it ground to a halt altogether. There was no doubt that Sheringham's account of the carp fisherman blending into his landscape is only the beginning. From there we are absorbed into the universe, into space and time, utterly, into Hawking's brief history.

The evening came on, nonetheless. My arm ached, my back and my knees ached. I sat on the soft ground and lay the rod on a projecting ridge of slate. I felt anxious. Was the bait still on? Had it survived the reckless cast? Had the crays made off with it? I hadn't taken my eyes off the rod tip for a second but now they were tempted to wander. I slid backwards slowly, watching the rod, back to the tree where once again I was hidden and able to search the water unseen. There were no shadows out there now. Carp vanish of course, being only in part flesh and blood. I sensed relief and disappointment. The few inches of line between the rod tip and the water twitched. I was on the rod instantly. It twitched again. My hand hovered over the smooth cork. The spool was loose, loose as loose. It was turning! The line pulled off, I grabbed the rod, turned the handle and struck hard. The rod bent over, bounced and tugged erratically and I was suddenly recovering like mad as the fish raced towards me. In no time it was splashing about in the shallows, a little silver gold carp of maybe half a pound. 'Lovely fish,' Bernard Venables said in my ear, and I agreed. I slipped him into the water and stood back to have another look at things. There was no sign of anything else at all.

I left my stuff there and half in a trance wandered round to the camping things. I assembled the long spidery poles ready to slide in and get the igloo pitched. The ground was good and I unrolled the tent, spreading it out carefully. The evening warmth was pleasant and I hadn't brought any sleeping things really, except a mat in case the ground was hard, which it wasn't. However lightly I travelled I always ended up with something I didn't need. A little while later, I had the few things I felt needed to be inside, stowed - clothes, for a pillow as much as anything else, and some of the fresh food.

I lay in the shade, though much of the heat had passed, and thought about the carp. It must have been more than four feet long and as wide across the shoulders as a labrador. I half thought, half dreamt about how I was going to fish the coming day, knowing that a fish that size was out there, knowing that he came up here to feed in the evening. And how many more fish of that sort of size might there be in the lake! I extracted a lovely forked branch from the bushes next to me and set to whittling a rod rest. The blades and the little saw of my Swiss army knife would soon produce the desired article.

The evening was drawing in, the light was beautiful with that bluer intensity that makes colours more vibrant in the last of the daylight. The scents seemed stronger too, a subtle blend of eucalyptus and pine and the heavier sweet dewy aroma of adelfas off the water.

I stirred myself and collected some brush tinder and a few bigger bits of dead wood and lit a tiny fire, to have the flickering company as much as anything. I boiled some water in the old pot, wondering as usual why I had never got around to a Kelly kettle or a Primus stove. A nice bit of slate served well to cut up chorizo with the skinning knife and I roasted the chunks at the end of a thin green stick. A cut of bread and some mint tea, what more could an angler ask for.

The heady presence of adelfas caused me to muse a moment on the deadly poisonous qualities of their wood. During the Napoleonic wars, many parties of unsuspecting French soldiers had apparently cut its excellent straight twigs to make wild rabbit brochettes. The poor devils all died as a result, poisoned on the very eve of the battle they had been mobilised for.

The light was almost gone and all sounds intensified. The crash of heavy fish. I jumped at least once at the thudding splashes which came from different parts of the lake. I couldn't help wondering just how many monsters there might be. A bat flitted past and wheeled abruptly before making another pass. It was big, a noctule, hunting high up, with considerable success, the insects I could see in the fire's glow. A churring call hung on the air with sudden changes of pitch, not far off, though I couldn't tell exactly from where really. A nightjar almost certainly. From the dark more and more sounds came; at intervals an owlish piping note, Scops possibly, but there were the mingled noises of various frogs and toads, birds and every other kind of creature. It could have been the Amazonian rainforest. I tidied up a bit, and making sure I knew where things were, decided to get some sleep. The next day would start with the dawn and in all probability before. Dreams of monster carp would accompany me meanwhile.

It was too warm in the tent and after a moment I found myself back outside. With a bundle of clothes as a headrest I stretched out in my private paradise. It was something, really, that you could still do this in Europe. There was still space. I remembered Ted Hughes wondering what he would do if angling was ever abolished. He would have to go and live somewhere else, he thought. 'In a land where I can still keep hold of the world [and] reconnect to the natural cycle.'

The night was really beautiful, though it wasn't quite dark yet. The sky still retained light, pastel blue; odd flimsy cloud banks, low and darkling, extended over the southern horizon. Their shapes were extraordinary, like other landscapes of rocky escarpments and abundant meadows, mirage upon mirage, echoing above and beyond. It was that kind of optical illusion where your senses picked first one part, then another to hold on to, each as real as the next. The light was an ever decreasing patch, at the edges of which, stars gradually established themselves. Cooling boisterous breezes sprang up, jostling the heavy hot stillnesses which lingered after the day. More bats flitted about among easier, more dispersed night noises after the clamorous nightfall overture. It had all become gentler, more symphonic, slightly brooding, certainly Romantic, featuring the kind of counterpoint of natural sounds never achieved by the composers. There was a bit for Beethoven, something for Vivaldi even, and a broad sweep of a palette for Mahler. All this moved against a deep rich and vibrant silence which seemed best conveyed by the presence of the lake itself.

I again remembered Rose Macaulay's *Fabled Shore* and a night she spent in the open air:

> It was already dusk. The wind whispered and sighed among the pines; a distant storm, I thought, for faint lightning flashed far off. I drove back to the cottages; they told me that the nearest inn was at Serra, ten kilometres away along a cart track through the forest. They advised me to return to Betera and sleep there. But I did not want to leave Porta Coeli, so I drove the car off the road into a clearing by a pool, half a mile from the convent, and prepared to spend the night there. A young man with a horn slung from his shoulder and wearing a badge that proclaimed him a Guardia de las Montanas passed by, and stopped to speak to me; he said I had better not sleep in the forest, a storm was approaching. I told him I should be all right in the car. When he had gone I spread my lilo and rug under a huge pine and lay there; the dim vault of pine roofed over me like a groined apse in the strange moonlight, making a dark pattern against the pale sky; its great boughs swept about me in a wide circle, their dark plumes almost on the

ground. The distant storm still flashed. All night the wind sang in the pines, frogs in the pool, mosquitoes round my bed. The air was warm, and smelt of pine. At about three the moon set, and I could no longer see the line of mountains against the sky, until, two hours later, a pale dawn began. An early donkey cart creaked by, with a great load of grass and a driver asleep on the top of it.

I was woken more than once through the night by crashing carp uprisings, or so I imagined. At some stage I had crawled back into the tent where I was safe against the one mosquito which had turned up to feast on me. Some other disturbance then shook me from my slumbers and, unsure of the cause, I unzipped the netted flap and peered out. With a jolt I noticed a slight lightening of the eastern sky and jumped up, anxious not to miss a thing. I crept down to the water's edge and wandered cautiously along the margin. Mysterious shadows seemed to move against the dark, contours unrecognisable, the water reflecting a still sky. I turned back to where I had left the rod. There were no signs of activity on the inscrutable face of the pool but I couldn't help imagining great cyprinoid fins moving gently deep down.

I stood there a while, looking along the margins. Several minutes passed before I realised I was staring directly into the eyes of a deer. It must have emerged from behind one or two big eucalyptus trunks. I had wondered when I would see one, and suddenly, there we were, face to face. Its eyes reflected tiny dots of pale blue, as did the water at its feet. It was a female, a red deer I thought, though I wasn't really sure. She wasn't looking at me in fact, but over my shoulder, but knowing full well I was there. I was in shadow, close to a towering stripped trunk. There was a slight wind rustle in a sapling behind me, and she took off in an instant. I stayed stock still, but there were no more. How lovely. Such a beautiful, graceful creature, but very timid and shy. She would doubtless let the others know there was a stranger about.

I sauntered back, sat on the dusty ground and wondered about a cast before breakfast. There was barely enough light to see and, all things considered, I decided on the latter. I sorted out bread rolls, cheese and peanut butter, and got the little fire going for coffee. After all, I was on holiday and I might as well get comfy down by the water, before chancing a cast. In my search for twigs, I noticed a bit of fishy activity along the bank. Leaving my bundle, I approached an intervening clump of reeds to get a better look. There were fry in the shallows, unidentifiable in their little cloud-like shoals. Small shocks of them occasionally burst through the surface further out, fleeing some predator, most likely bass. The survivors joined those I could see in barely an inch of water.

I had one other rod with me, a sort of multi-purpose telescopic effort called a Magic 390. That and a spare fixed-spool would be enough to try for large mouths, but they could wait. In the growing light I could see there were more of the reddish-brown American crayfish about. I wondered if they knew about corn, they certainly did at a tench water I fished back near Valladolid. Fingers crossed these critters knew nothing of it.

I slipped back quickly to the rod and got the fire going under the pot. It's funny how good instant coffee is, made like this out in the country; at home I couldn't stand the stuff. I had some equally ghastly UHT milk too and some yet worse, of the powdered variety, all of which was wonderfully welcome in the country. I made some cheesy rolls, a peanut one too, there was no sense in going hungry. Then I made the pot full of coffee, baited up with corn and cast out a way, since I was sure there was nothing in close. Then I sat back, coffee in one hand, cheese roll in the other and paused ready to drop both. The Mitchell spool incomprehensibly didn't turn and the rod didn't leap headlong into the mire either. So, I got on with my breakfast.

I munched away for a good while, listening to the dawn chorus, watching the shapes and shadows resume their recognisable selves as hills and trees. The sun rose quickly, odd rustlings coming to my ears of lizards getting to a nice spot to soak up some life giving warmth; others, already warmed, were hunting. There were grasshoppers moving, doubtless a staple on the local menu. Out where my line lay, meanwhile, there appeared to be no sign of diners. I cleared up and stowed all comestibles out of the way of any marauding ants, since there were already a couple of scouts about. There was the risk of vole incursions also. On one occasion I had lost a very fine tuna *empanada* from my picnic, to one of these furry fellows; though twice his size he had dragged it some yards away and devoured about half, leaving the rest somewhat chewed and unappetising by the time I found it.

I returned to the rod having hardly taken my eyes off it in the meantime, but my patience was inadequate and I reeled in to find the bait gone. I had put several grains on and the skins of two of them remained. It had to be crays. It turned out to be the beginning of a plague of them. Every bait I put out during the succeeding hour or more was demolished. I nearly caught several but they continually dropped off. The line would jiggle about most entertainingly until I decided they were on and I would reel in. Finally fed up, I left the lines alone while the nibbling went on, thinking that when the baits were gone then I might get some peace. One line then started to jag more violently. I watched it a while, unsure. It certainly didn't seem like a fish. Following a couple of good tugs, I struck and wound in, feeling only the slightest resistance. Up to my hand came the rather gory remains of a tiny hooked fish. There wasn't much to identify. I guessed it was a small carp, three inches long at most. The poor little blighter had taken the bait, hooked himself and then been devoured by the crays.

A glutton for punishment, I thought it might be fun to catch a few and get some pictures so I went back towards camp for the camera. Nearing the bike, a glimpse of movement stopped me in my tracks, but the animal bolted, a young fox it looked like, though I barely saw enough to be sure. It had obviously seen me first, its sudden start catching my eye. Then I noticed something else, just half on the crossbar of my bike and part on the tree, as though in mid step down. A black and white ringed tail dangled. It was a genet. This really was the place for things I had never seen before. It was watching me and seemed about to make a dash for it. I took a few steps slowly backwards, hoping it would stay and consider the situation a minute longer. My mind turned to the camera and the binoculars, too far away, as always. The little fellow wouldn't hang around long if I moved off. It was a youngster, maybe a foot of body and another of tail. It was peering at me nervously and still hadn't moved, perhaps it had been hurt by the fox. His pinky nose twitched. He would know whether the fox was still in the vicinity. We both just waited, his orangey eyes and pink ears with fine white tufts of hair in them, all trained on me and my every movement. Then a sudden bound down, apparently unhurt, and he scampered away and out of sight.

I breathed. It had been an extraordinary sighting and I resolved as I had done a million times, never to move more than a yard in any direction without the camera. Armed with both, the camera and the spare rod, plus some tackle I returned to the waterside and set up with a float. I set the depth to be well on the bottom, allowing a bit of loose line too since it was often by tangling themselves up in the line that I had caught crayfish in the past. Back in Valladolid I had a proper crayfishing net which I had found washed up downriver after some spring flooding. It was a circular affair of fine burgundy red mesh, about 18 inches in diameter and a foot deep. At its bottom was a small plastic plate, leaded underneath, for tying on the bait, a bit of meat or fish. The whole thing was then lowered into a likely spot, just about anywhere in this lake by the look of things. After an appropriate lapse of time you hoisted it up quickly and there would be your crayfish.

My methods now were somewhat less orthodox, however. I'd had the line out for only a few minutes when the float made something of a movement, shifting slowly across the surface, and I gently pulled in. I felt rapid jerks on the line as the creature's powerful tail attempted to propel him from capture. It was to no avail and I soon brought him up and on to the bank. It was as I expected, the American variety *Cambarus affinis*. As soon as it touched the ground it adopted its impressive defence stance, leaning back on its tail and raising its powerful pincers. It had hold of the line at various points in the tiny pincers at the end of its legs and the hook was just in the crease between one fore claw and the main shell of its body. I got the tackle clear and took a quick picture. He was quite a size, eight inches from claws to tail, mainly red but flecked with blue. I went on to catch several more, enjoying myself as I had done as a small boy fishing for shrimps in the murky river Medway. I have never forgotten the smell of that mud.

The memory of that distinctive aroma which accompanied my rummagings under rocks for ragworm and crabs, came back suddenly, jolting me off down the years. Shrimp fishing with a line, the year the M2 motorway bridge was finished, around 1966. As I threw out the float I recalled vividly peering down into a clear pool from an abandoned concrete pile under that huge bridge. The water there was clean; out further where the monstrous block pillars towered, it was muddy and there were eels.

I had a red plastic bucket with me from family trips down to Camber Sands near Rye, and I was kneeling, the dried muddy backside of my shorts drying. The edge of the pile was green and immediately below, a big crab repeatedly emerged and retreated. I was a few miles upstream from the immense estuary where codling and bass and all sorts of exciting things might be caught. But on these middle reaches where I lived, there were only eels and maybe a flounder. That was in later years though. As a small boy I remembered mostly lowering a handline off a plastic spool with a hook and a ragworm, down to the greyish, transparent bodied shrimps which abounded in those shallows. Their curious jaws sucked the worm in and I could lift them, flipping indignantly into my bucket.

On the occasion which so filled my consciousness while watching my float's antics, I was visited in my absorption by a local bully. A boy called, ironically enough, Dave Goody. He was a year or two older than me - I was 11 - and had rarely ever paid me any attention. That day though he hung around a good while and surprised me by being quite friendly. We even took turns at fishing and worm hunting but eventually he was suddenly bored and ran off. Time passed and the tide dropped, taking the shrimps with it and I had to give up. I didn't catch any more after Goody had left and had spent the interim lowering worms to the cautious crab who would not be tempted to leave his hiding place. He pulled the bait in to his hole a few times and after a brief tug of war, won for himself the worm.

The shrimps always shoved off just after the turn of the tide and I would go up on to the wooden jetty, negotiate the No Entry signs and the barbed wire before walking out over the thrillingly gapped boards to the end where I would usually release my captures. The jetty ran all the way to the low water mark where a ladder led down so there was never any hurry, even though the tide receded fast over the mud flats. It had been a great session and on this occasion I wandered back to the house with my bucket, keen to impress my mother with the catch.

As I approached the house, David Goody appeared and began the taunting routine he normally reserved for others, ridiculing my interest in fishing, my muddied clothes and anything else he could think of, while a couple of other kids who comprised his audience laughed. I carried on my way, taking no notice of his jibes, but noting at the same time a tremble of fear and that sensation of blood draining from your face. His abuse then turned to the shrimps - how pathetic they were, hardly enough to feed a mouse. I froze in my tracks as he taunted on, saying they wouldn't take five minutes to cook since they were already prepared or some such nonsense. Then he ran off with his cohorts in tow.

I was drawn to look into my bucket. To my horror I saw that he had pulled all the heads and tails off; the poor dismembered things were lying at the bottom, swirled in the moving water. In a towering rage I took off after him. There were several things against this course of action. He was much bigger than me, he was older, he was the neighbourhood bully, and he was a cross-country runner. Despite all this, he was the one running away and I was blind with fury. I somehow caught up with him and threw myself on to his back, my arm round his throat. He crashed to the ground and I laid into him like a demon. Very little time passed before I was dragged off, fists flailing and red faced in a mixture of burning tears and rage, eventually calmed by various mothers. It was the unexpected end not only to an afternoon's fishing but to David Goody's bullying days, at least around our neighbourhood.

While I had been remembering all this, I caught several more crays and had them all in the landing-net, though they were pretty good at getting out of it. I got them all together for what was really quite an amusing group photo, a very odd sight indeed. But it was time that I got back to some proper fishing. I would have to deal with the crayfish problem somehow or other though. I didn't have nearly enough bait to sling out to satisfy them as well as attract the fish. Perhaps I could just avoid the bottom. Surface fishing was always a pleasure and there was no sign of the blustery wind that had come up during the previous afternoon. Ideal conditions, just a slight ripple on the water off to the left, ten yards out.

I thought I would put the float out too, with bread flake and raising the depth and bunching the shot up at the top to allow nice slow sinking. But for the moment there was still no sign of fish, so I resolved to stalk off around the bank in search of action. With the rods and gear I headed away from my base camp following the path I had taken on my evening reconnoitre. It wasn't long before I found an attractive looking bay. There were reeds and a broad carpet of that pinky weed at the water's edge with a couple of frogs sunning themselves. Before getting closer, I paused to have a look at them through the binoculars. They were common marsh frogs and were busy calling with their extraordinary range of noises. They would start up without warning and fall silent just as suddenly. I attempted, as I so often have, over the years, to start them off by imitating them, but, this time, with only partial success. The best was to use a tape recording of their singing. I had done so on occasional field trips with some biologist friends, and the response could be overwhelming. It was as though the recording contained some scandalous item of gossip, maybe it did. Whatever they were chortling about, they were good and frequent company for the angler on nearly all the waters of Spain.

I crept down to the spot, the frogs leaping and plopping from view, and sent out my first cast. The line now carried a bubble float and a worm at the end of a couple of feet of tapered leader, made for salmon fishing, which I hoped would be strong enough for I hardly dared think what. I tweaked it back, leaving the bubble resting at the edge of the weeds and the worm dangling just in open water. Very carpy, I thought. I laid the rod on one of my newly crafted rests. It all looked most propitious; I was sure to get a bite.

I baited the other float line and scattered some corn around before casting straight out. I guessed the bait would sink to a foot or so clear of the bottom there, and I settled down to watch both lines intently. I put a bell on the bubble line just in case, clipped on to the rest with the bell held by the line, not too tight, so as to avoid any sense of resistance. Everything was primed for action, it was time to melt once more into the setting, to disappear, leaving only my senses in play.

The sky was bright and the sun hot, I donned my very silly hat to avoid actually melting into non-existence, and liberally applied my factor 20. The red tipped float wavered and twitched a few times making me jump to the rod, only to wait for nothing more to happen. The bubble remained absolutely still on the weeds where the frogs had reappeared, chuckling and croaking in the sun. The morning moved on and around ten I heard the first crashing rise of the day, like a clap of thunder, from a big carp somewhere out on the lake. Scanning the surface with the binoculars I failed to locate it. From then on, at longish intervals the sound was repeated and eventually one uprising came, not far away, back towards where I had been earlier. Then came that slurping, sucking sound of a carp in the reeds, taking something off the surface. Fish were very obviously on the move and feeding. I sank back and became a tree, a rock, a nothing, but totally alert. Sheringham's ginger beer crate would have been nice to sit on but the ground was comfortable enough.

I was confident, as only an angler can be, that something was going to happen. Sure enough a swirl came under the surface just several yards out in front of me, but a good distance from my float. The movement made the whole mass of the water in my chosen bay shudder, or so it seemed. It had to be another huge fish, perhaps the same one. Then came two or three more deep swirls further right, and alarmingly near the bank a dark scaled back broke the surface. I hardly dared breathe. These were very, very big fish, 40-pounders, or more. I had no frame of reference for these giants.

My eyes jumped from the bubble to the float and back again, convinced each time that I was missing some tremor, some hint of impending action. The activity continued to close in. I didn't dare bring the float nearer. It was way too far out. Did I dare . . . I very gently leant toward the rod and softly, softly pulled on the line, taking up the slack with the reel, not moving the rod from the rest. The fish were obliviously busy feeding, on bloodworm, all kinds of larvae, water boatmen, snails, then picking up bits of corn I imagined, grains that had fallen short. Bubbles rose near to the weed-bed. I could hardly stand the suspense. There had to be a take, at any moment. I glanced back to the float, back to the bubble, at the bell, its little spring held in a slight arc by the line. The tension was horrible. I wasn't sure if I didn't begin to feel ill, feverish.

A couple of swallows skated by, dipping their beaks into the water. Above me, where I daren't look, a million swifts swarmed like an epidemic, screeching, stupefying their winged victims with pulsewaves of sound. The bubble had moved. I was on the rod in an instant, my heart pounding. It was off the edge of the weeds, it bobbed and I struck. An eruption deep in the water sent shock waves into the reed bed. The run was frightening. Again I remembered Sheringham: 'hooking a big carp was terrifying, like being dragged out of bed by a grapnel from a passing plane.' The bow-wave rocked the whole bay, the reel screamed and in moments the fish had torn off more than 20 yards of line and was still going. Other waves powered off in other directions, my fish's companions spooked by this sudden turmoil.

I kept the rod high and the bend was rather more than just impressive. I held on but there was no stopping this fish. He was pulling steadily and hard, albeit more slowly than that first run. I kept up the pressure. I couldn't do anything else. It was way out and well down and I was very worried about all that slate. All I could do was wait, the fish was in control. By the feel on the line, it wasn't as yet on the bottom. The huge lunges and heavy turns suggested open mid-water. I could feel nothing else, nothing touching the line. That initial run though had been hard down; a long way down it had seemed, like a submarine.

It was not long before my arms began to ache. I switched hands a couple of times and even recovered a few yards of line. But the fish was staying put. Then came a new flurry of turns and lunges and I held on; resistance and stamina were all that were likely to pay dividends. The dull aching pulling kept up. It seemed at least well hooked. It was apparently in open water. No snags, at least so far, though those outcrops of knife-edge slate were never far away. Then it was nearer. After what may have been half an hour, the carp was back in the bay and I had one fleeting glimpse of a bronze-green common carp flank. Then the fish churned in close and in a dangerously powerful turn, sent up silty clouds from only a yard or two out. A tidal waved crayfish tumbled, flailing, into the shallows, and skipping backwards ran aground at my feet. The line sang, spray streaming as the rod yanked horribly up and down. Then it cut through the surface as my fish bow-waved in a bid for the weed-bed, where the whole skirmish had started. I sidestrained as much as I dared, the old Milbro bowing right round on itself but holding up surprisingly well. I prayed to all the gods of angling that the line too would hold and the carp swung out again, away from danger. I breathed; the tackle and I were at least, momentarily relieved. The ensuing run was as hefty as at the beginning, I was once again losing ground. The carp was out of the bay and cutting a great arc against me as I sidestrained again, to the other side.

A wave of hope broke over me. There came down the line the unmistakable feel of rolling. The fish was weakening, tiring. I recovered line and slid out the landing-net into the turbid shallows. Great heaving rolls, dangerous enough, came down the line and the carp came in, closer, but not close enough. It turned and made a few juggernaut lunges. I couldn't get any closer. I waded in, the edge was steep, the water lovely and warm. I had the rod high. I knew where the fish was in the seething cloudy water before me. It made a desperate lurch as I got the net down towards it. I took the handle between my legs, slipped on a sudden smooth slate and crashed down on to my back. The fish bolted, the reel screamed briefly but it was still on, I still had some control. I struggled back upright, fumbling about to get hold of the net which had somehow vanished in barely two feet of water.

More by luck than anything else, I still had my fish. It was definitely tired now, and rolled one way then the other, up on the surface. I could not reach him though and I pulled. I pulled his dead weight towards me. The great tail flapped slightly giving a helping propulsion. The carp came over the net, which was definitely not adequate to the task. The great gasping head came over the lip, then the humped shoulders. I ducked down and scooped his formidable bulk, doubling into the net. The rounded red tail and a fair bit of body remained out. I got hold of the frame, the rod under my arm and staggered and dragged all to dry land, frankly exhausted.

It was a tremendous fish. The hook came out so easily from the upper lip, I could hardly believe he hadn't thrown it. A dark-olive coloured common carp, a smoky purple sheen to his back, lay passively on the net. My first serious fish from El Campanario, and my first really big carp. It seemed huge, I hardly dared guess its weight. I thought of the one or two 20-pounders I had seen close to, fish I had caught at a gravel pit lake, near Valladolid. This fish was nearly double that size. I went for the scales but just as soon realised they would be no good, they only weighed to 12kg. I quickly set up the camera on its mini tele-scopic tripod and took several snaps to record the event. Then I measured the length, the depth and then I had a brainwave.

I had my Little Samson scale with me too, and it weighed to 10lb. I quickly got the fish into my flimsy old green nylon rucksack after soaking it and wring-ing it out. I hooked the Little Samson on one end and the brass Hardy scale on the other and heaved them up slowly. They both went down to their limits, but only just. They teetered there as I eased the weight one side then the other. A total of 34lb. Another second or two and I had the gasping, patient, king of carp back in the water. I gently held him there, his gills working strongly. Then I launched him like a cyprinoid *Titanic*, and in a few seconds he vanished below the waters. I watched the surface a while, then breathed deeply with relief and tremendous satisfaction. What a fish. What a place.

I returned to the scales and weighed the rucksack, 1lb 2oz, so my fish was 32lb 12oz, my personal best by more than 10lb. I got my zip-change trousers to shorts that had doubled as a pillow from the tent and changed into them. I hung up my wet shorts in the prickly branches of an encina and put my train-ers out to dry on a sun-facing slab of slate. The ground was ideal for going barefoot, soft and warming quickly as the sun climbed higher. To the right of my bay was a small peninsula and I sauntered over there to let the air blow through my mind. Breathing deeply, I gazed out across the water, across the surrounding landscape, as though I were the king of all I saw. I was filled with that oddly pleasurable sense of being alone, quite at one with the world, con-nected in some profoundly vital, immeasurable way with the infinite universe.

At my back it was shady, under the tall trees. Beyond the point was one of the lake's big cuts into the terrain that formed its zigzag. Across the water a domed hill rose, looking for all the world like a turtle, with an even covering of encina and jara bushes. The view was framed from where I stood by two euca-lyptus. I took the photograph, leaving just two frames to go. I would have to make sure I kept the spare film with me from now on. One thing that guaran-teed seeing something really interesting was to run out of film.

I had taken some trophy pictures of the carp. I could hardly believe now that it had really happened. I would believe it again when I collected the pictures from the shop, back home in the city. Then my thoughts wandered to the giant carp I had seen the previous day and the thought that if I were to hook such a fish, the tackle would never stand it. I wasn't sure if I would be able to stand it. And I wouldn't have any means of weighing it. All this speculation about the unlikely capture of such a fish had me feeling vaguely uneasy. It was surely just under such adverse conditions that a fish like that would be hooked.

I walked back to my pitch and manning the abandoned rod, baited up once more with a couple of lively worms and cast again to the weed bed. The fish seemed to like truffling and rooting about close in and though I would doubtless have to wait now until evening, there was a very good chance of more action. My heart then skipped a beat as I realised that the float on the other line was nowhere to be seen. I grabbed the rod and struck tentatively into a massy, thick, motionless weight. It was in the weed. Then the rod bounded into action and I was rewarded with another perfect little carp, like that of the previous evening. This one was a mirror, very prettily marked with three big glossy silver scales on his sides and bright orangey red fins. It had towed the line right round the bank and into the reeds, where I had been lucky to pull it free, only a small clump of weed remaining on the line, mainly wrapped around the float. Watching the little fellow go, its golden flanks glistening in the sunlight, I thought that in 30 years, he too would be a Campanario giant.

I re-baited and cast out once more, and immediately it touched the water the float lurched off and I struck. It was another madly erratic fight but not a carp this time. It felt more aggressive despite its small size and once into the shallows I saw, as I expected, that it was a bass, its jaws gaping; they were not known as large mouths for nothing. I hoisted it up, a small fish of under half a pound, full of fight which made its spiny form difficult to get hold of for a moment. I unhooked it, its dark, flecked flanks catching the light, and after slipping it back I suddenly felt hungry. The day was pretty well advanced, it might have been as late as two or three in the afternoon. Not having eaten for maybe eight hours, I was starving.

I lay aside the rod and watched the bubble out on the weed bed a while, then set up the bell. Confident there would be no interruptions, I nipped back through the cool shade of the trees to the tent for provisions. I was suddenly fantasising again, not about giant carp this time but food. Images crowded in. Salad with bacon bits, hot buttered toast with crunchy peanut butter, a BLT sandwich, those cinnamon scented hot cross buns . . . It was odd, the kind of cravings you felt at moments such as these.

I remembered being far from home as a boy, at least a couple of hours by bicycle, and having attacks of the hunger horrors. It was a day in the long summer holidays. I had raided the larder before coming out, but it must have been shopping day or something, because all I had been able to find was a sachet of sponge mix, a bag of raisins and an individual mini Christmas pudding. Each of these things proved unbelievably delicious that day. The uncooked pudding particularly, and the sponge mix started a fad during which I would organise raids on these packets behind my mother's back, dipping my finger into the vanilla tasting powder until I ended up having to make off with yet another packet. Meanwhile, bags of raisins have remained a tremendous pleasure to this day, alleviating the hunger of long angling expeditions almost better than anything else.

I had asked various friends what food item they fantasised about under such circumstances and the replies were most curious: fresh crusty bread, fresh banana sandwiches, coleslaw, ham and grated cheese baguettes, a pint of fridge cold milk or orange juice, a tin of sardines, chocolate . . . All these were cited before any kind of proper cooked meal. The one exception was Claudio, a dear friend, painter and fellow fisherman who was born in Napoli. His hunger fantasy was his mother's pasta, thoughts of her homemade lasagne would cause him to go starry eyed and miss bites one after another.

Practically slavering at the mouth, I grabbed some picnic packages from the tent and about-turned. The mid-afternoon heat was becoming oppressive, 40°C for certain, 110°F, no wonder the carp were doing well here, there was nothing they liked as much as warm water. I kept well back, making myself comfortable under the eucalyptus, the cooled wine bottle at hand. I had the bike's water bottle too, since thirst quenching with wine was never a good idea.

Ravenous, I ate eagerly, bread, ham and tomatoes. A glass of the wine too. Manzanilla as it should be, nice and cold. I had taken the precaution of slipping the bottle into a reedy shadowed spot in the water. It was cool enough, though it was hard to imagine anything truly approaching cold in this part of the world. A nice deep *bodega* would do the trick, a constant 12°C all the year round, even in Andalucía. I settled down, an eagle eye on the rods, and from my usual, near indestructible, tough Arcoroc glass tasted the wine. Its sherry tangy crisp flavour was a superb accompaniment and it seemed there was not so much as a fish to worry about. Just as well really, and so I enjoyed my lunch, or tea, or whatever it was, and then felt suddenly satiated and tired.

Through drowsy eyes I watched the landscape in a kind of stupor, more alert within than would have seemed apparent. There was a heat haze over the water which gained in intensity as I squinted beyond the reeds. My eye was drawn to the shimmering opposite bank, up the rounded hillside of thin sapling eucalyptus, their leaves and branches reflecting broken white glimmers. At the crest were tumbled-down ruins; 'Casa Umbrías del Pardo', the house had been called, according to my map. A lovely evocative name like 'Top Withens', the likely Yorkshire original of 'Wuthering Heights'. The fallen walls of crumbled adobe bespoke a once large dwelling. There might be a story there I pondered. Then I noticed a silhouette, a large bird perched on one of the piles of mud bricks which once had formed a corner. I peered through the binoculars. Still as a stone sentinel, it was an eagle, the same imperial eagle I had seen before, its white shoulders unmistakable. It too was scanning the hazy liquid landscape, on the look-out for a rabbit foolish enough to be abroad in the sense-numbing heat. Its vigil was calm and infinitely patient, fixed for long periods, then the head would turn a few degrees and the eyes fix again.

My own gaze returned to the rods. I stirred myself, re-cast the float newly baited and flopped down again. The other line lay still, across the weed beds, glistening with moisture, easy enough to see in the otherwise blinding light of reflections. The bubble too, was immobile. Even the frogs were quiet; around them were the little daisy like flowers of water crowfoot, all turned adoringly to the sun. Sun worship made considerable sense among religions. It really was both an omnipotently powerful giver and taker of life.

There were bubbles blistering the surface near the reeds, each one reflecting momentarily the burning white dot of the sun. It was like a tiny hint of hope under the mind dulling heat. A fish was truffling down there in the warm silt, steering pectorals as big as my hands as the barbuled lips blew gently, puffing up interesting morsels. The bubbles were coming nearer; a little more and I might be able to see what calibre of fish it was. I stayed stock-still, letting my eyes only cast around from line to line.

I had pinched a nice bit of doughy bread on to the float line, which had fallen from one of my *bocadillos*, scented with serrano ham and tomato, sure to be of interest to a giant carp. Some time had elapsed since that last cast and it had drifted, directed by a rising soft westerly breeze. It was nudged up against the reedy margin away to the right, several yards beyond the bubble float on the weeds. It stood still as still, the red and white tip showing up nicely against the green. All was stillness and peace. Nothing doing.

I looked back to the ruins and just as I did so, the eagle took off and after a few flaps, glided out of sight over the back of the hill. I seemed to remember reading that this Spanish race was in danger of extinction, its habitat diminishing and its food source too, which was mainly rabbits. The territory around and above the lake seemed good though. Coming in from the road I had seen new plantations of the indigenous encina, protected saplings on land cleared of eucalyptus. That would improve the habitat no end, though it would be a slow process. There were certainly plenty of rabbits, at least down here; there were scratchings and fresh holes all around. I wondered if the bird itself was trying to adapt, it really had looked as though he was having a go for those egrets. I wondered too if there was a mate or a nest anywhere; I would continue to be watchful.

There were bee eaters up at the ruins too. The syrupy calls carried on the air though I could only barely make out their pointy-winged silhouettes against the blue intensity of the sky. A watery ripple suddenly imposed itself on my senses and I lowered the binoculars, focusing instantly on the rings that remained of a rise near the weeds. Would I get another fish, I mused, that is, another really big fish. I was watching the lines once more, but there was still no sign of movement there.

The feeding fish was still about though. The odd bubble popped at the far end of the reeds. There was more than one fish there in fact, a couple of smaller companions moved at the surface. It was almost certainly one of these that had risen. Just then a snout protruded momentarily, slurping right in the thick of the weeds, causing an erstwhile comatose frog to leap head over heels backwards in fright and splash into the water. If a camera could have caught that moment, it would surely have been a prize winner. It had seemed an infinite moment, in slow motion, but had probably lasted no more than the blink of an eye.

The weed lurched, suggesting the carp too was alarmed but only very briefly, for the snout came again and with another resonant slurp. I watched through the binoculars, the glossy olive nose, the upper lip extending, but I couldn't see what it was taking. Maybe it was just weed, along with all the various diminutive creatures in it.

I observed the shadowy surface closely, a fraction further out, where occasional bubbles still showed. The water was at least a metre deep and although there was a bit of spangled eucalyptus shade, it was difficult to see well. However, there was a fish down there, a big one at that. The mass of water itself gave the game away, even without the intermittent bubbles; something heavy, something voluminous, displaced and wavered the liquid element. I imagined the nose going down, a cloud spilling out over the bottom. I hadn't dared make a sound, not to move a muscle, but it knew I was there, I was sure of that, and so did his consorts. The two of them were suddenly right in front of me, they cruised by, coquettish, a final tail thrust and they sped away in a wide arc.

I still didn't move. I knew all about this game. Carp would pretend they didn't know you were there, then suddenly skedaddle leaving you perplexed. They had gone towards the farther crop of weeds and my patiently waiting bread bait. I still didn't move but subconsciously I was on the 'Magic 390', my rod hand ready to strike, then check the drag tension. Once again, I somehow knew a take was imminent. I watched the float intently for what seemed an eternity, nearly jumping with electric shocks every time the breeze leant the quill over the tiniest bit. It moved, a slight jolt caused by I knew not what. I tensed, I crept forward, the game was afoot. Poised and waiting. Again a little jolt, the fish was near, very near the bait, touching, but not mouthing it, not yet. Then the long slim quill rose up, as though levitated by some invisible force, and lay flat. Tenchy, but too laboured really. Then it slid away from me, following the line of the reeds. I grabbed the rod and struck. The reaction was explosive, deep down; both fish, as I imagined, took off together creating a massive displacement of water. I involuntarily uttered a gasp of delight as I clamped down on that initial power run; it wasn't one of the smaller companions after all. I felt that indescribable surge of pleasure at connecting with a really big carp. The rod hooped over superbly, it was another Campanario giant, and certainly not one of the concubines, a caliph perhaps. But this time I was in trouble. Hardly before I had realised it, the run had ended and line went taut into the reeds where they curved round following the line of the bank and extended into a deeper broader bed of real triffids. Towering bulrush heads waved where my fish had thundered into their bases.

I saw in my mind's eye a sketch by Dick Walker in *Drop me a Line* entitled 'Fatal!' It showed a carp happily tying a clove hitch round the base of a reed, much as I felt mine was doing. 'Keep the fish's head up at all costs,' Dick had said. I held the rod at the vertical, maintaining the pressure in a terrific bend, and held on. The fish was well in there and I could feel the persistent heavy thud of its pulling, though it was making no ground. I just waited, not knowing what else I could do, just keeping up the tension. I couldn't afford for the fish to make a turn. If it weakened, I would have to roll it under or over itself, back out through the channel it had undoubtedly made, tearing in there like a rogue elephant.

I waited and waited, feeling less along the line until there was only dead weight. I couldn't pull any more, the line wouldn't take it, I had to hold on. I was dripping with sweat. Despite the factor 20, my forehead burnt and my eyes were stinging. I gingerly changed hands and gave my wrist a rest. I turned the handle a fraction, the rod tip pulling down, and all hell broke loose in the reed bed. The carp had evidently rested and was suddenly bursting with energy. The line jagged horribly and the reeds near the edge crashed down into the water and I suddenly, frantically, had to recover line. The fish was out, quite how I couldn't fathom. It torpedoed along the edge of the reeds. I had changed hands again and felt pretty much in control. It was pulling steadily like 'all the big ones do', as Chris Yates once said at Redmire. This one was getting a bit too far away for comfort and once again, I saw in my mind's eye, all those ghastly blades of slate. For the moment, I could feel nothing in contact with the line, the fish was in deep open water. It was gaining on me still, wrenching off a foot at a time against the drag. I had to stop it. If it got to the end of the reeds, it would be away round the far side and I'd be done for. I checked the drag, holding against the fish and it didn't like it. Sudden thudding tugs came down the line, the rod yanked down, I couldn't hold it. The carp was back in the reeds, more than 10 yards further along. Horrible abrasive sensations juddered along the nylon and . . . bang!

My line trailed away across the surface. Another moan escaped my lips. I had lost it, after all that. I wound in and laying the rod down, got the binoculars. The float was there, upright, just into the reeds. There was no sign of movement. I grabbed the landing-net and made off around the lake, soon arriving at what I judged to be the spot, behind a great wall of bulrushes. I slipped off my trainers, after all they hadn't completely dried out after the last monster encounter. I waded into the rather strange Brobdingnagian reed world. They were huge, 12 feet, at least 8 above the water. I stopped, catching sight of a little green blob that moved. It was a tree frog, the *ranita de San Antonio*, then it was gone.

I made my way slowly, prising the reeds apart, the net ahead of me. As I approached where I thought the float was, there was no sign of my fish. I had expected there would be, I had thought to catch a final glimpse. I got to the edge of the reeds, my shorts soaked again, the water up to my waist, not that I minded. I spotted the float and made my way along the edge until it was within reach; it was another foot deeper. There was a load of line there, above the float, coarse and jagged to the touch, yards and yards of it. It was a miracle it had lasted as long as it had. I wound it all up, round my hand, leaving the net lodged in the reeds. The fish was clearly long gone. I got hold of the float and finding the hook end stuck somewhere below the water line, set to pulling and persuading it free. Up it came, bringing shards of reed with it. The bend was well opened out, I hoped it had done the fish no harm. A formidable opponent, this time the carp had won the round.

I struggled back the same way I had come, though not before grazing a toe on a nice chunk of slate. The lake bed there was soft and solid for the most part though, matted with the roots of generations of king reeds. A short while later I was wringing out my shorts again and hanging them in the encina. I pulled on the spare pair and took a closer look at the line I had recovered, and the last few yards on the reel. There was far too much damage for it to have been only the reeds. The last 15 feet had been dragged in there but then there was a good stretch with no damage. Then came the worst part, really rough to the touch and giving it a yank it broke more easily. It had to be the slate, several feet had rubbed back and forth over it and it was there it had finally broken.

The water was still, the sun had dropped a long way and the evening was not far off. After all the commotion, I couldn't really expect any carp to be nearby. In fact everything was quite suddenly preternaturally silent. The carp were probably getting their heads together in a pow-wow. Word would have got around after that last encounter. For my part, I felt pretty tired and didn't want to go trekking off to another location with all the gear either. A little stalking could be interesting, armed with the Milbro and the net. There were the black bass too, they'd always take a worm. But maybe I should go looking for a big one, I did have some lures with me. I lay aside the Magic 390 and reeled in the bubble. The bait was gone, dropped off after so long probably.

Nipping back to the tent, I found the little box of lures I had brought along, among them a soft vinyl crayfish. It was a ghastly looking thing, pale reddy brown, semi-transparent wet look, flecked with multi-coloured glitter. A false bait indeed. It occurred to me that a bass would have to be dafter than a salmon to be taken in by such a thing. I settled down to re-tackle both rods. I ran the line, checking it as I went, back through the eyes of the Magic 390. I had to discard a few feet more, always better to be safe than sorry. I set up for carp, going for a small drilled bullet, thinking I might fish a little further out. The crays as a general rule, preferring the margins. Then on the Milbro, which would cast a lure really well (even a ridiculous one) I added 12 feet of spider wire, thinking to outwit the slate snags.

I had more than shaken off any sense of lethargy and found myself a few minutes later loaded up with both rods, a rucksack full of tackle, rod rests, bait, all ready to go. I donned the still slightly soggy trainers, took up the rods and the net and started off in the opposite direction to that I had taken at nearly the same time the previous evening. A light cooling breeze greeted me through the eucalyptus as I negotiated the occasionally steep bankside. Lizards again scuttled, startled by my appearance. I must have looked rather like the bird man in Gerald Durrell's *My Family and other Animals*. The truth is I often felt great affinity with that book, it was a shame there was no fishing in it.

I was soon panting and feeling that I didn't want to go much further. All the gear felt suddenly heavy and it was still very warm, the low sun streaming through the young trees. As the wood thickened it was a little cooler between the stripped and tattered trunks.

Pressing on, the trees changed to pines, many of them ancient and some leaning rather precariously on the steep slopes. I started to descend, nearing the water, cautious and alert to every movement and sound. At a safe distance I paused, and crouching down pulled off my rucksack to get at the binoculars. I studied the water carefully. I had come maybe half a mile round the lake, following the west bank nearly opposite my camp. The path had reduced to almost nothing and I had to pick out where deer had passed to make my way. The vegetation was quite thick right down to the water, low bushes with more adelfa and jara blooms as well as thyme and rosemary amongst the grasses. The warm air was deliciously scented. The margins were lined with reeds, but there were several attractive gaps where I might fish.

The dam was diagonally opposite and again I guessed that this spot overlooked the deepest part of the lake. It was hard to say but there might be 30 feet of water, before the point at which the long run up to the dam started. There might well be a big fellow down there, taking it easy before going on his evening foragings. I decided I should get on and fish, making a beeline for a perfect niche I had spotted among the reeds. A crayfish skipped away backwards at my approach and I heard what were probably some small black bass creating a bit of a commotion along the bank to the left. I could hear nothing carpy for the moment. I crept on into position and baited up with corn, slinging out a few free offerings to arouse any potential diners' interest. I cast, not too far, thinking that any fish would probably be moving out of the deepest water by this time. I eased the ledger along the bottom a fraction, feeling the soft sand. It felt clear. I perched the rod on the rests and sat on a most conveniently positioned chunk of slate, its flat surface jutting out at just the right angle, the bank behind forming a back rest. It had to be a good omen.

The evening was beautiful, the stillness and the quiet of the place was quite overwhelming. The noise of nature was plentiful but I had seen no trace of a human being for over 24 hours. Though I would have to be off in another 24 hours, I knew I would be coming back. The next day was Thursday and it would take a few hours to get back to Seville, where I rather fancied spending another evening around the bars. After all this blissful solitude I would doubtless be ready for the hustle and bustle, the music and of course, the cuisine. I reached into my bag and pulled out the last of the *bocadillos* I had made earlier. There were plenty more provisions back at the tent, but I knew that by the following evening I would appreciate a proper meal. I tucked in heartily to my sandwich and marvelling at my foresight, poured myself a glass of the *Manzanilla* too. It was still reasonably chilled and I popped the cork back and pushed the bottle into the water among the nearest reeds to keep it so. As I did so, I leant over and loosened the spool drag. I didn't want the rod to be dragged into the lake by a 50-pounder while I was savouring my supper. Carp power - I was half surprised that engines weren't measured by it. I'd had a rod leap into a lake before now at the first run of a mere 5lb tiddler.

No action now for a moment. A long moment in all probability. Carp angling above all was the contemplative man's recreation. Sand trickled imperceptibly through the universal hourglass and I watched the evening's display of gold and rose spread overhead. It had begun to cloud up a bit, diffusing the light and making it rather darker than the previous evening. I could see the line well enough and anyway the spool would sound should anything happen. It wasn't going to. How I knew that, I couldn't really say, maybe the carp conference was still underway. Whatever it was, I felt at leisure to enjoy the sunset, though I never let my attention wander too far from the line. You have to keep playing the game.

It got dark very quickly, or so it seemed. Stillness took over everything and the air became oppressive. There was a storm brewing, maybe a long way off. Summer storms in Spain were formidable, more in the massive pressure build up and the humidity than when they finally broke. As often as not, the rain would not come, or it fell so far away that only the scent reached you, sometimes hours later.

I thought about packing up. Nothing at all had happened and eventually, I reeled in a bare hook. I cast a few expletives on the doubtful parentage of crayfish and got ready to make a move. I collected everything with some difficulty, checking time and again that I hadn't forgotten anything. I couldn't make out the path at all, such as it was, and realising it would be shorter to go on round to the dam, began picking my way through the dark. It was pitch dark by this time, under a lowering night sky.

My ears were alive to every sound, rodent scuttlings and the fluttering wings of insects. I had climbed only a few yards from the water when all the delicate hitherings and thitherings were obliterated, a huge watery crash shattering the night. It sounded like an army of 50-pounders in some kind of aquatic stampede. My eyes widened expectantly as I turned to face the water, my pupils dilated to the extreme to somehow see, but it was just too dark. Continuing my way I could barely distinguish between the dark forms of bushes and open patches of ground. Deep shapes all, like terrestrial carp invading the land. My steps were unsteady, it was like sleepwalking among all the dreams that sleep is heir to. I was tempted to whistle a tune to myself as I had done all my life to keep my spirits up but it wasn't really necessary. The trees were all ogres, their arms clasping witches and spitting demons, but the best of all was the occasional sense that I was walking under water. When I reached the first of the eucalyptus, they seemed gigantic weed cables with monster carp lurking among them. I was no more than a crayfish hoping to reach my hiding place before being slurped up and devoured like the sons of Saturn.

Once into the trees, it was no time before I was crossing the old dam and back at my camp. Without further ado I turned in. I lay back in the igloo, tuned in once again to all the delicious sounds that whirled about outside. The temperature had eased and a fitful wind had risen, whipping around the eucalyptus tops. There had to be storms somewhere, though I could hear no thunder. That homely, comfortable sensation washed over me, just as when it is pouring down outside and you listen to the cacophony of raindrops on roof and window sills, from the shelter and safety of your room. I was asleep in no time and my next conscious thought was breakfast.

Over hot coffee, more bread and peanut butter, I resolved to go back round the lake to the point facing the dam. There were giant carp everywhere but those night sounds were just too much, I had to give the spot another try. It was just before six on my last day. To be on the safe side, I would have to leave around 7pm to get the 9 o'clock bus from San Juan del Puerto, the last one every evening for Seville. I packed up the tent and everything else I wouldn't be needing, and wheeled the still very heavy bike to the safety of a hidden nook among jaras and eucalyptus.

Collecting my tackle together I found the corn can upended and grains scattered here and there. Some little fellow had feasted quite well during my slumbers. Not only had I left it out but I had forgotten to snap on the lid. I collected up the remains feeling I was lucky there hadn't been a whole family of them, whoever they were. Armed with my gear and the food leftovers, I set off for the dam and the walk round. It took quite a while to get there, what with every kind of distraction in the undergrowth, although I only paused briefly for a glimpse of their scuttling retreats.

All was still at the water's edge. On my way down the final slope I heard another of Campanario's hefty uprisings, but saw nothing. I crouched by the reeds and looked out over the still surface. It was 6.30, the light was sweet and delicate, and a vague mist hung over the water at the margins. A slurp resounded across the water from the reeds near the dam. I organised rods and rests and threw out a handful of golden grains, rather rashly as it turned out. I found that there was very little corn left but I also had some worms. It would have to suffice. I had some bread left too, though it was no longer fresh; edible enough for me but too dry to make decent hook bait. I baited up the float line with a few bits of corn and cast long. I watched the tiny dot of carmine for a while as it drifted slowly towards the reeds along to my left, eventually stopping where the bait touched the bottom. It looked good, ten feet of water, a yard or so from the reeds. I baited the ledger with a biggish worm and flicked it out, not too far, a little to the right. Watching the line sink, I could see it was deep, 30 yards off and maybe 20 feet down. I pulled the lead gently and felt the soft bottom free of snags.

A sudden thought made me poke around in my worm baitbox, a lovely old, two-tone green Efgeeco, cracked as they always are through the base. It was as I had feared, that lob had been the last of the worms. I suddenly realised that I hadn't got anything like enough bait in fact. The sweetcorn was barely a handful, looking at it realistically, and the bread almost useless. I watched the rods and the water quietly pondering, wondering whether to go off in search of worms. Every hour left seemed almost too precious. Then it occurred to me to make up a kind of bubble and squeak breadmash, from some of my leftovers. I emptied out the baitbox and started concocting. There was some peanut butter, some biscuits and dryish bread, and I added some tuna, mainly the oil, keeping the rest for my lunch. I cut a bit off my one remaining apple too and mashed and mixed it in with the rest, then added a crushed acorn or two. It certainly smelt extremely interesting; if only it smelt half as good to a carp it might serve.

Upon arriving at Olhão on the Algarve, only 60-odd miles from where I was fishing, Rose Macaulay, with a little help from the ancient Greeks, had commented on the tuna fishing carried on there:

> The tunnies off Algarve are fine fat fish, perhaps acorn fed, for Polybius said that 'in the sea off Lusitania acorn-bearing oaks grow, upon which the tunnies feed and fatten themselves, which may well be called sea hogs, as they feed like hogs on acorns.'

If a tuna might be taken with acorns, then why not a carp?

Although it was still very early, the sun had risen quite high by the time I had the mixture prepared. The recipe was certainly unorthodox but nonetheless I had a very good feeling about it. Reeling in the lines, I found the worm gone but the corn bait still intact. The worm had been one of those rather white, fleshy ones and I feared it may simply have dropped off. I picked off the bits of corn and pressed some into my new bait, slinging most of the remainder of the tin out as groundbait, recklessly confident in the new preparation. I kneaded a good sized lump solidly on to both hooks and set about casting afresh.

The float line didn't give me a moment's peace, the crays and tiddler carp went at it as soon as it touched the water. I ended up cutting down the bait size drastically and eventually rather enjoyed catching little silvery carp of a few ounces. The ledger line, meanwhile, remained quiet in the deeper water. I pulled it gently once or twice and fancied I felt the weight of the bait still there. Time went by and eventually I could no longer resist the nagging doubt that the hook was bare. I wound in and found indeed that the bait had gone. The same thing happened with the next cast, there were tiddlers or crays down there too, I supposed, even though the rod tip gave no indication. At one point I thought I might give up on the big carp; either that or head off in search of worms. There could be bigger bass too, to while away the remaining hours.

I pulled out the vinyl crayfish from my bag. Surely no carp would be daft enough to take such a harlequin lump of soft plastic, even if it were craftily flavoured. I fancied that it did look a little like a crayfish . . . one that had shed its shell. I tied it on to the ledger line and pressed a wad of the fishy peanut scented mash under the lure's body, the point of the hook just at the surface. I wondered what sort of smell a carp picked up from a crayfish, one that had per-haps gorged itself on peanut butter. Well, it seemed worth a try. I cast the lure into the same area of deep water, a little further out, hoping to get beyond the crays, and followed up with a couple of small balls of the mash as groundbait

Around midday, I was nibbling at the last of the bread along with the tuna and some pitted black olives, when the reeds nearby heaved about suddenly, giving away the position of a big fish. A dark, golden brown back briefly broke the surface, a great sail of a dorsal fin rose and fell as the fish turned against the reeds. A massive swirling, sucking sound followed and reed stems juddered. There was more than one fish there and they were apparently feeding. I couldn't help a resurgence of that good feeling I had already felt so often at this place. A positive surge of electric optimism or foresight or something inexplica-ble. I swallowed my last scrap and sat transfixed in the presence of these formidable creatures.

I leant over and picked up my last apple. It was an unconscious action and when I bit into it, its cold, sharp, crispness made me shudder with surprise. The day had become hot, 40°C once again, the world burning in unending stillness. Nature, the air, the very earth knew what was going to happen as well as I did. I ate on, finally, almost carelessly tossing the core into the scrub. The cicadas stopped their churring. The whole filmy surface before me shifted. I saw it as though dizzy, like a moment when you stand up suddenly and seem to notice for the first time that the planet you are standing on is spinning. The float bobbed, jarred by ripples of concentricity. The entire volume of the lake echoed the slow bends and turns of a great fish. The reeds were still, a colossal carp was approaching the richly scented ball of paste, I could sense it as surely as if I were able to actually see it. I looked away from the line a bare micro-second. The spool was loose, the drag lightly set. Everything and nothing was happening.

A sprite breeze suddenly puffed into my face, the scent of wild thyme inter-mingled with peanut from the dough next to me. The cicadas had switched back on and a few swifts' distant shrieks came from high up. The float started to bob again, too playfully for a big fish, it ducked from view only to appear again a yard nearer. It began bobbing again and I nearly made a grab for the rod but I looked instead at the ledger line. Still, straight, tight into the water, at an acute angle, maybe 30°. There was a tiny tremble at the point of penetra-tion through the surface tension, the hint of a ripple, just one, a yard towards me. Something had happened. Something momentous in that period of utter stillness, and I had missed it.

I leant down to the rod and gave the line a slight pull. It ripped out of my fingers and the reel yelped as though from pain. A vast implosion buckled the water right before my eyes and then thundered into a tidal wave and bore out across the lake. The take had come all that distance out but I imagined I saw the water at my feet drop some inches as this fish torpedoed away. I had the rod, I tightened the drag, but the spool just kept spinning. The old hollow glass hooped over, I thumbed the spool tentatively. I knew the line, I knew it better than the reel did. The fish just kept going. I couldn't say how many minutes had passed. The spool held 200 metres of 0.35. This carp was a hundred yards away already. It was, thankfully, high in the water, but there was no let up in pace. The spool was looking empty. I couldn't believe it. I tried to force a stop to the run again and again but the line just sang out dangerously pulling the rod down. I couldn't stop it.

The fish was over 150 yards away . . . more every second. The line was com-ing to its end. I applied pressure once more and my whole being breathed with relief as the charge appeared to slacken. There were maybe a dozen turns left on the spool. I wound against the tension, recovering valuable line. The sweat poured off my brow, I was blinking madly, trying to see. I wound on. My fish had changed direction and was heading across the lake toward the near bank, but a long way away, towards the dam. He felt much deeper down now too but I couldn't be sure, my eyes were stinging and quite blinded. I had the rod high but had no idea where the line entered the water. The pull was dull, slow, and extremely heavy. I kept on winding, the fish was coming closer at least.

Some massive lunges came down the line, dragging the rod over, and ripping yards at a time off the reel, but for the moment it felt as though I had some control. The desire to at least see this fish was paramount. I had to keep it on this course, kiting round in a huge arc towards my part of the bank. Landing it would be another matter, of that I was sure, and anyway there was plenty of time yet. I had a hundred or more yards of line back on the spool but the fish still felt very deep down, in what seemed to be open clear water. I wiped my eyes, the sting of the sweat abating, and looked where the line entered the water. I saw and felt another run, powerful and fast, but luckily parallel with the shore. Then the lake bulged and broke open, and my fish thundered to the surface. I was recovering line wildly and nearly went over backwards. It was huge. I had never hooked such a fish in all my born days. No one would ever believe this. I would never get it to land. A bitter wave of despair broke over me. The rod bent low, the line pulling off, the drag wailing. My actions were all reflex, giving and taking line, holding on as though for dear life and hoping.

Physically, I was engaged in what seemed like mortal combat but my mind wandered all over the place, recalling great fishing moments: that sturgeon story in 1933, and the onlooker who fled for his life at the sight of it; Miss Ballantine's two hours with the still-standing UK salmon record, back in 1922; Bernard Venables's premonition and actual landing of a monster off Madeira in 1959.

I had more line back. The great carp was within 60 yards of me, very active, shudders and lunges never stopping, down in the depths of the lake. I thought too of *The Old Man and the Sea* :

> Now alone . . . he was fast to the biggest fish that he had ever seen and bigger than he had ever heard of.

I reeled and stopped, the line cutting fast through the surface and then giving, and I reeled again. Time had fled from this encounter, but time had passed. How much time? My brow, my face had felt very dry at one point, then was streaming with burning sweat once again. Time, its flaming face the sun observed me closely, burning its way across the sky. It burned the back of my neck then the right side and ear. I couldn't think what I had done with my hat. The reel shrieked; I felt thankful that the line was good as far too many yards flew out into the lake. I was failing, weakening. Too hot. Much too hot. It seemed like an age since the fish had shown itself, but it wasn't so far off. Still pulling steadily and heavily, making great turns and deep rolls, maintaining its distance at around 50 yards. I relaxed a bit. He was tiring too. In the very same second that thought occurred, the great carp tore up and through the surface once again. The water burst open and this immense fish came three-quarters out; it seemed more like a golden shimmering seal than a fish. I was sure I caught its eye; a big beautiful copper ringed iris drank me in. My resolve shattered like an old cane rod. I couldn't catch this fish. It bore away from me, straight across the surface, the water bowing out ahead, the rod wincing in its arc, line tearing off the screaming spool.

Maybe the roller would burn out. I wondered if I should splash water on it, as they do in those big game fishing programmes on TV. Everything held while the line was stripped off in an action-replay of the first run so very long ago. Then the carp began patrolling, back and forth a hundred yards away, as though pondering his next move. Back and forth. Again. He began to give and once again I was recovering line.

The cicadas were singing, and a slight breeze animated the surface. The world ticked along, quite indifferent to these momentous events. Yet I had known that all this was going to happen, like no other big fish encounter I had ever had. Some tremendous sense of the creature's presence had certainly been there. A monster approaching the bait from the reeds. It was the fact of being connected, Ted Hughes's connection to the natural cycle, it was the answer to the ultimate question, it was why I was here, why I was angling.

The rod bowed down and gave, following some shoulder barging down there in the green mist. I found myself wondering what this fish could weigh. Dangerous thoughts, not really permitted in the game: 70lb . . . 80 . . . it felt like a hundred, just lazing along. Turns and changes of depth, but all the time coming closer. I realised with a start I had lots of line back on the reel. The surface water was troubled, that whirlpool effect, the action of gigantic fins, only 20 or so yards out, right where he had first taken that ridiculous rubber crayfish. I felt he could see me. I barely dared to breathe.

The biggest carp ever caught on a rod and line, I believed, was a South African fish. If I remembered correctly it had been 86lb, over six stone. And then there was that famous 1950s' monster Hungarian specimen, talked about in *The Carp Catchers' Club*, at 'over 80lb'. The fish I had was bigger, I knew that. It was a common too, stocked here as far back as the Thirties probably, after the Civil War.

Suddenly, it was perfectly simple, I would have to beach this fish. It would have to be completely exhausted. A thud or two registered on the taut line, tail movements. Another few feet of line yanked off and then everything stopped dead, ominously still. I held the rod high and stepped into the shallows; the bottom began to drop away abruptly, only a few feet out. Feeling my way, there was something of a ledge to my left. The fish was stone still, but there - an immense presence, still, as though thinking, planning. I manoeuvred my position, bringing some sidestrain to bear, stepping cautiously through the silty clouds, I inched my way to the left. The water cleared slowly, the muddy swirls settling. The sun was lower. I thought about how long this had been going on. My arms ached, my neck was certainly red raw, my eyes were sore too. Despite a cooling steady breeze off the lake, it was still unbearably hot.

A cold sweat sensation ran down my back like an icy finger, sending an involuntary shudder through me, up the rod and down the line. The carp felt it and lurched annoyed and away, pulling off more valuable yards. He turned slowly, led back by straining pressure from the rod. The reel spun, whipping the line neatly on to the spool in my favour; he was coming ever closer. Then, once again, that unnerving dead stop, resting on the bottom. I dragged the sadly inadequate landing-net into the muddied water. Its 18-inch diameter frame on a dear old pine wood handle would be of small use really. I could scoop the tail in maybe.

The carp made some kind of inscrutable decision and became suddenly active again. He pulled hard but slow, giving, changing direction, measuring the ground, keeping up a tremendous strain on the rod through sheer weight. The bend was total, and numbingly still, no jerks or lunges. I changed hands for the umpteenth time and heard myself emit a groan. Everything ached. I daydreamed about that suddenly luxurious *pensión* in Seville and some anaesthetic glasses of *Manzanilla*. I felt hungry and thirsty, tired and vaguely disconsolate but I still had this fish on. It was close, only a few feet now. I would beach it in the hollow off the slate ledge; my footing seemed good enough. I backed away tentatively sidestraining, the rod low towards the bank. This fish, even when rolled over, would need a considerable draught, there were two or three feet of water beyond the ledge then a quick sandy rise up to a few muddy inches of shallows to where the rod rest was. The angle was right, now was the time. I pulled, not too hard. I could feel fin movements, heavy, slow, slipping towards the bank. I let it come. I could feel no contact with weed or slate, nor the bottom. He had to be touching the bottom. He was only feet away through the thin watery clouds.

There! Huge, a dark shape moving. I breathed hard, pulse racing, ready for everything. I brought the net round behind me, poised to push out behind. A few feet more. He was quite upright, perhaps a slight lean away from me. Again I felt a sickening sense of loss, of anguish and despair. This fish was too much for me. Four feet in front of me now, the head a foot wide. I couldn't see where the line went. Then I saw the crayfish lure, just at the corner of his great pouted lips. Everything stopped. He was run aground. He rested his great chin on the soft bottom. There were dusty grains of sand settled on his snout. The fleshy nasal openings seemed to flare slightly. His eyes looked up, then down. It was as though he were taking everything in. This new experience, oddly, seemed not to trouble the fish at all. His great sail-like dorsal rippled, his pectorals, as big as paddles, flexed slightly. Immense shoulders, the vast bronze plated bulk extended four, five feet to a tail I could not see. It was stalemate.

I thought of the cycle ride back to San Juan, and the bus, the driver amenable, or not, to stowing my bike. The looks of wonder on the faces of other passengers that some lunatic could cycle under such a load of gear in such heat. It was getting on, I knew it was time to go. The *pensión*, a good bath or a shower that beats into you, and a cooked meal. A late night walk around the bars.

The enormous fleshy mouth puffed open, the gills sighed. This extraordinary fish looked at me. I gently brought the landing-net round behind, letting the handle slip slowly through my fingers. The movement broke the spell. The water exploded. It splashed and rained everywhere, a sudden deluge drenching me utterly. The rod yanked, the reel yelped and the line went slack. I stood there and cried. No real melodrama, but big hot tears slowly running down my face. I wanted to stamp my foot like a child but I didn't. I didn't move at all in fact, for some while. A dying fall, merely, a whimper.

Eventually I packed up. The line was fine, the lure too, the hook bend slightly opened. There was no sign that anything much had really happened. The timing of the catastrophe was perfect, just before 7pm. All afternoon that fish had been on, six complete hours. I stood back at my original spot and looked out over the lake, thinking I would come back, wishing the great fish well, wondering if we met again, if that great carp would remember me.

Fishing and Travelling in Spain

Fishing licences
Arriving in Spain
Where to go and where to stay

Fishing licences

Getting a fishing licence for anywhere in Spain is not particularly easy and ideally needs to be done before you go. Fishing without a licence anywhere in Spain is not recommended since the Civil Guards, Forestry Guards or any other police officials are empowered to confiscate your gear at the very least, even your vehicle, or prosecute, which will lead to a heavy fine in excess of 6000 Euros, not to mention a minor criminal record and possible difficulties entering the country on future occasions. There is no national authority or licence and so you have to apply for the one that is right for the region you are visiting. Going online to *www.licenciascazaypesca.es/licencia-de-pesca.asp* is one option, and clicking 'translate this page' produces reasonable English. This is a private agency, Gestoria Apinaniz, and their charges vary from around 30 to 40 Euros per licence depending on the region. The actual cost locally is considerably less than this, around 7 or 8 Euros in most cases but this requires you to apply direct to the regional government department and this is not easy for non-Spanish speakers. In the middle of the agency's homepage you will see a simple map, with all the *'comunidades autónomas'* or politically autonomous regions of the country clearly delineated, and on the right-hand side a list in alphabetical order of these same regions. Clicking on these and thereby choosing the region you are planning to visit will take you to a page which indicates the cost for obtaining your licence by ordinary post or urgent delivery. Below, there is a button marked *'Solicitud de licencia'* that takes you to an application form, which is reasonably straightforward but you will need to provide a Spanish address. The address of the accommodation you will be using would be suitable. If you wish to fish anywhere in Andalusia you are obliged to provide proof that you are already a fisherman - a copy of your current UK fishing licence would be ideal - since failure to do so will result in your having to do a course and pass an exam prior to obtaining your licence, the total cost of which exceeds £75.00. By way of a 'Stop Press' addition to this information, the Apinaniz agency has stated that they will soon be providing their online service in English and offering postage of the licences to UK addresses.

A licence is also required for sea fishing everywhere in Spain, usually issued by the same authorities but often by a different department. You will need a licence in all regions with a sea coast in order to merely fish from the shore. These licences are for '*pesca maritima*' (saltwater fishing) as opposed to '*pesca continental*' or '*pesca fluvial*' (freshwater fishing). Further licences will be needed for anyone wishing to dive (*buceo*) or do any underwater spear-fishing (*pesca submarina*), or any kind of sea fishing at all from boats (*desde embarcación*). A special licence will be needed anywhere in Spain for having a boat, which can be applied for in the same offices where you obtain your normal fishing licence. These licences can be problematic for several reasons, not least the fact that the authority in question may be limited in the number they are allowed to grant. They are also expensive, depending on the size of craft, power of engine etc., with the cheapest costing around £200 and rising dramatically thereafter. In addition, the use of any kind of boat at a water, whether a small inflatable, a canoe or kayak, including the use of a manned boat, no matter what its size, merely to drop your baits, requires a special boating permit, or '*permiso de navegación*' from a further authority, namely the Hydrographic Confederation, or '*Confederación Hidrográfica*', of the region in question. It's a complex, difficult and expensive process, which it's very important to note, will *not* allow you, under any circumstances, to go afloat anywhere or at any time you like, since individual waters are subject to all manner of rules and restrictions, which only the local authorities can inform you about.

Regional inland licences allow you to fish in most places but there are of course waters where some kind of day-ticket or other permit is required. The word '*Coto*' on a sign at the water means something like 'reserve', and a special ticket will be required. These may be available from the same authority as the licence, or they may have to be obtained from a private angling club, as is the case, for example on the Ebro for catfishing, where the ticket has to be obtained from a bar in Mequinenza. A '*Vedado de pesca*' means no fishing is allowed under any circumstances.

All and any difficulties involved in obtaining licences can always be avoided by contracting local guided angling services and for first time visitors this approach is highly recommended.

Very general information for tourists and anglers alike is available from the Spanish Tourist Office in the UK at *www.spain.info*, where you can find Sports and Water Sports options for further information.

For those anglers with enough Spanish to get by while in the country, obtaining a licence is nowhere near as complicated and if you have time, you simply need to get along to the offices of the local authority, or apply directly via their websites. The following information is correct as of 2013:

If you are dialling Spain from abroad please add 0034 before the regional numbers given below.

Catalunya

Licences can be obtained online, by phone or in person from the Generalitat de Catalunya (gen-cat.), either the Department de Medi Ambient i Habitatge or the Department d'Agricultura, Alimentació i Acció Rural under the heading '*pesca recreativa.*' Payment is by credit card. In order to apply online you have to register at www.gencat.cat

The physical address is:
Palau Robert
Passeig de Gracia, 107
08008 Barcelona
Tel: (932) 38 80 91 / 92 / 93   Fax (932) 92 12 70
www.gencat.cat/palaurobert

Navarra

Online applications from:
www.navarra.es/home_es/Servicios/ficha/3748/Tramitacion-de-la-licencia-de-pesca#documentacion
You can apply for your licence by email, writing to: *cazaypesca@navarra.es*
The physical address for applying in person, if you happen to be nearby is:
Departamento de Desarrollo Rural, Industria, Empleo y Medio Ambiente
Mostrador de Licencias de Caza y Pesca:
C/Gonzalez Tablas, 931005 Pamplona (Navarra)

Basque Country

Getting a licence for fishing in the Basque Country can be an additionally complicated affair, as each of the provinces has its own rules and regulations, and its own licences both for sea and freshwater fishing. Searching the internet throws up horrible quantities of nearly indecipherable information in Basque and Spanish but relief came when I finally made the discovery that the Caja Vital, a bank of the provinces of Vitoria and Álava, handles freshwater licence applications for the whole region. Finding the address of the nearest Caja Vital to where you are in the Basque Country, as well as elsewhere around Spain, is easy enough, via the internet or the Yellow Pages and much to my surprise and pleasure there was one in Valladolid. I spent no more than ten minutes in the bank, where a passport or other identification was required, and I had to pay very little (under €10 in 2009) for my licence.

Asturias

Licences for Asturias can be obtained by going to *www.asturias.es* and then putting 'pesca' or 'licencias pesca' in the search box and following instructions.

The physical address is:
Consejería de Agricultura, Negociado de Pesca
C/ Coronel Aranda, s/n
33005 Oviedo (Asturias)
Tel: (985) 10 56 84

Cantabria

Licences can be obtained from:
Servicio de Montes, Caza y Conservación de Naturaleza
C/ Rodríguez, 5
39002 Santander (Cantabria)
Tel: (942) 20 76 81 / (942) 20 71 00 / (942) 20 75 91

Galicia

Licences for Galicia may be obtained at:
Consellería de Medio Ambiente
Juan Montés, 3
27071 Lugo
Tel: (982) 25 00 52
Fax: (982) 29 45 23

Information may also be found in the city of La Coruña:
Consellería de Medio Ambiente,
Edificio de Servicios Administrativos
Planta 5ª
Plaza Luis Seoane, S/N
15008 La Coruña
Tel: (981) 18 45 76
Fax: (981) 18 46 54

And at the regional capital city of Santiago de Compostela:
Consellería de Medio Ambiente
San Lázaro, S/N
15781 Santiago de Compostela
(A Coruña)
Tel: (981) 54 61 09
Fax: (981) 51 61 01

Information about licences for anywhere in Galicia can be found on the internet at: *www.xunta.es* by putting 'pesca' or 'licencia pesca' in the search box and following the instructions.

Castilla y León

Getting a licence to fish anywhere in Castilla y León, or day-tickets to the '*cotos*' or restricted fishing areas, has always been fairly straightforward, if you happen to be in Valladolid, since it has to be done there, in person, at the offices located at:

Delegación Territorial
Calle Duque de la Victoria, 5
47001 Valladolid
Tel: (983) 414463 / (983) 411079

Aragon

For Aragon a fishing licence can be obtained from:
Instituto Aragonés de Gestión Ambiental (INAGA)
Pza. Antonio Beltrán Martínez, 1, 5ª pta
50002 Zaragoza
Tel: (976) 71 41 11
Email: inaga@aragon.es

Contacting the INAGA by phone, letter or email or internet will be enough to obtain the 'solicitud' or application form and this must be completed and returned, whereupon the angler will receive a document which must be taken to a Spanish bank for payment within a certain period, approximately six weeks. Exactly which banks payment can be made at is indicated on the document. The cost is minimal: €10,69 or £9.00 for the year 2011/2012. All this paperwork is in Spanish, of course, and so the help of a Spanish speaker would be ideal. Payment can be made when the angler arrives in the country and the licence is valid from that moment.

Next, the angler wishing to fish the Ebro's most famous carp and catfish waters, namely the Embalse de Ribarroja, will also need a day ticket, or *Permiso de pesca*, currently €5.00 or a fraction over £4, issued by the Federación Aragonesa de Pesca y Casting. These tickets are also available on a weekly basis at a cost of €18.00 or around £20, in 2013. It is important to note that you are only allowed by law to fish from 6am to sunset, unless you are fishing for catfish, when the time extends to 12 midnight and, once again, the Civil Guard have every right to enforce the law, i.e. confiscate your gear. In rather typical Spanish style, the day or weekly tickets are available from certain bars, for example the Bar Sport in the village of Mequinenza.

Extremadura

Getting a licence for Extremadura is not as easy as in some Spanish regions, simply because you have to apply by post or go in person to a Caja de Extremadura, which is a regional bank. There is no Caja de Extremadura in Valladolid for example but there is more than one in Madrid and once you've located one, actually getting the licence could not be easier, or at least a receipt which proves you have applied for one (valid for 60 days) which serves until the actual licence arrives by post. You fill out a form issued by the Junta de Extremadura headed 'Tasas Licencias de Caza/Pesca 50' and pay out the princely sum of €4.85 for a one year licence. Licences can also be obtained which are valid for up to five years. My own licence for Extremadura lapsed some years ago and when I applied for a new one, my flimsy pink cover note substitute ran out long before the new licence arrived due to a major administrative overhaul in Extremaduran Local Government. My actual licence finally arrived eight months later.

The Autonomous Community of Extremadura is, I believe, unique in Spain in having a close season for coarse fish. The calendar month of April is off-limits to the angler, which is the period when the very popular black bass are nest-building, spawning and defending their progeny. The existence and enforcement of this close season seems a most enlightened policy and one which would do well to be adopted elsewhere in the Iberian Peninsula.

Alicante

Licences to fish in Alicante, which comes under the region of Valencia, can be obtained from the following:

Registro de la Dirección Territorial de Agricultura,
Pesca, Alimentación y Agua
C/ Gregorio Gea,
46009 Valencia
Tel: (963) 52 54 78   Fax: (963) 42 63 12   Tel: 012

The information service telephone number 012 is often the only number available for phone enquiries.

Registro de la Dirección Territorial de Agricultura,
Pesca, Alimentación y Agua (Alicante)
Profesor Manuel Sala, 2
03003 Alacant/Alicante
Tel: (965) 98 62 17   Tel: 012

Registro de la Dirección Territorial de Agricultura,
Pesca, Alimentación y Agua (Castellón)
Avda Hermanos Bou, 47
12003 Castelló de la Plana/Castellón de la Plana
Tel: 012   Fax: (964) 35 82 19

And, most conveniently, in any Correos office (the Post Office service) but, for the moment a licence cannot be obtained online.

Andalusia
Licences can be obtained by email from the Consejería de Medio Ambiente, *via: dggmn.cma@juntadeandalucia.es*

The physical address is:
Consejería de Medio Ambiente D. G. Gestión del Medio Natural
Av. Manuel Siurot,
5041071 Sevilla

Many of the Spanish licences that I hold can be renewed automatically by direct debit to my bank and the option for setting this up is usually available during the original application process with each local authority.

Arriving in Spain

Most tourists coming into Spain invariably fly into Barcelona, Malaga, Palma Mallorca or the centrally located Madrid-Barajas, but there are a great many other airports with frequent services to and from London, including Alicante, Bilbao, Santander, Seville, Valencia etc. For fishing the Ebro, Barcelona-El Prat, or Tarragona (Reus) are the most frequently used airports. For Galicia, La Coruna is the most accessible airport from the UK.

Driving into the country over the Pyrenees is also popular and immediately brings you into wonderful fishing country. Many then take the northern coastal route, following parts of the old pilgrim's way to Santiago de Compostela in Galicia. Heading inland to Aragon, Old and New Castile or into Extremadura is a less frequented route, which would include many locations well off the typical tourist circuit, with spectacular scenery, some truly historic cities such as Segovia, Salamanca or Trujillo to name but a few, and some first rate fishing.

There are some fine old converted railway lines known as *vias verdes* which have been converted into cycle paths and a particularly good 30-odd mile example connects Logrosan near Caceres and Serena near Badajoz in Extremadura, passing close to both lakes and rivers with very good fishing.

Another inland road journey would be to follow the *Ruta de Plata* or Silver Route, which in theory runs from Seville in Andalusia to Gijon, Asturias, on the Bay of Biscay but which is officially signposted nowadays between the Castilian town of Astorga and classical Merida in Extremadura, via Salamanca and Caceres. Astorga, of course, is home to Spain's most ancient angling text, Juan de Bergara's *Astorga Manuscript* of 1624, a more than sufficient reason for a stop in the town. A further driving route would be to follow the coast south-east from Barcelona along the famous '*Costas*', the Costa Dorada, Costa Brava, Costa del Sol and Costa Blanca, which are all very touristy of course but where some quieter, out-of-the-way spots can still be found.

Where to go and where to stay

For a huge number of anglers the place to fish in Spain is the Ebro, where they will be going for the giant wels catfish and large carp, although there are also good zander to be caught along with several other species.

Fly fishermen interested in salmonids mostly head for the northern highland regions extending from Catalonia to Galicia, although trout also occur in the mountain streams around Madrid, the sierras of Andalusia, the uplands of La Rioja and other similar regions. Salmon occur primarily in Asturias and a few rivers in Galicia and Cantabria but if the fly anglers would like to extend their range of species, there is excellent wet- and dry-fly fishing for several species of barbel almost anywhere in the country with the main targets being the gypsy barbel in Andalusia, the shorthead in Extremadura or the smaller comizos in both regions.

Carp fishermen tend to make for the huge reservoirs of Extremadura and Andalusia, as well as the river Ebro, although carp occur in practically every drop of water, with the exception of the highland trout streams, right across the country, usually in company with one or more of the country's many species of barbel. Getting to the Ebro's most famous carp and catfish waters, namely the Embalse de Ribarroja could not be easier, since Satnav GPS devices ensure you do not lose your way. Simply key in Mequinenza as your final destination and look forward to hearing your chosen voice announcing the turns and the straight ons along the way, plus, of course, an occasional 'Recalculating, recalculating!' The nearest main train and bus stations in the national network are in Barcelona, Zaragoza and Lérida (Lleida), with local services available from there.

Sea fishing usually means the coastal Mediterranean, where there are numerous species of sea bream, including the gilthead or rather more exciting species such as the voracious bluefish or the spectacular giant leerfish. Out at sea the boat angler can turn their thoughts to big game, with different species of tuna, as well as swordfish and dorado, or dolphinfish (no relation to the cuddly star of the *Flipper* series). There are sea bass to be caught in the Med too but Spain's north coast tends to be more productive, where there are also plenty of sea bream species too.

At risk of repetition, it cannot be stressed enough that for the best possible fishing experience anywhere around the country, guided services are a must. Contracting these services not only avoids the difficulties of obtaining licences but also enables you to get to the fishiest spots on the waters, as is the case with reservoirs such as the famous Embalse de Orellana, where locating 70lb carp in 12,500 acres most definitely requires local knowledge. There are a great many operators out there, as can soon be seen via a quick internet search. The experiences of other anglers are often a good guide when choosing services and internet forums and blogs are a very useful source of information.

Exactly where to stay for an angling holiday in Spain depends greatly on your budget and individual taste, as well as whether you are driving around the country or stopping at one particular location. At the top of the list, in terms of luxury, might be the nearest *parador*, which is often an historic castle or palace, offering the very best of everything but which will usually require considerable advance booking.

If your trip is to the north, along the coast between the Basque Country and Galicia, perhaps the many '*Casa Rural*' establishments might be best, which offer either self-catering or B&B facilities often within easy reach of river, lakes and the sea. Many cities, of course, have a wide range of accommodation available, and regional capitals will also have local government offices where regional licences can be obtained.

The *Casa Rural* option is also available throughout inland Spain and for the more popular coastal regions, there are numerous hotels or villa complexes, which will never be far from either the sea or inland beauty spots and historic towns and villages, as well as the numerous rivers and lakes. The Spanish Tourist Office mentioned above has useful information with regard to places to stay and there are, of course, numerous webpages offering every kind of accommodation in the country, including *www.booking.com* and *www.toprural.com* both of which I have used frequently, with the best possible results.

Tight Lines! or *¡Buena Pesca!*

Useful Spanish Phrases

Are the fish biting? Caught anything? - *¿Pican o no pican?*

Fishing tackle - *aparejos de pesca*

Fishing licence - *licencia de pesca/permiso de pesca*

Do I need a licence to fish here? - *Necesito un permiso/una licencia para pescar aquí?*

Where can I get a licence? - *¿Donde puedo conseguir una licencia/ un permiso de pesca?*

Rods, reel, line, lead weights, hooks - *Caña, carrete, sedal, plomos, anzuelos*

Fly line - *cola de rata*

Artificial flies - *moscas artificiales*

Landing net - *red sacadera*

Waders - *vadeadores*

Float tube (for going afloat) - *pato*

Bait - *cebo*

Corn, worms - *maíz, lombrices*

Stretch of river or 'beat' - *tramo de río*

No Fishing - *Vedado de pesca*

Ticketed water - *Acotado de pesca*

A managed water requiring a day ticket etc - *Coto (de pesca)*

Trout water - *aguas trucheras*

A managed trout water - *Coto de salmónidos*

A managed carp/tench etc water - *Coto de ciprínidos*

Tight Lines! - *¡Suerte! ¡Buena pesca!*

Barbel *(barbo)* - Black bass *(blas or perca americana)* - Brown trout *(trucha)*

Catfish *(siluro)* - Carp *(carpa)* - Gilthead *(dorada)* - Leerfish *(palometón)*

Mullet *(mújol)* - Pike *(lucio)* - Rainbow trout *(trucha arco iris)* - Salmon *(salmón)*

Sea bass *(lubina)* - Tench *(tenca)* - Tuna *(atún)* - Zander *(lucioperca)*

Selected Bibliography & Recommended Reading

Baedeker, Karl *Spain & Portugal* Scribner's London 1898

Borrow, George *The Bible in Spain* (1842) Dent, London 1961

Brenan, Gerald *South of Granada* Hamish Hamilton, London 1957

Coles, S. F. A. *Spain Everlasting* Hollis & Carter, London 1946

Delibes, Juan *Guía de la Pesca en España* Espasa Calpe, Madrid 1999

Ford, Richard *Gatherings from Spain*, Murray, London 1846

Ford, Richard *Handbook for Travellers in Spain*, John Murray, London 1845

Gibson, Ian *Fire in the Blood* Faber & Faber, London 1992

Graves, William *Wild Olives* Pimlico, London 2001

Hooper, John *The Spaniards* Viking, London 1986

Langridge, John *Lizarralde* Ediciones Fuente de la fama, Valladolid 2003

Langridge, John *Lizarralde* Medlar Press, Ellesmere 2005

Langridge, John *El inglés e la manga corta* Ediciones Fuente de la fama, Valladolid 2007

Lewis, Norman *Voices of the Old Sea* Hamilton, London 1984

Macaulay, Rose *Fabled Shore* Hamish Hamilton, London 1949

Morris, Jan *The Presence of Spain* Faber & Faber, London 1964

Orwell, George *Homage to Catalonia* Secker & Warburg, London 1938

O'Shea, Henry *A Guide to Spain & Portugal*, A & C. Black, Edinburgh 1838

Sciascia, Leonardo *Sicilian Uncles* Granta, London 2001

Various Authors *Spain Lonely Planet*, London 9th edition 2013

Index

General

Álava 33, 38, 343
Alicante 6, 8, 223, 267, 268, 269, 271, 273, 275, 277, 279, 281, 283, 346, 347
Ampolla 253, 254, 260
Amposta 253, 254, 255, 263
Aragón 6, 8, 35, 118, 171, 172, 173, 174, 175, 176, 177, 179, 181, 182, 183, 185, 186, 187, 189, 190, 191, 193, 195, 197, 199, 200, 201, 203
Astorga 180, 181, 348

Barcelona 8, 40, 41, 120, 171, 180, 186, 343, 347, 348
Bilbao 8, 33, 347
Biscay 33, 253, 348
Borrow, George 10, 220, 221, 222, 286
Burguete 14, 15, 16, 19, 23, 25, 26, 27, 28, 31

Cáceres 206, 216, 232, 233
Cádiz 140, 288
Cervantes, Miguel de 118
Chapman and Buck 5, 79, 86, 87
Civil War 5, 13, 33, 79, 93, 97, 106, 119, 290, 337
Columbus 118
Costa Blanca 177, 268, 348
Costa Brava 348
Costa de Azahar 254
Costa del Sol 348
Costa Dorada 254, 348

Dénia 6, 267, 268, 269, 270
Doñana 87, 253

Flamenco 6, 285, 287, 288, 289
Ford, Richard 221, 222

Gerona 40
Gibraltar 8, 207
Gibson, Ian 107
Guipuzcoa 37, 38
Gypsies 223, 285, 286, 287, 289, 290, 291, 293, 295,
297, 299, 301, 303, 305, 307, 309, 311, 313, 315, 317, 319, 321, 323, 325, 327, 329, 331, 333, 335, 337, 339

Hemingway, Ernest 5, 10, 13, 31, 119, 207
Huelva 300, 301, 303

La Coruña 80, 344
Lee, Laurie 5, 10, 79, 93, 119, 301
Lérida 176, 190, 191, 348
Lorca, Federico García 289
Luarca 52
Lugo 93, 95, 115, 344

Macaulay, Rose 222, 254, 264, 269, 301, 314, 333
Madrid 8, 26, 41, 85, 89, 93, 107, 118, 120, 140, 171, 180, 215, 216, 217, 218, 222, 227, 229, 231, 300, 303, 346, 347, 348, 351
Málaga 93, 107, 109, 171, 192, 290, 292, 295, 296
Mediterranean 10, 66, 173, 177, 202, 217, 234, 253, 254, 268, 275, 348
Mequinenza 176, 177, 178, 180, 184, 191, 192, 199, 203, 342, 345, 348
Mérida 205, 206
Mondoñedo 5, 52, 79, 81, 84, 94, 98, 105, 107, 108, 109, 111, 158, 162, 166
Monfragüe 206
Morris, Jan 216

O'Donnell, Red Hugh 118
Orwell, George 222
Ourense 90

Pamplona 8, 15, 18, 20, 28, 343

Reus 171, 347

Salamanca 120, 142, 233, 347, 348
San Sebastián 27, 40

Santander 8, 65, 173, 344, 347
Santiago de Compostela 13, 217, 344, 347
Segovia 120, 216, 347
Seville 6, 8, 140, 145, 172, 210, 253, 275, 285, 289, 299, 300, 301, 303, 331, 332, 338, 347, 348

Trujillo 206, 218, 347

Valencia 6, 8, 82, 173, 177, 192, 217, 256, 270, 346, 347
Valladolid 5, 8, 38, 83, 93, 115, 116, 117, 118, 119, 120, 140, 142, 143, 172, 174, 190, 210, 216, 217, 218, 226, 227, 231, 244, 267, 268, 269, 277, 286, 287, 291, 299, 300, 301, 316, 317, 322, 343, 345, 346, 351
Vigo 8, 80, 93, 109
Vitoria 38, 40, 343
Vizcaya 33

Woolf, Virginia 299

Zaragoza 177, 345, 348

Fish species

barbel 5, 6, 10, 33, 41, 48, 50, 82, 86, 87, 115, 116, 124, 125, 126, 127, 128, 129, 131, 132, 135, 136, 137, 143, 181, 182, 232, 239, 243, 249, 255, 271, 285, 296, 297, 298, 309, 348, 350
black bass 5, 6, 10, 79, 82, 87, 92, 93, 116, 138, 167, 182, 205, 215, 217, 218, 231, 232, 236, 239, 242, 243, 249, 255, 257, 303, 306, 308, 309, 329, 330, 346, 350
bleak 6, 176, 182, 205, 215, 224, 225, 228, 229
bluefish 349
carp 5, 6, 10, 49, 82, 87, 89, 90, 115, 116, 123, 124, 149, 152, 154, 171, 173, 175,

176, 178, 179, 180, 181,
182, 183, 184, 185, 186,
187, 188, 190, 191, 192,
193, 194, 195, 196, 198,
199, 200, 202, 205, 215,
219, 221, 223, 224, 225,
226, 228, 229, 230, 231,
232, 243, 255, 261, 263,
280, 285, 296, 299, 303,
307, 308, 309, 311, 312,
313, 314, 315, 316, 320,
321, 322, 323, 324, 325,
326, 327, 328, 329, 330,
331, 332, 333, 334, 335,
336, 337, 338, 339, 345,
348, 349, 350
catfish 6, 10, 171, 173, 179,
180, 181, 182, 189, 190,
191, 192, 193, 194, 195,
196, 197, 198, 199, 200,
201, 202, 203, 204, 217,
244, 254, 345, 348, 350
comizo barbel 239
conger eel 5, 51, 75
crayfish 6, 43, 232, 236, 265,
285, 303, 308, 309, 316,
317, 319, 322, 329, 330,
331, 332, 334, 337, 338

eel 5, 51, 56, 57, 62, 63, 75,
104, 105, 272

gilthead 6, 254, 255, 263, 267,
269, 271, 272, 273, 275,
277, 278, 279, 280, 281,
283, 349, 350
gudgeon 5, 115, 124, 129, 130,
243
gypsy barbel 285, 297, 348

leerfish 6, 253, 254, 258, 260,
261, 349, 350

mullet 5, 10, 51, 53, 67, 68,
70, 71, 72, 73, 74, 75, 77,
78, 87, 217, 254, 256, 265,
270, 274, 350

nase 5, 79, 82, 83, 85, 87, 88,
91, 124, 181, 297

pike 5, 10, 33, 41, 43, 44, 49,
87, 88, 89, 115, 116, 135,
136, 137, 138, 139, 140,
143, 145, 147, 148, 149,
150, 151, 152, 154, 155,
156, 157, 167, 168, 169,
174, 185, 215, 225, 228,
229, 230, 231, 232, 236,
237, 239, 240, 241, 249, 350
pumpkinseed 124

rainbow trout 10, 87, 217, 244,
350

salmon 10, 80, 87, 94, 97, 217,
257, 320, 329, 336, 348, 350
sunfish 124, 125, 244

tench 10, 143, 181, 227, 278,
316, 350
trout 5, 10, 13, 14, 17, 21, 22,
27, 30, 31, 33, 39, 41, 43,
52, 60, 79, 80, 85, 86, 87,
94, 96, 97, 101, 102, 103,
104, 105, 106, 109, 111,
116, 141, 143, 160, 161,
162, 163, 164, 165, 166,
173, 180, 181, 185, 194,
216, 217, 244, 274, 348, 350
tuna 10, 153, 173, 254, 316,
333, 334, 349, 350

wels 10, 171, 192, 195, 202,
203, 204, 231, 244, 254, 348

zander 10, 176, 182, 217, 231,
232, 233, 237, 239, 240,
241, 242, 243, 244, 245,
246, 247, 248, 249, 255,
256, 348, 350

Rivers and stillwaters

Alcántara Reservoir 6, 205,

231, 242
Canal de Castilla 135, 143,
167
Cinca river 176, 179, 187

Duero river 8, 9, 82, 83, 85,
116, 120, 121, 122, 124,
134, 142, 143, 144, 173,
212, 242, 244
Duratón river 116

Ebro river 6, 8, 116, 120, 171,
172, 173, 174, 175, 176,
177, 178, 179, 180, 181,
182, 183, 185, 187, 188,
189, 190, 191, 192, 193,
195, 197, 199, 200, 201,
202, 203, 204, 253, 254,
255, 257, 259, 260, 261,
263, 265, 342, 345, 347, 348
Esla river 8, 116

Guadalhorce river 296
Guadalquivir river 8, 296, 301
Guadiana river 8, 82

Júcar river 82

Miño river 83, 97

Orellana Reservoir 224

Pisuerga river 8, 116, 117, 118,
123, 141, 142, 143

Ruecas river 215, 219

Segre river 179, 180, 187

Tagus river 206, 235
Tajo river 8, 116, 232, 235
Tormes river 142
Turia river 82

Zadorra reservoirs 45